Folk Music in Overdrive

FOLK MUSIC IN OVERDRIVE

A PRIMER ON TRADITIONAL COUNTRY AND BLUEGRASS ARTISTS ✺

Ivan M. Tribe

THE CHARLES K. WOLFE MUSIC SERIES   *Ted Olson, series editor*

The University of Tennessee Press / Knoxville

The Charles K. Wolfe Music Series was launched in honor
of the late Charles K. Wolfe (1943–2006), whose pioneering
work in the study of American vernacular music brought a
deepened understanding of a wide range of American music to a
worldwide audience. In recognition of Dr. Wolfe's approach to music
scholarship, the series will include books that investigate genres
of folk and popular music as broadly as possible.

All photographs are from the author's archives unless
otherwise credited.

Frontispiece: James and Martha Carson, WSB, Atlanta, late 1940s.

Library of Congress Cataloging-in-Publication Data

Names: Tribe, Ivan M. author.
Title: Folk music in overdrive: a primer on traditional country and
bluegrass artists / Ivan M. Tribe.
Description: First edition. | Knoxville: The University of Tennessee
Press, [2018] | Series: The Charles K. Wolfe music series | Includes
bibliographical references and index. |
Identifiers: LCCN 2017057793 (print) | LCCN 2017058601 (ebook)
| ISBN 9781621903987 (pdf) | ISBN 9781621903970 (pbk.)
Subjects: LCSH: Country musicians—United States—Biography. |
Bluegrass musicians—United States—Biography.
Classification: LCC ML385 (ebook) | LCC ML385 .T74 2018 (print)
| DDC 781.642—dc23
LC record available at https://lccn.loc.gov/2017057793

In memory of Pete Kuykendall,

who in a sense made this book possible

and

To the Charles K. Wolfe family

for their hospitality

Contents

Foreword   *Ted Olson*   xi
Acknowledgments   xiii
Introduction   xv

PART ONE: Leaders, Solo Singers, and Composers   1

Hylo Brown   4
Roy Hall   11
J. D. Jarvis   19
Mac Martin   27
Charlie Monroe   37
Clyde Moody   47
Lee Moore   54
Mac Odell (Odell McLeod)   63
Jimmie Skinner   70
Buddy Starcher   78
Carl Story   89
Lillie Mae Whitaker   99

PART TWO: Sidemen   105

Billy Baker   108
Claude Boone   115
Buddy Griffin   122
George "Speedy" Krise   133
Curley Lambert   139
Joe Meadows   146
Natchee the Indian (Lester Storer)   153

Red Rector   158
Clarence "Tater" Tate   166
Chubby Wise   174

PART THREE: Husband-Wife Duets   181

James and Martha Carson   183
Wilma Lee and Stoney Cooper   195
Joe and Stacy Isaacs   206
Bonnie Lou and Buster Moore   214
Molly O'Day and Lynn Davis   222
Doc and Chickie Williams   232

PART FOUR: Brother Duets   247

The Bailes Brothers   249
The Callahan Brothers   259
The Goins Brothers   267
Mel and Stan Hankinson—The Kentucky Twins   283
The Lilly Brothers   290
J. E. and Wade Mainer   301

PART FIVE: Families and Groups   317

The Briarhoppers   320
The Coon Creek Girls   334
Betty Fisher and David Deese   343
The Lewis Family   351
The Masters Family   364

Further Reading   373
Index of Names   375

Illustrations

Hylo Brown, ca. 1959   5
Hylo Brown, mid-1960s   5
Roy Hall   12
J. D. Jarvis with Rusty York   20
J. D. Jarvis   20
Mac Martin and the Dixie Travelers, ca. 1971   28
Charlie Monroe   38
Clyde Moody   48
Lee Moore at WCHS, Charleston, West Virginia, 1938   55
Lee and Juanita Moore, WHIS, Bluefield, West Virginia, 1941   56
Mac Odell, WLAC, Nashville, 1949   64
Jimmie Skinner   71
Buddy Starcher, ca. 1949   79
Carl Story   90
Lillie Mae and The Dixie Gospel-Aires   100
Billy Baker and Del McCoury, the Shady Valley Boys, 1964   109
Billy Baker, 1977   109
Claude Boone with the Rambling Mountaineers, late 1940s   116
Buddy Griffin with Lester Flatt, ca. 1970   123
Buddy Griffin with fiddle   123
George "Speedy" Krise, 1946   134
Curley Lambert with the Goins Brothers, 1977   140
Joe Meadows with the Goins Brothers, 1973   147
Natchee the Indian (Lester Storer)   154
Red Rector, late 1940s   159
Tater Tate with the Shenandoah Cutups   167

Chubby Wise   175

James and Martha Carson, WSB, Atlanta, late 1940s   184

Wilma Lee and Stoney Cooper, WSM, Nashville,
    Grand Ole Opry, 1958   196

Joe and Stacy Isaacs, 2011   207

Bonnie Lou and Buster Moore, mid-1960s   215

Molly O'Day and Lynn Davis, WHAS, Louisville, 1943   223

The Border Riders, 1947   233

The Bailes Brothers   250

Homer "Bill" and Walter "Joe" Callahan   260

The Callahan Brothers with band, ca. 1940s   260

Melvin and Ray, the Goins Brothers, ca. 1971   268

Mel and Stan Hankinson, The Kentucky Twins,
    WSM, Nashville, 1947   284

Everett and Mitchell B. "Bea" Lilly, WWVA, Wheeling,
    West Virginia, 1948   291

Wade and J. E. Mainer, probably late 1940s   302

The Briarhoppers, 1977   321

The Coon Creek Girls, 1939   335

The Dixie Bluegrass, 1993   344

The Lewis Family, ca. 1970   352

Owen, Lucille, and John Masters, probably late-fifties   365

Foreword

The Upland South—that somewhat amorphous geo-cultural region en-
compassing the western part of the Carolina and Virginia piedmont; the
Southern Appalachian foothills, highlands, the valleys; parts of the Cumberland and Allegheny plateaus; the Upper Cumberland River area of central Tennessee/Kentucky; and the rolling lands that extend westward to
the Ozarks—inspired vernacular regional music traditions that have played
vital if often uncredited roles in influencing mainstream American music.
As Ivan Tribe illustrates in *Folk Music in Overdrive*, talented if overlooked
musicians from the Upland South have contributed significantly to the evolution of commercial country and bluegrass music.

The main title of this book alludes to Alan Lomax's identifying label for
bluegrass, which at the time of Lomax's coining of the phrase (1959) was
emerging from the shadow of the genre—country music—that had spawned
it. Lomax's expression, of course, was soon supplanted by a new, though
arguably problematical genre title (because the term "bluegrass" inadvertently acceded the lion's share of genre creation to Kentucky's Bill Monroe,
whose band was famously called The Blue Grass Boys). The coopting of
Lomax's phrase, nonetheless, is entirely appropriate because this book primarily focuses on the post–World War II generation of musicians from the
Upland South who extended the revolutionary musical sound and style
first popularized by Bill Monroe and his band in mid-1940s recordings for
Columbia Records. Tribe rightly explores early bluegrass as the creation
of many people—some of whom had personal connections to Bill Monroe
(Charlie Monroe, Chubby Wise, Clyde Moody, Billy Baker, and others), but
many of whom were unaffilliated with Monroe.

Folk Music in Overdrive compiles just under forty separate articles—profile essays, for the most part—that were researched and written by Tribe

and that originally were published in leading periodicals devoted to understanding the roots and branches of traditional country and bluegrass music. The majority of this book's essays—thirty-two in all—originally appeared in *Bluegrass Unlimited*, a leading print periodical devoted to the genre. Five other pieces were first published in other important periodicals (including *Old-Time Music* and *Goldenseal*), while the pieces on The Coon Creek Girls and on The Lewis Family were previously unpublished. Tribe carefully revised the previously published works, updating them and incorporating thematically relevant historical photographs. In *Folk Music in Overdrive* the various essays are, rather uniquely, organized by type of musical configuration: profiles on solo acts are joined together, as are pieces on instrumentalists ("sidemen"), larger musical units (including family groups), and duos (husband-and-wife acts and brother acts).

Readers will note the lack of separate profile essays focused on the most widely recognized pioneering bluegrass acts (Bill Monroe, The Stanley Brothers, Reno and Smiley, etc.). Tribe, through decades of dedicated research, understood that certain people and certain stories were receiving much of the scholarly and popular attention. What makes this book so valuable is its detailed documentation of the lives and careers of many unsung or forgotten yet essential talents. Knowledge of and appreciation for traditional country and bluegrass music will be profoundly enhanced because Tribe cared about such people and their contributions to our collective musical culture. In *Folk Music in Overdrive* Tribe has admirably filled wide gaps in the existing scholarship of American roots music.

Ted Olson
East Tennessee State University

Acknowledgments

When I started writing articles for *Bluegrass Unlimited* in 1973, incorporating them into a book was about the farthest thing from my mind. I simply wanted to highlight the careers of significant musical figures who it seemed had often been overlooked. As the years went by these articles in *Bluegrass Unlimited* but also in additional outlets such as *Old Time Music*, *Precious Memories*, and *Goldenseal* began to accumulate. Fellow music historian Charles K. Wolfe suggested that a selection might be compiled for a book as he had done in his collections *The Devil's Box: Masters of Southern Fiddling* (1997) and *Classic Country: Legends of Country Music* (2001). The project lay dormant until March 2015, several years after Dr. Wolfe died, when during a convention conversation Dr. Ted Olson, East Tennessee State University professor of Appalachian Studies, and Thomas Wells, University of Tennessee Press acquisitions editor, brought it up as a possible volume in their Charles K. Wolfe Music Series.

I soon began revising and updating thirty-nine articles for inclusion. Most had been originally built around interviews with the musical figures and their close associates and it is to them that the greatest appreciation is in order. Additional revision information came from a variety of sources, much found in additional biographical and discographic information used in Bear Family boxed sets as well as counsel, advice, and knowledge shared with experts in the field including Fred Bartenstein, Norm Cohen, John Lilly, John Morris, Wayde Powell, Tony Russell, Linda Shaw, and Richard Spottsword as well as Dr. Kevin Kehrberg and the late Archie Green, the late Guthrie Meade, the late W. K. McNeil, and the late Gene Wiggins. And, of course, the late Charles Wolfe, who along with Bill Malone set the pattern for scholarship in country music history.

Closer to home, my wife of fifty years, Deanna, has always proven helpful as has colleague Jacob Bapst, a professor at Rio Grande Community College. Scott Beekman, Jean Ann Vance, and Barry and Judithe Thompson have offered encouragement as have past and present University of Rio Grande presidents the late Dr. Paul Hayes, Dr. Barry Dorsey, and Dr. Michelle Johnston. Special thanks go to the late Pete Kuykendall of *Bluegrass Unlimited*. I am certain that this volume would not exist without him. The Wolfe family always had insightful information, good conversation, a spare bed, and a place at their table in the many research trips made to Nashville over the years. All of these persons have earned my gratitude including anyone I may have inadvertently omitted.

Introduction

Ron Thomason, the leader and witty spokesman of the Dry Branch Fire Squad, once said there was a fine line between country music and bluegrass and, likewise, between old time music and bluegrass. From the late 1930s through the early 1960s even those fine lines were practically nonexistent. Numerous musicians played music that contained elements of two and sometimes all three styles.

Bluegrass as a musical art form has been described in a variety of ways. Writing in a 1959 *Esquire* article Alan Lomax became one of the first scholars to single bluegrass out as a distinct form of country music, labeling it "Folk Music with Overdrive."[1] In 1982 another academic wrote that bluegrass "is an acoustical string-band type of music which usually features a prominent three-finger Scruggs style banjo and some combination of guitar, banjo, mandolin, and string bass."[2] In 1998, Richard D. Smith, who wrote a 2000 biography of bluegrass founder Bill Monroe, wrote, "Bluegrass is a traditionally oriented country music initially created as the string band sound of Bill Monroe & His Blue Grass Boys, which became widely imitated and evolved into a distinctive musical genre."[3] Norm Cohen, writing from over four decades of perspective, added in 2005 that it seemed as if bluegrass was "old-time string band music but at a faster tempo, with greater instrumental technique, with . . . rotating solos (or 'breaks') among the various instruments—in particular mandolin, banjo, and fiddle."[4] Finally, Neil V. Rosenberg, a leading academic expert on the topic, wrote "Bluegrass is part of country music. . . . During the [nineteen] fifties it was named and recognized as a unique form—a music in which singers accompany themselves with acoustic rather than electric instruments, using the fiddle, mandolin, guitar, five-string banjo, Dobro, and bass. Its performance demands mastery of virtuoso instrumental techniques . . . , often executed in rapid tempos. . . . Bluegrass singing is high pitched [and] lonesome sounding; it often involves tightly arranged harmonies."[5]

Bluegrass musicians, less academic, but nonetheless immersed in the sound, have also made commentary on the idiom. Pioneer vocalist, the late Red Allen said, "There's no difference between a bluegrass and country song often in terms of the feeling or emotion it evokes: It's just the way I do it. I just hear a song and if I like it, it sticks in my mind. I'll go home and it will ring in my head and I won't be able to go to sleep. I just feel that it's a grass song." David McLaughlin, a younger mandolin picker and formerly with The Johnson Mountain Boys, writes that real bluegrass "is about soul and honest emotion. It's the kind of sound that gives you goosebumps and makes the hair stand up on the back of your head."[6] A dedicated fan might not be able to provide a simple definition, but would instead say, "I know it when I hear it."

What music listeners term bluegrass, according to connoisseurs of the style, originated in 1946 when *Grand Ole Opry* star Bill Monroe assembled the following personnel in his band the Blue Grass Boys. Monroe played mandolin, sang some lead and high tenor in the chorus. Lester Flatt played guitar and sang some lead solos as well as lead duets with Monroe. Earl Scruggs sang baritone when the song called for it and played an exciting three-finger style five-string banjo. Chubby Wise played a bluesy fiddle while Howard Watts, who went by the stage name "Cedric Rainwater," played a solid rhythm bass fiddle and enlivened shows with bucolic comedy.

This form of acoustic string music attained considerable popularity, especially in the Appalachian South and Piedmont regions where string-band music had flourished for at least a generation and probably longer. Influential recording artists in the 1920s included Charlie Poole's North Carolina Ramblers, Ernest V. Stoneman's Blue Ridge Corn Shuckers, and Gid Tanner's Skillet Lickers. In addition to *Opry* appearances and tours, the sounds of the Blue Grass Boys could be heard on Columbia Records. Soon other bands were adapting the style of Monroe and his associates. Initially they were primarily imitative, but quickly they developed their own innovations to the sound.

The best-known and influential of the other early day bluegrass bands were Lester Flatt, Earl Scruggs and the Foggy Mountain Boys, the Stanley Brothers and the Clinch Mountain Boys, and Don Reno, Red Smiley, and the

Tennessee Cut Ups. Next were Jim and Jesse McReynolds and the Virginia Boys, the Osborne Brothers, Jimmy Martin and the Sunny Mountain Boys, Mac Wiseman and his Country Boys, and Carl Story and the Rambling Mountaineers.

While Bill Monroe and his band ranked as musical innovators, what came to be called bluegrass did not emerge from a total vacuum. Monroe was always quick to credit the influence of his fiddling uncle Pendleton Vandiver, a Kentucky fiddler Monroe immortalized in the song "Uncle Pen," and Arnold Schultz, an African-American fiddler and guitarist whom Monroe had frequently heard during his youth in Western Kentucky. Monroe could also have credited the string-band music that he and his older brother Charlie who performed on radio and recorded as the Monroe Brothers in the Carolinas, had heard from their fellow musicians. Like the Monroes these groups worked on such radio outlets as WBT Charlotte, WIS Columbia, and WPTF Raleigh. They included Mainer's Mountaineers, Roy Hall and his Blue Ridge Entertainers, and Byron Parker's Mountaineers. Also included in this category were the Coon Creek Girls of Kentucky's *Renfro Valley Barn Dance*, a creation of radio entrepreneur John Lair.

Harmony vocal duets with mandolin-guitar accompaniments like the Monroe Brothers also shared radio air time with such duos as the Blue Sky Boys, the Callahan Brothers, and the Morris Brothers among others. In fact, Monroe's radio and record performances from 1939 to 1945 also contained much that went into the bluegrass sound prior to 1946.

The aftermath of the Second World War witnessed not only young musicians returning home from military service, but also numerous additional radio stations being licensed. Most of the newer broadcast outlets were hardly powerful enough to sustain musical careers (with the possible exception of WCYB Bristol) such as 50,000 watt giants WLS Chicago, WLW Cincinnati, or WSM Nashville, but they could serve as a springboard to work at larger stations. By all accounts, the second bluegrass band, the Stanley Brothers and their Clinch Mountain Boys, formed by a pair of young World War II veterans from southwest Virginia, initially worked briefly on radio at Norton, Virginia and soon moved on to WCYB Bristol which became a career launcher for several noted bluegrass aggregations. Knoxville with WNOX and WROL as well as WWNC Asheville also served as a proving ground for new bands as did the aforementioned stations in Charlotte and

Raleigh. By 1948, Lester Flatt and Earl Scruggs had left the Blue Grass Boys and started their own band, the Foggy Mountain Boys. They, too, worked for a time at WCYB. Bill Monroe, thinking the new bands were simply imitating him, resented this competition and many years passed before he felt appreciated for creating an innovative musical form.

By 1950, other bluegrass bands were forming. Although the majority was comprised of younger musicians, there were a few older ones among them such as Stanley fiddler Leslie Keith and Flatt and Scruggs' tenor vocalist Curly Seckler. Some older pickers still active like Wade Mainer moved closer to the bluegrass style, even replacing himself on banjo with Troy Brammer on one recording session. What is undeniable is that nearly all of the early bluegrass pioneers came from the Appalachian and Piedmont regions. Exceptions were the Monroes who came from the Pennyroyal region of Western Kentucky and original Blue Grass Boys Chubby Wise and Howard Watts who hailed from Florida. The aforementioned bluegrass bands along with those of Jimmy Martin, Jim Eanes, the Lonesome Pine Fiddlers, Don Reno and Red Smiley, Carl Story, and Hylo Brown all hailed from the uplands as did those who picked in their band.

By the time Alan Lomax authored his *Esquire* article, bluegrass music had become increasingly distinct from the country music mainstream. In the years between 1945 and 1960, a number of musicians and groups who might be labeled "traditional country" shared many traits with bluegrass in either style or song repertoire. This term requires some explanation. It is the form that prevailed in the decade between the end of World War II and the emergence of rockabilly and the "Nashville Sound." It co-existed beside what scholars like Bill Malone have termed "honky-tonk" which was designed for nightclubs and the jukebox trade. Practitioners of the form included such stars of their time as Webb Pierce, Hank Snow, Ernest Tubb, and Hank Williams. Less well known but attuned to the older forms were traditional country musicians who were more oriented toward radio audiences and sometimes early local television. One might describe this music as designed more for home listening around the fireplace and hearth. It often included a generous amount of sacred song.

Groups and/or solo traditional country musicians influenced bluegrass music or were in turn influenced by it. Perhaps the key figures in this regard were Ira and Charles, the Louvin Brothers, natives of the Sand Mountain region of Alabama, who further refined the harmony styling of the duos who had attained popularity in the 1930s, used some electric instruments, and contributed numerous original songs. The Louvin career has been well documented by the late country music scholar Charles K. Wolfe. There were also numerous others some of whom included the Bailes Brothers and Mel and Stan—the Kentucky Twins. The brother-in-law team of Johnnie [Wright] and Jack [Anglin] also made notable contributions to the blue-grass sound and repertoire.

Also retaining much traditional sound were such husband-wife teams as Wilma Lee and Stoney Cooper, James and Martha Carson, Bonnie Lou and Buster Moore, the Masters Family, Molly O' Day and Lynn Davis, Lulubelle and Scotty Wiseman, and Doc and Chickie Williams. Although these groups sometimes used electrical instruments, they also had in their musical support acoustical instruments such as mandolin, resonator guitar and in one instance accordion. Radio singers, who had initially been supported only by their own guitar accompaniment, often added electrical instruments to their recorded efforts. They managed to retain a tradition-oriented sound and also compose songs that became bluegrass standards. Typical figures among these vocalists included Lee Moore, Mac Odell, Jimmie Skinner, and Buddy Starcher. Like the pioneer bluegrass musicians, the majority of these figures attained their initial popularity in the Appalachian and Piedmont regions.

The following narrative incorporates updated, revised profiles of thirty-nine musicians and/or bands that were both bluegrass pickers and singers themselves, or were those who fall within the realm of traditional country. Some led bands for all or part of their careers while others ranked as noted "sidemen" or band members. Others composed songs that have become popular—indeed often standard fare—in the bluegrass field.

In its early years, bluegrass music was almost exclusively male domi-nated. Murphy Hicks Henry in her study about women in bluegrass, *Pretty Good for a Girl: Women in Bluegrass*, identified the first one as Wilene "Sally Ann" Forrester, who played accordion with the Blue Grass Boys dur-ing World War II when there was a scarcity of male musicians. The better known girl artists tended to be part of husband-wife duets whose music was closer to bluegrass such as Molly O'Day and Wilma Lee Cooper. Others made a name within family groups such as Donna, Veronica (Roni), and

Patsy Stoneman of the Stonemans or the sisters, Miggie, Polly, and Janis within the Lewis Family. This situation, in large part, reflected the traditions of the rural culture from which bluegrass music and its initial fan base originated. By the late 1960s and early 1970s, regional bands with female leaders and male sidemen had begun to emerge such as those led by Betty Fisher and Lillie Mae Whitaker followed by the Lynn Morris Band and the Dale Ann Bradley Band. Later, there came the Wildwood Girls, the New Coon Creek Girls, and the initially bluegrass Dixie Chicks, as well as such Ohio Valley regional favorites as Ma Crow and the Lady Slippers. All of these individuals and bands paved the way for Rhonda Vincent, who as leader, picker, and vocalist by 2016 has reached about as high a pinnacle in the bluegrass world as any man in the trade.

The profiles herein, in their initial form appeared mostly—thirty-two— in *Bluegrass Unlimited*, which has been the leading publication for that type of music since its founding in 1966. Two more first appeared in the now defunct *Precious Memories: Journal of Gospel Music*, one in Tony Russell's British magazine *Old Time Music*, and two in *Goldenseal: West Virginia Traditional Life*. Finally, those dealing with the original Coon Creek Girls and the Lewis Family appear here for the first time. Grateful permission for reprinting the revised versions is owed to the late Pete Kuykendall of *BU*, Wayde Powell of the defunct *Precious Memories*, Tony Russell of *Old Time Music*, and John Lilly, recently retired from *Goldenseal*. Additional special thanks is due to Kuykendall who provided the pages of his magazine to profile otherwise overlooked bluegrass and influential traditional country figures beginning in 1973 when I was a cash-strapped graduate student. In a sense he made it all possible. Also thanks to the late Charles K. Wolfe and his family who provided a spare bedroom and a place at their table on numerous research trips to Nashville. Information initially came mostly from the musicians themselves, or in the case of those already deceased, to their nearest available kin. Additional information came from detailed discographic data such as that found in Bear Family reissues or updates and corrections from various sources. Since the original articles were done for journals that did not utilize footnotes, that practice has been continued here.

Those profiled range from fairly well-known figures such as Carl Story, Wilma Lee Cooper, and Molly O'Day to those who are nearly forgotten typified by Lester Storer known as the Natchee the Indian, once a noted contest fiddler, and Mel and Stan Hankinson, the Kentucky Twins, who recorded for Capitol and spent time as regulars on such 50,000 watt stations as WLAC, WSM, and WWVA. Sadly the Kentucky Twins's music has not been reissued and Natchee never made any commercial recordings. Others, such as Lillie Mae Whitaker and Mac Martin and the Dixie Travelers, had their fame confined to three or four states.

Most of the articles were initially based on first-person interviews. Supplemental information came from secondary sources ranging from songbooks to news clippings and eventually published discographies. The latter proved especially useful for establishing correct dates and personnel for record sessions as artists do not always recall such details. The late Melvin Goins demonstrated a rare capacity for recall. He could remember minutia within a few days of virtually every important incident in his musical career.

In some instances of partner figures, such as Molly O'Day and Lynn Davis, Bonnie Lou and Buster Moore, and Doc and Chickie Williams, both musicians talked as much as they wished although not necessarily equally. Stan Hankinson was the only one of the Kentucky Twins interviewed because he was in my living room at the time while brother Mel was some 250 miles away. I did no formal interviews with the Lewis Family, but as a close observer and friend for some forty-five years, I felt sufficiently confident to put the essay together.

Surviving relatives and musical associates filled in the essential gaps for those who had already died. A significant example would be Rufus Hall, the younger brother of Roy Hall, and the unrelated Clayton Hall who served as a key member of the Blue Ridge Entertainers Band. The brief article on Lester "Natchee the Indian" Storer was some two decades in the making. Data was derived from oral sources such as Johnnie and Walter Bailes, contest rivals like Curly Fox, genealogical websites, and John Roger Simon's book, *Cowboy Copas and the Golden Age of Country Music*.

Some subjects such as John Masters and Charlie Monroe died before the articles actually appeared in print, but fortunately they had the opportunity to review and check typed copies before their demise. In the case of musicians such as the Callahans, the Mainers, and the Coopers, the surviving brother or spouse served as the oral source. In the case of some multiple survivors, one person was the primary source while the other was more taciturn. Ray Goins and Bea Lilly readily come to mind.

All of the subjects ranked as people or groups in which I had long held a strong interest and wished to do more to document and share their careers. All of those living at the time cheerfully assisted in their own way, having some awareness that they were a part of history and wanted their story told. Whether moderately well known or confined to relative obscurity, whether bluegrass or traditional country, they have made significant contributions to making the music what it has become today.

NOTES

1. Alan Lomax, "Bluegrass Underground: Folk Music with Overdrive," *Esquire* 52 (October 1959), p. 108.

2. Ivan M. Tribe, "Bluegrass Music," Jim Stokely and Jeff D. Johnson, eds., *An Encyclopedia of East Tennessee* (Oak Ridge, TN: Children's Museum of Oak Ridge, 1982), p. 52.

3. Richard D. Smith, "Bluegrass," *The Encyclopedia of Country Music*, Paul Kingsbury, ed. (New York: Oxford University Press, 1998), p. 40.

4. Norm Cohen, *Folk Music: A Regional Exploration* (Westport: CT: Greenwood Press, 2005), p. 145.

5. Neil V. Rosenberg, *Bluegrass: A History* (Urbana: University of Illinois Press, 1985), p. 3.

6. Red Allen quoted in liner notes to *Red Allen: The Folkways Years, 1964–1983*, Smithsonian Folkways SFW CD 40127, 2001, and David McLaughlin, quoted in liner notes to *Danny Paisley and the Southern Grass: Weary River*, Patuxent CD 270, 2015.

PART ONE

Leaders, Solo Singers, and Composers

Bluegrass music first emerged in 1946 with Bill Monroe and his Blue Grass Boys which included Lester Flatt and Earl Scruggs as key band members. The latter formed their own group in 1948 and other groups including the Stanley Brothers adopted the style. As other bands emerged they created their own version of the bluegrass sound, adding their own twists to the original creation and developing their own fan base. Lovers of the style tended to be widespread, but were especially concentrated in the Highland and Piedmont regions of the South.

The urban industrial areas that attracted Appalachian migrants also came to contain large numbers of bluegrass lovers. These locales in the Midwest included Cincinnati, Dayton, and Detroit among others while farther East, Baltimore, Washington, and Pittsburgh ranked as most prevalent. Soon folks in these locales furnished not only an audience, but musicians and bands as well. Although Nashville was in the process of becoming Music City, USA, cities in the South such as Charlotte, Knoxville, Raleigh, and Roanoke as well as the Bristol-Johnson City region in Tennessee and Virginia, all had significant radio stations and later television outlets with an audience for down home music.

Four of the figures profiled in this section led bluegrass bands while a fifth recorded with almost exclusive bluegrass accompaniment. Carl Story and his Rambling Mountaineers had an active musical career of more than fifty years doing bluegrass and near-bluegrass, based mostly in Appalachian and Piedmont locales and placing much of his music on such major record labels as Mercury, Columbia, and Starday with a high but not exclusive proportion of his repertoire being sacred. For much of the later fifties, Hylo Brown ranked among the best traditional country and bluegrass vocalists on the scene and for a couple of years carried an outstanding band, the Timberliners. After his Capitol Records and Starday contracts ended, Brown slowly descended into obscurity and was unable to capitalize on the growing bluegrass festival movement.

Mac Martin led a quality regional band, The Dixie Travelers, in the Pittsburgh area for a half-century and recorded a number of stellar traditional albums on labels that specialize in bluegrass. Since he and the band members held day jobs, their area of personal appearances were largely confined to the Steel City and the adjacent region. As he turned ninety, Martin remained a semi-active musician. The late Lillie Mae Whitaker also performed mostly regionally. She used her west-central Ohio home as a base playing mostly churches and regional festivals with the all-male Dixie Gospel-Aires. Yet she made five guest appearances on the *Grand Ole Opry* and deserves recognition as one of the first women to lead a bluegrass band. Kentucky migrant and sacred vocalist J. D. Jarvis also used his southwest Ohio home as a regional base. He also recorded extensively and composed songs, some of which have become standards.

Other artists were better known as solo performers on radio, but made significant recordings and also composed songs that have become favorites among bluegrass musicians and fans alike. Mac Odell became known as a studio star mostly at WLAC Nashville and made some two dozen recordings for Mercury Records and King Records with support from several musicians known in bluegrass including Don Reno, Buster Moore, and George "Speedy" Krise. Odell's musical timing was not exactly bluegrass in form, but many of his original lyrics have become standards. Buddy Starcher plied his trade as a vocalist who accompanied himself on guitar. He was also an on-air salesman for radio stations in his native West Virginia and elsewhere for several decades. His most effective recordings featured only his singing and simple guitar accompaniment. Yet he attained widespread popularity and also wrote some marvelous songs still widely heard in bluegrass circles.

Charlie Monroe never attained the fame of his younger brother Bill, but for a dozen years he ranked as a significant figure in the field of traditional country music with the Kentucky Pardners band, based most often in East Tennessee and the Carolinas. Monroe never played as a bluegrass artist until his later years, but his string of RCA Victor discs often found favor with the fan base. Such bluegrass figures as Lester Flatt, Curly Seckler, Red Rector, and Slim Martin served apprenticeships in his band.

Jimmie Skinner may seem to have been closer to the country mainstream, placing ten numbers on the *Billboard* charts over a dozen years. His style was atypical with instrumental support dominated by the electric mandolin of Ray Lunsford in the earlier years and the steel guitar of Rusty York later. Remembered today more for his original songs and the Cincinnati Record Store that bore his name, Skinner did record with bluegrass band accompaniment in later years, with only minimal impact on his overall career.

As country musicians go, Clyde Moody never became a major star, but proved himself adaptable in a variety of stylings. He first made a name as a band member for Wade Mainer and as part of a trio within the Sons of the Mountaineers known as the Happy-Go-Lucky Boys. Moving on to becoming a Blue Grass Boy, he sang solo on the blues number "Six White Horses" and sang lead to Bill Monroe's high tenor during the World War II era. Going solo in 1945, he recorded for Columbia, King, and Decca adopting the country crooner approach being popularized at the time by Eddy Arnold. He became known as the Country Waltz King with his own hit "Shenandoah Waltz" and similar songs. As the years passed he switched effortlessly from bluegrass to traditional country.

Lee Moore was a good traditional country singer who may be best remembered as the longtime all-night deejay at 50,000 watt WWVA in Wheeling. Like his friend Buddy Starcher, Moore and his first wife Juanita, who was sometimes billed as the Girl from the Hills, worked live radio on stations from West Virginia to Iowa and North Carolina for years prior to making their first records in 1953. Lee Moore soon went solo and like Starcher did his best recordings accompanied only by his guitar although he did make a couple of albums with bluegrass backing in the 1960s.

More than seventy years have passed since bluegrass music first evolved in 1946. In addition to Bill Monroe, Lester Flatt, Earl Scruggs, and the Stanley Brothers, many other folks contributed to making the great music that fans have come to love. Some led bands, others composed classic songs, and some while not quite bluegrass still made significant contributions to the sound and style. Those profiled here rank as representative of those individuals.

⤙ Hylo Brown

1922–2003

For somewhat more than a decade beginning in 1954, Hylo Brown ranked as a major force in bluegrass music. An Eastern Kentucky native, he migrated to Ohio and worked as a part-time musician, signed with Capitol Records, and playing on his high, lonesome vocals turned out excellent bluegrass and traditional country songs. He continued to record solid bluegrass material in the 1960s, but as time passed production quality declined. In the 1970s, Brown began a slow descent into relative obscurity. By the time of his death, much of the bluegrass community had virtually forgotten his early contributions to the style.

In November 1954, a young Kentucky-born factory worker living in Springfield, Ohio, Brown journeyed to Nashville hoping to get an established country singer to record a song he had written. Although he had made something of a reputation as a part-time performer on Ohio radio stations and parks, and had once assisted a recently retired country star on recordings, Brown really had no other aspirations for a full-time career in music. Yet much to his own surprise, young Brown soon found himself in the Castle Studio doing a session for Ken Nelson of Capitol Records. In the next few years Brown made some of the highest quality bluegrass and hard country music ever recorded. Unfortunately, the musical trend of the times was not in the direction of the style of young Brown, and his share of fame would be much smaller than that of Elvis Presley and Johnny Cash who began recording at about the same time. Nonetheless, for those who appreciated the older vocal and instrumental styles, Brown became a popular and significant entertainer.

Frank Brown Jr. began life in River, Kentucky, part of mountainous Johnson County on April 20, 1922. He attended grade school there and went to high school in nearby Oil Springs, where he began to take an interest in

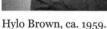

Hylo Brown, ca. 1959.   Hylo Brown, mid-1960s.

music, especially of banjo, mandolin, fiddle, and guitar. Like other pioneer artists, Brown came to love the sound of the Blue Sky Boys, the Monroe Brothers, and, perhaps atypically, the Sons of the Pioneers. He also liked ballad singers such as Doc Hopkins and Bradley Kincaid as well as the Coon Hunter of Uncle Henry's Original Kentucky Mountaineers.

At age sixteen, Brown first sang on the radio at WCMI in Ashland, Kentucky. The next year he and friend Doug Saddler had a weekly program at newly opened WLOG in Logan, West Virginia, which paid them a fifteen dollar salary. However, this ended with the coming of World War II. The Brown family moved to Springfield, Ohio, as part of the great Appalachian migration who found work in defense plants. After the war, Brown continued factory work, but also played music in the area's parks and on local radio.

For years a popular joke circulated among natives of the Buckeye state that the "three R's" as taught in Kentucky consisted of "readin'," "'ritin'", and the "road to Ohio." Although economic opportunity and industrial employment were obviously the major factors in this movement, it resulted in heavy concentrations of bluegrass and country musicians in southwestern Ohio and radio programs that appealed to this clientele. Radio station WPFB in Middletown took to the air in 1947, and featured such musicians as Cincinnati's former *Renfro Valley Barn Dance* favorites Smokey Ward and Little Eller Long. Ward could not remember names very well. When Frank Brown was a guest, Ward began calling the vocalist with the wide voice range "Hi-Lo" or "Hylo." Henceforth, the singer with the lonesome mountain sound became known as Hylo Brown.

Another popular entertainer in the area was Bradley Kincaid, the Kentucky Mountain Boy, a veteran singer whose career extended back to the early days of the WLS *National Barn Dance* and Gennett Records. In 1949, having spent some five years at the *Grand Ole Opry*, Kincaid came to Springfield, purchased an interest in station WWSO, and opened a music store. He sang on his own station, played shows, and opened a music park. In 1950, Brown was one of the local musicians who assisted Kincaid on his last record session for Capitol when the Kentucky Mountain Boy recorded such songs as "Legend of the Robin's Red Breast" and "Red Light Ahead." Brown often credited Kincaid for providing him with valuable experience in the music business.

Brown continued playing locally on weekends with fiddler Shorty McCoy and also dabbled in songwriting. One of his early efforts was a description of WSM's popular Saturday night radio program, which he titled "Grand Ole Opry Song." He had hopes that it might be recorded, but *Opry* management was not enthusiastic. Later in 1956, Jimmy Martin recorded it for Decca and it became a minor classic. Brown included it in his final album in 1977.

Hylo continued writing songs and playing music throughout southwest Ohio. In 1954 he came up with "Lost to a Stranger." Dayton deejay Tommy Sutton suggested the song had possibilities and took it to Joe Allison in Nashville who believed it was a good fit for Kitty Wells. However, Ken Nelson of Capitol preferred that Brown do it himself and scheduled a November 7 session with experienced bluegrass musicians providing support including Red Taylor on fiddle and Joe Drumwright on banjo. Both "Lost to a Stranger" and a second release of another Hylo original "Lovesick and Sorrow," while hardly hits, encouraged more recording sessions. Some later efforts that did well in the Appalachian region had Grady Martin's electric guitar on them. Brown's 1956 recording of "The Prisoner's Song" featured him singing a falsetto tenor on part of the vocal and it became a staple in his repertoire for the rest of his career. Fiddler Tommy Jackson and sometime Blue Grass Boy Jackie Phelps also worked on some Brown recordings. A 1957 single, "Stone Wall," had Lester Flatt and Earl Scruggs joining Hylo for a trio on the chorus.

Following the release of "Lost to a Stranger," Brown organized a band the Buckeye Boys with Sonny Collins on fiddle, well-known comedian Smoky Pleacher on bass fiddle, and the Shepherd Twins on mandolin and banjo. They secured a spot on the WWVA *Jamboree* and played through-out Ohio, West Virginia, Kentucky, and Pennsylvania. Since most of the band members kept their day jobs, they did not record. By early 1957, the Bluegrass Balladeer, as he was becoming known, disbanded his group and joined Flatt and Scruggs and the Foggy Mountain Boys as a featured vocalist.

By this time, Flatt and Scruggs were becoming so popular with their Martha White live television shows that their sponsor formed a second band, the Timberliners, with Brown as leader. This included the superb fiddle and mandolin combination of Tater Tate and Red Rector along with slightly lesser-known Jim Smoak on banjo and Joe "Flapjack" Phillips on bass fiddle and comedy. They initially worked a television circuit from Jackson and Tupelo, Mississippi, to Jackson, Tennessee. After six months, they switched places with the Foggy Mountain Boys and worked the Appalachian cities of Chattanooga and Knoxville, Tennessee; Bluefield and Huntington, West Virginia. The fifth city rotated between the West Virginia towns of Clarksburg, Parkersburg, and Wheeling and was seemingly less successful, but Huntington was as popular for Brown as it had been for Flatt and Scruggs. Comedian Charles Elza, known alternately as Kentucky Slim or Little Darling, was also a popular attraction on this circuit. In 1959, the use of video tape caused Martha White to syndicate Flatt and Scruggs in both circuit areas and Brown's best days came to an end. However, he soon rejoined the Foggy Mountain Boys as a featured vocalist.

Brown and the Timberliners did their best recordings for Capitol in early August 1958 at Kincaid's studio. The album simply titled *Hylo Brown* is often considered one of the best traditional bluegrass offerings of all time. Only two or three songs were of recent vintage with most dating to the Carter Family or earlier. Both Brown and Rector vocalized in their best form and Tate added baritone on the chorus of most songs. A week later the Timberliners did an additional eight numbers for single releases. Although they included some good numbers such as "I've Waited as Long as I Can," "Shuffle of My Feet," and "Thunderclouds of Love," choral overdubbing by the Jordanaires diluted the purity of the traditional approach taken by Brown and the Timberliners.

After the Martha White connection ended, both Rector and Phillips left the band. The Timberliners kept television programs in Clarksburg and Parkersburg for a few more months. The band still had a very good sound as evidenced by both a recording of a WSIP program out of Paintsville, Kentucky, that was later released on John Palmer's Grassound label and a live stage show that was released on a Copper Creek Records compact disc. Family illness led Tate to leave the band, but Brown found competent new band members such as banjo picker Billy Edwards, fiddler Louie Profitt, bass man Bill Lowe, and young resonator guitarist Norman Blake. Brown's popularity remained high in central Appalachia and he still attracted crowds. The band did a final four-song session for Capitol in late October 1960, but the material wasn't released until 1992 when it appeared on a two disc Bear Family collection. Soon after the 1960 recording, Hylo disbanded the Timberliners and returned to his old role as a featured vocalist with Flatt and Scruggs. Capitol did not pick up his option, so he signed with Starday Records in December 1961.

Through mid-1963, Brown did four bluegrass albums with Starday Records, three of them with Nashville session musicians that included such notables as Joe Drumwright, a sometime Blue Grass Boy who had worked on Brown's first Capitol session, fiddle legend Chubby Wise, later Nashville Brass banjo picker Curtis McPeake, and Dobro player Shot Jackson. Songs included Hylo's version of the Flatt and Scruggs hit "Cabin on the Hill" that he had actually first brought to the Foggy Mountain Boys via Rector. Although of Mississippi origin, it had been sung on Knoxville radio by more than one group for some years. A fine Jimmie Skinner song "Picture in the Wallet," and a bluegrass version of the later country stan-dard "Truck Drivin' Man" ranked among his Starday fare. The third of the four albums recorded on Thanksgiving weekend 1962, *Hylo Brown Meets the Lonesome Pine Fiddlers*, had band support from a pioneer Appalachian bluegrass group that had musical roots similar to Brown. The Fiddlers lead vocalist Melvin Goins had earlier as well as later worked with Brown doing comedy as "Hot Rize Charlie." Since the Fiddlers re-corded an album of their own the same weekend, Brown did a guest vocal at their session on "Coal Dust Blues."

After leaving Flatt and Scruggs, Brown worked a lot of club dates, local jamborees, and drive-in theaters. He also began supplementing his mid-week income by performing musical programs in public schools always doing a few folk songs of Appalachian origin thus providing some educa-tional content. Through the 1960s and 1970s, he did many of these venues throughout the tri-state region of Ohio, West Virginia, and Kentucky. About 1966, Brown began to record for Uncle Jim O'Neal's Rural Rhythm label. This company produced long-play albums containing about twenty num-bers—some rather short—with many of the songs drawn from the public domain. By 1970, he had turned out seven of these albums all with varying quality of bluegrass accompaniment. Some sessions used musicians who were part of the Columbus, Ohio, Appalachian migrant community such as Dobro player Danny Milhon, banjo picker Ross Branham, and guitar-ist Jack Casey. Three albums used the services of Roy Ross and his Blue Ridge Mountain Boys, a popular local band from Pike County, Ohio. The final one, *America's Favorite Balladeer*, briefly reunited him with two for-mer band members, Tater Tate and Billy Edwards who were then part of the Red Smiley band. While these recordings were competent, they were a far cry from his Capitol classics or even the Starday material. Keeping one foot in the country camp, he made some singles for smaller Nashville-based labels such as King's Music City and K-Ark.

The advent of bluegrass festivals saw Brown on stage occasionally, but he never really connected with the festival scene. He appeared at Bean Blossom in 1970 with banjo picker Gary Brotherton who had played on some of his Rural Rhythm records, but he generally played solo or with whatever musicians he could pick up. He shared a gospel album with Crum, West Virginia, banjo picker Lowell Varney. In the early 1970s, he made an LP on the Jessup label in Jackson, Michigan, backed by musicians from the Detroit bluegrass community and looked forward to doing more. In the meantime, he moved his home to a farm near Jackson, Ohio.

After 1974, Hylo continued a slow slide into musical obscurity. In 1977, he made his final bluegrass album on Carl Queen's Atteiram label. Entitled

A Tribute to My Heroes it included his original "Grand Ole Opry Song" and well-known hits of various country stars. With support from better-known Nashville pickers, it was best described as a valiant effort that had little effect in reviving his sagging career.

My last visit with the Bluegrass Balladeer took place at a small festival near Logan, Ohio, in the summer of 1981. The city is remembered as the place where a riot occurred a few weeks earlier as the result of a last-minute show cancellation by George Jones. Brown's voice quality had declined and he could no longer naturally sing the higher keys, a real problem for a bluegrass vocalist. He usually sang in low keys and as a result sounded like an Appalachian version of Johnny Cash. He divided his later years between Eastern Kentucky and Springfield, Ohio and suffered a stroke in 1990. Later interviewers found him somewhat disillusioned and embittered.

Brown was not totally forgotten as in 1992 Bear Family Records of Germany issued his entire Capitol output in a two-CD set. In his notes, Colin Escott correctly observed that Brown had been "less well-served by the history business." In 1995 Copper Creek released a compact disc of a live show at New River Ranch on August 9, 1959, that included support from band members Tater Tate, Jim Smoak, and Jay Bailey. In February 2003, the Society for the Preservation of Bluegrass Music of America planned to honor him. He died on January 17, 2003. That year, Gusto Records released a CD of some of his best Starday sides and in recent years some of his Rural Rhythm material has been reissued, but to again quote Escott, he remained "still shortchanged by official histories of bluegrass." Nonetheless, for a decade Hylo Brown was a shining light of musical tradition.

SELECTED RECORDINGS

Hylo Brown & the Timberliners, 1954–60. Bear Family BCD 15572, 1992. Brown's entire
Capitol output with unissued and some alternate takes.
Hylo Brown: In Concert. Copper Creek, CCCD-0135, 1995. Recorded at New River Ranch,
August 9, 1959.
Hylo Brown: Lovesick and Sorrow. Starday SD 0124–2, 2003. A good sampling of sixteen
songs from his four Starday albums, 1961–1963.

✐ Roy Hall

1907–1943

The country music group of Roy Hall and his Blue Ridge Entertainers achieved tremendous regional popularity from their radio base of WDBJ in Roanoke, Virginia, in the two years prior to Pearl Harbor. Their recordings sold well over an even wider area and one song, "Don't Let Your Sweet Love Die," achieved hit status. The group's music, while rooted in traditional Appalachian mountain styles, also contained a mixture of more modern influences, much of which evolved into bluegrass by the end of the decade. Unfortunately, the war forced the breakup of the band, and Hall's untimely death in an automobile crash prevented any possibility of a reunion. As a result, Hall and his musicians are somewhat neglected. Nonetheless, the Blue Ridge Entertainers in their brief existence exercised considerable influence in the Piedmont and mountain areas of Virginia and the Carolinas.

The Hall Family, which included twelve children, came from Waynesville in Haywood County, North Carolina, some twenty-five miles west of Asheville. Three went on to enjoy some renown as musicians—Roy Davis born January 6, 1907, Jay Hugh born November 13, 1910, and Rufus born September 1, 1921. The boys came by music naturally as several paternal uncles played a variety of instruments at local venues. More importantly, the entire area was steeped in a rich tradition of mountain instrumental and vocal music. As Rufus Hall aptly explained the situation, the family grew up in the same environment as J. E. and Wade Mainer, Homer and Walter Callahan, George, Zeke and Wiley Morris, and Clyde Moody. From the mid-1920s, area musicians also received exposure to mountain music on phonograph records that acquainted them with the sound of such Carolina groups as Charlie Poole and the North Carolina Ramblers and Dock Walsh and the Carolina Tar Heels.

Roy Hall. *Photo Courtesy of David Freeman.*

As Roy and Jay Hugh Hall grew to adulthood, to earn a living they followed many rural working-class men into the cotton textile mills. At the same time, they continued to play and sing locally and for their own amusement. Roy Hall was thirty and Jay Hugh twenty-six when they went full time as musicians.. Rufus Hall recalled that his older brothers still worked in the mills at the time they recorded their first Bluebird session on February 16, 1937. The duo recorded a dozen numbers that day using only their own guitars for accompaniment. The numbers ranged from traditional folk songs like "Little Mohee" to the recent Sons of the Pioneers' hit, "Way Out There." Using the name the Hall Brothers, they exhibited a flair for comic novelty songs in "Whistle Honey Whistle," a number reminiscent of some of the material then being performed by the popular Tobacco Tags group.

Eight to ten weeks after their initial session, the Hall Brothers went to work for radio station WSPA in Spartanburg, South Carolina. Jay Hugh Hall had some previous radio experience having played as a duet with Clyde Moody. He later rejoined Moody and the two worked as the team of Bill and Joe, the Happy-Go-Lucky Boys part of the more established Wade Mainer and the Sons of the Mountaineers. Nonetheless, Jay Hugh Hall got together with his brother Roy to do two more Hall Brothers sessions on Bluebird on January 27, 1938 and September 26, 1938. Since the Wade Mainer group also recorded on these same days, Steve Ledford, Wade Mainer's fiddle player, was present and helped out on three numbers. One of the more memorable tunes recorded with Ledford, "The Wrong Road," reflected the recently passed gangster era and told of a youth's entry into a life of crime utilizing the old tune, "Little Stream of Whiskey." In all, the Hall Brothers made twenty-four songs for Bluebird, with eighteen issued.

With Jay Hugh Hall's departure, Roy Hall began to gather a string band known as the Blue Ridge Entertainers to perform with him at WSPA. Clato "Bud" Buchanan had joined on fiddle somewhat earlier, but switched to the tenor banjo after the more accomplished Tommy Magness became a member of the band. Others in the group included Bill Brown on Dobro and Wayne Watson on bass. In addition to their radio work at WSPA, the Roy Hall group also worked brief stints at WWNC Asheville and WBIG Greensboro, both in North Carolina.

By the fall of 1938, the Blue Ridge Entertainers had a half-hour early morning show at WAIR Winston-Salem, North Carolina, sponsored by Dr. Pepper. In November 1938, the band journeyed to Columbia, South Carolina, and made their first recordings for the American Record Corporation. Likely personnel on this initial session—directed by Art Satherly—included Roy Hall on guitar, Tommy Magness on fiddle, Bud Buchanan on banjo, Talton Aldridge and Bob Hopson, both on guitar. This latter duo was apparently borrowed from Fisher Hendley's Aristocratic Pigs and did not perform regularly with the Blue Ridge Entertainers. The group recorded eighteen numbers, only eight of which were released. One of their unreleased tunes seemed as intriguing as those songs that were issued—the now standard fiddle tune, "Orange Blossom Special." This Hall-Magness rendition preceded that of the Rouse Brothers by more than seven months. The record company files contained the notation, "Hold Release, Rouse Brothers refuse to sign contract" while the A. & R. director's ledgers contain the handwritten words, "Don't Release—Pub. Promises Trouble." The whole story behind these two brief comments may never be known, but it seems likely that only a slight stroke of fate kept this now famous tune from being identified with Roy Hall in the public eye. In 1999, Columbia released the number in an anthology *Country, the American Tradition*. Most critics were disappointed as Magness had not yet mastered the tune and it lacked the zip that characterized his later fiddle work. Clayton Hall perhaps said it best when his grandson played the recording for him in old age, "Boy, Tommy didn't do much with that one."

The numbers that Columbia did release on their Vocalion label included "Come Back, Little Pal" which has been most identified with Roy Hall. Some doubt exists as to whether Hall or Hanford Wilson composed the song, but Roy Hall owned the rights to it. Subsequent versions by Wade Mainer, Roy Acuff, and several bluegrass artists have made the song a standard. Roy Hall's recordings of "The Lonesome Dove," "Wabash Cannonball," "Where the Roses Never Fade," "Sunny Tennessee," and "Answer to the Great Speckled Bird" also came from that session.

Soon after the Columbia session, Buchanan left the band and the Hall Twins, Clayton and Saford, joined the Blue Ridge Entertainers. This duo (no relation to Roy) born on May 4, 1919, already had previous experience on WSJS and local entertainment venues. They added new variety to the group by doing their own duets as well as duets by Clayton and Roy. The twins played many instruments although Clayton favored the banjo and Saford the fiddle. This kept at least one fiddler in the band at all times since Magness left for a time to play with Bill Monroe. He returned later, although he eventually departed a second time, going with Roy Acuff and his Smoky Mountain Boys.

During Roy Hall's Winston-Salem stint, the Delmore Brothers often appeared on his show. Alton and Rabon Delmore had left the *Grand Ole Opry* in September 1938 and headed for North Carolina to play personal appearances. In his autobiography, which was published posthumously in 1978, Alton Delmore recalled Roy Hall as "a nice fellow and a good businessman."

In 1939, the Blue Ridge Entertainers moved from Winston-Salem to WDBJ Roanoke, still working for Dr. Pepper. The group found it challenging to make ends meet prior to the Virginia move. Within a few weeks after settling in Roanoke, they won acclaim which they had not achieved before. Soon they played to packed crowds everywhere. Clayton Hall recalled that they found appreciative audiences at theaters and schoolhouses every night of the week and were booked nearly a year in advance. Clayton Hall contended that in one unusually good week his share of the band's earnings provided him with a new automobile.

Roy Hall also inaugurated a live Saturday night show in Roanoke, *The Blue Ridge Jamboree*, which featured both local acts and big name guest entertainers. Both Rufus Hall and Clayton Hall recalled that individual stars and groups from Hollywood musical westerns ranked among the favorite guests including Jimmy Wakely, Tex Ritter, Ken Maynard, Gabby Hayes, Roy Rogers, and Ray Whitley as well as the Sons of the Pioneers. Regional practitioners of mountain and country music also were guests on the Jamboree, such as the Blue Sky Boys, the Carter Family, the Tobacco Tags, WBT Briarhoppers, the Callahan Brothers, the Delmore Brothers, and both the J. E. and Wade Mainer groups. From their fond memories of the *Blue Ridge Jamboree*, it is obvious that both Clayton Hall and Rufus Hall considered the show to be among the highlights of their careers as entertainers. By the spring of 1941, the Blue Ridge Entertainers had attained a level of popularity so great that one band could no longer supply the demand for personal appearances. Roy Hall formed two units. No. 1 consisted of himself on guitar, the Hall Twins on guitar and fiddle, Bill Brown on Dobro, Wayne Watson on bass, and Tommy Magness on fiddle, after returning from his stint with Monroe. The second unit consisted of Jay Hugh Hall, having returned from his Mainer work, on mandolin; Rufus Hall on guitar, who had returned to music after spending two years in professional baseball in Asheville (a St. Louis Cardinal farm team in the Piedmont League); Steve Ledford (another Mainer alumnus) on fiddle; and Hank Angle on bass. According to Rufus Hall, each unit received equal time and billing on the Blue Ridge Entertainers' daily radio shows and the *Blue Ridge Jamboree*. Another musician who sometimes worked as a featured act with the Entertainers was Rafe Brady, the Cherokee Rose, who performed heart songs such as his own "Traveling Through Life."

Roy Hall also became a sort of regional entertainment manager for Dr. Pepper by organizing musical groups under company sponsorship to work on other stations in the area. One group, the Blue Mountain Boys, had Burk Barbour on fiddle, Joe Johnson on bass and Dobro, Bob Hopson on guitar, and a comedian known as Happy Gad. Jay Hugh Hall also worked with this group for a few weeks until it got established. Paul Smith and the Tinker Mountain Boys was a second such band.

Roy Hall and his Blue Ridge Entertainers did two recording sessions, both for Bluebird in Atlanta, during their years in Roanoke. The first on October 9, 1940, resulted in a dozen numbers including Hall's two best-known titles, "Don't Let Your Sweet Love Die" and "Can You Forgive." The former song had been a country-pop number that Roy Hall rearranged to his own style and his version gave it the country-bluegrass standard status that it has attained. "Can You Forgive," a Roy Hall original, achieved enough popularity to inspire an answer written by Eva Nichols and although un-recorded, appeared in Roy's *Melodies from the Hills* Songbook. Both these recordings have become bluegrass standards, the former by several art-ists, most notably Mac Wiseman, and the latter by Wilma Lee and Stoney Cooper and also the Stanley Brothers. Roy also did an early cover of Bob Wills' hit, "New San Antonio Rose," at this session. The Hall Twins recorded a pair of duets.

Roy Hall recorded eight numbers at his final session of October 1, 1941. Memorable tunes recorded then included two Tommy Magness fiddle orig-inals, "Polecat Blues" and "Natural Bridge Blues" and the recent Johnny Bond composition, "I Wonder Where You Are Tonight." Jimmy Wakely re-corded it first, but the Hall rendition doubtlessly furnished the model for the countless bluegrass versions that one hears today although he included an additional verse no longer used.

Besides the previously mentioned musicians, other aspiring pickers or singers played brief periods with the Blue Ridge Entertainers. Rufus Hall remembered one in particular, a teen-age youth who did a few shows with the band one summer playing guitar and harmonica using a homemade holder made from a coat hanger. The fellow later attained worldwide fame as television and movie actor Andy Griffith. Jim Eanes also received some early experience with the group.

During the Roanoke years, the group issued a number of song books for sale via their daily radio broadcasts. The songs contained in these book-lets suggest that Roy Hall performed a goodly amount of currently popular Texas and Louisiana country material such as "Sweethearts or Strangers," "It Makes No Difference Now," and "Sleepy Rio Grande." He also did old tra-ditional lyrics and newer material by contemporary artists of Appalachian background such as the Coon Creek Girls and Roy Acuff. Roy Hall per-formed songs composed by local writers, too, such as "Don't Let It Be

Goodbye" by Allie May Belton of Mount Airy, North Carolina, and "When the Silver Moon Is Shining" by Lois Warrell of Woodlawn.

The coming of World War II ended the great days of the Blue Ridge Entertainers. The Hall Twins entered the service shortly after Pearl Harbor and by June 1942 the two units consolidated into a single band. After Rufus Hall entered the service on October 24, the group ceased to play on a regular basis. Jay Hugh Hall joined Charlie Monroe and the Kentucky Pardners at Renfro Valley for a brief time until he, too, entered the service. Roy Hall died in an automobile accident near Roanoke on May 16, 1943.

After the war, Jay Hugh and Rufus Hall reorganized as the Hall Brothers and the Blue Ridge Entertainers. The group played at WROV and WSJS in Winston-Salem. The Halls also worked for a few months at WNOX Knoxville and WCYB Bristol with such musicians as Curly King and Jack and Curly Shelton. They also did a few shows at the *Barrel O' Fun* show at Elizabethton, Tennessee, with J. E. Mainer. However, things never seemed the same without Roy Hall and the remaining brothers dropped out of music in June 1947. Jay Hugh Hall worked in construction until his death in the spring of 1972. Rufus Hall went to work for the Norfolk and Western Railway. In 1979 he resided in Vinton, Virginia, and was interviewed for an early version of this essay.

Of other prominent band members, Tommy Magness went on to work several years with Roy Acuff and then led his own band, the Tennessee Buddies. For a time, he had a band at WDBJ Roanoke called the Orange Blossom Boys which included the Hall Twins. Magness died in 1972 at the age of 61, one of the more respected fiddlers of his era. Bill Brown resided in Roanoke and Wayne Watson in Winston-Salem, North Carolina. Clayton Hall lived near Ararat, Virginia, and his twin brother Saford in High Point, North Carolina. They often played at local gatherings in the North Carolina-Virginia region. Saford died in 1999 and Clayton in 2003. In 2010, the latter's grandson, Ralph Berrier, wrote a biography of the twins entitled *If Trouble Don't Kill Me* (Crown Publisher), which related much about Roy Hall's life as well as their own. Until 1978, the Roy Hall group remained relatively neglected in the field of record reissues. RCA Victor included "Can You Forgive" on their *Early Bluegrass* (LPV569) anthology. That song and "Don't Let Your Sweet Love Die" appeared on an inadequately circulated Roan Mountain EP in the early seventies. County Records had a full reissue album released in 1979. It included Roy Hall's best-known tunes from the 1938–1941 era as well as lesser-known songs such as "Neath the Bridge at the Foot of the Hill" and "The Best of Friends Must Part Someday."

The musical legacy of Roy Hall rests largely in his contributions to bluegrass music through influence on other musicians, band style, and song repertoire. The sound of crisp clear vocals, bluesy fiddle, and Dobro often bear the mark of the Blue Ridge Entertainers. In fact, one might even typify the group's sound as almost bluegrass. Songs like "Come Back Little Pal," "Can You Forgive," "Don't Let Your Sweet Love Die," and "I Wonder Where You Are Tonight" have become bluegrass classics. In addition, Hall himself was fondly remembered by those who faithfully heard his shows on WDBJ Roanoke from 1939 through 1942.

Acknowledgement is gratefully extended to Rufus Hall, Clayton Hall, and David Freeman for their help in gathering this information. The photo is courtesy of Freeman from the collection of the late Mrs. Roy Hall.

SELECTED RECORDINGS

Roy Hall & His Blue Ridge Entertainers. County LP 406, 1978. Out of print vinyl album containing fourteen of his original Vocalion and Bluebird recordings from 1938–1941.

✂ J. D. Jarvis

1924–2010

Although gospel music has always been a significant part of bluegrass, beyond the Lewis Family and the late Carl Story, few individuals or groups have gained renown for a long-term association with the genre. Family acts such as the Forbes and the Marshalls made an impact for a few years and then moved on to other endeavors. By contrast, J. D. Jarvis devoted much of the last four decades of his life to gospel music. From the mid-1960s into the early 1980s, Jarvis recorded heavily—usually with bluegrass accompaniment—and along the way composed a few songs that have become classics. In later years, Jarvis slowed down, but still made himself available for church performances as his health permitted.

Like many folks whose bluegrass roots are in the earliest years of the music, John Dill Jarvis hailed from Eastern Kentucky. Born five miles from Manchester in Clay County on April 21, 1924, he was about eight years old when he began to play guitar and then clawhammer banjo. As far back as he could remember he had a knack for composing rhymes, which certainly came in handy when he began writing song lyrics. Since Jarvis did not have a very good guitar, his parents arranged to buy a better one for him from an uncle who lived in Brookville, Indiana, returning home to surprise him with it. Like many young country pickers, "Wildwood Flower" was the first tune he mastered. Within a few months, he went into nearby Manchester on Saturdays and joined other pickers on the town square. Sometimes he would receive tips.

Thirteen-year-old Jarvis's happy youth came to a sudden end in January 1938 when his coal miner father died in a hospital from a gunshot wound he sustained following an argument alongside a highway. The family experienced difficult times. As soon as Jarvis turned sixteen, he persuaded his mother to let him join the Civilian Conservation Corps. He went first to

J. D. Jarvis with
Rusty York.

J. D. Jarvis.
*Photo courtesy of
John Morris.*

Indiana and then to Wyoming. During his absence, his mother remarried and moved to Cincinnati. Jarvis took his guitar with him and entertained his fellow CCC members in their idle moments. When his service ended, he headed east and fondly recalled the kindness of a motorist who not only transported him to Muncie, Indiana, but also bought him a train ticket to Cincinnati's Union Terminal.

Jarvis worked for a time with his stepfather in Cincinnati, briefly returned to Kentucky, and then moved back to Cincinnati. World War II had started by then and Jarvis decided to enlist. His mother agreed to sign enlistment papers for him and he left Manchester for a four-year hitch in the U. S. Army. Like many country boys, he took his old guitar along and with others managed to keep morale high in the army camps with his picking and singing. From Kentucky and Indiana to Florida and eventually England, the process repeated itself. Like many Appalachian youth, Jarvis had his wilder moments and became involved in more than his share of drinking and fighting incidents, but surprisingly came through in pretty good shape. One time in Scotland, Bob Hope and Tex Ritter came to entertain the troops. Jarvis got so enthusiastic when the latter sang "Pistol Packing Mama" that he ran up on stage, shook hands with the cowboy film star, and told him in front of the whole unit how much he appreciated his "down home music."

Meanwhile the Allies prepared for the Normandy invasion. Jarvis was among the thousands who swarmed onto the beaches of Normandy that memorable morning of June 6, 1944. Almost a month later on July 5 at a place that became known as "Purple Heart Hill," the aggressive young Kentuckian as a soldier in Patton's army got hit by shell fragments and was thrown through the air some thirty feet. As Jarvis modestly explained it, he was "torn up pretty bad." His combat career came to a sudden end, and he spent several months recovering from his multiple wounds. After recovery, he spent his remaining service time in the USO.

Back in civilian life early in 1946, Jarvis rotated for several years between residing in his Kentucky mountain homeland and the Greater Cincinnati area. Eventually he settled permanently in Hamilton, Ohio, moving into his suburban home in 1959. Jarvis had married Rosie Owens in Corbin, Kentucky, on May 25, 1946, and they eventually had a son named Lucky. While working for the Newport Steel Company, the transplanted mountaineer began playing in a variety of country bands on the hillbilly bar scene in the greater Cincinnati area. He also played in various musical groups during periods of living back in the mountains. His indulgence in a rounder's lifestyle also continued, and he found himself involved in a variety of fights and brawls. But that all changed in 1953.

Jarvis probably began to reflect upon the way he was living in 1951 when he came home from a musical job late one night and found a note pinned to the door screen informing him that one of his brothers had been killed in a car wreck back in Kentucky. However, the real change came in 1953 when Rosie told him one morning that he had almost "killed them all" with his driving the night before. He recalled telling her that "it won't happen again" and he quit drinking immediately. A few weeks later he was saved in a tent revival. Thereafter, he primarily sang, played, and composed sacred music.

In one of his first post-salvation musical experiences, Jarvis participated in one and possibly both of the more unique collections of Appalachian gospel music ever recorded as a support musician for Brother Claude Ely (1922–1978). Ely, a powerful mountain preacher from Pennington Gap, Virginia, had two King Record sessions in church services on October 26, 1953 and June 16, 1954. The songs included the first recording by a white musician of the now standard "There Ain't No Grave Gonna Hold My Body Down." Earlier versions had been done for the U. S. Library of Congress and also by a black gospel duo, the Two Gospel Keys on Apollo. Some years later Jarvis assisted Ely again on an album recorded in Rusty York's Jewel studio. Jarvis said that Reverend Ely was "a wonderful man" and a great preacher.

As a newly converted Christian, J. D. Jarvis put his singing and composing skills to work in churches. Whether in his mountain homeland or in the Greater Cincinnati area, Jarvis put in hundreds of weekends at gospel singings as far away as Tennessee, Michigan, and Missouri. He also donated his vocal talent to many gospel radio and television shows in the region including Cincinnati, Dayton, Hamilton and Middletown, Ohio, and Covington and Newport, Kentucky. His raw, primitive vocals found special appreciation among the transplanted mountain folk that had relocated to an urban-industrial environment. Some years elapsed before he tried his hand at recording, making a demo about 1956, and then doing a session for commercial release about four years later.

According to Jarvis's nearest recollection, he did his first session for release on the Ark label about 1960 when he cut a four-song EP. One song was his original titled "Life of Ransom," which he had put to the tune of "Sunny Side of the Mountain." Another was a cover of the then new Stanley Brothers recording of "A Few More Seasons." He did not recall the other numbers, but did remember that Walter Hensley picked the banjo. Wayne Metcalf fiddled, Gene Sweet played resonator guitar, and Art Wydner played the bass. The mandolin work was done by a guy he recalled only as "Juicy Fruit" who normally worked with Dave Woolum's Laurel County Boys. In addition to Jarvis, veteran guitarist Jim McCall played rhythm. He subsequently did some more recording for Ark including an LP, but his first album was for Harp Records and bore the title *Walk the Streets of Glory*; it was released without a cover.

Over the next twenty years, J. D. Jarvis recorded more than thirty albums for many different labels. His most widely distributed releases were cut for Uncle Jim O'Neal's Rural Rhythm Records in Arcadia, California, most of which were recorded at Rusty York's Jewel Studio in Cincinnati. Most were straight bluegrass although some contained a piano. The one most musically satisfying to bluegrass purists would likely be *More Bluegrass Gospel Songs* which had Ralph Stanley's Clinch Mountain Boys furnishing the instrumentation. One Rural Rhythm album featured Jarvis's vocals on one side and Rusty York on the other. Support musicians on the Rural Rhythm sessions were Vern McIntire on banjo; Harley Gabbard on resonator guitar; Frank Wakefield on mandolin; Fred Spencer and Rusty York on rhythm guitars; and Jack Sanderson on bass. Since Uncle Jim usually had a minimum of twenty numbers (some rather short time-wise) per album, Jarvis had a total of 112 cuts on Rural Rhythm not counting those on which he furnished backup for Rusty York's vocals.

If O'Neal managed to get the Jarvis albums out to a broader audience, those on Rusty York's own Jewel label may have surpassed most of the others in terms of quality. Although more than a decade younger than Jarvis, York was also a Kentucky mountain boy who had come to Cincinnati while still in his teens, mastered the bluegrass banjo and other instruments, and recorded not only bluegrass, but country and rockabilly as well. He also learned the technical skills associated with record engineering and over the years turned out some high quality traditional products at his little studio in Mt. Healthy, Ohio. Jarvis not only cut a considerable volume of material at Jewel studio, but he and York became close friends. Since quantity was less a factor on the Jewel albums, quality tended to be better. Jarvis did five albums for Jewel including one he shared with Lillie Mae Whitaker and her group. In addition to some of the aforementioned sidemen, Jarvis also had some help on his Jewel recordings from fiddlers Paul "Moon" Mullins and Art Stamper and guitarist Dennis Hensley.

Over the years J.D. had musicians on his recordings that read like a who's who of bluegrass in the Dayton-Cincinnati region. These included Ralph King, George Brock, Billy Thomas, Curly Tuttle, Billy Holmes, and Junior Spivey, plus Joe and Lily Isaacs. At times he also scheduled musicians from Nashville to participate in his sessions including Josh Graves, Kenny Baker, Glen Duncan, and Blake Williams. In addition to the aforementioned labels, Jarvis had album releases on his own Down Home trademark and Lou Ukelson's Vetco Records, as well as one album for the Nashville-based Heart Warming Records. When his friend Dennis Hensley opened a studio in Covington, Jarvis made some recordings for his Sagegrass Records. Since many of these companies wished to have a recording of Jarvis's best-known originals in their catalog, he actually made several renditions of his most popular efforts such as "Six Hours on the Cross" and "Take Your Shoes Off, Moses," sometimes to the chagrin of record reviewers.

Jarvis's recording output generally contained a broad spectrum of well-known country and bluegrass gospel numbers and lesser-known chestnuts. He not only borrowed from the sacred repertoires of the Stanley Brothers, Bill Monroe, and Flatt and Scruggs, but always turned out several fine originals. Some of the latter included "Life of Ransom," "Six Hours on the Cross," "I Am the Man, Thomas" (usually credited to Stanley and Sparks who re-arranged Jarvis's rendition), "Come on Little Children," and "The Space Ship Song." By far the best-known Jarvis original is "Take Your Shoes Off, Moses."

Jarvis wrote "Take Your Shoes Off, Moses" in 1963. While he cut the song several times himself over the years, the recordings by others have done even more to make the song a standard. Ralph Stanley and the Clinch Mountain Boys used it on their popular *Cry from the Cross* Rebel album in February 1971 and the Lewis Family on their *High in Gospel Country* on Canaan in 1974. Other versions are those of George Brock, the Easter Brothers, and the Isaacs who included a verse and a chorus in "Bluegrass Medley" on their *Live in Atlanta* album. A compact disc collection of Canaan various gospel numbers kept the Lewis rendition in print for several years. Jarvis also got word that Elvis Presley had intended to do the song in a gospel album, but died prior to its being completed. He heard that Presley may have made a demo of it but did not know if that rumor was true or not. Floyd Whited of Gospel Gems Music in Dayton originally had the publishing rights to the song, but Jarvis later placed it with Quentin Weldy's company. It yielded steady, if unspectacular, royalties through the years.

As Jarvis became better known through his records and songs, he made several trips to Florida and as far southwest as Jackson, Mississippi, and northwest to Wisconsin. When he did the country gospel album for Heart Warming, their producers wanted him to go into music full time and travel all over the country. However, J.D. preferred to remain a part-time musician. His war experiences had taken some toll on his nerves and he had a prospering paint contracting business in Hamilton.

Although Jarvis confined most of his writings to sacred lyrics, he did compose a few topical and patriotic songs. "Tragedy of Sandy River" dealt with the same 1958 school bus wreck in Floyd County, Kentucky, that the Stanley Brothers had sung about in "No School Bus In Heaven" and the Phipps Family memorialized in "Yellow Tomb." "In Memory of LeRoy Allen Lykens" told the story of a child who suffered fatal internal injuries in an accident with a bulldozer. As Jarvis recalled, the boy's father came to him with a newspaper clipping about the tragedy and asked him to compose a song-poem about it. "Thank God for Old Glory" reflected on Jarvis's war experiences and was his patriotic tribute to the American flag.

The most touching of the Jarvis topical items, however, also proved to be his own individual best seller. "The Hyden Miner's Tragedy" concerned the major coal mine disaster that happened in Eastern Kentucky on December 30, 1970. As soon as Jarvis heard of the incident he drove immediately to Hyden to assist with rescue efforts. He had numerous friends and relatives who worked in that mine and as he sadly phrased it, "put two first cousins in their casket." The inspiration to write a memorial followed soon after the funeral. Jarvis related that he and Rosie took a station wagon loaded with the singles to a mountain record shop and found buyers lined up awaiting their arrival. They sold the entire carload in a day and some 14,000 copies of the 45 RPM version and a considerable volume of albums as well.

As the years passed and Jarvis grew older, he slowed down a bit, but continued to be active as a writer and singer. Son Lucky took over the paint contracting business and Jarvis had more time to relax at home. He no longer played churches on a nightly basis, but did a few each month. He continued to write songs and made a few cassette tapes in the 1990s. Many of his gospel originals had combined the country penchant for topical ballads with biblical narrative. He put the finishing touches to a lyric titled "Old Daniel Read the Writing on the Wall."

In retrospect, Jarvis is one Appalachian migrant who overcame his wilder habits of earlier days and through faith put his skills to use at building a successful business and an avocation of singing and songwriting that has inspired thousands. John Dill Jarvis was closely identified with bluegrass and gospel music for some five decades. As a singer, he exemplified the rough-hewn mountain singing style that typified the older musical forms of the Appalachian region in much the same manner as Ralph Stanley. As a composer, he contributed some standard songs to the field that rank as significant additions to the genre which have been under-recognized. My own appreciation for Jarvis reached its height during the 1978 Christmas season when my wife and I visited the Chapel of the Burning Bush in St. Catherine's Greek Orthodox Monastery at the foot of Mt. Sinai. In that hallowed space is a large mosaic of Moses reaching down to remove his sandals. "This is an inspiring sight," I said to myself, "but it could be improved if they only had a background soundtrack of J. D. Jarvis singing "Take Your Shoes Off, Moses."

In 2007, Jarvis suffered several strokes. He died three years later on December 31, 2010. According to one obituary, he had recorded forty-six albums and managed to get two compact discs of his best work released. He was buried with full military honors.

SELECTED RECORDINGS

J. D. Jarvis: Mother Needs No Marker. Old Homestead OHCD 4018, 1999. Anthology of his better numbers.

J. D. Jarvis: You Get the Best of Me. Down Home DH 501029, [ca. 2001]. Another collection of Jarvis recordings.

∾ Mac Martin

1925–

Whereas bluegrass band leaders and some musicians have long had an enduring quality about them—Bill Monroe being the most obvious—continuity of personnel in bands is much less common. One quite atypical group in bluegrass music that has long endured with a consistent quality product may have been only a part-time band, but they gained respect among fans around the world.

Mac Martin and the Dixie Travelers became a virtual institution in the Pittsburgh area. The key members of the band on guitar, banjo, and fiddle played together for more than thirty-five years. Other members remained for over ten years. Through more than four decades of recording, the Dixie Travelers released about a dozen albums of quality music.

Although Pittsburgh maintains a well-deserved reputation for ethnic diversity, particularly Eastern European, the Steel City can also boast its share of Appalachian migrants to provide an audience for the music of the Dixie Travelers. Mac Martin comes from Galway, Ireland stock. His real name is William Colleran, and his forebears made up a part of the great Celtic exodus that emigrated from the Emerald Isle over several decades beginning in the 1840s. Born in Pittsburgh on April 26, 1925, Martin reported that some of his first cousins who reside in Ireland also play music, so his musical talents are in the blood.

As a youngster in Pittsburgh, Martin listened to country music on the radio. His favorite programs included the *Grand Ole Opry* and the *Wheeling Jamboree*. He also gained a great appreciation for the recordings of folks like the Carter Family and the Monroe Brothers as well as being attracted to the songs of lesser yet still significant duets like the Dixon Brothers and the West Virginia team of Bill Cox and Cliff Hobbs. By the early forties, Mac had taken up the guitar and began to try re-creating the music of his

Mac Martin & the Dixie Travelers, ca. 1971. *Top row from left*: Billy Bryant, Mac Martin, Bob Artis. *Bottom row from left:* Mike Carson, Frank Basista.

favorites. At the time, he pursued this interest pretty much as a hobby or for pastime with little thought of a professional or a semi-professional career. However, in this process Martin picked up a tremendous song repertoire. Bill Vernon quoted an unidentified Dixie Traveler fan that Martin "knows 'at least a verse and a chorus' of every song he has ever heard." Even if this claim constitutes a slight exaggeration, it still comprises an esteemed compliment to his mental storehouse of song lyrics.

About 1942, Martin met a fellow named Ed Brozi. The two spent a lot of time picking and singing together. They also looked around in the used record departments of stores and Martin developed fondness for harmony duets. Brozi had some experience as a medicine show entertainer and helped the young Irish-American further develop his still increasing repertoire. In the early seventies, Martin and Brozi made several home recordings some of which were released in 2010 on a Patuxent Music compact disc. The title song *Sun Racer* was taken from an airplane crash ballad by WWVA's Happy-Go-Lucky Joe Barker.

After finishing school, Martin entered the U. S. Navy. His experience as a Seabee eventually took him to Okinawa. His guitar reached the occupied island, too, and Martin continued to add new lyrics and tunes to his repertoire. Not long after the war when he returned to civilian life, Mac put his first country band together and in 1948 bought a new Martin D 28. Bill Monroe's classic band of Lester Flatt, Earl Scruggs, Chubby Wise, and Cedric Rainwater had performed at the *Grand Ole Opry* and immediately after Flatt and Scruggs formed their own group. The Stanley Brothers were also getting started although it took a little longer for their sounds to reach Pittsburgh. The revitalized form of traditional country that these bands played came to be the musical style that Martin and his band would favor for the next fifty years. He described his first band as playing bluegrass music without the banjo.

This group went by the name Pike County Boys. In 1949, they began playing regularly over WHJB radio in Greensburg, Pennsylvania. This station had a sizable audience in southwestern Pennsylvania and like WMMN in Fairmont, West Virginia, it might be described as a miniature WWVA. Band members also included Bill Higgins on fiddle and Bill Wagner on bass. Three "Bills" were too many for one band, so Bill Colleran took the name Mac Martin and has since used it as a stage and musical name. In 1950, a mandolin player from Kingsport, Tennessee, named Earl Banner rounded out the band. He and Martin often did Monroe Brothers duets or as Martin deemed them at the time Lilly Brothers duets. The Lilly Brothers played at WWVA in that period and Martin considered them really tops in their prime with a very broad repertoire, hardly ever singing the same song twice, at least on radio. Martin came to know the Lillys pretty well, but only later did he realize that many of their songs had been recorded earlier by the Monroe Brothers, the Callahan Brothers, or the Blue Sky Boys. Martin's band played on the station gratis and advertised their few show dates—dances and occasional parks—and finely honed their feel for the music. Martin always worked a day job, being an accountant for A & P Food Stores from 1948 until 1969 and afterward for Volkwein Brothers Music Store.

After two or three years of weekly radio work, the Pike County Boys stopped going to Greensburg. For a brief time Martin, Banner, and Higgins played on station WHOD in Homestead, Pennsylvania. Then for a time

Martin also began to play some banjo although he never considered himself very good. Following the short stint on the Homestead radio outlet, Martin and Banner worked for several months just as a mandolin-guitar duet, mostly in clubs on the north side of Pittsburgh.

Martin had married in 1952 and the first of his five children was born in 1954. About this time a young fiddler named Mike Carson, originally from McKeesport, Pennsylvania, where he had been born on June 27, 1937, heard Martin and joined forces. A little bit later, a banjo player named Billy Bryant also became part of their group. Born on May 4, 1938, young Bryant had some prior radio experience at WEIR in Weirton, West Virginia. Carson had played country fiddle from childhood, but became a convert to bluegrass about 1952, developing, in the words of Bill Vernon, a knack for being "particularly adept at writing original fiddle tunes with unusual and intriguing chord changes." Bryant had played guitar before learning banjo and could do fine lead guitar work when an arrangement called for it in addition to what Vernon termed "his crisp, lean, bright 'attack' on the banjo." The addition of a local Pittsburgh bass player named Slim Jones brought the Dixie Travelers bluegrass band to maturity.

Irregular club and radio work in the greater Pittsburgh area characterized the first two or three years of the Dixie Travelers operation as a semi-professional band. Beginning in 1957, the group played Saturday nights at Walsh's Lounge, 6018 Broad Street. This club became their principal base for the next nineteen years. Sometimes they also played on Fridays as well and in later years the management took a congenial attitude toward the band whenever they received an opportunity to make a festival or concert appearance elsewhere. In the process, a traditional band made up of part-time musicians perfected their talents and techniques making themselves a bluegrass institution and Walsh's the bluegrass locale in the Steel City.

The Dixie Travelers had been together as a group for nine years and at Walsh's for six when they made their first records. The National Record Mart in Pittsburgh's parent company had a label called Gateway (not the same as the Carl Burkhardt's similarly named firm in Cincinnati that released early efforts of the Osbornes, Red Allen, and others). The Dixie Travelers recorded sufficient material for two albums; one album plus an additional single was released.

Much of the material on the Gateway recordings consisted of standard fare that the folks running the company wanted such as "Roll on Buddy," "Salty Dog Blues," "Orange Blossom Special," "Banks of the Ohio," and "Bluegrass Breakdown." Still, Martin managed to sneak in a pair of rare gems from the early years of recorded bluegrass, the Lonesome Pine Fiddlers' "Nobody Cares," and the George "Speedy" Krise song by way of Mac Wiseman, "You're Sweeter than Honey" as well as the classic Stanley song, "The Angels Are Singing in Heaven Tonight." The single included an original instrumental, "Mustang," backed with the common favorite, "Sittin' on Top of the World."

Continuing their regular appearances at Walsh's, the Dixie Travelers experienced their first personnel change in 1965 when Slim Jones left the group. His replacement, Frank Basista, had known Martin since his radio days at Greensburg. Only a few months younger than Martin, Basista played mostly bass with the band, but also had a flair for comedy. He could also play mandolin and guitar, and sometimes got in a few licks on the fiddle during his seven years with the band. Banner left the group about 1967, leaving the band without a regular mandolin player for several months.

In 1968, the Dixie Travelers began a four-year association with Rural Rhythm Records which was owned by the late Uncle Jim O'Neal of Arcadia, California. At the time O'Neal had some fine bluegrass talent, including Red Smiley's Bluegrass Cut Ups, Don Reno and Bill Harrell, and Mac Wiseman as well as that durable old-timer J. E. Mainer along with some lesser knowns. O'Neal liked twenty-song albums and Martin generally liked the format of two-thirds of his repertoire consisting of vocal numbers and one-third instrumentals. While some of the instrumentals tended to be a bit brief, Mac believes that the Dixie Travelers gave record purchasers a good deal musically for their money. Tom Knight, a fan and longtime friend in Pittsburgh, engineered and produced the albums for them, all of which were recorded locally. The initial offering, *Traveling Blues* (RR 201), consisted of instrumentals featuring the talents of Carson and Bryant. Although Earl Banner's picture appeared on the album cover, he had actually left the band by the time of the sessions which contained only the foursome of Basista, Bryant, Carson, and Martin.

By the time Mac Martin and the Dixie Travelers did their second Rural Rhythm album in 1969, they had returned to full strength. Shortly after the recording of *Travelin' Blues*, a twenty-two year-old native of Santa Monica, California, began sitting in with the group and within a few weeks became a regular member. Bob Artis brought an intellectual interest to the band that rivaled Martin's as well as a strong tenor voice and an excellent mandolin style. Artis became interested in bluegrass at fifteen and within three years had taught himself to play several instruments and organized a band. He spent several years with the band and became leader after Martin took a leave of absence in the summer of 1972. Artis also possessed a fine talent as a writer and penned the first respectable book on the music, *Bluegrass* (Hawthorn Books).

In the meantime, Mac Martin and the Dixie Travelers continued playing their once and sometimes twice weekly stint at Walsh's and occasional appearances elsewhere. Their second Rural Rhythm album, *Goin' Down the Country* (RR 214), featured bluegrass arrangements of such tasteful old-time numbers as Bill Cox and Cliff Hobbs' "Drift Along Pretty Moon" (as "Southern Moon"), the Delmores' "Blue Railroad Train," and George Morris and Leonard Stokes' "We Can't Be Darlings Anymore," among its twenty cuts. Their third album, *Just Like Old Times* (RR 232), was released in 1970 and contained such rare classics as Jake Landers's The Last Request," Connie Gateley's "How Will the Flowers Bloom," and Charlie Monroe's "Is She Praying There." The 1971 last effort for O'Neal, entitled *Backtrackin'* (RR 237), included such forgotten classics as Molly O'Day's "If You See My Savior," the Carlisle Brothers' "She Waits for Me There" (as "A Silent Place"), and Melissa Monroe 's "Guilty Tears." The last two Rural Rhythm albums can be counted among the few which contained liner notes, both uncredited, but from Artis's expert pen.

In 1972, the Dixie Travelers switched to David Freeman's County Records. Freeman and Bill Vernon came to Pittsburgh to see them a couple of times and the band went to New York City twice. Martin's skills at song selection perhaps peaked on this well-recorded album. Highlights included a fine rendition of Roy Acuff's "Just to Ease My Worried Mind," Buddy Starcher's "A Faded Rose, a Broken Heart," Walter Bailes's "Pretty Flowers," and Charlie Bailey's "Have You Forgotten." Mike Carson contributed a fine new rendition of his original fiddle tune "Natchez" and Billy Bryant's "Dixie Bound" ranked among the instrumental showcases. Bill Vernon contributed a sensitive set of liner notes which explained the true essence of what made the music of the Dixie Travelers so compelling to fans of traditional bluegrass. The album *Dixie Bound* (County 745) rolled off the presses in 1974.

By that time Mac Martin had taken a leave of absence from the Dixie Travelers. Twenty years of weekend playing had convinced him that he needed a rest from the musical grind. He departed in September 1972. Frank Basista left around the same time. The band continued under Artis's leadership, adding Tim Nesiti in the lead singer-guitar spot and Norman Azinger on bass. In 1974, the band cut an album for Paul Gerry's New York state-based Revonah records *Wheeling* (Revonah 914). Band members continued to display excellent expertise in song selection. Billy Bryant contributed the title tune, an original banjo number, while Mike Carson played a fine rendition of a Tommy Jackson adaptation of an older tune, "Run Johnny Run." Vocal showcases included the Church Brothers' "Way Down in Old Caroline," the Kentucky Travelers's "Dreaming," and a popular number done by many country artists in the thirties, "Rattle Snake Daddy."

Bob Artis left the group in October 1975 to play with the Dog Run Boys, a more progressive style band. Edgar "Bud" Smith, a mandolin picker and tenor singer from Wellsburg, West Virginia, who had previously worked with other bands in the Wheeling area, became a regular Dixie Traveler in October 1975. For a few months in the summer and fall of 1975, the band restyled themselves as the Steel City Grass, a name that never quite caught the public fancy and led them to soon revert to their original moniker. Billy Bryant also branched out somewhat in the mid-seventies, starting a separate band called the Bluefield Boys while retaining his older affiliation as well.

By 1977, Martin got back into the swing of things, appearing at Walsh's on Friday nights while the Dixie Travelers worked there on Saturdays. By the end of the year, the entire ensemble switched their principal base of operations to Gustine's, a club run by former Pittsburgh Pirate third baseman (1939–1948) Frank Gustine, located at 3911 Forbes Avenue. The band worked at this locale for about six years. Although the group never toured extensively on the festival circuit, they did play at a few festivals each year, chiefly in Pennsylvania and surrounding states. They also did concerts at colleges and universities over the years.

In October 1977, the Dixie Travelers returned to recording their *Travelin' On* album for Revonah (RS 928). Outstanding cuts included a bluegrass arrangement of the early Marty Robbins song, "At the End of a Long Lonely Day," the Lonesome Pine Fiddlers' That's Why You Left Me So Blue," and a lesser-known Bill Monroe number from 1964, "Mary at the Home Place." "Gethsemane" constituted a fine gospel cut that Byron Parker's group recorded in the forties, but the Dixie Travelers learned it from the Columbia 1957 recording by the Carl Smith Trio.

Moving into the decade of the 1980s, the Dixie Travelers continued playing the brand of bluegrass that has caused them to achieve regional acclaim and wide acceptance if not widespread fame. By this time, younger musicians like the Johnson Mountain Boys had appeared on the scene and won broad audiences for the kind of sound and style that Martin and his boys had always favored albeit with youthful appeal. Mac became a strong booster of the Johnson Mountain Boys, Larry Sparks, and other younger musicians who showed respect for the traditional brand of bluegrass.

Following the long stint at Gustine's, the Dixie Travelers spent a year or so as an itinerant band with no permanent place to play. This ended in 1984 when the Dixie Travelers settled at the Elizabeth Moose Lodge where they appeared at least monthly and often every-other-week for many years. Name bluegrass bands from outside the Pittsburgh area appeared there with some regularity, too, including the Country Gentlemen, Bluegrass Cardinals, and Larry Sparks's Lonesome Ramblers. Martin reflects with some pride that the Johnson Mountain Boys played one of their last concerts there. He also thinks that such quality "competition helps keep the Dixie Travelers on their toes."

In 1987, after a near decade of absence from the recording studios, the same five musicians as had cut the *Travelin' On* disc did a new album. For the first time, the Dixie Travelers utilized the services of guest musicians, namely Ron Mesing on Dobro; Bob Martin on lead guitar; and Larry Zierath on rhythm mandolin. The result was another excellent album. Released as *Basic Blue Grass* (Old Homestead OHS 90178), the record received favorable reviews with the same superlatives that greeted the earlier efforts. Somewhat surprisingly, a trio of songs—"Big City," "Roustabout," and "Simon Crutchfield"—were relatively new—meaning written after 1960. Still, the presence of a pair of lesser-known Monroe Brothers songs, "Some Glad Day" and "The Old Man's Story," remind us that Martin retained his skill to choose "new old material." His rescue of an obscure Lilly Brothers tune from their WWVA days, "I'll Forgive You" and Mike Carson's rendition of an infrequently heard Chubby Collier tune, "Two O 'Clock," demonstrated the band's capacity to draw from memories of old radio broadcasts. In 1989, the Dixie Travelers finished another album *Traveler's Portrait* designed to commemorate their thirty-fifth anniversary as a band.

None of The Dixie Travelers have ever been full-time musicians. In one sense, Martin believes that the semi-professional character of the Dixie Travelers has enabled them to develop themselves. Their leader says they exemplify the advice offered in the 1973 Country Gazette album, *Don't Give up Your Day Job.* In addition to Martin's work as an accountant, Mike Carson served as assistant manager of a supermarket while Billy Bryant worked in construction for Martin's brother-in-law. Norm Azinger worked for the telephone company, and Bud Smith worked for the employee-owned Weirton Steel Corporation. In the winter of 1988–1989, shift work became something of a problem and Buzz Matheson, a veteran bluegrass musician from Warren, Ohio, filled in for Smith. Martin and Matheson recorded a cassette of old-time duets. Besides their work in the clubs and sometime festival appearances, the Dixie Travelers worked several times at the annual bluegrass night held on station WWVA's *Jamboree U.S.A.* Billy Bryant played his last show with the Travelers on February 19, 1994, subsequently becoming ill and passing away on March 31, 1994. After Bryant died, Keith Little, a young banjo picker from across the West Virginia line became the band's major banjo picker. Little was already a proven guitarist with his *Distant Land to Roam* on Copper Creek. He displayed his banjo work on the Dixie Travelers' studio album *Venango* in 2004. By this time, Martin's son Bob had become a regular on guitar and Martin had switched to mandolin. Azinger and Carson completed the ensemble. The Dixie Travelers turned out their usual quality product.

Mac Martin and the Dixie Travelers continued to be an active band through 2015 although many of their old locales seemed to dry up with changing times. "Besides," as Martin said in early 2016, "he would soon be ninety-one and maybe it was time to slow down some." Nonetheless, many of his recordings remain in print. In 2015, Rural Rhythm reissued his first two albums on compact disc in their *Classic* series.

One can positively reflect on the sixty plus years of Mac Martin and the Dixie Travelers. It has not been their fate to achieve the fame of Monroe,

Stanley, or Flatt and Scruggs. However, there can be no doubt that they have carried on the tradition in a most high manner. They also exemplify a capacity for creativity and innovation while remaining true to the spirit of the founding fathers of bluegrass. In the aesthetic sense, we as adherents of the bluegrass sound can expect no more from its practitioners.

SELECTED RECORDINGS

Mac Martin & the Dixie Travelers: 24 Bluegrass Favorites. Rural Rhythm RHY 267. Anthology of the best of his 1968–1971 recordings.

Mac Martin and the Dixie Travelers: Travelin' On. Copper Creek CCCD 0928, 2004. Reissue of 1977 Revonah album.

Mac Martin and the Dixie Travelers: Basic Bluegrass/Portrait Old Homestead OHCD 90178/95, 2006. Reissue of mid-1980s albums.

∽ Charlie Monroe

1903–1975

For the last eight decades the name of Charles Pendleton Monroe has ranked high on the list of those who have made important contributions to old-time, traditional country music. First as a member of the famous Monroe Brothers duet and second as a vocalist and bandleader in his own right, Charlie's record is an impressive one. Emerging from a long period of semi-retirement in 1972, his comeback in his last years not only was successful, but he quickly re-established himself as a top artist until the grim reaper intervened.

James B. Monroe (1857–1928) and his wife Melissa Vandiver (1870–1921) reared a family of eight children. Born on July 4, 1903, Charlie was number six, making him a couple of years younger than brother Birch, but eight years older than Bill. The elder Monroe owned a large farm near Rosine, Kentucky, where the boys were exposed to agricultural chores as well as timber cutting and sawmill work at an early age. Charlie, along with the other children, attended grade school at nearby Horton.

Music constituted another fare to which the Monroe youngsters received exposure. Their father liked to dance and their mother played accordion, fiddle, and harmonica as well as sang old ballads. However, their mother's brother, Pendleton Vandiver, known as Uncle Pen, was a renowned local fiddler who provided the main musical inspiration for the Monroe boys and girls. Charlie favored the guitar, which he recalled taking up at about age eleven. Birch played the fiddle while younger sister Bertha also took up the guitar, leaving young Bill, so the story goes, with the mandolin.

Throughout his teens and early adulthood, Charlie Monroe remained at home, working on the farm or at his father's coal mine and sawmill. In the latter part of the 1920s, he and Birch went to Detroit where they worked for some time at the Briggs Motor Company, which manufactured Ford parts.

37

Charlie Monroe.

While there they often played their fiddles and guitars for local parties and dances. By this time, they had heard phonograph records of artists such as Charlie Poole, the Carter Family, Jimmie Rodgers, Bradley Kincaid, and the Skillet Lickers as well as the music learned back home. After a while, the boys got laid off and returned home just in time for Christmas.

Soon, however, the lure of the northern industry drew Charlie and Birch back to the city. This time they went to Hammond, Indiana, and the Sinclair Oil Company where Charlie also played on the baseball team. Kentucky seemed less attractive to the boys as both their parents had died. Not long afterward, Bill, now eighteen, moved and went to work at Sinclair. Charlie, however, was fired for fighting and went to work for Standard.

Charlie was working and playing on the company baseball team. The brothers weren't playing much music; they did attend area square dances.

At one, Tom Owens, square dance caller at the WLS National Barn Dance, saw the Monroes, their partners, and friends Mr. and Mrs. Larry Moore. He asked the four couples to dance with the WLS Road Show. Their acceptance led to the Monroe Brothers being introduced to professional show business. In addition to their dancing, the boys also did some singing. As Monroe recollected, they did a lot of Carter Family and Karl Davis-Harty Taylor numbers. Among other places, they worked at the 1933 Chicago World's Fair with the exhibition square dance team.

Not long afterward, a representative of the Texas Crystal Company asked the Monroe Brothers to go into radio work under their sponsorship. Birch preferred to keep his job at the oil refinery, but Charlie and Bill accepted and were soon broadcasting from station KFNF in Shenandoah, Iowa. Three months later, still working for the same company, they switched to WAAW in Omaha where they remained for approximately a half-year. During this time the Monroe Brothers became an exceedingly popular radio group. Although they worked only as a duet, they had the able assistance of Byron Parker, The Old Hired Hand, as announcer. By all accounts, the latter was one of the best radio salesmen of his era and played an instrumental part in the radio success not only of Bill and Charlie Monroe, but also the Mainers, Snuffy Jenkins, and Homer Sherrill. Parker died in 1948.

In 1935, the Monroe Brothers switched their base of operations to the Carolinas. This change to the South probably constituted an extremely decisive move for them. For Charlie Monroe, the move placed him in a geographic area whose people took him to heart as it did few entertainers. For the brothers, it placed them on Bluebird Records and also on a series of regionally popular radio stations including WIS, Columbia; WBT, Charlotte; WFBC, Greenville; and WPTF, Raleigh for the next three years. Although the Carolinas boasted a great deal of homegrown talent including the Callahans, the Mainers, the Bolicks a.k.a. the Blue Sky Boys, the Morrises, the Dixons, and the Tobacco Tags, while Bill and Charlie Monroe more than held their own with the competition.

While at Charlotte the Monroes left Texas Crystals and went to work for J. W. Fincher's Crazy Water Crystals. Early in 1936, Eli Oberstein of RCA Records approached the brothers about recording on the Bluebird label. Seemingly unenthusiastic, they finally entered the temporary studio at Charlotte on February 17, 1936. They cut ten numbers that day, including their biggest hit, "What Would You Give in Exchange for Your Soul." This old hymn became so popular that the next year they recorded three additional versions and the Dixon Brothers added three more. In four more sessions over the next two years, the Monroe Brothers recorded a total of sixty sides, all of them released on RCA's Bluebird label. All have since been released on a Bear Family boxed set along with Bill Monroe's other Bluebird and Columbia material.

The recorded repertoire of the Monroe Brothers was composed of nearly equal divisions of sacred and secular material. As Charlie Monroe remembered, the brothers did little songwriting in this period of their lives, but tried to select material suited to the Monroe style. In so doing, they helped a number of important old-time songs to eventually become bluegrass standards. Such numbers included Buster Carter and Preston Young's "I'll Roll in My Sweet Baby's Arms," which, contrary to bluegrass and country neophytes, originated with neither Flatt and Scruggs nor Buck Owens, as well as John Foster and Leonard Rutherford's "Six Months Ain't Long," "Watermelon on the Vine," "New River Train," and "Darling Corey." They also recorded a number of songs previously released by the Carter Family such as "Foggy Mountain Top," "Little Joe," "Weeping Willow Tree," and "Will the Circle Be Unbroken." Old hymns transmitted from one generation to another with the help of Monroe Brothers' records included "How Beautiful Heaven Must Be," "What Would the Profit Be," and "When Our Lord Shall Come Again," plus their memorable first hit "What Would You Give in Exchange for your Soul" which dated from 1912.

Since many other acts of the time had begun to add some variety to their stage shows, Charlie and Bill Monroe followed. They remained a two-man group, but for a time, Bill Monroe did some fiddle playing and Charlie Monroe took up the banjo as part of a comedy routine. However, this seemed something less than a great success and as a result they returned to the more familiar duet singing and the mandolin-guitar instrumentation.

Like most other brother duos at one time or another, Bill and Charlie Monroe began to have some differences in mid-1938. They were working in Raleigh when the split came; each going his own way—Bill Monroe to Little Rock, Arkansas, and Charlie Monroe to Knoxville, Tennessee. In the metropolis of East Tennessee, the latter was hired by Lowell Blanchard at WNOX. In Knoxville, he added band members and took the name for radio and recordings as Monroe's Boys while retaining as much of the Brothers' sound and style as possible.

Charlie had only two band members in Knoxville—Bill Calhoun, a guitar player and tenor singer, and Lefty Frizzell, not the better known Lefty Frizzell who came along in the 1950's, but a southpaw mandolin player. After Frizzell's departure, Zeke Morris joined Monroe on mandolin. Morris had previously been with the Mainer Mountaineers and his own brother group. From WNOX, the Monroe Boys went to Roanoke, Virginia, where they worked at WDBJ for nearly a year.

Charlie Monroe cut two more sessions on Bluebird at Rock Hill, South Carolina, in September 1938 and February 1939. Morris and Calhoun assisted him both times recording a total of eighteen sides. All the songs fell into the sacred or sentimental category and included such titles as the beautiful "No Home, No Place to Pillow My Head," a song probably learned from Karl Davis and Harty Taylor; a cover of Roy Acuff's popular hit, "Great Speckled Bird," which combined both the No. 1 and No. 2 versions; and the old sentimental ballad, "Black Sheep." Although of excellent quality, these records probably did not sell as well as the Monroe Brothers recordings or Charlie Monroe's later efforts on Victor since they are more difficult to find today.

In mid-1939 Charlie Monroe went to the *World's Original Jamboree* at Wheeling, West Virginia, and stayed about three months. By this time, he had replaced the three-man group that had worked on his last Bluebird session with a full-sized band, the Kentucky Pardners, that included Dale Cole on fiddle, Tommy Edwards on mandolin, Tommy Scott on guitar, and Curly Seckler on four-string banjo and as tenor singer. During the next decade, Charlie Monroe continued to maintain a full band for his personal appearance schedule frequently adding a comedian and a female vocalist. Charlie strived to entertain his audiences by offering them a wide variety of talent. His popularity with the fans of that period attested to his success as a country showman.

Charlie Monroe appeared on a variety of radio stations during the following decade. From Wheeling, he went to WHAS Louisville in November and the *Renfro Valley Barn Dance*. Oddly enough, he recalled this radio venture in his home state as being the only one where he lost money. Leaving Kentucky in the spring of 1940, he put together the first of his now legendary tent shows which opened at Almo, Georgia, in May. The tent seated 2,000 spectators. At a dollar a ticket, Monroe managed to keep it filled six nights a week all summer. When the tent show season ended that fall, Charlie brought the Kentucky Pardners to Greensboro, North Carolina, and station WBIG. This remained his major base of operations for the next twelve years although he occasionally left to do stints on other radio stations including WNOX Knoxville; WBT Charlotte, and WBOK Birmingham. For quite some time during the war, he worked on a series of seven stations in Virginia and North Carolina including WBIG and WSJS Winston-Salem, doing his own daily show, *The Noonday Jamboree*. Man-o-Ree, a laxative which Monroe had manufactured, sponsored the show, and he made up transcriptions to play when unable to do the shows live. Fortunately for Charlie Monroe fans, these transcriptions were preserved for posterity and David Freeman of County Records released two albums from them in 1974. During the winter months, the band played school houses. Monroe contended that there was "not a school house in the radius of 200 miles around Greensboro we didn't play." In fact, the Kentucky Pardners usually played them several times with little or no loss in crowd appeal.

Except for a summer vacation and a two-week Christmas break, the Kentucky Pardners maintained a heavy personal appearance schedule. Monroe operated a large tent show with its own light plant. His wife, the former Elizabeth Miller whom he had married in 1935, handled the bookings and the troupe usually played to capacity crowds for two shows daily, six days per week. The tent show operation was a costly one, but through hard work and thousands of loyal fans, they made it pay.

Charlie Monroe played an important part in the training of many young traditional musicians through those persons employed in the Kentucky Pardners. Mandolin players and tenor singers in particular gained valuable professional experience in their work with Monroe including Curly Seckler, Ira Louvin, and Red Rector. Lester Flatt, most famous as a lead singer, played mandolin and sang tenor with Charlie for some time and thus widened his professional horizons. David "Stringbean" Akeman also worked with Charlie prior to going to Nashville to join the Blue Grass Boys and then the *Opry*. James Slim Martin, a notable fiddler, harmonica player, and comedian who also worked with Molly O'Day and with the Bailey Brothers, played with the Kentucky Pardners off and on for several years as did his wife Wilma Martin. Other longtime stalwarts with the Charlie Monroe band at various times included fiddlers Paul Prince, Birch Monroe, Lance and Maynard Spencer; guitarists Larry "Tex" Isley, Rex Henderson and Orne "Buddy" Osborne; and bass player Lavelle "Bill" Coy.

Charlie Monroe and his Kentucky Pardners did forty-four additional sides for RCA Victor between 1946 and 1951. As with the early recordings, both secular and sacred materials were cut with a slight dominance of the former. The repertoire contained train songs such as "That Wild Black Engine" and "Bringin' in the Georgia Mail," both of which featured Slim Martin's spirited harmonica. It also included sentimental classics like "I'm Comin' Back but I Don't Know When" and "Mother's Not Dead, She's Only Sleeping," the latter performed as a duet with Curly Seckler and actually composed by the aforementioned Spencer Brothers. Probably his most popular number, "Down in the Willow Garden," the old murder ballad, was recorded at his March 1947 session in Chicago with the aid of Robert Lambert, Tex Isley, Slim Martin, and Ira Louvin. At his two Nashville sessions in 1950, Jerry Rivers and other members of the Hank Williams band provided instrumental assistance. At Charlie Monroe's final RCA session in Atlanta during May 1951, former sidemen Osborne, Isley, and Martin returned to back him along with Clyde Baum, an excellent mandolin player who had formerly worked with Johnnie and Jack and the Bailes Brothers at KWKH. Although most of Charlie Monroe's post-war recordings featured an electric guitar, this seems to have antagonized few of the old-time fans who continued to enjoy his special brand of music.

In the early fifties, Charlie began to relax somewhat from his heavy schedule and to spend more time at his farm at Beaver Dam, Kentucky. In 1952, he switched to Decca, recording "I'm Old Kentucky Bound," one of his most popular numbers. He cut "Find 'Em, Fool 'Em and Leave 'Em Alone"/"These Triflin' Women," the only recordings made in his heydey with bluegrass banjo—played by Joe Medford. These sides are the only ones which Decca failed to include on the album, *Bill and Charlie Monroe*. Charlie Monroe did his second and last Decca session in August 1956.

In 1952, Charlie Monroe left Greensboro and went back to Kentucky. Soon, however, he got a call from J. L. Frank and went to KWKH in Shreveport and the *Louisiana Hayride*. Buddy Osborne, Tex Isley, Slim and Wilma Martin, and the Spencer Brothers also went along. After about a year, Charlie Monroe returned to WNOX and Lowell Blanchard's *Mid-Day Merry-Go-Round*.

From Knoxville, Monroe went to WPAQ Mount Airy, North Carolina, doing daily noon-time radio shows. He also did a Wednesday evening half-hour television show at Roanoke, Virginia, for Bunker Hill Beef. He made personal appearances on other week nights while following his time-honored practice of taking off on Sundays.

In March 1957, Charlie and Betty Monroe retired to their Beaver Dam farm. For the next decade and a half he made only a few public appearances. Monroe ran the farm, operated a coal mine, and generally enjoyed rural living.

A notable exception to his absence from the musical world came in 1962 and 1964 when with full bluegrass backing, Monroe recorded two albums for Bob Mooney's Rem label in Lexington, Kentucky. J. D. Crowe played banjo on both albums. The first album also featured Moon Mullins and Bee Lucas of the *Renfro Valley Barn Dance* on fiddles. The songs were a mixture of Monroe's old hits with five that had not previously been recorded including "Mother's White Rose" and "We'll Love Again Sweetheart." After appearing on Rem, the albums were released on Starday and later appeared on A. L. Phipps's Pine Mountain label and John Morris's Old Homestead Records.

Had Charlie Monroe's wife Betty not become ill with cancer in the middle sixties, he might well have stayed content with retirement in Kentucky. However, the bout with illness proved to be a losing one and Betty Monroe died in 1967. During her illness, the Monroes moved to Martinsville, Indiana, and medical expenses forced Charlie to work for Howard Johnson's Restaurants and the Otis Elevator Company.

After Betty Monroe's death, Monroe still did not emerge from retirement although he played occasionally at the *Brown County Jamboree* at Bean Blossom, Indiana. He also played at the O'Tuck's Day Celebration in Hamilton, Ohio, in the fall of 1969. In the meantime, he remarried and moved to Tennessee. His new wife, Martha Gammon, claimed that the town of Cross Plains, ten miles south of the Kentucky border, was "as far into Tennessee as I could get him" to go. A few of his recordings were re-issued including a Camden album of late 1940s Victor materials entitled *Who's Calling You Sweetheart Tonight*. In addition, six cuts on the Monroe

Brothers' album actually featured Charlie and his band. Two numbers in the Vintage series and six songs on Decca were also by him. These helped to maintain interest in the man and his music. For all practical purposes, Charlie remained in retirement until the summer of 1972.

In 1972, Jimmy Martin, an old fan of Monroe's from the Knoxville days, persuaded him to appear as a special guest at two Carlton Haney festivals— one in Gettysburg, Pennsylvania, the other in Camp Springs, North Carolina. Martin's group consisting of Ronnie Prevette, Kenny Ingram, and Gloria Belle backed Monroe and he made a tremendous impression. He sang some duets, Monroe Brothers style, with Everett Lilly at the Pennsylvania event. At Camp Springs, he acquainted thousands of old fans with his music and also won hosts of new admirers. Before many weeks had passed, Monroe's two guest spots seemed to be expanding into a whole new career.

In the winter of 1972–73, Charlie continued to make occasional appearances with Jimmy Martin and the Sunny Mountain Boys. In early spring, he cut a new album for Starday with backing by the Martin band, released under the title *Tally-Ho*. This recording included some of Martin's best numbers from the old days like the beautiful "Time Clock of Life," which Victor had never reissued and some other songs previously unrecorded.

Charlie Monroe appeared at many bluegrass festivals in the summer of 1973 and was very well received. Gloria Belle, longtime vocalist with Jimmy Martin, worked with him, singing tenor, and playing mandolin. Part of their appearance at the Hugo, Oklahoma, festival was shown on NET television. Monroe moved to Reidsville, North Carolina, started a local jamboree, and continued to work at the Carlton Haney festivals.

Throughout the summer of 1974, Monroe worked another heavy schedule of festivals with a full band, the Dominion Bluegrass Boys—Clarence Hall, J. A. Midkiff, Grady Bullins, Cliff Mabe, and Ron Pinnix. Two of the old Kentucky Pardners, Slim and Wilma Martin, also appeared frequently with their former leader. Monroe worked with this band until September 1974, alternating weekends with festivals and the jamboree at Reidsville. An album *Charlie Monroe Live at Lake Norman Music Hall* came out on the Pine Tree label.

In 1975, Monroe worked mostly with some of his original Kentucky Pardners: Slim and Wilma Martin, Olen Gardner along with Grady Bullins, Audine Lineberry, Roy Russell, and Charlie Chaney. From the time of his

Camp Springs appearance of 1972, Charlie endeavored to reunite as many of the group as possible on shows at which he worked. Although plagued by illness through that winter, he kept hard at work for the next three years providing the people of North Carolina and the rest of the country with the type of entertainment and traditional string music which had made him so popular and well liked in bygone years.

Monroe continued working at music through the summer of 1975 as long as his health allowed, but his days were numbered. He played his last show in Rosine, Kentucky, in mid-September. Back in North Carolina he entered the hospital and died on September 27, 1975, the same week that a new *Bluegrass Unlimited* cover issue with the initial version of this biographical piece appeared. Perhaps his most unique Kentucky Pardner, Slim Martin who had given "Bringin' in the Georgia Mail" such a distinctive touch, preceded him in death on June 29, 1975. Charlie Monroe's remains were interred in the family plot in Rosine where brother Birch joined him in 1982 and his off-and-on again estranged brother Bill joined them in 1996.

Much of Charlie Monroe's musical legacy has been revived. At the time of his death only the recordings made after he came out of retirement were in print. In 2002 Bear Family Records of Germany included all of the original Monroe Brothers' material in a box set as well as Bill's solo efforts for Victor and Columbia (BCD 16399). In 2012, Bear Family produced another box set that covered all of Charlie Monroe's Victor and Decca sides, augmented by two live shows at New River Ranch in 1955 and 1956. In the accompanying booklet, Richard Spottswood reflected that "Charlie Monroe knew how to create enduring music on his own terms and the best of that music is some of the best there is."

SELECTED RECORDINGS

Charlie Monroe: I'm Old Kentucky Bound, Bear Family BCD 16808, 2007. Includes all of
Charlie's Victor and Decca recordings, plus a live show from the mid-1950s.

⌒ Clyde Moody

1915–1989

In more than fifty years as a professional entertainer, Clyde Leonard Moody showed himself to be a versatile performer who significantly contributed to various forms of country music. His professional experience ranged from old-time duets and string bands to bluegrass and the pioneering sounds of modern country music. Through it all—unlike many performers who seem to be most at home in a single style—Moody demonstrated comfort in several types of country music. This phenomenon appears all the more remarkable when realizing that his individual style was much the same throughout his career.

Moody was born September 19, 1915 in Cherokee, North Carolina. His parents, Lynn and Lou Moody, who were of Indian and Scotch-Irish descent respectively, reared a family of twelve children with Clyde being eleventh in line. The elder Moody sang and played old-time banjo and an elder brother, Fred, played guitar. A year after the family moved to Marion, North Carolina, in 1923, Clyde learned to play guitar. Among the friends young Clyde made in Marion were the Hall Brothers, Jay Hugh and Roy. Although the Halls sang together, Clyde and Jay Hugh also did duet work. Not many years passed before Jay Hugh Hall and Clyde Moody became known as Bill and Joe, the Happy-Go-Lucky Boys.

Moody left home at fourteen, his stern father telling him not to bother to return as he did not believe his son could make it on his own as a musician. Moody went 69 miles to Spartanburg, South Carolina, hitchhiking the entire distance. He had never eaten in a restaurant and recalled that he first learned to eat out by ordering what he heard others order. For a while, Moody worked in a logging camp, but in those early years, he had two loves, baseball and music. As a pitcher, he threw about as hard and fast as anyone, but had control troubles. He did try professional baseball for a while

47

Clyde Moody, probably
during his days as a
Blue Grass Boy.

playing for the Asheville club, but after a good rookie season and a poor
sophomore year, he decided to concentrate on music.

About 1933, Moody and Jay Hugh Hall landed a radio job in Spartanburg,
South Carolina, doing a half-hour show daily. It required a lot of walking in
order to get there and back, but they enjoyed the opportunity to entertain.
After a while the Happy-Go-Lucky Boys began to get requests for personal
appearances and were able to make a living. Since neither drove nor owned
a car, they had to depend on a friend who Moody lived with them until they
saved enough to get their own auto. Soon they acquired a sponsor, the Blue
Front Liquor Stores, who paid them a salary for their radio show. About this
time, Moody recalled doing a recording session for Art Satherly of A. R. C.
who happened to be in the area recording. This session, which may have
included Moody's first recording of "Six White Horses," remains unissued.

In the fall of 1937, Wade Mainer, who had become one of the most famous radio and recording personalities of the Carolinas, was looking for a singer and guitar player to replace Zeke Morris in a new group he was forming called the Sons of the Mountaineers. Mainer apparently had heard Moody on the radio and inquired about him through Mainer's brother James who lived near Moody's family in Marion. Moody had heard of Mainer and knew of his popularity so he jumped at a chance to join him; he also talked Mainer into using Jay Hugh Hall. They formed a quartet with Steve Ledford from Mitchell County, North Carolina, on fiddle, Clyde and Hall on guitars, and Mainer on banjo which became one of the most successful groups of the late 1930s. They recorded many sides for Bluebird, mostly featuring Moody as lead vocal. The group's version of the Bill Cox song, "Sparkling Blue Eyes," became one of the most popular country songs of 1938.

During the time Moody was with Wade he also experimented with Jay Hugh in different vocal styles. For instance, on the recording of "Mama You're Awful Mean to Me," there is a strong Callahan Brothers influence and on the recording, "That Kind," a strong resemblance to the Delmore Brothers can be noticed. Moody boasted of Hall's and his ability to yodel in harmony. It was also at this time that Clyde was able to develop his distinctive two-finger guitar style that has been used in bluegrass by musicians such as Charlie Moore among others.

Moody remained with the Wade Mainer band for two years during which time they did radio work at WIS-Columbia, South Carolina, WWNC-Asheville and WPTF-Raleigh, North Carolina. They split their earnings evenly after expenses and enjoyed a good relationship. The group also experienced excellent radio popularity, especially at Raleigh. In addition to their musical numbers, the group did comedy, some of which included blackface routines.

Besides his recordings with Wade Mainer's band, Clyde also helped J. E. Mainer do his last session on Bluebird. In February 1940, the Happy-Go-Lucky Boys, who had continued to work as a duet within the Sons of the Mountaineers, did a session of their own for Bluebird in Atlanta, Georgia. Steve Ledford helped "Bill and Joe" on fiddle and they did six numbers, two of which were instrumentals. The session allegedly was made with only these three musicians because Wade Mainer sat it out due to a financial argument with Victor. Not long after this, the band broke up, but Moody and Hall joined with J. E. Mainer, going to WAPI in Birmingham, Alabama. Moody soon fell out with Hall and Mainer and resolved not to work with them again. Returning to North Carolina, he accepted an offer to join Bill Monroe and the Blue Grass Boys on WSM's *Grand Ole Opry.*

Moody made arrangements to meet Monroe in Bluefield, West Virginia, on the night of September 6, 1940. Bill Monroe's group at that time consisted of Cousin Wilbur Wesbrooks on bass, Tommy Magness on fiddle, and Mack McGar who also worked separately on the *Opry* playing both fiddle and mandolin. After playing the Friday night show in West Virginia, the Blue Grass Boys took off for Nashville and the *Opry*, working it also, all before Moody had the opportunity to rehearse with the group.

After Moody had been with the group about a month, the Blue Grass Boys recorded their first Bluebird session in Atlanta in the fall of 1940. The group cut eight sides with Moody doing the solo vocal on "Six White Horses," a number Georgia Tom Dorsey had written several years earlier. He also did a couple of duets with Monroe and sang lead on the gospel quartet number, "Cryin' Holy unto the Lord." Although this was the only session that Moody did with the Blue Grass Boys, it, along with the heavy radio and show date schedule, made him probably the best-known Blue Grass Boy prior to the Flatt and Scruggs years. On the same Atlanta sessions, Clyde also helped Arthur Smith cut some fiddle instrumentals by playing rhythm guitar behind him.

The four or five years that Moody spent with Bill Monroe and the Blue Grass Boys turned out to be extremely busy ones. The group averaged about 3,000 miles on the road per week, doing two or three shows daily much of the time. In the summer months they also had a baseball team on which Clyde served as pitcher. Monroe and Moody enjoyed a good relationship and the lead singer-guitar man sometimes helped in obtaining sidemen. Moody was instrumental in the hiring of both Carl Story and Chubby Wise as the band's fiddlers.

For one brief period, Moody returned to North Carolina and formed a group of his own at WBBB in Burlington. Lester Flatt was part of this band and the two did a lot of duet numbers. However, after about six months, the "Carolina Woodchopper" went back with Bill Monroe and WSM.

By the beginning of 1945, Moody resolved to try to make it on his own as a solo artist. He went to Harry Stone, manager of the *Grand Ole Opry,* and obtained a spot for himself on the *Opry*. Roy Acuff hired Clyde at $200 weekly to be a featured solo artist with his troupe for a few weeks until Moody could line up some show dates for himself. It was not long until Moody began to make a name as an individual artist.

In February 1945, Moody did his first record session as a solo artist cutting four sides for Art Satherley on Columbia. Only two of the four were issued. A little later Moody did four more numbers for the Bullet label, one of the earlier Nashville-based operations. On the latter recordings he used instrumentation which featured Owen Bradley on piano and trumpet in addition to more standard country instruments. The music on the records is much like western swing although Moody's own style is little changed from those recordings which featured a more Appalachian sound. Songs from the session included "I'm So Lonesome" and "If I Had My Life to Live Over."

Perhaps the most important new record company in the 1940s as far as country music was concerned was Syd Nathan's King Records of Cincinnati. Nathan built his label into a major company with a strong line of rhythm and blues and hillbilly records. Major country artists who joined the King roster early included the Delmore Brothers, the Carlisle Brothers, Grandpa Jones, and both J. E. and Wade Mainer. In 1947, Moody signed with King and soon became one of its major artists. Although none of these recordings are bluegrass, one may nonetheless appreciate the quality of the vocal work and the smooth fiddles of Chubby Wise and Tommy Jackson who worked on many of the sessions. During Clyde's King days he also worked on some gospel recordings with the Brown's Ferry Four and as part of the King's Sacred Quartet (along with Johnnie and Jack and Ray Atkins).

The first Moody release on King, "Shenandoah Waltz," written by himself with an assist from Chubby Wise, proved to be a hit and firmly established him as a recording artist. The song was widely covered by other artists ranging from Lulubelle and Scotty, Charlie Monroe, and Jimmy Martin to Lawrence Welk and Frankie Yankovic. By 1952, it became a million seller. Not surprisingly, it ranks as a bluegrass standard although Moody's original rendition of it fits more into the country crooner style.

Clyde Moody along with fellow *Opry* artists Eddy Arnold and Red Foley helped to popularize the crooner style in country music during the mid-forties. Most of the sixty or so sides Clyde cut with King fall into this stylistic category. Today one suspects that it was artists who had a background in more traditional musical forms such as Moody and Red Foley, which helped to sell this newer sound to hard-core country fans. Clyde gained some fame for his waltz type numbers such as "Cherokee Waltz," "Carolina Waltz," and "West Virginia Waltz." For several years, he was known as the "Hillbilly Waltz King." Other songs have become standard bluegrass fare like "Next Sunday Darlin' is my Birthday" and "I Know What It Means to be Lonesome." The old Jimmie Davis number, "Where the Old Red River Flows," probably entered the repertoire of bluegrass vocalists via Clyde's recording of it.

About the end of the decade Clyde left the *Opry* to work television in the Washington, D.C., area for Connie B. Gay including the Constitution Hall *Gay Time* and other *Town & Country Time* shows. Chubby Wise worked there with him. He also worked on several radio stations such as WDBJ in Roanoke and WDVA in Danville where he was the star of the *Virginia Barn Dance*, a half hour of which was broadcast over the Mutual Broadcasting System. A number of well-known bluegrass musicians also appeared on this show including Bobby Hicks and Hubert Davis who were part of a band known as the Flint Hill Playboys.

In 1951, Moody cut his last session with King, having been promised an excellent deal by Paul Cohen at Decca. As a result he bought his own contract from Syd Nathan and signed with Decca. Although he had been promised six single releases yearly, he had only five releases in three years with the company that had put him on the shelf to keep his records from competing with those of certain longer established Decca artists. He then dropped out of country music for several years, about 1957–1962. During this time, Clyde made a foray into the mobile home business.

Moody returned to the record studio in 1962 by doing an album for Don Pierce at Starday Records, *Songs that Made Him Famous*. He also became more active, working a daily television show in Raleigh called *Carolina in the Morning*. During the sixties, he did two more recording sessions— one for Ray Davis at Wango and the other on the Little Darlin' label. And while the tradition oriented fans generally liked the Wango release, neither recording received very good circulation. In the fall of 1971, after a long absence Moody returned to Nashville. The following year with the instrumental assistance of the Sunnysiders, a Detroit-area band, he cut his first bluegrass album for Old Homestead, *Moody's Blues*. Clyde made some guest appearances on Lester Flatt's radio show and the *Opry*. Although in ill health from the early 1970s he continued to work as circumstances permitted.

In the late 1970s, Moody toured extensively with Ramblin' Tommy Scott, a country music veteran whose friendship went back to Carolina radio stations prior to World War II. During this time, the pair cut two albums, one on Starday, *We've Played Every Place (More than Once)*, and one on Old Homestead, *Early Country Favorites*. Given Moody's delicate health, Scott's heavy touring schedule must have been a trial on his physical strength.

Moody continued recording in his later years beginning with a country album, *Tribute to Fred Rose*, on Old Homestead which was primarily a bluegrass label. In 1985, he fulfilled a long desire to record an album of waltz songs, *Country Waltz King* on Longhorn, normally a western swing label. Although a country album, it suggested that Moody could have been a competent vocalist along the lines of a Tommy Duncan or a Bill Boyd. His final effort, not released until after his death on April 7, 1989, *A Sacred Collection* on Old Homestead, could best be described as bluegrass lite. Mostly Moody's own guitar with banjo and fiddle on some cuts supported a light gospel album. Since Moody's death, five compact discs of his material—mostly from King masters—have been released, two in Britain, two in the United States and one in Germany, in addition to all he did with the Mainers and Bill Monroe.

Besides being a superb vocalist, Clyde Moody's flat-top guitar work was also outstanding. His active career as a performer covered more than fifty years, during which time he influenced and contributed much to vernacular music. He did it all with a style that fits into several types of country music. He helped bridge old-time with bluegrass and modern country music. Through it all, he demonstrated himself as an outstanding vocalist.

SELECTED RECORDINGS

Clyde Moody: The Hillbilly Waltz King. Gusto GT 7-2012, 2009. Reissues numbers from his
   King and Starday country recordings
Clyde Moody: Shenandoah Waltz. Gusto GT 7-20542, 2011. More country sides from King
   and Starday numbers.

Clyde Moody also recorded with Mainer's Mountaineers, the Happy-Go-Lucky Boys, and Bill
Monroe on the Bluebird label.

✂ Lee Moore

1914–1997

Lee Moore experienced a long career in country and bluegrass music as a performer. Furthermore, for nearly two decades, he served as one of the most influential and best-liked disc jockeys on one of the largest stations. This background made Moore one of the best informed and most knowledgeable artists on the whole musical range of a half century. As a solo performer still around in the 1990s and blessed with broad credentials and a friendly personality, listening to Lee Moore—either on or off stage—proved a real delight.

Walter LeRoy Moore called Circleville, Ohio, home. He was born there on September 24, 1914, in a section of town known as The Field. He first developed an interest in music through a radio network show known as *Hawaii Calls*. This led to Moore taking Hawaiian guitar lessons and playing locally with a friend who picked Spanish guitar style. Moore also got extensive exposure to early country music in central Ohio via the pioneering Columbus station WAIU. Numerous acts performed there, most notably the duet of Hank and Slim Newman. This pair of Georgians had toured with the Skillet Lickers and based themselves in Columbus from 1931 with occasional forays to other areas. Another duo, Handsome Bob and Happy Johnnie Zufall, also worked in Columbus quite early before the latter established himself in the Baltimore, Maryland, area. Frank Dudgeon, the West Virginia Mountain Boy, recorded for Champion and worked in Columbus as well as Wheeling, West Virginia. Montana Meechy and his wife Myrtle also played in the area as did the team of Horseshoe Mike and Cowboy Joe. The Tweedy Brothers—Big Red and Little Red—with their entertaining piano and fiddle act did some local radio work and also appeared each fall at the Circleville Pumpkin Show. Even though Lee grew up in the flatland country several miles from the Appalachian foothills, he managed to

Lee Moore
at WCHS,
Charleston, WV,
1938.

receive ample exposure to hillbilly music. He began playing music, appearing from 1931 as a Saturday guest with Jimmie Smith on WSEN Columbus. In the early thirties Moore also had a strong interest in athletics, excelling in both football and track. At one point he held the league record in the 440 yard dash and on the mile relay team. The University of Cincinnati offered him a scholarship, but he chose a career in entertainment. His first regular job came with a traveling tent show group called Doc Schnieder and his Texas Yodeling Cowboys. Based in Eagle Pass, Texas, where they had

Lee and Juanita
Moore, WHIS, Bluefield,
WV, 1941.

some border station radio exposure, the Cowboys advertised themselves as
from Coahuila, Mexico. However, the group traveled more extensively than
Moore really wished so he returned to Ohio in 1935 and landed a job at
WPAY Portsmouth.

The Portsmouth station had recently moved there from Mount Orab,
Ohio, and Moore received a salary of $12 weekly for his daily show. He also
often had an opportunity to make an additional $2 nightly playing in beer
joints or during the summer on show boats between acts of dramas. On
Saturday nights a jamboree took place in a skating rink adjoining the studio. Moore sang a lot of Gene Autry numbers in those days and recalled that

M. M. Cole Publishing Company used to push Autry songs by furnishing radio entertainers with copies of his songbooks. Moore adopted the cowboy image in those years which stayed with him throughout his career. This led Lynn Davis, a colleague when both were later in Bluefield, to refer to Moore as the "two-gun yodelin' cowboy from Circleville, Ohio." Moore remained in Portsmouth until after the famous flood of January 1937.

Moore then moved up the river some 39 miles to WCMI in Ashland, Kentucky. There he worked weekdays with a group called Chief Skaggs and the Mountain Melody Boys. Led by Dolpha Skaggs, the chief of police in nearby Catlettsburg, this band had several notable musicians pass through its ranks over the years including Slim Clere, Chuck Wiggins, and the trio of Bob Shortridge, Curly Wellman, and Big Foot Keaton. In Ashland he also first met Juanita and her sister, Ann Pickelsimer, "the Gal from the Hills" and "Sister Ann," and Juanita would eventually become his wife. On Saturdays Moore went over to WSAZ in Huntington, West Virginia, and performed on a show sponsored by a bakery.

By the end of 1937, Moore had moved again, this time to WCHS in Charleston, West Virginia. Other entertainers there at the time included Buddy Starcher, Frank Welling, Cowboy Copas, and Grandpa Jones. From Warren Caplinger, head of the Cap, Andy, and Flip trio, Moore learned a guitar technique he continued to use. After a few months at this station, Moore began to hit what he then considered real prosperity, an $18 weekly salary plus income from sales of pictures and personal appearances. Under such conditions he managed to purchase his first Martin D-45 and also help his friends and fellow entertainers Budge and Fudge Mayse—a Delmore styled duet—with their car payments. When Juanita, the Gal from the Hills, came to WCHS, Moore announced her show, and they soon became husband and wife. They also worked as a duet for two decades, during which time they became one of the more memorable husband-wife duets in traditionally oriented country music.

Not long after their 1938 marriage, the Moores relocated to WHIS in Bluefield, West Virginia. They did exceedingly well in Bluefield drawing good crowds in the surrounding coal camps, having Tomchin Furniture as regular sponsor on their radio programs, and selling lots of pictures and friendship ball point pens. Dixie Lee Williamson, known later as Molly O'Day, who arrived at WHIS months after the Moores became established recalled that they literally carried their mail in by the basket full. Moore said the station management finally had them get their own post office box because the secretaries could not handle it. This produced another problem because a delinquent youth found a key to a neighboring box and began stealing money out of the letters. Finally, the crook was arrested and sent to the federal reformatory.

Another unfortunate incident took place at Bluefield in September 1941 when Dale Roseberry, leader of a group called the Campfire Boys and formerly closely associated with the Moores, died in an auto crash. The Moores also had an addition to their family, son Roger Lee who was born May 1, 1940, and began working with his parents almost from infancy. He learned "Down in Union County" as his first song and played with his dad and mom until reaching sixteen years old. The Moores did excellent duets in that period and each sang solos. Moore recalled that "The True and Trembling Motorman," a song sometimes credited to McDowell County miner Orville Jenks, tended to be his most requested number for several months. He also had his last serious fling with athletics in Bluefield, playing briefly with the town's baseball team which was in the Class D Mountain State League. The Moores remained at WHIS until after the December 7, 1941, attack on Pearl Harbor. They then turned their spot over to another newlywed duo—Rex and Eleanor Parker—and headed for that northern West Virginia station which also made so many contributions to traditionally oriented country music, WMMN Fairmont.

During the war years, the Moores alternated between their work at Fairmont and a station with a similar format, WSVA in Harrisonburg, Virginia. They remained at each location about six months on their first go-round, but stayed about a year and a half at both places the second time. Lee Moore had a band during his second stint in Virginia that contained some notable members such as the famous fiddler, Leslie Keith, and the future notable bluegrass fiddler, Buck Ryan. Another Moore sideman, Daniel "Zag" Pennell, the Ozark Mountain Boy, later recorded for Columbia records and worked as a featured vocalist on the *Old Dominion Barn Dance* at Richmond. At Fairmont, Moore had the honor of serving as president of the local musicians union. He also had fond memories of the WMMN entertainers having a baseball team that played a team from the Fairmont newspapers. With a straight face, he related how Little Jimmie Dickens played shortstop.

After a brief stay at WPAQ in Mount Airy, North Carolina, in October 1946, the Moore family went to KFNF in Shenandoah, Iowa. Lee Moore considered this to be something of a mistake because the population was too scattered for many personal appearances. Although he enjoyed the rabbit hunting, he decided to return to Charleston, West Virginia, and WCHS in the early spring of 1947. Things did not seem as prosperous there either, and they soon returned to Harrisonburg, Virginia, where he reorganized his band, the Sandy Valley Gang. During this period Lee Moore also spiced up his show by adding a few magic acts. This made him one of the few—if not the only—country musicians to double as a magician.

Lee and Juanita Moore's next moves again took them farther South. First they worked at WPAQ in Mount Airy, North Carolina, once more. The so-called Granite City station served as a home base for several solid traditional and bluegrass acts in the decade following World War II. Then in late summer 1949 they moved to Knoxville where they formed one of several acts working for the supermarket tycoon Cas Walker. Here they replaced Lynn Davis and Molly O'Day who moved on to WVLK in Versailles, Kentucky. They labored several months for Walker before receiving a call from Wilma Lee and Stoney Cooper who had more than they could handle at WWVA Wheeling. Late in 1949, the Moores joined that 50,000 watt station whose *World's Original Jamboree* ranked only slightly behind the *Grand Ole Opry* and *National Barn Dance* in prestige. It also proved to be their last move for a long time. The Moores caught on fairly quickly at WWVA both in terms of morning shows and the Saturday night *Jamboree*. Like their friends, the Coopers, their earlier stay at WMMN had exposed them to a portion of the same listening audience.

Lee and Juanita Moore did quite well during the early years at Wheeling. The station had a strong appeal throughout Pennsylvania, upstate New York, and rural New England as well as into Canada. Lee Moore recalled 1953 as being an especially good year. That same year also became memorable for when he initiated his all-night deejay show. Another WWVA personality, Uncle Tom George, previously had the show, but the hours apparently began to get to him. This curtailed Lee's mid-week personal appearance schedule somewhat, but he still had some close-in shows at first since he did not go on until 2:00 a.m., but later his shift began at midnight. Nonetheless, he still had weekends and the Sunday park trade did very well in the 1950s. Many weekends saw Lee Moore do his stint on the *Jamboree*, go home for an hour, return to the studio and do his all-night deejay show, take off at 6:00 a.m. for a Sunday afternoon park appearance, and get back to WWVA at midnight for his next all-night show. Weekends frequently became real endurance tests.

As a deejay, Moore became something of a legend during the remainder of the fifties and most of the sixties. This also earned him his famous nickname of "the Coffee Drinkin' Night Hawk." He had a brief experience at deejay work at WMMN, but at WWVA he obtained the opportunity to develop a real personality with his occasional live picking and singing, individualized style of commercials, and taste for hard country music that made him a favorite of truck drivers and insomniacs all over the Northeast. Like Nelson King of WCKY and Randy Blake of WJJD, Lee Moore soon ranked as one of America's truly great country disc jockeys.

Another memorable event of 1953 in Moore's life came with his first recordings. Like many other radio personalities, the Moores gave little thought to records during much of their career. He said in retrospect that he recalled back in 1940 and 1941 when at Bluefield how he often bought and listened to the Bluebird cuts of Roy Hall who worked at WDBJ Roanoke, the next big station to the South. Although Hall's rank as an artist was only roughly equivalent or slightly ahead of Moore's at the time, he never gave any real thought to do the same thing himself. Unfortunately, by the time Moore entered the Cross Country studios, it was becoming increasingly difficult for hard country acts to get on the major labels. As a result, all of his and Juanita's efforts were on smaller labels. His first recording featured his virtual trademark song "The Cat Came Back" with the forgettable "Stop Cracking Peanuts," on the flip side. Later he recorded more singles as well as several duets with his wife. Some of this material later appeared on a Point album in Canada. Moore also recorded a four-song EP for Doc Williams's Wheeling Records.

In 1959 Lee Moore took a six-month leave from WWVA and worked for that time at a station in Mount Jackson, Virginia. In retrospect this seemed to have also been a trial separation from Juanita. By most accounts the Moores had not been happy for some time. Lee Moore later worked as a solo act and would marry twice more before his death.

Lee recorded more in the 1960s. Two albums on the Arc Label in Canada of just Moore and his guitar probably represent his best work on wax. They contained a mixture of old and new songs done in a simple arrangement.

The material ranged from oldies like "Treasures Untold" to the then new "Hello Vietnam." For real collector items, Moore recorded three singles in 1962 for Joe Bussard's Fonotone label in Frederick, Maryland. Two of these cuts have appeared in a Fonotone box-set from Dust-to-Digital. A little later he did a pair of albums for Uncle Jim O'Neal's Rural Rhythm label. On the first, he had some help from Charlie Moore and Bill Napier, while the second featured the Red Smiley group of Tater Tate, John Palmer, and Billy Edwards augmented by Dobroist Dan Milhon of Columbus, Ohio. Like the Arc recordings, these albums featured a broad cross section of material from Moore's extensive song repertory. Old-time songs such as "Gathering Flowers from the Hillside" and "Little Girl Dressed in Blue" blended well with middle-period songs like "Strand from a Yellow Curl" and "Down Where the River Bends." It even contained a few newer compositions typified by Harlan Howard's "The Deepening Snow" which other vocalists have also adapted well to bluegrass arrangements. Moore continued as WWVA's night-time deejay until 1969. He did not feel comfortable with the modern format he had been forced into a couple of years earlier and expressed no regrets when WWVA's management decided to replace him.

Lee Moore continued as a WWVA *Jamboree* artist through 1973 and then decided to leave for two reasons. First, a high proportion of his bookings tended to be in upstate New York, central and eastern Pennsylvania, New England, and adjacent parts of Canada, so relocation cut down on his travel. Second, he remarried about this time and third wife Thelma lived in the Albany, New York, area. As a result, Moore became and remained a resident of Wynantskill, New York, for the rest of his life. By this time, WWVA's headlong plunge into modernization had pretty much run its course and the management seemed increasingly determined to make itself into a Nashville satellite. However, while the *Grand Ole Opry* continued to revere its Roy Acuff and Bill Monroe, the new crowd at *Jamboree USA* never seemed to know what to do with its own legends like Doc Williams and Lee Moore.

From 1973 forward Lee Moore continued to be either semi-active or semi-retired. He did club work and also played some bluegrass festivals, both as performer and emcee. His recording efforts were limited to a pair of singles and some 8-track tapes. The latter consisted of solo performances of a good mixture of old and newer songs that fit his style. The tapes could best be described as nothing fancy, but nonetheless good traditionally oriented country music that sounded highly pleasing to those who appreciated Lee Moore's simple and pleasant approach to a song. In the 1980s, Cattle Records of Germany released two albums of his earlier material.

In May 1979, as part of the Vandalia Gathering in Charleston, West Virginia, Lee again appeared with older radio legends that he had been so closely associated with in the Mountain State: Buddy Starcher, the Bailes Brothers, Rex and Eleanor, Slim Clere, Doc and Chickie Williams, and others. For this writer who assisted the West Virginia Department of Culture and History in organizing the show and for many older fans, it seemed almost like a dream come true. For a few brief moments at least the sounds once heard on *the World's Original Jamboree* and the *Old Farm Hour* were heard again. Somewhere it seemed that the spirits of Big Slim McAuliffe, Billy Cox, Stoney Cooper, Frank Welling, and Warren Caplinger must have nodded their heads approvingly!

As Lee Moore's career wound down, he continued to play a few shows, attended the Doc Williams Reunion in Wheeling a few times, made custom cassette tapes for friends, and called them and sang happy birthday over the phone. A lingering habit from his deejay days often led him to go to bed at about six or seven in the early evening. This writer visited Lee and Thelma at their Wynantskill home in 1987 and found them to be a retired couple at peace with the world. The "Coffee Drinking Night Hawk" died in New York on August 17, 1997. As his longtime friend and *Jamboree* colleague Doc Williams reflected, "Lee was unique in his style."

SELECTED RECORDINGS

Lee Moore Sings Radio Favorites of Country Music. Rural Rhythm RUR 137, 1998. Reissue of 1966 long play album.
Lee Moore: The Coffee Drinkin' Night Hawk. Rural Rhythm RHY 202, 2013. Reissue of 1968 album.

✎ Mac Odell (Odell McLeod)

1916–2003

To the contemporary bluegrass fan, the name of Mac Odell will probably not mean much. He did not lead a band, and he never played at a festival until well past his prime. Only those who closely examine composer credits on record labels or jackets may have caught the name Mac Odell or Odell McLeod. Composer credits always used his real name, Odell McLeod, but artist credits and later radio shows used the name Mac Odell. Many recollected his daily radio shows at Nashville's other important country station, WLAC, whose television studio was the home of *Hee Haw*. Odell made recordings of many of his excellent original songs on the Mercury and King labels. The best of those became hits for other country artists of the era. Many of these compositions have become bluegrass standards. Known as Mac Odell the Ole Country Boy, or the One Man Band, Odell made significant contributions to country and bluegrass music for more than a decade.

Born Odell McLeod, he first saw the light of day on May 31, 1916, in Roanoke, Alabama. His father, a section foreman on the Central of Georgia Railroad, moved to LaGrange, Georgia, when Odell was small so Odell grew up in the Peach State. As a boy, he learned to play harmonica. He also grew to appreciate phonograph records, especially those of the Skillet Lickers and such individual members as Riley Puckett, Clayton McMichen, and Lowe Stokes. Later, Odell and his father—his mother died when he was seven—moved to Hogansville, Georgia, where he often attended local dances. He also listened to early *Grand Ole Opry* radio broadcasts, and harmonica player DeFord Bailey became his favorite.

As a result of this early musical influence, he and a friend, Jay Bassett, began to play music together. Calling themselves Mac and Slim, they worked at local events with Odell on harmonica and Bassett on guitar. Later Odell traded a bicycle for an old guitar and even later he got a mandolin. He and

Mac Odell, WLAC,
Nashville, 1949.

Bassett eventually fell out, and Odell began to drift around, finally going as far north as Virginia. But he got homesick and came back to Georgia where he worked in the cotton mill at LaGrange. A wildcat strike closed the mill and many of the workers went to Atlanta including Odell's sisters and their families. Soon he met his old friend Bassett and the two got more serious about their music, working as a mandolin-guitar duet. They auditioned for WGST, but no openings were available. They nonetheless continued to play in the area on street corners, at farmer's markets, and in wagon yards where they made a living of sorts by passing the hat following their performances.

Finally, Mac and Slim decided to hitchhike around the country and see America while they picked and sang. They first went to Charlotte, North Carolina, where they worked for several days. Deciding to go to Seattle, Washington, the boys went first to Bristol, Virginia, where they played a program on a local radio station. Moving northward through Kentucky, they arrived in Columbus, Indiana, where they entertained firemen in the local station house. Also stopping in Indianapolis and Kokomo, they moved north-ward along Highway 31. At Benton Harbor, Michigan, they secured a regu-lar job at a local night spot called the Jungle Inn. Here their cross-country progress stopped. Both Mac and Slim met girls in Benton Harbor who quickly became romantic interests. After several months in Michigan, they left for their Georgia home on Labor Day 1934. After a few days in Atlanta, they again hitchhiked westward, going to New Orleans where they got their first big break at radio station WWL. The New Orleans station had just be-gun live programming of country music in a major way and several name acts appeared there. Artists on the roster of the *River Revelers* shows included Rex Griffin, Lew Childre, Curly Fox, Asa White, Leon Chappclear, and the Shelton Brothers, as well as others. For Mac and Slim one of the most in-teresting performers was one of their boyhood idols, Lowe Stokes, a former Georgia fiddler who now played under the handicap of a missing hand. Mac and Slim played early morning shows by themselves and then beginning at 10:00 p.m. played with the other groups. After several months, the duo got lonesome for their girls in Michigan and left WWL just prior to an opportu-nity to record for Decca that recorded many WWL artists in the mid-thirties. Odell went to work in Benton Harbor and eventually married Addie.

While working in Benton Harbor, Mac and Addie formed a duet fre-quently playing locally. After winning an area talent contest they made a guest appearance on the *National Barn Dance* at WLS. The *Supper Time Frolic* on WJJD, Chicago also proved to be a popular program and they gained a regular spot there with the help of Irvin Victor, an announcer whom Odell had known in New Orleans. Others appearing on the show in-cluded ballad singer Doc Hopkins, the famous duo of Karl Davis and Harty Taylor who had first popularized such great songs as "Kentucky" and "I'm Just Here To Get My Baby Out of Jail," Shelby Jean Davis, and the Flannery Sisters. After about a year, the couple, who had built up quite a reputa-tion and made several personal appearances at a much better salary than at WWL, found themselves victims to a change in station policy. The Pickard Family came to Chicago and several groups including the McLeods found themselves out of a job.

Since Addie's family came from Arkansas, the duo decided to try their luck in that part of the country. They secured a job at KBTM in Jonesboro, Arkansas. Numerous opportunities for personal appearances were available in local schools and while the profits did not make them wealthy, the remuneration seemed sufficient and a relaxed atmosphere made the work there a lot of fun. Roy Acuff came over from WSM and played a few shows and Mac first made the acquaintance of the man who would later make one of his songs famous.

After several months in Jonesboro, the duo returned to Michigan and Mac went back to his old job. They continued to play music on weekends in the Benton Harbor area. Odell's old partner, Bassett, who had also married a local girl, played some with them. One weekend in early December 1941, they and their group went to Kalamazoo to play for a convention of Eckrich Meat sales personnel. Upon their return home, they learned that the Japanese had bombed Pearl Harbor.

During the war, Odell remained out of the music business, working in a Michigan Power Shovels defense plant. Although in industrial work, he took a serious interest in songwriting. Over a period of several months, he worked on five songs: "Money Won't Buy This Soul Of Mine," "That Glory Bound Train," "The Battle Of Armageddon," "We Planted Roses On Our Darling's Grave," and "Radio Station, S-A-V-E-D." Recalling his earlier meeting with Roy Acuff, Odell sent the songs to him at WSM, not knowing that Acuff and Fred Rose had entered the music publishing business. After a long correspondence, Acuff-Rose published the songs. Roy Acuff took considerable interest in the material and recorded four of the songs although only "That Glory Bound Train" was released at the time, becoming a hit of some significance. Hank Williams later recorded the fifth song, "Battle of Armageddon," although the number's release came out only after the singer's tragic death. All the songs appeared in sheet music and in Acuff song books. An excellent rendition of "Radio Station, S-A-V-E-D" by the Blue Sky Boys finally found its way onto an album released in 1963. The impact made by the songs at the time of their publication in 1944 managed to launch the career of Odell McLeod as a successful songwriter.

Following the war, Odell endeavored to secure a spot as an artist at WSM. However, after being advised by Fred Rose that it might be some time before he could be worked in, he decided to audition at Nashville's CBS affiliate, WLAC, instead. His tryout proved to be successful and in the winter of 1946, the Odells and their three children moved to Nashville.

When he went to work at WLAC as Mac Odell and Little Addie, the duo received a salary of more than one hundred dollars weekly and one minute on each show to sell songbooks and harmonicas. These mail order sales proved to be highly profitable. Odell later claimed to have purchased a substantial brick home from the songbook proceeds. Although the station never seriously competed with WSM, WLAC did boast the presence of several important country acts doing primarily daily shows including Jack Henderson, Big Jeff Bess, and Ted and Wanda Henderson among others. Grady Martin and Benny Martin, two important instrumentalists, also played with various groups at the station early in their careers. Since WLAC relied heavily on daily shows, their artists did not travel as far afield as did those at the *Opry*, but nonetheless still played numerous personal appearances within a hundred miles or so of Nashville.

Mac also continued his career as a songwriter. Three of Cowboy Copas' most popular gospel numbers—"From the Manger to the Cross," "Four Books in the Bible," and "Purple Robe"—all came from Odell's fertile imagination. These numbers have become standards in the bluegrass field as recorded by Carl Story, the Stanley Brothers, the Lewis Family, and others. Another song of Odell's, "Cora Is Gone," became one of the early Flatt and Scruggs Mercury classics.

Other artists and groups also recorded Odell McLeod songs. Wilma Lee and Stoney Cooper recorded "Thirty Pieces of Silver" on Columbia as did the Harmony Gospeleers on Victor and Milton Estes on Coral. Bonnie Lou and Buster Moore cut "Wolves in Sheep's Clothing" on Mercury. At the Columbia studios, Little Jimmie Dickens recorded "Sign on the Highway."

Odell also recorded in his own right. In 1948, he cut two sides for Mercury: "Wild Rose of the Mountains" and "Thirty Pieces of Silver." In the next two years, he did two more Mercury sessions, one of them with backing by Bonnie Lou and Buster Moore. Generally his records featured musical accompaniment similar—albeit somewhat less complex—to contemporary Acuff records. Only "Prayer for Freedom" among Odell's Mercury recordings was not his own, having been written by Knoxville nurse, Ruby Moody, who is probably best known as composer of "Walking My Lord Up Calvary Hill." A train song of Odell's, "Red Ball Rocket Train," became much admired for the Dobro work of George "Speedy" Krise, best remembered for his instrumental support on Molly O'Day's recordings.

In 1952, Odell switched to King Records and recorded four sessions for Syd Nathan's label. On the first four recordings, Don Reno and Red Smiley helped out and Don's pronounced tenor singing on "Be on Time" and "Let's

Pray" along with his mandolin playing make that session of special signif-
icance to bluegrass fans. Another trip to the King studio saw the Delmore
Brothers and Wayne Raney assisting. Their guitar sound is especially
prominent on "Life's Elevator." The only King master not containing an
Odell McLeod original was his rendition of the old Carter Family standard,
"Wildwood Flower."

Many of Odell's songs reflected a continuing theme in country gospel
music, associating technological innovations—railroads, radios, elevators—
with religious lessons. Others consisted of poetic retellings of key Bible nar-
ratives. Some dealt with moral teachings such as "I Wish My Mommy Did
Not Smoke" or then current topical items like "The Tattoo Hand," about
a notorious criminal with an identifying mark. One of his more unusual
songs told in humorous fashion of the new wonder drug, "Penicillin." In
fact, Odell's compositions constituted some examples of the type of old time
songs that entered tradition. Perhaps this explains why several have become bluegrass standards.

Odell performed other tunes than his own material on radio. His songbooks indicated a preference for older material mixed with newer gospel
and heart songs. He listed some of his favorite soloists as Molly O'Day and
Bill Monroe and favorite contemporary groups as the Blue Sky Boys, the
Bailes Brothers, and the Louvin Brothers.

Mac continued working at WLAC, but had some aspirations to switch
over to the *Opry*. WSM gave him an audition and he got some of his best
friends from among the local corps of musicians including Zeb Turner,
Grady Martin, Mac McGar, and Benny Martin to assist. He was offered an
early morning show at WSM, but lost his enthusiasm upon finding out that
he would have to take about a 50 percent pay cut. As a result, he stayed with
WLAC, much more satisfied than before. His only appearance on WSM
came as a benefit show for the March of Dimes.

Eventually, Odell's work at WLAC included a little deejay activity and
either one or two daily shows. After a while, Addie Odell tired of radio and
Mac Odell continued doing the shows alone working at the station for a
decade in all. The program drew mail from all over the South and into
the Midwest. He believed his best responses came from Virginia and West
Virginia. Oddly enough, he only played one show in that area, a tobacco
festival in Richmond and as a guest on the *Old Dominion Barn Dance*.

Mac's closest friends in the business tended to be those who shared his love for hunting and fishing. He hunted and fished most often with John "Lonzo" Sullivan and Grandpa Jones. He and Jones remained friends until Jones died.

As live country music began to fade from the scene in the middle 1950s, Odell left WLAC, and he and Addie moved to Florida. For some months, he taped his shows and had them played back from Nashville. He entered the sign business and more or less dropped out of the entertainment world except for a few guest appearances on Ernie Lee's Tampa television show.

In 1957, the Odells returned to Benton Harbor, Michigan, and remained there for the rest of their lives. Staying in the sign business, Odell prospered in that trade until illness in the fall of 1974 forced him to curtail his physical activity. It was then that he renewed his interest in songwriting and music publishing even though country music had changed. He also liked bluegrass which he never actually played, but still influenced with his style of singing heart songs and especially his songwriting.

Little came of Odell's reconnection with the music world. Older fans showed interest in his Mercury and King sides which were reissued on the German label, Folk Varieties; BACM later put them on a compact disc. Old Homestead released an album of his old radio shows. However, two albums of his newer songs, recorded in 1977 and 1981 on Folk Varieties, made little impact. His one known festival appearance at Charlotte, Michigan, failed to generate any more bookings. One problem derived from his not being able to remember lyrics of his own hits very well. As a result, Odell McLeod returned to Benton Harbor and lived out his days. By the time of his death on January 11, 2003, the Old Country Boy could look back on years of real achievement as an artist and composer in the 1935–1957 eras.

SELECTED RECORDINGS

Mac Odell: The Old Country Boy. BACM CD D 309, 2010. A collection that includes all of
Mac's 1949 Mercury recordings, his 1952–54 King efforts, and two additional cuts.

✎ Jimmie Skinner

1909–1979

Although Jimmie Skinner had not been a bluegrass artist until late in his career, his contributions to the music have nonetheless been considerable. His unique style of country singing appeals to both bluegrass lovers and traditionalists. Many of Skinner's musical compositions found their way into the bluegrass repertoire. A few of his many recordings had bluegrass accompaniment. His partly owned business enterprise, the Jimmie Skinner Music Center, long provided a place for bluegrass fans to purchase records. During the lean period of the mid-fifties through the early sixties, the Cincinnati store was one of the few places where the buyer of bluegrass could get satisfaction. Skinner's own background, like that of many bluegrass artists, remained deeply rooted in traditional instrumental and vocal music.

Born near Berea at Blue Lick in Madison County, Kentucky, on April 27, 1909, James Skinner grew up in an area that probably produced more pioneer recording and radio artists than any other part of the United States with the possible exception of the section around Galax, Virginia. For a generation after 1925, Berea and surrounding communities turned out such notables as Marion Underwood, Doc Roberts, Asa Martin, Edgar Boaz, Green Bailey, Welby Toomey, Ted Chestnut, James "Carson" Roberts, Doc Hopkins, Karl Davis, Harty Taylor, Bradley Kincaid, and Red Foley and the Coon Creek Girls as well as Jimmie Skinner. Such bluegrass bands as John Cosby and the Bluegrass Drifters, the Van Winkle Brothers, the Russell Brothers, and the New Coon Creek Girls together with many performers who were on John Lair's *Renfro Valley Barn Dance* also came from this portion of east-central Kentucky.

Skinner's particular childhood favorites were fiddler Doc Roberts and banjoist Marion Underwood. He recalled Roberts playing for square

Jimmie Skinner.

dances at his parents' home and those of other neighbors before he ever recorded anything. He remembered hearing Underwood play at local functions, known even then for the banjo tune "Coal Creek March" which he later recorded for Gennett. The Skinner family all played a bit of music and Jimmie learned to frail the banjo at age six or seven. Although he absorbed much of the music of his native area, his own vocal stylings contained more Jimmie Rodgers influence than any of the locally heard vocalists.

After Skinner turned sixteen, the Skinner family moved to Hamilton, Ohio, taking their musical heritage with them. Jimmie had already learned to play guitar, banjo, and fiddle and his father and three brothers also played a variety of instruments. One brother, Esmer, picked the banjo in a fashion similar to Underwood and Skinner seconded him on guitar. In the early 1930s, the duo went to Richmond, Indiana, and performing as the Skinner Brothers they recorded two instrumental numbers—"Coal Creek March" and "Blue Banjo Rag"—in the Gennett studios. Unfortunately, neither master was released, the company being in financial straits as a result of the Great Depression. Later a representative of Gennett called Jimmie Skinner and asked him to record "99 Years," but he did not know the song and turned down the opportunity.

For some ten or twelve years after moving to Ohio, Skinner played music as an amateur. He worked square dances and other local events with his brothers and area musicians. From time to time they also worked on radio stations, occasionally having regular programs. Among the stations on which Skinner played was one at Mt. Orab, Ohio. This little station operated out of the back of a grocery store and called itself the "hundred watt station that covers the nation." The station played a lot of Gennett records and occasionally featured live acts, including a group of which Skinner was part. He worked some at WLW and WKRC in Cincinnati, WCKY in Covington (later in Cincinnati), WPFB in Middletown, and WHTN in Huntington, West Virginia. For a decade or so, Jimmie Skinner contented himself with being a part-time performer.

In the mid-1940s an incident occurred that led to Skinner's becoming a full-time performer. He made a few custom recordings on a label called Red Barn accompanied by Ray Lunsford, an electric mandolin player who worked with Skinner for years, and his brother Esmer playing old-time banjo on a song Jimmie Skinner wrote called "Doin' My Time." To Skinner's surprise, another original song called "Will You Be Satisfied That Way" became especially popular in Knoxville and he was invited to join Cas Walker's *Dinner Bell* show on WROL with Carl Butler, Carl Smith, and Archie Campbell.

Not too long after the release of "Doin' My Time," Lester Flatt and Earl Scruggs learned the song from Skinner's record and cut it in bluegrass style on Mercury. From Flatt and Scruggs, the song found its way onto recordings by groups ranging from Jimmy Martin and the Sunny Mountain Boys to High Country and to Wilma Lee and Stoney Cooper. The number has entered the repertoire of most other bluegrass groups as well and even Johnny Cash recorded it during his early years with Sun.

Jimmie actually wrote the number back in the early thirties while visiting a cousin in Grand Rapids, Michigan. One day the relative showed him an article in *True Detective* magazine called "I'm a Fugitive from a Georgia Chain Gang" by Robert Burns, not the Scottish poet. From this story, in part an expose' of the chain gang facet of the southern penal system, came the basic ideas for an all-time country classic. At one time, he became disgruntled with the song and "started to throw it away," but a guitar-playing friend named Maeford Cole convinced him to hold on to it. Skinner sang the song locally for years and somewhat miraculously it escaped being picked up by someone else and stolen.

After working in Knoxville for a while, Skinner returned to southwestern Ohio. For the next twenty years he alternated between personal appearances scattered throughout the South with a schedule in the Hamilton-Middletown-Cincinnati and Northern Kentucky area where he had already become established.

In Cincinnati, Skinner acquired an astute manager named Lou Epstein and the two soon entered into a couple of notable business enterprises—both involving records. First, they took control of the Radio Artist Records label, a local company that had recorded local country performers such as the Turner Brothers, Roy Lanham, Barefoot Brownie Reynolds, and radio personality Ruth Lyons. Henceforth, Radio Artists became an exclusive Jimmie Skinner label. Most of his classic original compositions: "Doin' My Time," "Will You Be Satisfied That Way," "Don't Give Your Heart to a Rambler," and "You Don't Know My Mind" as well as many other numbers originally came out on this label in the later 1940s. The musical format of Skinner's early records also was the style that would come to be most identified with him—solo vocals and Lunsford's electric mandolin providing most of the backing. For several years Lunsford's mandolin, Skinner's rhythm guitar, and a bass fiddle provided the only instrumentation heard on Jimmie Skinner discs.

The second venture, a record shop first opened in 1950, soon grew into the Jimmie Skinner Music Center. This company, through radio advertising on Cincinnati's WCKY and Newport, Kentucky's WNOP, developed into one of the major mail order houses for bluegrass and hard country. The late evening deejay shows on the 50,000–watt WCKY by Nelson King, Marty Roberts, Wayne Raney, Jimmy Logsdon, and sometimes Skinner himself (via pre-taped presentation) attracted a nationwide audience of traditional country music fans until the station changed its format in the mid-1960s. During the day, Skinner had daily shows broadcast directly from the Center and reached an area containing many Southern migrants who were drawn to Jimmie's down-home style. From the mid-fifties to the mid-sixties, the Jimmie Skinner Music Center was the one place where blue-grass records could always be obtained. Although Skinner was quick to give Lou Epstein, who ran the store until his death in 1963, most of the credit for the store's success, it cannot be denied that Skinner's name was a definite asset. Another business venture which gives some idea of Skinner's popularity in the Cincinnati area was "Jimmie Skinner's Vacuum Packed Coffee" which was sold in that area for a time in the late 1950s.

In 1950, Skinner signed with Capitol and in the next three years had thirteen single records released. Although none of these songs became a giant hit, they managed to sustain his popularity to the point that he ranked fifth in a 1951 *Country Song Roundup* magazine poll following Hank Snow, Eddy Arnold, Hank Williams, and Ernest Tubb respectively. In 1953, he ranked seventeenth in the same poll. In addition to new versions of his older numbers, Skinner's Capitol recordings included a popular sacred song "Hem of His Garment," "Send Me a Penny Postcard," "Women Beware," and a tribute song entitled "Hank Williams is a Singing Teacher in Heaven."

After three years with Capitol, Skinner switched to Decca. He had several more notable recordings including "John Henry and the Water Boy," a recomposition of the old ballad which featured a bluegrass banjo along with electric mandolin and fiddle. A second song with this instrumentation, "Too Hot to Handle," later received full bluegrass treatment from the Lonesome Pine Fiddlers.

Beginning in 1956, Skinner began to record for Mercury. During the late 1950s, he had several chart makers, the most important being "Dark Hollow" which was somewhat based on the older "East Virginia Blues" which Luke Gordon had originally recorded on a small label. The Jimmie Skinner recording reached No. 7 on the *Billboard* charts and has entered the repertoire of many bluegrass groups. Another Mercury hit of Skinner's, "I Found My Girl in the U.S.A.," was written in response to the many popular tunes of the time about foreign love—"Fraulein" and "Geisha Girl" for example—but in a sense nearly ended the cycle for that type of song. One remaining answer song, "I'm the Girl in the U.S.A.," became a hit for Connie Hall a.k.a. Inez Hellman, who subsequently recorded four Mercury duets with Skinner.

In the latter part of 1958, a falling out took place between Skinner and longtime electric mandolin accompanist Ray Lunsford. Over a period of months, Skinner had to pay a sizable sum in back pay to Lunsford, and he never worked for Jimmie again. Thereafter, Rusty York became Jimmie's principal associate. York could handle anything from traditional bluegrass to rockabilly and filled the role well, but the electric mandolin was gone.

Traditional country fans found the album *Jimmie Skinner Sings Jimmie Rodgers* a generally admirable album. Recorded just prior to the death of Jimmie Rodgers's widow Carrie in 1961, the album featured York on steel guitar and did much to recapture the mood of the original classics. Nonetheless, it was distinctly in the Skinner style and not imitative. In many respects, it could be compared to the Merle Haggard effort that appeared nearly a decade later.

Skinner's association with Mercury led to a friendship with executive Don Pierce who subsequently reinstituted Starday Records as an independent label. It was largely at Skinner's urging that Pierce recorded so many bluegrass artists in the early 1960s. Jimmie knew that a market for that type of music existed because he and Epstein had sold bluegrass records steadily in their store. After his Mercury contract ended, Skinner also went with Starday and had a couple of albums and several singles on that label including a good bluegrass rendition of "Fallin' Leaf."

When Skinner's contract with Starday ended, he continued to record largely on the smaller labels. Two of his more interesting albums were on Lou Ukelson's Vetco label; Ukelson eventually succeeded Epstein as the principal owner of the Jimmie Skinner Music Center. *Jimmie Skinner Sings the Blues* illustrated one side of his talents; *Jimmie Skinner Sings Bluegrass* reflected another. The latter album featured bluegrass instrumentation including Harley Gabbard on Dobro and Vernon McIntyre on banjo, and contained a variety of standards and lesser-known songs. Skinner also recorded some material in a more contemporary vein including some singles for the Nashville-based Stop label and the albums *Requestfully Yours* and *Jimmie Skinner's Greatest Hits*. In the 1970s, he started his own label known as Well Done although it's not clear if he ever had any releases on it.

During the late sixties and early seventies, Jimmie continued to play personal appearances in Ohio and adjacent states. He sometimes worked package shows and also did club work, often with a guitar player named Warren Ellison. He also worked a few bluegrass festivals and did some deejay work on WCNW, the leading country station in the Cincinnati-Hamilton, Ohio, area.

As a record spinner, Skinner exhibited a high degree of independence. He did this because either he or the sponsor bought the time and often did remote broadcasts from the sponsor's place of business. This permitted him to choose his own material which included considerable bluegrass and such hard country singers as Hank Williams, Ernest Tubb, and himself. Skinner contended that he could probably never do deejay work directly for a station since he would lack the freedom to choose his own material. One of his Vetco singles, a song and recitation entitled "I'm Gonna Tell It Like It Happened," told of a country station disc jockey who played real country music on the air and lost his job. Although the song was not auto-biographical, Skinner believed it would become so were he to be a deejay and be restricted to the format prevalent on most of the so-called country radio stations.

Jimmie decided to move to the Nashville area in 1974, mostly because of his interests as a songwriter. He said he still worked a lot of shows in the same areas he always had. However, being in Music City gave him the opportunity to get more of his songs recorded by other artists. Skinner was always interested in songwriting for others—one of his first successes was doing "Let's Say Goodbye Like We Said Hello" for Ernest Tubb. He was one of the first writers to go with Acuff-Rose Publishing Company in the 1940s although he later had his own company.

Skinner signed with the Monroe Talent Agency in 1976 and worked a lot of bluegrass festivals that year and in 1977. Since he had such a close relationship with it, he found the move to bluegrass a comfortable one. He wrote a new song entitled "I'm Proud to Be a Bluegrass Loving Man" while his wife, Betty, contributed "It's Blowing Away (in a Lonesome Bluegrass Wind)." According to Skinner, the latter song "kind of tells the story of what's happened to country music." He planned to record both. He and Betty had a son James, a talented singer who Jimmie said "can do justice to the old songs of mine."

In the summer of 1979, Jimmie visited in Hamilton and had a chance meeting with Ray Lunsford. Supposedly Lunsford apologized and they shook hands, yet, the two never saw each other again. Skinner was beginning to feel his age. On October 27, 1979, he played a show in Shepherdsville, Kentucky. He and Betty had originally planned to visit his one-time duet partner Connie Hall in nearby Butler, Kentucky. However, as Skinner did not feel well, they returned to Nashville where Jimmie died the next day. A truly unique vocal stylist was gone, but it was saved in 2003, when Bear Family Records released a box set that included all of his early recordings on Capitol, Decca and Mercury.

Outside of "Doin' My Time" which many artists have recorded, Jimmy Martin probably did more to make Skinner an important bluegrass composer than any other artist. "You Don't Know My Mind" was one of Martin's most requested numbers. Martin's rendition of "Don't Give Your Heart to a Rambler" has also been noteworthy. The Osborne Brothers recorded two of Skinner's later songs—"Little Trouble" and "A Born Ramblin' Man"—on MCA. These songs together with his own style and the long presence of the Jimmie Skinner Music Center have all endeared the genial gentleman from Blue Lick, Kentucky, to the bluegrass and traditional country music world.

SELECTED RECORDINGS

Jimmie Skinner: Doin' My Time. Bear Family BCD 16513, 2003. Contains all of Skinner's commercial recordings through 1962.

✂ Buddy Starcher

1906–2001

Buddy Starcher ranked as one of those country singers who appealed to numerous bluegrass lovers over the years. His simple, unvarnished, traditional-rooted vocal style together with a sizable number of original old-time sounding songs went a long way toward explaining his popularity. Retiring in the mid-1970s, Buddy's musical career extended for about a half-century. Starcher spent much of his radio and television days in his native West Virginia, but at times traveled as far afield as Iowa, Texas, Florida, and Pennsylvania.

Born near Ripley in Jackson County, West Virginia, on March 16, 1906, Oby Edgar Starcher's family moved considerably in his early years before finally settling down in rugged Nicholas County, midway between Charleston and the Virginia state line. Starcher's dad, Homer Francis Starcher, played a pretty good old-time fiddle and the son first learned music by providing rhythm—first on banjo and then on guitar.

From his own memory, the youngster seemed to have always been called Buddy. And Buddy Starcher soon took up singing although there were few vocalists in his section of the state. He learned most of his songs from phonograph artists such as Riley Puckett, Jimmie Rodgers, and the Carter Family. Starcher recalled that his earliest public performances, in addition to country dances and parties, were made over the telephone party lines. Several neighbors tuned in simultaneously and he and his dad would play requests over the wires. Radio coverage had not yet penetrated that part of West Virginia, but the party lines were utilized for similar albeit more limited purposes.

In the fall of 1928 Starcher left his native state and went to Baltimore in search of work. A local department store sponsored a talent contest as a means of advertising the newly developed home recording machines.

Buddy Starcher,
ca. 1949.
*Photo courtesy
of John Morris.*

Although there were quite a number of entries, only Starcher sang country songs to his own guitar accompaniment. The man at the store seemed impressed and secured an appearance for him on local radio station WFBR. Buddy remembered singing three songs that day in October 1928: "Wildwood Flower" and "Midnight Special," learned from newly released recordings by the Carter Family and Otto Gray's Oklahoma Cowboys, respectively; and "Those Brown Eyes," a song he arranged himself. It would be many years before he had the opportunity to record the latter song by which time Billy Cox had cut it and the Dixon Brothers had made a variant, "Those Dark Eyes." However, the radio debut soon resulted in Starcher having a daily show.

Buddy received no salary for this early radio work, but he managed to exist by playing for food and drinks in local speakeasies. Later he found a job selling insurance. After several months of this meager subsistence, he returned to his West Virginia home.

In 1930 Starcher went to Charleston looking for work and again found himself playing on radio. Station WOBU had been in operation since 1927 and several musicians of note already played at the station including Clark and Luke Kessinger and also Billy Cox, all of whom had made records by that time. Starcher recalled some lesser-known performers there, too, such as the fine singer and yodeler Willie Tyler, Hayes Young, and Jimmy Stamper. Although it was interesting, radio singing still paid nothing, so after a few months Buddy went back to Nicholas County.

By 1932 the country was in the depths of depression and an unemployed and wandering Starcher found himself in Washington, D. C., along with that large horde of unemployed veterans known as the Bonus Army. Buddy, a sympathizer, provided entertainment for the men. He also wrote a number of social protest songs such as "Bonus Blues" and "Hoover Blues." The lyrics of these numbers were printed on broadsides to help support the Bonus Army. Oddly enough, none of these songs seem to have found their way onto records like that other Bonus Army ballad, "Forgotten Soldier Boy." Starcher did not even know of the existence of the latter song written by Bert Layne.

Later that year Buddy drifted to North Carolina where he found a place at WSOC then in Gastonia. As usual the so-called job paid no money, but the manager let Starcher sleep in the station in return for doing the janitor work. On his daily show, he permitted Starcher to sell typed copies of his songs for a small fee and this brought in just enough to keep him eating. He did encounter the Carolina group, the Tobacco Tags, who later recorded an unreleased Bonus Army song which may have been a Starcher lyric.

Starcher returned to Charleston in the fall of 1933 and managed to land a sponsor—Certified Crystals—for his show and a regular job as an announcer and flunky at WCHS, changed from WOBU. In addition to his daily picking and singing, he also performed daily dramatic skits with station manager Gene Ferguson on a show called "The Better Health Hotel" which might be described as a forerunner of *Hee Haw*'s "Empty Arms Hotel" skits.

On Wednesday nights Starcher auditioned local talent which went on the air on Friday evenings. In time, this show developed into the *Old Farm Hour.* By the end of the decade, the program became one of the more important hillbilly jamborees on radio. With Frank Welling as emcee the *Old Farm Hour*, gave a start to such significant performers as the Lilly Brothers, the Bailes Brothers, and Red Sovine. Older local favorites like the Kessingers and Bill Cox as well as Cap, Andy, and Flip played on the show, too. Up until the mid-thirties Starcher never gave much thought to playing personal appearances. When the vaudeville team of Salt and Peanuts came to WCHS, they also booked into area theaters. They told Buddy that people asked for him at their shows. Afterward, he, too, began playing show dates.

In the fall of 1935, Starcher went to Washington, D. C., where a friend from his Gastonia days now worked. He took over a daily radio show which was heard on the regional CBS-controlled Dixie Network. After several months, he returned to West Virginia and station WMMN Fairmont. Following a few months there, he went to WPAY Portsmouth, Ohio, a newer station recently relocated from the Brown County village of Mt. Orab.

Buddy remained in Portsmouth until after the great Ohio River Flood of January 1937. During his stay he met several notable musicians with whom he would cross paths over the years. Chief among them was Lee Moore, then in his first professional job. Like Starcher, Moore went on to enjoy a lengthy career, much of it at WWVA. Another, Bill Stallard, also had a notable radio and recording career. Stallard and his wife worked on several stations as Indian Bill and Little Montana and recorded on King as Bill and Evalina. Later as a solo artist, Stallard recorded for Columbia and other labels under the name of Billy Starr. Another Portsmouth artist, Ervin Staggs, co-authored the song "Pale Horse and His Rider" and played a part in the early careers of Johnnie Bailes, Skeets Williamson, and Molly O'Day.

Starcher returned to WCHS in the spring of 1937 and put together his first band, the Mountaineers. He picked up three members from a medicine show band, Doc Grayfeathers and his Cowboys, who had just broken up in Charleston: Jack Carter, Robert Rutland, and Anthony Slater, a.k.a. Smiley Sutter. The former remained in music only a short time, but Rutland played a pretty good fiddle and eventually attained wide fame as Georgia Slim. Slater first took the name Smiley Sutter and attracted much attention as a vocalist and yodeler. From the 1940s he specialized in comedy using the name Crazy Elmer until his death in 1980. After coming to WCHS and getting his own show, Lee Moore rounded out the group.

By this time, Starcher performed a good deal of his own material as is indicated by his 1937 *Mountain Melodies* songbook. This booklet, the fourth in the series, contained twenty original songs, few of which have since been recorded. Oddly enough, he never recorded prior to World War II. The Kessingers and Billy Cox made several trips to the studio, but not Buddy. Quite a number of Cox's recorded repertoire bears a resemblance to some of Starcher's material, but are clearly not the same songs. For instance, Starcher wrote his most famous song, "I'll Still Write Your Name In the Sand," in the early thirties. Billy then wrote and recorded a different song bearing the same title. Since the same publisher, Dixie Music, held the copyright to both songs, considerable confusion resulted. Both men also had a song called "Beautiful Blue-Eyed Blonde" with different lyrics. On one occasion, however, Billy Cox and Cliff Hobbs did record a Starcher composition entitled "Smiling Through Tears."

In 1938, Buddy moved on to WMMN Fairmont for a second sojourn in northern West Virginia. By this time the Fairmont station had become home base for quite a number of musical acts and soon boasted a jamboree show entitled the *Sage Brush Roundup*. Starcher kept a pretty good band together which included Smiley Sutter with whom he sang numerous duets. Another member was fiddler Ted Grant who had formal musical training and once recorded with Texas Swing pioneer Milton Brown, but preferred hillbilly tunes. Mary Ann Estes first worked with Starcher at WMMN. She sang as girl vocalist at various times with Hugh and Shug's Radio Pals and also the Prairie Ramblers. She later became Buddy's wife in June 1946. Lennie Aleshire, Indian Bill and Little Montana, Rusty Gabbard, and Natchee the Indian (Lester Storer) also worked with Starcher at that time.

Other headline acts at Fairmont in those years—all friends of Starcher's—included Murrell Poor, Cowboy Loye (Pack), and Grandpa Jones. The first two ended their careers tragically. Poor was killed in an auto wreck in 1939, returning from a personal appearance. Pack died following a stomach ulcer operation in March 1941. Both men had reputations as excellent radio salesmen in addition to being good entertainers. Buddy also developed this knack for being able to sell sponsors' products and it proved to be an asset throughout his career. Other friends and sometimes closer associates of Starcher included Budge and Fudge Mayse, and Little John Graham.

Starcher left Fairmont in 1941 for WIBC in Indianapolis. However, since he worked solo and was the only country act on the station, he became somewhat lonely. He shortly took advantage of a chance to return to the mountains and went to WSVA Harrisonburg, Virginia. In the Shenandoah

Valley, he gathered a band that included Dolph Hewitt, later of WLS fame; Paul Buskirk, the legendary mandolin picker; Mary Ann Estes; Margie and Mary Humes; and for a time, Mac Wiseman. This group worked together for about a year.

Starcher then took the entire group except for Wiseman, along with fiddler Sleepy Marlin and Bill and Evalina Stallard to KXEL Waterloo, Iowa, where they had a daily show late in the evening and what amounted to a nationwide audience. After a few months, however, the draft began to cut into his personnel. Starcher recalled that Paul Buskirk received his draft notice the day after he had bought the talented sideman a brand new mandolin. With his band breaking up because of the war, he moved on to KMA Shenandoah, Iowa, where he also did daily radio work and transcriptions for Spark-o-Lite which were played on several stations including WWVA Wheeling back in his home state.

In 1944, Starcher moved back to WSVA in Harrisonburg where he managed to assemble a new band. This version of Buddy Starcher's All Star Round Up included Red Belcher and the Franklin Brothers. Belcher later had a group at WWVA that included the Lilly Brothers and Tex Logan among its members. The Franklin Brothers—Clyde, Bill, and Delmas— eventually formed one of the early pre-bluegrass bands; Bill Franklin became known for his gospel composition, "That Moon's No Stopping Place for Me." Starcher's comedian at Harrisonburg was Emory Stroup, known as "Stroupy."

Buddy moved back to WMMN Fairmont in 1945 taking Estes, Belcher, and the Franklin Brothers along. He filled out his group with bass player Herman Redman and fiddler French Mitchell, two veteran Fairmont radio performers. Starcher also hired a new comedian, Dusty Shaver, alias Oscar August Quiddlemurp.

It was during his last hitch at Fairmont that Starcher first made recordings. In the spring of 1946 he went to Chicago and cut a session for Four Star. That fall he went to Hollywood and did more recordings for the same firm. The assisting musicians on the first session included Dolph Hewitt and some other people from WLS while Tex Williams and Smokey Rogers from the Spade Cooley band helped out on the second. The music, while something less than a traditional Appalachian sound, does not obscure Starcher's fine clear country voice. Several of the fourteen songs Buddy recorded on Four Star feature only Starcher and his guitar and it is these numbers that are most musically satisfying. "I'll Still Write Your Name in the Sand" is undoubtedly the most memorable although all of the songs are quite good, especially those composed by Starcher. The latter include "Song of the Waterwheel," "In Memory of Halloween," and "Fire in My Heart." At the time, his theme song, "Bless Your Little Heart," was recorded and released from both sessions. Buddy also recorded the old Carter Family song, "Wildwood Flower," with only his own guitar backing. For a brief time some of his younger fans even thought he composed the number.

By the time Starcher made his second session on Four Star, he had left radio work and became affiliated with a new record label, Dixie. Starcher lived in Marietta, Ohio, during this period. Although he recorded several other artists on Dixie including Budge and Fudge Mayse, the Franklin Brothers, Rusty Gabbard, and Big Slim McAuliffe, he made no recordings of himself. Dixie recorded some excellent artists and some vintage 1940s music, but never got the distribution necessary to make a financial success.

In August 1947, Starcher was persuaded to return to radio at newly opened WPDX Clarksburg, West Virginia. At this station he did both singing and deejay work. Many of his old friends from Fairmont and Charleston also worked at WPDX including Budge and Fudge Mayse and the husband and wife team of Cherokee Sue and Little John Graham. During Buddy Starcher's Clarksburg stay, he became one of the first country singers to have a biography written about him. His fan club president, Marion R. Goddard of Marietta, put together a forty-eight page booklet entitled *Bless Your Little Heart: The Story of Buddy Starcher.* Although it is not what one might call a definitive biography, it does contain a great deal of information and some interesting photos of Starcher, his friends, and his two prize horses, Chief Highland and Dawn.

Starcher's sponsor was Sunway Vitamins and his super salesmanship won him a new automobile, a Frazier Manhattan—the Edsel of the 40s—in June of 1948. By the spring of 1949, Sunway decided to place their best radio salesman on a big station. As a result, Starcher wound up at WCAU in Philadelphia spinning records and selling Sunway products. He recalled that the Philadelphia station had different ways from those of the more down-home style stations he worked at in past years. However, once he got used to the formats, things worked out about as well there as anywhere else. During the more than two years he spent in the City of Brotherly Love, he again became involved in radio drama, on a kiddie western, and with recording on Columbia.

Starcher had two sessions on Columbia, recording a total of ten songs. Some of these like "New Wildwood Flower" featured only Buddy and his guitar. Another was a recitation of an old sentimental poem, "The Colored Child's Funeral," that dated back to the 1880s. He first remembered Murrell Poor doing the song at WMMN more than a decade earlier. Hank Williams and Red Foley did versions of it, too. Starcher also covered the gospel favorite "Beyond the Sunset" which Chickie Williams had made popular at WWVA along with the recitation "Should You Go First." He also recorded original heart songs like "Oh, Leave One Token of Your Love" and gospel numbers typified by "Isn't He Wonderful" and "I Planted a Rose in the Garden of Prayer."

After a couple of years in Philadelphia, Starcher took a job as manager of a new radio station in Apollo, Pennsylvania. This job seemed like an almost natural step upward since he had frequently been involved in several phases of radio besides singing. His success in Apollo led to his accepting a similar position at WMBM in Miami, Florida.

Throughout much of the 1950s, Starcher worked primarily as a radio station manager or management consultant. After a few years in Florida, he moved on to Fort Worth, Texas, for a couple of years. He then served short stints at several other stations in such varied locations as Greenville, South Carolina, and Chambersburg, Pennsylvania.

During those years, however, Buddy never completely dropped out of performing. He often placed himself on a short radio show in both Florida and Texas. Starcher had only one record session on July 19, 1954, during his Florida years on the King-related DeLuxe label. Two of the four sides recorded at this time were released, but went nowhere. Finally, he decided to get primarily back into entertainment.

In 1958, Buddy Starcher returned to WSVA Harrisonburg, Virginia. He got a new band together which included Mary Ann Starcher, fiddler Joe Meadows, and steel player-comedian Herman Yarbrough. The group soon maintained a busy schedule of six weekly television shows and two radio shows per week. Starcher found that he still had plenty of fans around from the old days as he kept busy at personal appearances, too. He also began to record on the Starday label.

The Buddy Starcher Show in January 1960 moved back to another old location where he had an early morning television show on WCHS in Charleston. Here Starcher's popularity soared to new heights and the local ratings generally placed his show third in the region of West Virginia, Eastern Kentucky, and southeastern Ohio. Starcher recalled that his main competitor, the NBC network's *Today Show*, never even came close to his own for attracting a morning audience. In addition to Meadows, Mary Ann, and Yarbrough, who doubled as comedian Roscoe Swerps, support musicians were lead guitarist Norman Chapman; drummer and vocals Dorsey Ray Parsons; bass player Butch Lester; and autoharpist Wick Craig. Eventually others joined the cast including Lori Lee Bowles and Harry Griffith as well as the Davis Twins (Honey and Sonny), and Sleepy Jeffers, who also doubled as comedian Little Willie. Actually, only Yarbrough was a regular for the entire thirteen-year run of the show and *The Sleepy Jeffers Show* which continued after Starcher went to Nashville in 1966. The group kept busy with almost nightly personal appearances throughout the entire WCHS listening area. Only two shows, both night-time network programs, out-rated *The Buddy Starcher Show*.

Starcher also continued to record for Starday. Craig, Meadows, and Yarbrough played on some sessions and helped make the songs appealing to traditional country music lovers. Buddy had several single releases on the Starday and Nashville labels, at least one EP, and the highly listenable album *Buddy Starcher and His Mountain Guitar*. The Starday recordings contained a mixture of material: new songs and recitations, older country tunes, and new arrangements of songs he had either written or recorded in earlier years.

After his contract with Starday ended, Starcher and the group recorded a gospel album on the Heart Warming label. Recitations dominated the album, a talent in which Starcher had long specialized. In all, Starcher spent six pleasant and rewarding years in his last stay in Charleston. Then in 1966, a chance recording of his became a national hit. He had recorded an original recitation on the small Boone label entitled "History Repeats Itself." Essentially a comparison of the martyred Presidents Lincoln and Kennedy, the record had wide appeal to a nation still largely under the spell of the Kennedy mystique. Starcher now found himself in demand for personal appearances all over the country. He moved briefly to WHTN-TV Huntington and then gave up local television altogether for a career in

Nashville. He signed a new contract with Decca records who bought the master of "History Repeats Itself," and he recorded enough recitations to fill out an album released by Decca. Two of these numbers also made an impact—"Day of Decision" and "A Taxpayer's Letter." Starday quickly had Minnie Pearl do a cover of "History Repeats Itself" and released it on an album with some of Starcher's earlier material. Sheb Wooley a.k.a. Ben Colder, obviously trying to sound like Senator Everett Dirksen, did a parody entitled "Great Men Repeat Themselves" which was a witty comparison of President Lyndon Johnson and Batman. After nearly forty years in show business at the age of sixty, Starcher suddenly found himself on the verge of stardom in Nashville.

Buddy soon discovered that Nashville stardom can become very much a here today and gone tomorrow phenomenon. Eventually he gave up his career in Music City and returned to his former occupation of radio station management. He did record an album for Bluebonnet Records of Fort Worth, Texas, featuring simple vocals with guitar accompaniment. In a sense, this album contains some of his best performances along with his solo efforts on Columbia and Four Star.

Starcher worked in radio management until his retirement in 1976. From Nashville he went to the Florida cities of Ocala, Lakeland, and Sebring. He then managed a station in Baytown, Texas, and finally in Albany, New York.

After retirement, the Starchers decided to do the things they never had time to do when working. They settled in the village of Craigsville in Nicholas County, West Virginia. Buddy worked some as a salesman for a local Ford dealer. He continued writing songs and recorded a bit. In the later 1970s, he cut some material for Richard Weize's Bear Family label in Germany. He also recorded some material at Lowell Varney's Riverside Studio which was released only on eight-track tape. It was mostly just Buddy and his guitar, although Mary Ann Starcher joined in on a couple of numbers and Bill Clifton, a longtime admirer, played a little autoharp and helped on some vocals. Buddy, the Boy from Down Home, who had a couple of reissue albums on the German Cattle label, also played a personal appearance now and then. The first of these included a re-creation of the *Old Farm Hour* in Charleston at the May 1979 Vandalia Festival where he received the most applause of any of the old timers who played. He also attended a revived *Sagebrush Roundup* on Bunner's Ridge near Fairmont and a distant reunion at KMA in Shenandoah, Iowa.

About the time he reached the age of ninety, he and Mary Ann moved one final time to Harrisonburg, Virginia, where Mary Ann's son from an earlier marriage resided. Closer access to health facilities was the principal reason for the move. Buddy lived there until his death at ninety-five on November 2, 2001. Mary Ann passed away in January 2003. In 2005 Cattle Records reissued his Columbia material in a collection and in 2010 BACM issued more of his originals with sensitive notes by longtime admirer Bill Clifton. In 2013, *Goldenseal: West Virginia Traditional Life* ran a long feature on his Charleston television show. Two years later, he was inducted into the West Virginia Music Hall of Fame, a well-deserved and somewhat overdue honor.

Many other artists recorded Starcher's songs over the years. One of his earlier compositions, "Sweet Thing," was recorded by the Callahan Brothers on Decca in 1941. Subsequently T. Texas Tyler, Fiddlin' Arthur Smith, Cowboy Copas, the Osborne Brothers, and the Stanley Brothers also performed it on record. Mac Wiseman has made "I'll Still Write Your Name in the Sand" into a bluegrass standard and also recorded "The Fire in My Heart." Slim Whitman's version of "Song of the Waterwheel" became one of his better-known standards

Over a half-century in country music, Buddy Starcher had a very significant career. As a radio artist and performer, he spanned the gap from old-time music to modern country and western. As a writer, he displayed talent for composing songs that seem almost like traditional folk material. His stylings have had an obvious influence on such vocalists as Wiseman and Clifton. Throughout his career, Starcher remained a modest and hospitable gentleman who retained a host of friends among both artists and fans.

SELECTED RECORDINGS

Buddy Starcher: Battle of New Orleans. BACM CD D 311, 2010. A collection drawn from Four Star, Columbia, De Luxe, and Starday singles.

Buddy Starcher: Just Me and My Guitar. Old Homestead OHCD 320, 2001. A reissue of a 1968 Bluebonnet album

The Golden Age of Country Music. Cattle Compact Disc CCD 307, 2005. Presents tracks by three different artists, including all ten of Starcher's Columbia numbers.

✄ Carl Story

1916–1995

When thinking of people who have spent the greater part of a long professional life in bluegrass music, one probably most often thinks of Bill Monroe. The attention directed to the Father of Bluegrass Music is both correct and deserved, but there are others who have also given much to this musical style for some three decades or more. Among them is Carl Story, one-time Blue Grass Boy and longtime leader of the Rambling Mountaineers. Nicknamed the Father of Bluegrass Gospel Music, this North Carolinian spent nearly sixty years as a professional musician. Despite his title, not all of Story's recordings have been either gospel or bluegrass although the majority clearly falls into that category. It seems likely that only the Stanley Brothers, Don Reno, and perhaps Bill Monroe, Flatt and Scruggs, or the Lewis Family, have recorded more numbers than Carl Story and the Rambling Mountaineers. In the role of bluegrass leader, Story has provided a training ground for many of the super sidemen of the trade, for example Red Rector, Bobby Thompson, Tater Tate, Johnnie Whisnant, and the Brewster Brothers to name just a few.

Born Carl Moore Story at Lenoir in Caldwell County, North Carolina, on May 29, 1916, he was the son of Arthur C. Story, a local old-time fiddler of some renown. The younger Story developed his interest in the fiddle from his father. The elder Story admired the string band music of the time and seems to have bought and frequently played virtually every Columbia record by Charlie Poole—"Monkey On A String" was a favorite—and the North Carolina Ramblers as well as the Carolina Tar Heels and Grayson and Whitter among others. Carl's mother, Omie, was also a musician, being proficient on both guitar and organ. Carl also remembered hearing Uncle Dave Macon and Uncle Jimmie Thompson during the early days of the *Grand Ole Opry,* but had less opportunity to hear the radio in childhood

Carl Story.

than those artists who were younger than he. As a result of his parents' musical talents and interests, the younger Story gained a familiarity with some of the best old-time music available from the first decade of commercial country music.

Carl was nine years old when he learned to play the fiddle, his first instrument. Later he learned the guitar and clawhammer banjo, although for the first decade of his career the fiddle remained his main instrument. When he was about fourteen, he met young Johnnie Whisnant who was playing banjo at the age of nine. A few years later when Story formed his first band, Whisnant became a key member.

Furniture factories and related businesses provided most of the employment opportunities in the Lenoir area. Story wanted something different and drifted north to Lynchburg, Virginia, where he worked at the Mead Corporation's paper mill. The town also had a small 250-watt radio station, WLVA, which had a Wednesday night talent contest at the local theater. Carl entered one week and won not only the ten dollar first prize, but also he impressed the manager of a local furniture store so much that the store manager secured Story a fifteen-minute weekly Monday evening show with a sponsorship. After several months of the weekly show as a solo artist and more work at the paper mill, Story returned to Lenoir with both experience and ambition.

Back in his hometown, Story and Johnnie Whisnant became part of a group known as J. E. Clark and the Lonesome Mountaineers. Clark headed the group, but was not a musician himself. They did their first radio work at WSPA Spartanburg, South Carolina, in 1935. Dissatisfied with the poor pay received, Story and Whisnant withdrew and reorganized as the Rambling Mountaineers with Ed McMahan and Dudley "Uncle Dud" Watson, two guitar players whom they had met at fiddler's contests in Morganton and Boone, North Carolina, respectively. Watson was a good tenor singer and occasionally played a little mandolin as well. They continued to play on radio at Spartanburg, sponsored by the Vim Herb Company, manufacturers of "Scalf's Indian River Medicine," of Lafollette, Tennessee. This company continued to be Story's radio sponsor for the next several years on four different stations.

About this time the Rambling Mountaineers got their first opportunity to make records and journeyed to Atlanta where they cut an estimated six masters for the American Record Corporation featuring Story on fiddle, Watson and McMahan on guitars and Whisnant on banjo. Unfortunately for bluegrass fans and historians, these cuts were never released and the masters have reportedly been destroyed. If they existed today, some persons might well consider them to be the first bluegrass recordings. That early sound of the Rambling Mountaineers has not been totally lost, however, for Dave Samuelson was able to issue some material from home recordings reportedly made in 1941 which preserves a sampling of their work.

In 1940, the band moved on to Hickory, North Carolina, and the new radio station WHKY where they continued to be part-time radio performers, working at other jobs and playing personal appearances only in the immediate area. Story worked at the local furniture factory. Soon, however, they were approached by Hall Houp who began to book them for more distant shows. After making a particularly successful show date in Taylorsville, North Carolina, where they made an unheard of sum of fifty-five dollars, they decided to become full-time performers. Story recalled that their farthest-from-home performance was in the Washington, D. C., area and that they were forced to subsist on a quarter's worth of bologna until they were paid!

In the first part of 1939, the Rambling Mountaineers moved to WWNC—the call letters stood for Wonderful Western North Carolina—in Asheville, a station that already pioneered shows by such country greats as the Callahan Brothers, the Blue Sky Boys, and Wade Mainer. They continued to work for the same sponsor and booking agent as before and also on the *Farm Hour* with some success until the coming of World War II. Young musicians were susceptible to the Selective Service Act of 1940. McMahan was the first to leave the group. Jack Shelton, previously of Wade Mainer's band, replaced him. Then after Pearl Harbor, Whisnant followed McMahan. However, Carl struggled on for a time trying to hold a band together. Hoke Jenkins joined the group for a while picking banjo and after he was drafted, they did without a banjo and used sixteen-year old Ray Atkins of Erwin, Tennessee, on Dobro. Buster Moore, subsequently best known as half of the Bonnie Lou and Buster duo, worked with them briefly. Claude Boone, who had earlier worked and recorded with Cliff Carlisle, also saw the first of many years as a Rambling Mountaineer in that war-torn year of 1942.

Late in 1942, Bill Monroe and his Blue Grass Boys played a show in the area. Story was having lunch in Burlington with another North Carolinian, Clyde Moody, a former Wade Mainer sideman who had moved to Nashville. They discussed the problems of keeping a band together in war time and Carl surmised that his time to go was not far either. The Blue Grass Boys needed a fiddler and the meeting led to Story joining the band. Story's fiddle style was slower than that of Monroe's band and he had some reservations as to whether he could play that fast. However, he recalled Monroe as being quite patient. He enjoyed his stay as Monroe's fiddler and remembered the leader as being very helpful to him and whenever he did a fiddle tune on the *Opry* Monroe always insisted on introducing him as Carl Story, the North Carolina Tar Heel. The band also included Stringbean as banjo player-comedian and Cousin Wilbur Wesbrooks on bass in addition to Story, Moody, and Monroe. Story wound up serving nearly a year with the band before he was called to serve in the Navy in October 1943.

When Story was discharged in October 1945, he reorganized the Rambling Mountaineers at WWNC and went to work for his old sponsor, Scalf's Indian River Medicine. Jack and Curley Shelton, Hoke Jenkins, and Claude Boone comprised the remainder of the group. Even before the war, Story had prevailed upon his sponsor to get the group's radio show switched to WNOX Knoxville, Tennessee, and in December, after only two months at Asheville, an opening came and the Rambling Mountaineers moved to Knoxville's *Mid-Day Merry-Go-Round*, an extremely popular and significant show in the annals of country music history.

The next five years were labeled by Story as the good old days and accurately so for the *Mid-Day Merry-Go-Round* was a hit show and WNOX artists were excellent drawing cards in East Tennessee and adjacent parts of Kentucky, Virginia, and the Carolinas. Like other country acts of the time, the Rambling Mountaineers featured quite a bit of comedy. Claude Boone, who worked for Story for about nineteen years, did comedy and for a time Charles Elza, known as Kentucky Slim, the Little Darling, also did comedy and tap dance routines. Quite often they played to packed houses and sometimes had to put on two shows, especially on Friday nights when the Rambling Mountaineers sometimes teamed up and did package shows with Molly O'Day and the Cumberland Mountain Folks. During this period Story and Lowell Blanchard wrote the song "I Heard My Mother Weeping" which O'Day recorded on Columbia. A little later Story also recorded it on Mercury and again on Starday. It did well for both artists. With a heavy personal appearance schedule, daily radio shows, the *Merry-Go-Round* and the *Tennessee Barn Dance,* they had about all the work they could handle. They also got the opportunity to record and did several sessions for the new Mercury label.

Dee Kilpatrick was A and R man for Mercury in those early years and he signed Story to a contract after hearing the group on WNOX. The persons who worked on that first session in 1947 were Story, Claude Boone, and Jack and Curley Shelton. Only guitar and bass instrumentation were used on the quartet numbers. Songs recorded at that time included "I Heard My Name on the Radio," "Who's That Man," and "Keep on the Firing Line." Bluegrass music as we know it today had not yet evolved as a unique and distinct form of country music. As a result Story's early Mercury recordings do not qualify as true bluegrass since they have no banjo, but they are nonetheless good traditionally oriented country music of the period which usually featured lead guitar or mandolin. A few of the earlier numbers had electric steel added. Carl's first full bluegrass band backing on record in a technical sense came in the mid-1950s when Bud Brewster played banjo on his Mercury session. The instrumentation varied because the personnel in the band changed and so did the instruments they played. Examination of Carl Story's early Mercury and Columbia recordings provide documentation that the line between bluegrass and country music in the late forties and early fifties was not finely drawn.

Story's name also came to be widely associated with gospel and sacred material during these years although he seldom confined himself solely to gospel material. He also recorded such country standards on Mercury as "Faded Love," which gave a mountain sound to a western swing number, and "Tennessee Border," apparently the first recording of this on a major label. He also co-authored "I Overlooked an Orchid" which was not only Carl Smith's first country hit, but also became a top hit in 1974 by Mickey Gilley.

Through the years at WNOX the personnel of the Rambling Mountaineers changed somewhat. Hoke Jenkins departed and later young "Bud" Brewster came in on banjo together with his brother, Willie on mandolin. In all, the Brewsters worked with Story three different times, most often when he worked out of the Knoxville area. Still another brother act that worked with the group at the *Mid-Day Merry-Go-Round* was the Johnson Brothers, Clyde and Hack. When this twosome plus Story and Boone performed quartet numbers, they called themselves the Melody Four. Cotton Galyon played electric steel for a time and Fred Smith played guitar. Story left WNOX after five years at the station. The band included Red Rector on mandolin, Claude Boone on guitar or bass, and Ray Atkins on Dobro or electric steel.

From Knoxville they went to WCYB in Bristol where they appeared on *Farm and Fun Time.* Their tenure there, however, was brief for they soon got a much better paying deal at WAYS, a 5000-watt station in Charlotte where they received a salary as well as being able to plug their show dates. During this time they sponsored a contest to give away a television set and received some 27,000 pieces of mail, reminiscent of the thirties and forties when country acts received so many thousands of letters in a short time. Also at Charlotte they started a Saturday Night Jamboree show, the *Tar Heel*

Barn Dance, which did quite well. It was about this time that they switched from Mercury to Columbia Records for which the Rambling Mountaineers cut several sides. Included among their Columbia recordings were the gospel number that Story recorded several times, "My Lord Keeps A Record;" the excellent Claude Boone composition, "Have You Come to Say Goodbye" later recorded on RCA Victor by Lester Flatt; "Step It Up and Go," an old blues number; and "Love and Wealth," an original Louvin Brothers composition on which Red Rector sang lead and which has become a bluegrass standard.

Story stayed at Charlotte for about two years. Roughly in the latter part of 1953, Lowell Blanchard of WNOX came to Charlotte and enticed him to return to Knoxville. By this time, the *Tennessee Barn Dance* was carried over the CBS radio network every third week and booking opportunities were becoming available in more distant locations like Sunset Park and New River Ranch. So he returned to WNOX for another four-year stint although he lost part of his band in the process. Ray Atkins and his wife remained in Charlotte, going to work for Arthur "Guitar Boogie" Smith. Red Rector also departed. However, when Story and Claude Boone returned to Knoxville, they found the Brewster Brothers again ready to play music with them.

During the second stint in Knoxville, Story switched back to Mercury and recorded such memorable numbers as "Light at the River," "Banjolina," and "Mocking Banjo," giving the first full bluegrass band treatment to the latter number originated a couple of years before by Arthur Smith and Don Reno and later immortalized by Eric Weissberg. Tater Tate came in to play fiddle and Bobby Thompson replaced Bud Brewster on banjo playing on some of the aforementioned instrumentals recorded on Mercury that are now legendary. Story also worked at more than one place during this Knoxville tenure, putting in some time at WROL, and on Cas Walker's television show in addition to WNOX

In 1957, Carl left Knoxville to play a daily forty-five minute midday television show at WLOS-TV Asheville known as the *Dinner Bell*. He stayed there for about three years during which time his recording activities moved from the Mercury label to Starday. For a time in the mid-fifties the two labels had been combined and when Don Pierce made Starday a separate entity in the late 1950s Carl went along doing his first session with them in October 1958. In the next decade or so Story made about a dozen albums with Starday including one with the Lewis Family almost all of which was straight bluegrass gospel.

By 1960, it had become difficult for hard-core bluegrass groups to get steady bookings even in the mountainous area of the southern Appalachians. Story decided to give up extensive road work, became a disc jockey, and played out mostly on weekends. He first did deejay work at WFLW Monticello, Kentucky, and when playing shows he picked up musicians who were available. Shows in Kentucky often found him working with Clyde and Marie Denny. He also worked quite a bit with Bonnie Lou and Buster Moore and recorded some sides with them on both Starday and the small Acme label. Farther to the South he continued to work with Willie and Bud Brewster, Claude Boone, and often Tater Tate. It was this group of longtime friends and musical associates that he continued to record with on Starday. Like one or two other name bluegrass bands especially the Stanleys, Story took the opportunity to make records in between contracts and as a result had several albums released on more obscure labels such as Spar, Scripture, Sims, Songs of Faith, GRS, and Rimrock. Most of these records utilized the talents of Tate, Boone, and the Brewsters.

After 1965, the Brewsters and Claude Boone did not want to travel the road so much and Story's deejay work switched to WEAS Savannah, Georgia, and then to WCKI in Greer, South Carolina, where he made his home for most of the remainder of his life. During the latter part of this period he utilized the services of the Jones Brothers and their band on personal appearances and together they made three albums, two for Starday and one for Pine Tree. This band included Bruce Jones, mandolin; Lee Jones, bass; Frank Hamilton, fiddle; and either C. E. Ward or Frankie Belcher, banjo. Dewey Farmer, later of Al Wood's Smoky Ridge Boys, also worked with him for a while playing mandolin on his *Daddy Sang Bass*. This album was one of Story's better-selling records although he was the first to admit that his rendition of the title song was not his best. Starday executives persuaded him to record it with an electric guitar as a quick cover to the Johnny Cash hit. Being an alternate selection for the Capitol Record Club, it enjoyed good sales and made his music available to a wider audience.

Story and the Jones Brothers also did a weekly show at WCCB-TV in Charlotte. Story worked with the Joneses and Hamilton throughout the fall of 1971. After that he used several musicians in the Rambling Mountaineers. Harold Austin, a Pennsylvania-born resident and minister in Liberty, Kentucky, worked with him semi-regularly singing lead and playing rhythm guitar for several years. Austin had a good lead voice of the high lonesome type. Larry Beasley played banjo and Mitchell Moser did the bass fiddle work. Austin's voice can be heard on half of an album which was recorded live by Jessup and on Atteiram as well as on an unreleased Starday album. Red Rector, an old associate of Story's from way back, also helped out on these records with his top-notch mandolin work.

One of the more obvious things that strike one who listens to a great number of Carl Story records or has watched his shows is that with the passing of time he did less solo and lead singing. Red Rector, Willie Brewster, Bruce Jones, and Harold Austin are among those who have been featured on the lead vocals of Rambling Mountaineers records. Story did quite a bit of lead singing, too, but sang more tenor, becoming especially known for his high falsetto.

In 1973, Story moved to Germantown, Ohio, for a few months, but found that his family preferred the South and soon returned to Greer. In the winter, he did deejay work at WMCT in Mountain City, Tennessee. This is in the heart of a region that was famous for fiddlers' conventions in the late 1920s and produced such famous old-time greats as G. B. Grayson, Clarence Ashley, and Doc Watson. Story enjoyed work in this area because he could play bluegrass and old-time music in a place where it was appreciated. From the mid-1970s, he generally did winter deejay work and made summer personal appearances and festivals.

In the mid-seventies, Martin Haerle, a former associate of Starday's Don Pierce, started a new label CMH (from his initials) and signed several name bluegrass artists including Carl as well as a few new ones. He did a double album and two single ones for CMH, but the albums did little to boost his career. Through no one's fault, Story's voice and that of new lead vocalist Mike McKellar did not blend well. Veteran Stanley Brothers sideman Curley Lambert experienced a similar problem when he worked a few months as a tenor singer with Lester Flatt in the Foggy Mountain Boys. The third album, *Lonesome Wail from the Hills*, was an improvement as guitarist McKellar and mandolin picker Jeff Dalton were replaced by veteran vocalist Bill Millsaps of the Snowbird Mountain Boys and fiddler Eb Collins.

Through several years in the 1980s, Story had a good corps of Rambling Mountaineers in his group that included George Hazelwood on mandolin, either Randy Grindstaff or Fred Richardson on banjo, longtime bass man Mitchell Moser, and high-quality fiddler Billy Baker. They recorded a live cassette album and a good bluegrass secular album that included "I Overlooked an Orchid." Ironically, while the band made fewer recordings in those years, several of Story's earlier efforts were reissued on various labels including Country in Canada, Cattle in Germany, Mercury in Japan, and Old Homestead in the United States.

Although Story was aging into legendary status, he put a new band together in the early 1990s that included fine mandolin picker Danny Arms, Brett Dalton on banjo, and young Jim Clark on bass. They did a quality bluegrass album on a new Minnesota-based label, Pure White Dove, *Thank the Lord for Everything* that was a credit to his long career in music. Sadly, it turned out to be his musical swan song as the "Father of Bluegrass Gospel" passed away on March 31, 1995. Helen Story, his widow, kept the Rambling Mountaineers going for a time. She subsequently married one of Carl's former sidemen and has since been widowed a second time. It was Helen Story who accepted Carl Story's plaque when he was inducted into the Bluegrass Hall of Honor. Bear Family Records of Germany has kept his entire classic Columbia and Mercury material in print and Gusto released a well-produced disc containing his first twenty Starday numbers and some other cuts.

In six decades in old-time, country, and bluegrass music, Carl Story has been a very significant figure. He and his musicians had quite an impact on bluegrass music. While never quite attaining the recognition of Monroe, Flatt, Scruggs, or the Stanleys, only a few others could equal or surpass Story's longtime devotion and contribution to this art form.

SELECTED RECORDINGS

Carl Story & the Rambling Mountaineers: Bluegrass, Gospel, and Mountain Music.
   Bear Family BCD 16839, 2011. Contains Story's Mercury, Columbia, and early Starday recordings.
Carl Story: The Father of Bluegrass Gospel Music. King KSCD 5111, 1999. Good sampling of 1960's Starday efforts.
Carl Story: Angel Band. Gusto GT7-0548, 2008. Story's first twenty Starday cuts from 1958–1959 (also included in the BCD collection).

✄ Lillie Mae Whitaker

1939–2014

In more than seventy years of bluegrass music history the genre has been very much dominated by males. To be sure, a few women have been on the scene for some time, usually as part of a family group such as the Lewis's, Stoneman's, or Sullivan's. Two bands—Jimmy Martin and Jim and Jesse—have sometimes featured a female vocalist—Gloria Belle, Carol Johnson, and Lea Seagrave—but the female-led group appears to be a phenomenon that emerged in the 1970s. Among those ladies who never reached stardom, but managed to establish themselves firmly on the scene were Betty Fisher of Georgia and the subject of this profile, Lillie Mae Haney Whitaker of Ohio.

Born near Roundhead, Ohio, on March 23, 1939, Lillie Mae's parents immigrated to the Buckeye State from Magoffin County, Kentucky. Her father picked guitar in the Maybelle Carter style. Her parents named their daughter after Lily May Ledford of the *Renfro Valley Barn Dance* and Coon Creek Girl fame. The group influenced Lillie Mae and her sister, Wilma Jean, one year younger, in old-time picking and singing almost from infancy. Leroy Haney taught his daughters to chord the guitar and mandolin quite early. By the time Lillie Mae reached the age of eight, she and her sister, standing on chairs, had begun to sing duets in church. The duo achieved considerable local popularity, largely because of the novelty of their youth.

As a child, Lillie Mae had two especially preferred singers, one male and one female. Bill Monroe was her first choice whenever she had extra money to buy records. From this love of Monroe music came her love for bluegrass instrumentation and the coupling of that style with the gospel quartet. She also developed a strong appreciation for the music of Lester Flatt and Earl Scruggs. As for females, Lillie Mae Haney's own vocal style owed much to a Molly O'Day influence and also to Wilma Lee Cooper and Rose Maddox. She once heard and met O'Day at a church service in Indiana and even

Lillie Mae and the Dixie Gospel-Aires. *From left:* Junior Stennett, Curnie Collins, Charles Whitaker, Noah Hollon, and Lillie Mae Haney Whitaker.

corresponded with her for a time following a personal tragedy. Although she sang many of O'Day's songs, Lillie Mae Haney endeavored to avoid too close an association or imitation, a course of action of which O'Day herself would have heartily approved.

Soon the Haney Sisters and their father were asked to play and sing in other churches. Before long they received offers to appear at more distant revivals, special services, tent meetings, various reunions and Sunday school picnics. Occasionally, they even traveled to adjacent and Southern states and also sang on a local Sunday radio broadcast for several years. During this time, the sisters favored the songs and stylings of the Louvin Brothers although they performed a wide variety of gospel material. Looking back on those years, Lillie Mae considered them to be tremendous experiences although the family never made more than expenses and sometimes not even that. After Wilma Jean married, she gave up traveling which terminated the sister act. Lillie Mae and her father continued on, however, and soon acquired the services of Charles Whitaker, a very good mandolin player and native of Prestonsburg, Kentucky. After Lillie Mae and Charles were married on January 29, 1955, Leroy Haney retired from the group. Noah Hollon, another transplanted Kentuckian, became a third member of the band as banjoist, giving them a bluegrass sound. Although only a beginner at the time, Hollon eventually developed into a fine banjo player whom Lillie Mae Whitaker believed to be one of the most underrated pickers in the business. The three worked together until the Whitakers lost their eldest son, Charles Jr. in an auto-train accident and Lillie Mae in a despondent state gave up playing for about a year and a half.

Eventually, Lillie Mae decided to pick up the pieces and she and her husband began to play again with Hollon and Curnie Collins as bass player. Adopting the name Southern Gospel Singers, the foursome managed to stay busy playing gospel music at local church services and radio stations. Although they had previously recorded a couple of single records, one as early as 1959, an album recorded with J. D. Jarvis in 1966 entitled *The Old Crossroad* sold exceedingly well and provided an inspiration to do something more than just play music as a hobby and for spiritual fulfillment. At Hollon's suggestion, they decided to take bookings outside the church and to change the name of the group to the Dixie Gospel-Aires. At the same time Junior Stennett, an excellent tenor singer, joined the band.

In 1967 and 1968, Lillie Mae and the Dixie Gospel-Aires recorded two more albums. The first on the Arco label of Cincinnati bore the title *Lo I Am with You*. It contained songs from a variety of sources such as "Snow Covered Mound," "I'll Meet You in Church Sunday Morning," and "Just Over in the Gloryland." The second album, *Jesus Has Called Me*, produced by Rusty York and released on Uncle Jim O'Neal's Rural Rhythm label, featured eighteen songs including Lillie Mae's rendition of "Teardrops Falling in the Snow" and an old favorite once recorded by Carl Butler and the Webster Brothers "Looking Through the Windows of Heaven."

When bass player Curnie Collins left the group and George Smith of Brookville, Indiana, took his place, the Dixie Gospel-Aires endeavored to add a bluegrass quartet to the show, thereby increasing their appeal. With Smith, lead; Stennett, tenor; Hollon, baritone; and Charlie Whitaker on bass together with Lillie Mae now had a gospel act with more variety in their sound. This group recorded an album, *Working On A Road*, on J. D.

Jarvis's Down Home label. When Stennett left the band for the Motor City Bluegrass, Joe Isaacs joined the Dixie Gospel-Aires. An excellent lead singer in the Carter Stanley tradition, Isaacs, who had a wealth of experience from working with the Greenbriar Boys, Ralph Stanley, and Larry Sparks, now led the quartet and George Smith switched to the tenor. When Isaacs left to reform his own gospel group, Lillie Mae Whitaker was forced to become part of the quartet for a time until Jimmy Dutton joined as lead singer and fiddler. A veteran musician who had worked with Red Allen and Lawrence Lane as well as being half of the Dutton Brothers team, Jimmy filled an important role with the band for two years until leaving to start his own bluegrass gospel band, the New Gospel Ship, in 1975. For a time, Marty Townsend, formerly of the Bluegrass Alliance and the Kentucky Grass, replaced George Smith as bass player and tenor singer.

In 1974, Lillie Mae and the Dixie Gospel-Aires began recording for Jack Casey's Rome Records with their efforts being released on the gospel subsidiary Gloryland. The first album, *There's A Big Wheel*, included the old Wilma Lee and Stoney Cooper favorite as title song and also contained a variety of gospel standards and some originals by Lillie Mae Whitaker and Jimmy Dutton. Hollon, Smith, Dutton, and Whitaker performed the quartet numbers plus Tommy Boyd assisted on the session with his Dobro work. The next album, *Hymn Time with Lillie Mae*, featured Wayne Lewis singing lead on the quartet songs. A young bluegrass musician from Sandy Hook, Kentucky, Lewis had experience with Paul Mullins, the New Frontier, and a brief stint with Ralph Stanley. He later joined Bill Monroe's Blue Grass Boys.

Like many other artists who have stuck with bluegrass music for a long time, things did not always go well for the Dixie Gospel-Aires. Over the years, there was a lot of lost sleep, long rides in crowded vehicles, breakdowns, stolen instruments, little compensation, and changes in personnel, but Lillie Mae and Charles Whitaker, and Noah Hollon managed to stick together. Lillie Mae Whitaker once recalled when a key band member quit, the bus broke down, and her Martin guitar had been stolen that Hollon reminded them that only a few musicians had the dedication to hang together through the difficult times. Conditions improved and the band traveled in relative comfort working at fairs, conventions, churches, and bluegrass festivals. They also worked package gospel shows in which Lillie Mae occasionally played a Jerry Lee Lewis style gospel piano.

Lillie Mae Whitaker got along well with virtually all the bluegrass musicians she encountered. She made one of her few boasts in contending that the Dixie Gospel-Aires were as free from internal friction as a band could get. Nonetheless, there were a few changes she would like to have seen in the bluegrass world. For one, she did not nurture a high regard for those musicians who had to depend on alcohol and drugs in order to appear before an audience. Second, she felt it to be tough being a woman in bluegrass and welcomed more ready acceptance of women in the field. Third, she desired more recognition for lesser-known musicians who were as equally skilled as the better-known ones.

All of the Dixie Gospel-Aires were Kentucky natives; aside from George Smith, all of them lived in Ohio. Lillie Mae and Charlie Whitaker resided in Ada, Ohio, with their three sons, all who followed in their parents' footsteps and became adept bluegrass instrumentalists. Lillie Mae's goals remained simple and yet were not easy to attain in the hectic musical world: make a success while confining oneself to bluegrass gospel and take it to more and more places, perhaps around the world, but especially to Nashville's *Grand Ole Opry* which by the time of her death, she had appeared five times as a guest.

By the late 1970s, Lillie Mae had switched her recording allegiance to John Morris's Old Homestead Records of Brighton, Michigan. She also added a pair of veteran bluegrass pickers from southern Michigan to the band. Eddie Carroll had worked with a variety of Michigan bands, and he played both lead and rhythm guitar as well as singing lead in the quartet. James Miller, a veteran of the Miller Brothers, a band that had several albums to their credit, played bass and sang tenor in the quartet. The Dixie Gospel-Aires Quartet and Lillie Mae's vocal leads each shared billing on the recordings. The first album dated from 1978 and the second titled *Lord Lead Me On* came off the press in 1983. After that the recordings tapered off, but the music and singing at smaller festivals and churches continued unabated for many years.

Lillie Mae and Charlie kept the Dixie Gospel-Aires, with some changes in personnel, together for a total of fifty-four years, except for a period of time when Charlie Whitaker worked as a bus driver for Bill Monroe. In later years, they moved to Kenton, Ohio, and the children worked in the band. Lillie Mae and Charlie Whitaker had other occupations; Lillie Mae worked as a real estate broker. Diagnosed with a terminal illness, she died at the Kobacker House in Columbus on October 16, 2014. Her obituary in the *Lima News* stated "her passion was music, especially Bluegrass Gospel." Sadly, her oldest son Ron who had been a key band member in later years followed her in death a few months later. Although she never became a *Grand Ole Opry* regular, Lillie Mae Whitaker did help blaze a trail for females as band leaders that eventually led younger women such as Rhonda Vincent to reach the top of her profession.

SELECTED RECORDINGS

Lilimai [sic] *Whitaker & the Dixie Gospelaires: Jesus Has Called Me.* Rural Rhythm RRLW 238, ca. 1970. Perhaps her most widely distributed long play album.

Lillimae and the Dixie Gospel Aires: Lord Lead Me On. Old Homestead OHS 70038, 1983. Lillie Mae's most recent long play album.

PART TWO

Sidemen

One might say that most bluegrass bands are no better than its individual members. Some of the most notable bluegrass musicians have served the majority of their careers as members of someone else's band rather than leading a group themselves. In doing so, they helped define the sound that made their employers giants in their field. Some of the best known—not profiled here—have been Kenny Baker, who fiddled so many years with Bill Monroe's Blue Grass Boys; Curly Seckler, whose tenor vocals with Lester Flatt made their duets so distinctive; and Josh Graves, who provided Lester Flatt and Earl Scruggs with a whole new dimension to the sound of the Foggy Mountain Boys and in the words of historian Fred Bartenstein, made them "hip" as if Scruggs's banjo hadn't been doing that since 1948.

The sidemen considered here may have provided less drama, but had no less significance. Curley Lambert and Joe Meadows gave the Stanley Brothers quality mandolin and fiddle work, respectively, before moving on to other name bands. Chubby Wise has often been termed the original bluegrass fiddler for his work on Bill Monroe's 1946–1949 Columbia recordings. He spent an even longer time as fiddler for country star Hank Snow's Rainbow Ranch Boys and also did a great deal of session work. Wise also reinvented himself as a solo fiddler recording numerous albums and as a guest musician demonstrating skills in western swing that equaled his efforts in bluegrass and mainstream country.

Other fiddlers also demonstrated quality *extra ordinaire*. Clarence "Tater" Tate spent a half century in bluegrass working for a variety of name bands, often outside of Nashville, until 1977 when he joined Lester Flatt's Nashville Grass. He then worked with Wilma Lee Cooper and spent several years with Bill Monroe. Earlier he had been a mainstay with various bands including those lead by Carl Story, Hylo Brown, and Red Smiley among others as well as serving seven years as front man with the Shenandoah Cutups. Billy Baker fiddled extensively with bands in the Washington, D. C., area as well as with Del McCoury and Carl Story among others. West Virginia fiddler (and banjo picker) Buddy Griffin worked extensively with the traditional Goins Brothers and the more progressive Katie Laur Band before eventually going to Nashville and playing with Jim and Jesse's Virginia Boys and Bobby Osborne's Rocky Top Express. In between times, Griffin started and taught in the Glenville State College Bluegrass Music Program.

The other featured sidemen made up a varied group. Claude Boone came out of an old time music background with Cliff Carlisle and Leon Scott. He then settled into a long career as a bass man with Carl Story and the Rambling Mountaineers and on daily morning television in Knoxville with *Cas Walker's Farm and Home Hour*. Another longtime Cas Walker associate, mandolin picker Red Rector, had earlier spent notable stints with Charlie Monroe, Hylo Brown, and Carl Story, where he often sang lead. He could likely have led his own band, but preferred to work as a duet partner with Fred Smith, Don Stover, or Bill Clifton. West Virginia's George "Speedy" Krise made his name as a resonator guitarist, most notably with Molly O'Day on her first two Columbia sessions, but worked on radio both in West Virginia and in Knoxville. He also recorded with other noted traditionalists such as Bonnie Lou and Buster Moore, Mac Odell, and especially Carl Butler, the latter sessions dominated by bluegrass instrumentation. Krise composed songs that became bluegrass standards.

Somewhat in a category by himself, Lester "Natchee the Indian" Storer gained legendary status as a contest fiddler for a decade prior to 1945. Natchee never played bluegrass although he was often associated with future country star Lloyd "Cowboy" Copas and promoter Larry Sunbrock. Never commercially recorded, he often appeared on Cincinnati and West Virginia radio stations not only with Copas, but other musical figures of his era before a slow drift into obscurity.

All side musicians are worthy of attention. Those included herein might well be considered a representative cross section although somewhat light on banjo pickers (David Deese, Ray Goins, and Joe Isaacs are discussed elsewhere in this volume). Sidemen like Chubby Wise as well as Kenny Baker, Josh Graves, and Curly Seckler have their own niche in the Bluegrass Hall of Honor while Buddy Griffin remains quite active as of 2017. Others are nearly forgotten. Yet all discussed here and many others did their part in making bluegrass music what it is today.

✎ Billy Baker

1936–

Among the better-known but underrated bluegrass musicians who have more than paid their dues, the name of Billy Baker must rank as one of the more significant. At one time or another, this Virginia native worked as a regular or a fill-in with about every group that played in the Washington, D. C.–Baltimore area. Baker also recorded with many of them, served a stint as a Blue Grass Boy, fiddled on Del McCoury's first solo album, and can still wield a bow with the best of them.

Billy Baker was born near Pound, Virginia, on July 5, 1936, to Eddie and Esther Baker. Some may recall Pound as the birthplace of the now nearly forgotten fated U-2 pilot Francis Gary Powers who made national headlines in 1960. Nearby Pound Gap is on the state line, only a few miles from Jenkins, Kentucky, the hometown of the late fiddle legend Kenny Baker. In fact, the fiddling Baker boys are third cousins. Billy Baker had musical influences in his immediate family and first took up the fiddle at age six and played with his parents and siblings for home entertainment and community events such as pie suppers.

Outside the family circle, Billy Baker began playing fiddle as a teenager in a band that included the Cooke Brothers. This threesome was comprised of Hubert Cooke, a future Southern Gospel legend, on bass; Curtis Cooke, the eldest brother, also on bass; and Jack Cooke, who would be known for his decades with the Clinch Mountain Boys, on guitar. As Baker told it, Jack was the baby of the family. Playing a regular program on WNVA in Norton from 1951, the four adolescents developed their musical skills. After his service with the Cookes ended, Baker worked in another group at WCYB Bristol with banjo picker Porter Church, who like himself later made a name in the Washington, D. C., area with such bands as the Bluegrass Champs and Red

Billy Baker, 1977. *Courtesy of John Morris.*

Billy Baker and Del McCoury, the Shady Valley Boys, 1964.

Allen. From the mid-1950s Baker lived in Manassas, Virginia, becoming a close friend of banjo-picking policeman Smiley Hobbs.

With considerable experience behind him, Baker reunited musically with Jack Cooke who had broadened his own musical horizons as a member of Bill Monroe's Blue Grass Boys and recorded three Decca sessions with the master of his trade. The two journeyed to Baltimore where they became members of Earl Taylor's Stony Mountain Boys and were playing a radio show and working the clubs. The band at the time consisted of Walter Hensley on banjo, Porky Hutchins on guitar, Boat Whistle McIntire on bass, and Taylor himself on mandolin. After a time, Hutchins departed and Jim McCall took his place. At some point, Bill Monroe passed through the area and Billy did a show with him. The Father of Bluegrass offered Baker a job as a Blue Grass Boy, but he did not take it. A couple of years later, the offer came again and this time Baker accepted the opportunity. Like most other bluegrass musicians in this period, Billy usually had a day job to support his bluegrass habit; in this case, road construction and asphalt were what occupied his daylight hours.

After his stint with Earl Taylor ended, Baker continued to fiddle with numerous other bands in the Baltimore-Washington area. Perhaps one of the most significant from the point of his recording career was a combination known as the Shady Valley Boys. This band was started by Baker and Del McCoury, a young musician from Glen Rock, Pennsylvania. At various times personnel included Charlie Tomlinson on bass, Jack Cooke on guitar, Smiley Hobbs on banjo, Russ Hooper on resonator guitar, and Baker on fiddle. McCoury did not appear on any of the band's recordings, but Baker and McCoury worked together off and on for more than a decade.

Rebel recordings by the Shady Valley Boys and Billy Baker made up over twenty percent of the cuts of the four albums on the *70 Song Bluegrass Collection,* with nine numbers credited to the Shady Valley Boys and seven fiddle tunes to Baker. In addition, his fiddling was heard on selections by Red Allen, Bill Carroll, Pete Pike, and Buzz Busby. Although never part of the Country Gentlemen, he did play fiddle on some their recordings of Christmas songs. While Billy sometimes played shows with the Franklin County Boys and Benny and Vallie Cain's Country Clan, he does not recall being on any of their recordings.

Three Rebel singles in the 1960s bore Baker's credit as did half of an album on Rebel's budget label Zap. The Shady Valley Boys also made a budget album under Dick Freeland's direction that eventually saw release on the Sutton label entitled *Hootenanny with the Van Dykes*. It was marketed with a cover designed to appeal to urban folk music buffs. The Zap album was shared with resonator guitar player Kenny Haddock under the title *Dobro and Fiddle* (Zap 103). Baker recalled that Smiley Hobbs did the banjo work on both sides of the album. Fiddle tunes on this LP included some of Billy's signature numbers such as "Blackberry Blossom" and "Patty on the Turnpike." Baker also fiddled on Buzz Busby's "Mandolin Twist," which like the Zap album was apparently made after Baker's later Nashville and California experiences. Whether there was any overlap on the varied Rebel and Sutton releases cannot be determined at this writing.

In 1963, both Baker and McCoury accepted offers to join Bill Monroe's Blue Grass Boys. As Billy recalled, Del had originally been hired to play banjo, but ended up playing guitar and singing lead. While Baker made no studio recordings as a Blue Grass Boy, some of the material from live shows in July 1963 at the Newport Folk Festival did feature his fiddle work with Monroe. It was later issued in a Bear Family release and according to Neil Rosenberg and Charles Wolfe, showcased one of his best bands.

In February 1964, McCoury and Baker left the Monroe band and traveled to California to become members of the Golden State Boys. This aggregation at one time or another included such notables as Don Parmley and Vern and Rex Gosdin, but they were not part of the band at that time. The time spent in the Golden State held little if any gold. As McCoury recalled the experience, in a June 1973 *Bluegrass Unlimited* article:

I left Bill to go to California with Billy Baker (fiddle) and joined the Golden State Boys, whose manager promised me a pretty good living. But when we got there, they didn't have much work at all, so then Billy and I got a band up in Norwalk, Calif., the Shady Valley Boys [a West Coast version of their earlier group comprised of Steve Stevenson on banjo and Mel Durham on bass]. We played the bluegrass portion of a TV show every Sunday. We played clubs and the TV show but there wasn't enough work out there for a bluegrass band. In June we came back . . . .

Baker returned to the D.C. area working the club scene during which time he fiddled on Buzz Busby's "Mandolin Twist"/"Blue Vietnam Skies" and worked with Patsy Stoneman and Red Allen in a group that also contained his old band mate from WCYB, Porter Church.

Bill also continued working on a part-time basis with Del who went into logging with his dad after their misadventures in the Golden State. They played the area in McCoury's adopted homeland of York County, Pennsylvania. Baker also played some shows with Alex Campbell and Ola Belle Reed in the late sixties, but did no recording with their New River Boys.

Baker did, however, play fiddle on *Del McCoury Sings Bluegrass* on the Arhoolie label. Recorded in December 1967, this album went a long way to secure McCoury's reputation as a top-notch traditional vocalist. The instrumentation provided by Billy Baker, Bill Emerson, Wayne Yates, and Dewey Renfro complemented McCoury's high lonesome sound that won the hearts of hard core fans who had heard his live performances with the Blue Grass Boys four or five years earlier. Baker's kick-off on several of the numbers and tasteful fiddling helped make this album one of the real bluegrass classics of the sixties. Another album on which Baker fiddled in 1967 did not see release for six years, *Won't You Come and Sing For Me?*, the second Hazel Dickens and Alice Gerrard release on Folkways. The first one had dated from 1963 on their Verve subsidiary and the second was not issued until the pioneer girl team had signed with Rounder. Lamar Grier and David Grisman played on both discs with Baker replacing Chubby Wise who had fiddled on the 1963 effort. In addition to quality fiddle work throughout, Baker was featured on the old Fiddlin' Arthur Smith tune "Sugar Tree Stomp" which Neil Rosenberg noted "preserves all the features of Smith's performance" but "adds a few twists of his own."

In 1969, on the strength of his successful Arhoolie LP, McCoury put together his band the Dixie Pals. Given the fluctuating nature of personnel, the band could almost have been called the Dixie Bills. For several years alternating fiddlers included Billy Baker, Bill Sage and Bill Poffinberger while Bill Runkle often did the banjo work. There were other sidemen too—Dick Staber, Don Eldreth, Dewey Renfro, Jerry McCoury—but almost always one or two Bills. Baker can be seen and heard with the Dixie Pals and numerous fiddlers on the Carlton Haney-Fred Bartenstein motion picture recorded live at Camp Springs, North Carolina, in September 1971.

Although Baker had played some with Al Jones and the Spruce Mountain Boys over the years, he was not a regular member at the time, but he did the fiddle work when Al and Frank Necessary recorded their Rounder album in 1975. His work contributed to the quality of the entire project and was especially notable on such cuts as "Crying My Heart out over You," the old Ernest Tubb favorite "Letters Have No Arms," and Al's own signature song "How the Story Had to End." Baker has also recorded some new material with Al Jones that remains unreleased.

Baker filled in with many country and bluegrass groups over the years. This included a tour with Don Reno and another with Jimmy Martin. One memorable country appearance consisted of a week-long engagement in November 1971 with country star Bobbie Gentry of "Ode to Billy Joe" fame at a Washington, D.C. hotel.

Later in the seventies, Baker moved back to southwest Virginia, settling first in Pound and then Norton, not far from his birthplace. In 1976, he joined a band from Grundy, the Bluegrass Kinsmen. In addition to Baker, this ensemble included Shelby and Ebby Jewell on guitar and banjo, respectively with Danny Anderson on mandolin and James Cole on bass. The Kinsmen recorded an album on Old Homestead and backed Baker on one of his *Fiddle Classics* projects on that label. The other, recorded at the Rome Studio in Columbus, Ohio, had the support of Lawrence Lane and his Kentucky Grass. In addition to traditional fiddle tunes, these recordings featured arrangements of newer slow-paced country hits such as "Help Me Make It through the Night" and "Early Morning Rain" along with his original "Baker Hill."

Baker's main exposure to the larger bluegrass audience from the late seventies into the early nineties came as fiddler with Carl Story and the Rambling Mountaineers. During this period Story did not record at the frantic pace that sometimes characterized his career, in part because so much of his earlier work was being reissued. Nonetheless, he did cut three projects with Baker's fiddle including *Songs of the Blue Ridge Mountains* (Maggard 5903) in 1979 and *Live at the Lincoln Jamboree*, in Hodgenville, Kentucky, released on a Plantation cassette in 1984. Ironically, both of these contained renditions of "Orange Blossom Special" which Billy had done on his Zap offering in the late sixties. Baker also recorded another fiddle album, *Wise County Special* (Maggard 5902), with support from the Rambling Mountaineers.

After Carl Story's passing, Baker remained regionally active. He played numerous times for dances at the Carter Family Fold near Hiltons. He also played shows with a Kingsport band, Tennessee Skyline, recording one compact disc with them, *It's a Long, Long Way to the Tennessee Line.* It included one of his original fiddle tunes, "Digging Up Gold," which he described as essentially a reworking of Bill Monroe's "The Gold Rush."

In recent years, the semi-retired fiddler who lives in Norton, Virginia, with his wife Nora Sue has often been heard wielding the bow with young East Tennessee traditionalist Kody Norris and his Watauga Mountain Boys. In fact, it was Norris who insisted that Baker deserved more credit for his contributions to the music than he has hitherto received. Baker fiddled on Norris's 2011 compact disc release *Live on the Road.* Baker also participated in a traditional music in the public schools project with younger traditional musician Jack Hinshelwood under sponsorship of the Virginia Foundation for the Arts.

With sixty years of bluegrass fiddling behind him—fifty of it with recording bands—Billy Baker has more than paid his dues. From Norton and Bristol to Baltimore and Washington with side junkets in Nashville and California, and finally back to Norton, he has distinguished himself in his field. He remains one of those from the first decade of bluegrass who is still active.

SELECTED RECORDINGS

Billy Baker and Kenny Haddock: Dobro and Fiddle. Zap ZLP 103, 1967.
Billy Baker: Fiddle Classics, Vol. 1. Old Homestead OHS 90100, 1978.
Billy Baker: Fiddle Classics, Vol. 2. Old Homestead OHS 90103, 1978.

Billy Baker also recorded with the Shady Valley Boys, Franklin County Boys, Del McCoury, Bill Monroe, Carl Story, Al Jones, Kody Norris, the Bluegrass Kinsmen, and perhaps others.

✎ Claude Boone

1916–2007

Bluegrass musicians who spend their careers as sidemen do not typically attract a great deal of attention. Exceptions include those who fit into the super picker category and also those with unusual durability. Claude Boone ranks among the latter having spent a quarter century playing either rhythm guitar or bass with Carl Story and the Rambling Mountaineers. In addition, Boone served an earlier stint with Cliff Carlisle and for many years was a stalwart fixture on Knoxville's *Cas Walker Show*. Boone's writing credits would make many Nashville writers envious. In addition, he did a few notable recordings of his own. Finally, in a profession where tempers and tensions sometimes run high, his easygoing, unexcited mannerisms also marked him as a man of distinction.

Born in Yancey County, North Carolina, about 25 miles north of Asheville on February 18, 1916, Claude William Boone lived his childhood in a region rich in musical tradition. At sixteen, he obtained his own homemade banjo and he later got a guitar. Boone grew up loving virtually all types of country music, but in the early years the songs and stylings of Jimmie Rodgers—a somewhat foreign sound in that Carolina mountain environment—made the major impact. Given such influence, it is not surprising that when Boone moved toward preforming professionally in the mid-1930s, he joined forces with Cliff Carlisle. This Kentucky-born steel guitarist's own successful career always remained closer to the Rodgers sound than it did such other early imitators as Gene Autry and Ernest Tubb who eventually evolved into a quite different style in their music.

Boone first joined the Cliff Carlisle troupe at WWNC radio in Asheville, North Carolina. The band also included "Sonny Boy" Tommy Carlisle, and Joe Cook. Most important to Boone was Leon Scott with whom he teamed to form a duet. Known as Scott and Boone, the Elk Mountain Boys, this

The Rambling Mountaineers, late 1940s. *Counterclockwise from left:* Claude Boone, Ray "Duck" Atkins, Red Rector, and Carl Story.

duo sang in a style rather similar to that of the better-known Wade Mainer and Zeke Morris. Boone also did solos, many of them Rodgers' songs and also yodeled a bit. The group played daily radio shows and nightly personal appearances mostly in school houses throughout the mountain section of western North Carolina.

Boone also participated in Charlotte recording sessions. He helped Carlisle on Bluebird in 1937 (and perhaps also 1936) and Decca in 1938. He generally played rhythm guitar behind Cliff's louder steel and vocal and in a couple of instances shared label credits with him. Joe Cook did a pair of solos and Scott and Boone recorded duets of "Carolina Trail" and "Memories of a Shack on the Hill" (Bb 6885). He also did a pair of duets with Walter Hurdt. The Elk Mountain Boys recorded ten songs of their own in addition to those with Carlisle and His Buckle Busters the following June for Decca. These latter duets have strong vocals although the guitar instrumentation is not as strong as that of the Delmores. The songs included "Don't Dig Mother's Grave before She Is Dead" which despite its title is not a spoof on mother songs, but a rather sound piece of practical advice. "Father Dear Father Come Home," an old temperance song by Henry Clay Work, later appeared in cover form by the Blue Sky Boys on Bluebird. Boone and Scott also did an early rendition of Albert Brumley's "Jesus Hold My Hand," uncommon songs like "Sin is to Blame," "Mary In the Wildwood" and "Prepare Prepare" as well as a cover of the Monroe Brothers' "God Holds the Future" and Wade and Zeke's "Only a Word." Although the records did not sell especially well they did help extend their reputation. Not long after the Decca sessions, the Buckle Busters broke up with Hurdt and Cook remaining in North Carolina. Boone, Scott, and Cliff and Tommy Carlisle went to Charleston, West Virginia, with Cliff's Brother Bill. After a short time, Scott and Boone returned to Asheville where Claude joined Carl Story's Rambling Mountaineers, a relatively new group. His association with Story's band lasted for twenty-five years—with time out for World War II.

At that time Story generally fiddled with the Rambling Mountaineers. Boone and Dud Watson played rhythm guitars. The Selective Service Act and the War eventually made it difficult to maintain a band and the Rambling Mountaineers disintegrated. However, Story worked briefly with Bill Monroe in Nashville so Boone went to WNOX, Knoxville with Smilin' Eddie Hill and Buster Moore for a few months before returning to Asheville where he was drafted into the U. S. Navy.

Both Story and Boone returned to WWNC, Asheville in 1945 and Story reorganized the Rambling Mountaineers with Hoke Jenkins on banjo and Jack and Curly Shelton on guitars in addition to Claude Boone. Within a few months, they moved to WNOX, Knoxville and the ever popular *Mid-Day Merry-Go-Round*. Story's group became one of the more popular bands on the show. Numerous musicians worked in the band at various times: the Sheltons, the Johnsons, Red Rector, Cotton Galyon, Ray Atkins, and Fred Smith were regulars. Boone played his rhythm guitar and bass fiddle as well as performing featured vocal solos and bass voice in the quartets and taking on comedy roles. And he helped Story with bookings and other business matters

For a time in the early 1950s, the Rambling Mountaineers left Knoxville and went briefly to WCYB, Bristol and for a longer period at WAYS,

Charlotte and the *Tar Heel Barn Dance.* Then they returned to WNOX and the *Merry-Go-Round* as well as the Saturday night *Tennessee Barn Dance.* The latter show shared alternate Saturday nights on the CBS radio network for a time with WRVA Richmond's *Old Dominion Barn Dance.* By this time, the Brewster Brothers and Tater Tate had joined the group, finally giving the Rambling Mountaineers a full bluegrass band sound. They had already hovered on the periphery of that brand of music for a dozen years or so. Later in the decade, Story went to Asheville again doing television at WLOS-TV. Only Claude went with him. Bobby Thompson and Lloyd Bell comprised the remaining Rambling Mountaineers at that location.

During those years, Carl Story and the Rambling Mountaineers recorded extensively for both Mercury and Columbia. From the first session on September 14, 1947 to the last on August 3, 1957, Claude participated in every one of the masters cut for Mercury and Columbia. The first song Carl actually recorded, "You're a Prisoner In My Heart," bore Claude's name as composer. Subsequent Story Mercury recordings with writer credits to Claude included "Heaven's My Home," "Heaven's Inside," "The Day Is Coming Soon," and the memorable "Why Don't You Haul Off and Get Religion." This song featured Claude's vocal and owed something of a debt in title at least to Wayne Raney's popular country hit of 1949, "Why Don't You Haul Off and Love Me." Claude's stylistic borrowings came more from the older talking blues tradition. On the Rambling Mountaineers's Columbia recordings which produced some of their more outstanding secular songs, Boone owned "Have You Come to Say Goodbye" on which Red Rector sang lead and "Love Me Like You Used to Do" which featured Boone's own solo vocal. The former number ranks as a minor bluegrass classic and Flatt's rendition on the *Before You Go* album on RCA Victor constituted one of his better performances from the later years.

Another pair of songs owned by Claude also made some impact on country music generally. Bill Carlisle recorded "Wedding Bells"—which Boone allegedly purchased from Arthur Q. Smith—for King early in 1947. Although one could hardly call it one of Carlisle's more memorable recordings, it did bring the song to the attention of Hank Williams who recorded it for MGM on March 20, 1949. As a follow up to "Lovesick Blues," it reached No. 2 on the *Billboard* charts. In a sense, Margaret Whiting and Jimmy Wakely's version did even better. While it reached only seventh place on the country rankings, it did well in the pop field and as the reverse side of their song "Slipping Around" it earned equal royalties to Floyd Tillman's hit composition of 1949. Despite Hank Williams' biographer Roger Williams' attack on the song as excessively cliche-ridden, it has stood the test of time as well as many of Williams' originals and remains a country standard. A bluegrass rendition was done by Carl Story and the Rambling Mountaineers on the Mag Label. The second song, "You Can't Judge a Book by Its Cover," became one of Mac Wiseman's early Dot recordings and has appeared on a Statler Brothers album.

In 1949, with "Wedding Bells" doing well on the charts, Mercury signed Boone to a separate contract. He recorded six numbers featuring essentially the same type of instrumentation used by the Rambling Mountaineers. However, Mercury officials used different musicians to avoid making the sound too much like that of Story. As a result, Jethro Burns played mandolin rather than Red Rector and Homer Haynes on rhythm guitar along with Anita Carter on bass fiddle rounded out the personnel. The songs tended toward the comic novelty numbers that Boone had featured on Story shows like "Burglar Man" and "Ground Hog." He also did Tennessee Ernie Ford's hit "Milk 'Em In the Morning Blues" and the lesser heard "Down Where the Watermelons Grow"—rereleased on the Library of Congress Bicentennial album *Songs of Hilarity and Humor.* Two heart songs featuring Jerry Byrd on electric steel "You'd Better Get Your Kisses While You Can" and "Answer to Wedding Bells" completed the list of Boone's solo recording efforts.

Boone continued with Story's Rambling Mountaineers in the 1960s. His recording career continued without interruption as they, like some other hard country acts, moved from Mercury to Starday. The brief merger of those two firms ended with Starday becoming a separate company again. Although Boone and the Brewsters were not on Story's first Starday efforts, they, and usually Tater Tate, but sometimes Tommy Jackson, cut about one-hundred masters for Don Pierce's Nashville-based label. These included new renditions of many of Story's earlier songs, but numerous new ones as well. Unlike the Mercury and Columbia recordings which struck a balance between secular and sacred material, virtually all of the Rambling Mountaineers Starday efforts fell into the bluegrass gospel category.

Like the Stanley Brothers in this same era, the Rambling Mountaineers also recorded extensively for smaller labels between contracts. As a result an almost discographically bewildering amount of material also came out on such labels as Rimrock, Scripture, Spar, Songs of Faith, Sims, and perhaps rarest of all an EP on the tiny GRS label of Richmond Dale, Ohio. In all, Boone seems to have recorded about 300 songs with Story of which at least two thirds also featured the Brewster Brothers. On stage shows Boone continued to play the comedy role of Homeless Homer. However, as increasing amounts of their work tended to be in churches and gospel sings, this aspect of Claude's career slowly died out. As they traveled more widely Boone used an electric bass.

Times, however, were changing and as mid-week school house shows became more a thing of the past, Boone, Tate, and the Brewsters depended more heavily on television employment furnished by Cas Walker in Knoxville while Story did deejay work to supplement his income. They continued to work as bands primarily on weekends until the mid-1960s when Carl shifted his main base of operations eastward to the Carolinas again. This time, however, Boone and the Brewsters remained in Knoxville with the *Cas Walker Show*. Story and Boone finally parted company after a close association of some 25 years. The album *My Lord Keeps a Record* (Starday 411) was Claude's last. Carl subsequently joined forces with the Jones Brothers and Frank Hamilton.

Working with Cas Walker on early morning television, Boone played electric bass and participated in trio numbers with Red Rector and Danny Bailey. He sometimes played straight man to Fred Smith's comedy. In 1983, the program terminated and as Boone and his wife Grace's five grown children were all on their own, it provided Boone with even more fishing time. An avid angler, he delighted in recounting the fishing experiences he had with Ray Myers, the noted armless musician who worked some with the Rambling Mountaineers back in the 1950s Myers could handle the equipment as well with his toes as others could with their hands

Boone's active musical career spanned some fifty years. Throughout this long experience he retained his quiet easy-going manner with modesty rare in some musicians. He and Grace proved themselves gracious and genial hosts that cold snowy February 1981 day when James (Carson) Roberts and I visited their suburban Knoxville home. Roberts later told me that he considered Boone one of the finest people he had known in his long career. Later that year, Story told me that in the more than forty years he had known Claude, and he never saw him get upset or mad. This approach to life served Boone well in a stressful occupation for the man Mercury Records billed as "Claude Boone from the Smoky Mountains." He lived to ninety, passing away on February 23, 2007.

SELECTED RECORDINGS

Claude Boone's recordings under his own name on Decca (with Leon Scott) and on Mercury have been out of print for decades. However he appeared on selected recordings with Cliff Carlisle, and numerous recordings with Carl Story on Mercury, Columbia, Starday, and perhaps other labels through 1966 (see BCD 16839).

⌁ Buddy Griffin

1948–

One of the most notable figures in bluegrass—in the past four decades—is Buddy Griffin, mostly known as a fiddler, but equally skilled on other instruments as well. In recent years the West Virginia native—mostly known for sideman work—added academics to his resume by developing and teaching in the nation's first full-fledged four-year degree-granting program in bluegrass at his *alma mater*, Glenville State College. After retiring from this career, he returned to a sideman role at the *Grand Ole Opry*.

Buddy Mason Griffin was born in Richwood, West Virginia, on September 22, 1948. Although Buddy is often a nickname, it is real with him having been named at the behest of a hospital nurse who promised the Griffins that if she could name the newborn infant she would buy the baby a new set of clothes. So Buddy he became.

At home in Summersville, Griffin had several siblings who survived and all received ample musical exposure at an early age. His parents, Richard and Erma Griffin, played Carter Family style music and the children fell into line. Griffin developed skills on all the standard acoustical instruments beginning with bass fiddle and he can hardly remember a time when he could not also play guitar. Best known for his fiddle skills today, it comes as something of a surprise to learn that the five-string banjo is actually and ideally his instrument of choice. Griffin said his main musical influences among professionals were Lester Flatt and Earl Scruggs along with the Carter Family and Don Reno and Red Smiley. He added that "Dad's favorites were Carter Stanley and Red Smiley."

The Griffin Family played traditional country and bluegrass music in the general area of Nicholas and Braxton Counties for several years, not only on their front porch but also at local and community events and dances. In addition, they appeared on radio programs in Oak Hill, Sutton, Richwood, and

Buddy Griffin
with Lester Flatt,
ca. 1970.

Buddy Griffin
with fiddle.

Weston. In April 1963, they appeared on WOAY-TV in Oak Hill. When Red Smiley and the Bluegrass Cutups had a program on WOAY-TV, the Griffins did some guest spots on their show as well. From June 1964, they also made semi-regular appearances at the weekday morning WCHS-TV the *Buddy Starcher Show*, undoubtedly the most popular and watched live country music program in Mountain State history. As a result, Ken Davidson of Kanawha Records, who had made new recordings of fiddle legend Clark

Kessinger and Billy Cox and hitherto undiscovered traditional figures such as Phoebe Parsons, Jenes Cottrell, and French Carpenter, approached the Griffins about cutting some material for his label. But Richard Griffin turned him down because he did not feel his family group was ready yet.

Meanwhile, the family continued as before and hit another milestone on June 1, 1965. They did a guest spot on the *Top O' the Morning* show at WDBJ-TV in Roanoke, Virginia, then starring Red Smiley and the Bluegrass Cutups whom they knew from Oak Hill TV. When Buddy, his dad, and his brother Johnny added a non-family member in the person of mandolin picker Jerry Butler or occasionally someone else, they became known as the Sunny Valley Boys.

As a high school freshman, Griffin and friend George Ward had been enlisted to teach some lessons in string music at a nearby elementary school. When the family moved to Sutton as Buddy was entering his last year of high school for what he termed "the best year of education I got," it led him to decide to become a teacher. Accordingly, he went to Glenville State College in adjacent Gilmer County, well known as primarily a teacher training school in north central West Virginia. Glenville was also the home of the West Virginia Folk Festival, an event that had been the brainchild of Dr. Patrick W. Gainer, Folklore and English professor. Initiated as part of a class project in 1950 it continues today. Gainer also wrote the book *Folk Songs from the West Virginia Hills* (Seneca Books, 1975). The good professor was adamant about his advocacy of true folk music as opposed to his distaste for hillbilly music, failing to see any similarity between the two forms. Nonetheless, some intermingling occurred anyway. Buddy kept his feet firmly planted in both camps. During his college days Griffin began to play fiddle more because as he said most of the local banjo players played the "chromatic style which made no sense to me." So he took up the fiddle as "there was nothing else to do" and stayed with it. Griffin finished college in August 1971 with a degree in English and history. He then began teaching English at the junior high level in the Nicholas County schools.

Not long after he began teaching, Buddy started to get more serious about country and bluegrass music. On December 1, 1971, he and his old friend George Ward did their first recording as support musicians for former Stanley Brothers fiddler Joe Meadows who was getting musically involved again after several years of relative inactivity. Griffin played banjo and Ward rhythm guitar on this album. Meadows would go on to work with the Goins Brothers, Larry Sparks, Jim and Jesse, and Senator Robert Byrd of West Virginia. Griffin continued to work with his family and also with a Randolph County country family outfit, the Heckels.

The Heckels included father Pee Wee Heckel, son J-Bird, and daughters Susan and Beverly, the latter who would eventually be married for a time to country singer-songwriter Johnny Russell of "Red Neck, White Socks and Blue Ribbon Beer" fame. As regulars at WWVA's *Jamboree USA*, Griffin worked with them at the venerable program which led to his becoming a member of the staff band. He also recorded on their eight-track tape *The Heckels Sing!* In addition to backing regular performers such as Freddy Carr, Darnell Miller, Gus Thomas, Bob Gallion and Patti Powell, Griffin got to back such noted figures as the legendary Maybelle Carter and trucker favorite Dave Dudley. He also won both West Virginia state fiddle and banjo contests in October 1973. Buddy also did a recording session with popular *Jamboree* performer Slim Lehart, known as the Wheeling Cat, which gave Griffiin his first opportunity to fiddle the "Orange Blossom Special" on disc.

One of the *Jamboree* regulars was country singer Landon Williams who also played regularly at a couple of night clubs he owned in the Cincinnati area. This led to Griffin's going to Cincinnati to work for Williams and his band Hardtime on the club scene in the Queen City. Then in April 1975, Buddy began his career in bluegrass when he joined the Goins Brothers as a regular fiddler. Melvin and Ray Goins were becoming favorites on the festival circuit with a quality band that included younger brother, Conley Goins, on bass fiddle and also veteran mandolin picker Curley Lambert. In addition to festivals, the Goins group worked during slack moments in winter playing school shows in Eastern Kentucky and adjacent locales which gave the young fiddler not only the opportunity to introduce traditional fiddle music to numerous children, but also to participate in the somewhat corny dramatic comedy skits when he and Lambert often portrayed ghosts.

On the more serious side, Griffin did his first of many recording sessions with the Goins Brothers on Memorial Day weekend in May 1975 on the double Rebel, multi-artist album *Live at McClure*. Subsequently, he did three more Rebel albums with Melvin and Ray Goins on this initial stint with the band: *All the Way Home, Take This Hammer,* and *The Wandering Soul.* He also fiddled on a Lambert album *Bluegrass Evergreen* for Old

Homestead. Melvin Goins' wife Willia and her sisters had a quartet—the Woodettes—that often performed at Goins-promoted festivals and Griffin worked on one of their albums titled *Halfway Home*. In addition to playing some excellent fiddle with this band, Buddy also injected a degree of humor into the stage shows by playing a few notes from some classical tune or the Gillette Razor Blade commercial in the midst of a fiddle instrumental. This sojourn lasted until 1978 and represented some of the best work that the Goins Brothers did. Griffin credits Melvin Goins as really getting him into bluegrass professionalism as well as having opportunities to mix and mingle with members of other bands on the festival circuit.

Griffin also demonstrated a willingness to help on an informal basis other young musicians whom he encountered. He taught youthful pickers and fiddlers how to improve style and technique. A good example of this was teenage-fiddler Alan Stack, then with his family group, Frog and the Greenhorns, but who with older brother Jim eventually matured into the nucleus of the Rarely Herd band. Such efforts served Griffin well in later phases of his career.

During these years, Buddy also continued to work and record in Cincinnati with the Katie Laur Band. If the Goins Brothers provided Griffin with immersion in hard-core traditional bluegrass, Katie Laur gave him an opportunity to exhibit innovation within the genre. With such young pickers as Jeff Roberts on banjo, Jeff Terflinger on mandolin, Katie Laur on guitar, and sometimes Dr. Jim Huey on resonator guitar, the band worked at Aunt Maudie's and other clubs in Cincinnati, recording three, and possibly an unreleased fourth, albums on Vetco. The Laur band turned out an exciting brand of innovative music. Some years later Griffin did another project with Katie Laur that included her tribute song "When Earl Taylor Played the Mandolin for Me."

Being in Cincinnati so much in the late 1970s also gave Griffin an opportunity to do some session work for Vetco, often done at Rusty York's Jewel studio. These included one album each with Josh Graves and Earl Taylor. No doubt the most significant were two albums with Mac Wiseman when he mostly did twin-fiddling with Tater Tate, but also played autoharp on a few numbers currently available as *Classic Bluegrass* (Rebel CD-1106). In addition to the Vetco efforts, he and Meadows made a fiddle-guitar album *Two O'Clock in the Morning* released on Old Homestead 90081. Some of the cuts on this album featured a third fiddler, a concert violinist named Curl Snail, who sometimes sat in with Katie Laur's group but did not want to use her real name on the record.

Since Griffin was hardly getting rich as a sideman and session musician, he returned in the fall of 1979 to the classroom, teaching middle school social studies at Gassaway in Braxton County. Still, he did some musical work on a part-time basis including an appearance in the Carter Family documentary film *Keep on the Sunny Side* with the Griffin Family. The Griffins also made an appearance on Garrison Keillor's *Prairie Home Companion* of NPR fame. He left the school room in 1982 with intentions of obtaining a graduate degree, but that did not happen.

Buddy received a call from *Grand Ole Opry* artist Johnny Russell who needed a fiddler. Griffin had known Russell since he had been affiliated with *Jamboree USA* when he had been a staff musician there. This led to frequent work with Russell sporadically for several years including appearances on the *Opry* and also at the Gold Coast Casino in Las Vegas.

During his intermittent country music work with Johnny Russell, Griffin also kept a foot in the bluegrass camp through off-and-on work with the Doug Dillard Band, playing either bass or fiddle. A highlight of those years included a July 1983 appearance at the Winnipeg Folk Festival which was also televised on Canadian Broadcasting. In between times, he served as director at Camp Washington Carver in Fayette County, West Virginia, for the state's Department of Culture and History. He also appeared numerous times on the West Virginia Public Radio program, *Mountain Stage*. In 1988 Griffin released *The Buddy Griffin Band* on his own Braxton label which consisted of his doing all the instrumentation. Two decades later, he re-released it with eight additional cuts.

Given Griffins' talent to unexpectedly appear virtually any time at any place, it did not come as a tremendous surprise to me that on a visit to Branson, Griffin came on stage as a part of Albert Brumley Junior's daytime show. In addition to his fiddle work, Buddy did a bit of comedy with a mirror and toothless comb, grooming his increasingly hair-challenged cranium. He also worked for Christy Lane at her theater. In the evenings, he performed as a staff band member at the *Ozark Mountain Hoedown* some miles to the south at Eureka Springs on the Arkansas side of the Ozark region. At the time, he talked as though he might remain in the area permanently, but despite being nominated for and receiving musical awards for his fiddle and mandolin work at Branson, remaining in that locale was not to be.

Even while Griffin was still based in the Ozarks, he made periodic visits back in the East for special events. These occasions included a couple of appearances at the Kennedy Center in Washington, D.C., with the Katie Laur Band and on the *Prairie Home Companion* NPR programs with both the Griffin Family and Katie Laur. Another NPR experience came on *Rider's Radio Theater* with Ranger Doug of Riders in the Sky fame. Griffin also secured a stint as a performer and musical director of *At Home in the Country* on the Fine Arts Radio Network in Chicago. The actual program was made at the Ozark Folk Center in Mountain View, Arkansas.

What eventually brought the fiddler back to West Virginia was the declining health of his parents and the need to be near them. When Ray Goins became ill, Griffin returned to work with Melvin Goins as a fill-in on banjo and also completed a Goins Brothers' album on the five-string that Ray Goins had started. By the time *We'll Carry On* (Hay Holler HH CD 502) was completed, Griffin had picked banjo on nine of fourteen cuts and fiddle on eight. In April 1997, Griffin and Art Stamper shared fiddle duties on Melvin and Ray Goin's *Run Satan Run* (Hay Holler HH CD 1338). Since then he continued as a fill-in musician with Melvin Goins and Windy Mountain as occasion and circumstance permitted.

The year 1997 found Buddy back in a regular sideman role as he had joined Jim and Jesse and the Virginia Boys in July. A month later he became a part-time string music instructor at his alma mater, Glenville State College. As the school's traditional music program grew, this would eventually evolve into a full-time position, but in the meantime, he enjoyed the pleasures of being a regular member of a legendary bluegrass group and *Grand Ole Opry* act.

During his years with the Virginia Boys, Griffin worked on two recordings. The first in 1999 was essentially a project of Luke McKnight, Jesse's grandson, while the second in 2001 was titled *Our Kind of Country*. He considered the work with Jim and Jesse McReynolds as the highlight of his work as a sideman up to that time. The downside of being with the Virginia Boys was the fact that both of the McReynolds' were experiencing serious health problems. Jim's problems culminated in death on December 31,

2002. Griffin along with other band members served as pall bearers as Jim was laid to rest in the Virginia mountains. Griffin continued to work with Jesse McReynolds in the Virginia Boys band for a time and still does a few shows with him.

Buddy's increasing work at Glenville State had already become his top priority. After his work as an adjunct had been going on for about a year, Chair of the Fine Arts Department, Dr. John McKinney, suggested that Buddy might want to think about the possibility of expanding the program. Griffin recalls that he was so enamored of the idea that he went home and worked all night coming back the next day with a complete proposal. An astonished McKinney later stated, "I had only mentioned it in passing to plant the seed in his mind and was totally surprised when he walked in with the document the very next day!" It took some time to get it developed into a workable proposal. To help bolster the program, the college booked Jim and Jesse to give a concert—whose band just happened to have Griffin as a key member. Jim and Jesse then invited the Glenville State Percussion Ensemble—incidentally directed by John McKinney—to play at the Ryman in Nashville. Both concerts were a success and the foundation continued to be laid.

Academic proposals typically move slowly through a complicated committee process. Three years of editing and rewriting ensued. Finally in 2002, it had evolved into the Glenville State College Bluegrass Music Certificate Program. As growth continued, on August 3, 2007, the West Virginia Higher Education Policy Commission approved a Bachelor of Arts in Music in bluegrass music. "The first in the country," Griffin noted with considerable pride. East Tennessee State University and Morehead State University already had bluegrass music courses and soon followed with degree-granting programs of their own.

In addition to music courses, program requirements included audio and video production. Band organization and marketing also formed key elements in the curriculum. Buddy pointed out that the program only accepted students who had prior musical training and experience. Elizabeth "Lizzy" Long, now of the duo of Little Roy and Lizzy, became the first student to complete the Certificate program. Somewhat later, her sister Rebekah Long became the initial recipient of the four-year degree.

In 2003, with more students added, the first official Glenville State College Bluegrass Band had been formed. It consisted of Lizzy Long on banjo and fiddle, Eileen Marsh on guitar, Rachel Singleton on mandolin, and Aaron Miller on bass. Mack Samples, a former director of admissions at GSC as well as co-leader of an old-time band, the Samples Brothers, sometimes played with them as well. Griffin said all of the members "were good singers and had great chemistry on stage." Among the highlights of their first year was performing as a backup band for Mac Wiseman when he played a concert at the college.

The three women with the addition of Rebekah Long on bass became the first professional band to come out of the program. Taking the name Mountain Fury, the group played concerts, festivals in several states, and recorded a pair of compact discs. With Lizzy Long teaming up with Little Roy Lewis and Rebekah Long taking a bigger interest in the technical phases of the music as chief engineer for Tom T. Hall's studio, that band is more or less inactive today, but it provided Glenville's operation with a good beginning. Later GSC bands have played in such venues as *Jamboree USA* at WWVA in Wheeling, the year before the show's demise in 2005; the Mountain State Arts and Crafts Fair at Cedar Lakes near Ripley; Mayberry Days at Mount Airy, North Carolina; several county fairs; the annual Jesse McReynolds Benefit in Gallatin and concerts at GSC. In 2010, the band, re-creating the earlier years of a nearly vanished bluegrass tradition in Appalachia, appeared at some of the few remaining drive-in theaters.

While the program has produced several quality musicians, two others perhaps merit special mention. The first, Luke Shamblin, mostly known for mandolin work, turned out two solo CDs on Blue Circle Records with support from Buddy Spicher, Don Rigsby, and mentor Griffin. According to Griffin, Shamblin, who is also adept on fiddle and guitar, is perhaps the first person to really master the Jesse McReynolds cross-picking style. The second, Megan Murphy, an Ohio native and musician, is the person who became Griffin's successor as director of the GSC program.

Buddy Griffin has had some additional musical achievements on his re-sume. For instance, in 2004 he did the banjo tracks on a Disney animated film *The Fox and the Hound 2*. He says most of the musical tracks were done in Nashville where voices included Reba McEntire and Trisha Yearwood, but his efforts were done in a studio at Denison University in Granville, Ohio. He also continued session work ranging from a bluegrass album with former *Jamboree* star Patti Powell to recording with Mountain State comedian George Daugherty a.k.a. the Earl of Elkview.

After his mother passed in 2005, Griffin released a two-CD set of the family's recordings. His older brother Johnny died in 2008 followed by his father in March 2011. Two months later, his contributions to traditional music in West Virginia led to his being named the recipient of the Vandalia Award, the highest recognition made to a traditional musician by the Mountain State.

As a musician, Griffin has also formed a partnership with Ashley Messenger, a retired commercial airline pilot whom he has known for about thirty years. Griffin describes Messenger as a fine tenor singer and guitarist who once worked with the Butler Brothers. Together they have done three tribute discs to two of their heroes, Don Reno and Red Smiley. These were initially released under the pseudonym "Retro and Smiling and the Tennis Shoe Cut-Ups." Despite the humorous sounding name these are quite serious collections of Reno and Smiley songs. The first in 2008 bore the title *Wanted* (named after the old King LP 718) and featured Griffin and Messenger overdubbing all the instrumentation. The second one *Please Remember . . .* has Buddy on vocals and banjo, with some lead guitar in the Reno style; fiddle by Corrina Logston, naturally a Mac Magaha emulator; Luke Shamblin on mandolin; and Jon Weisburger on bass. A third gospel CD *Get Ready* released in 2013 had a cover photo taken in the same church in Terrace Park, Ohio, that adorned a 1963 Reno and Smiley album. Their "Retro and Smiling" efforts have received considerable airplay on XM satellite radio among other places. It is intended that the three discs be repackaged for a boxed set.

After retiring from Glenville State "completely" as he puts it, Griffin moved to Gallatin, Tennessee, in the spring of 2015 where he continues to work full-time as he had since 2013 at the *Opry* and on personals with Bobby Osborne and the Rocky Top Express and sometimes with Jesse McReynolds. For a time Ashley Messenger moved to Michigan's Upper Peninsula and he and Buddy did not play much together. However, Messenger returned to Ohio in the fall of 2015 and the two are working on a compact disc of original songs. Still a very active musician, one thing always holds true for Buddy Griffin: he is always full of surprises!

Reflecting over a four decades-plus musical career, Griffin can look back over some achievements that might seem remarkable. From working with his family group in the hills of home to working at *Jamboree, USA* and the *Grand Ole Opry*, from concerts ranging from the Kennedy Center to Las

Vegas and Disney soundtracks, one can safely say that this guy has been around. Buddy says in typical modest fashion that while he has never been a drinker, if he had been he might well be a legend, but he probably also would be dead. From being the bluegrass professor at Glenville State College to being on stage with Bobby Osborne or Jesse McReynolds when circumstances permit, he has become both an educator and a sideman *par excellence.*

SELECTED RECORDINGS

The Buddy Griffin Band. Braxton CD 001, 2008. Originally released as a cassette in 1988 that featured Griffin overdubbed on all the instruments. The compact disc includes eight additional numbers with other musicians.

Buddy Griffin Plays Hank Williams. [Braxton 002], 2012. Hank Williams compositions as fiddle tunes.

Buddy Griffin and Ashley Messenger (as Retro and Smiling). 2009–2013. A three-disc tribute to Don Reno and Red Smiley with Buddy on vocals and banjo.

Buddy Griffin also appears on selected recordings with Slim Lehart, Patti Powell, the Goins Brothers, Melvin Goins, Curley Lambert, Joe Meadows, Jim and Jesse, the Samples Brothers, The Heckels, The Woodettes, the Griffin Family, Jennifer Lilly, and perhaps others.

⤶ George "Speedy" Krise

1922–2011

When bluegrass music was in the developmental stage some seventy years ago, only five instruments were associated with the music. Those were the ones that appeared in the famous Bill Monroe band of that period—guitar, banjo, mandolin, fiddle, and bass. Somewhere along the line a sixth instrument, the resonator guitar—often called by the name of its most popular brand, Dobro—came to be accepted in bluegrass bands. From 1955, the Foggy Mountain Boys with Josh Graves on the old hound dog revived the instrument's popularity. However, this certainly was not the first use of the Dobro in bluegrass. During the forties, the Dobro was used in such non-bluegrass groups as those of Roy Acuff, the Bailes Brothers, Molly O'Day, and Esco Hankins. On the Hankins records the dobro was played by Graves. Two early users of the Dobro in bluegrass were Ray Atkins of the Carl Story band and George "Speedy" Krise who played mostly with non-bluegrass bands in the Knoxville and West Virginia areas. However, in 1950 and 1951, he made a number of recordings with Carl Butler which are excellent examples of vintage bluegrass. With the possible exception of Carl Story's radio shows, these recordings constitute the earliest known examples of the Dobro in bluegrass. Krise, who spent most of his active musical career as a sideman, also composed a number of fine songs that were recorded by such notables as Roy Acuff and Mac Wiseman.

George Edward Krise was born on May 7, 1922, near Hinton, West Virginia. Bradley Kincaid and J.E. Mainer were among his early favorites and somewhat later he developed a tremendous appreciation for Bashful Brother Oswald of the Roy Acuff band for obvious reasons. At age twelve, he learned to play guitar, but he subsequently became attracted to the Hawaiian guitar through the influence of his future brother-in-law. During this time he and his sister, Rene, won first prize at an amateur contest at

George "Speedy" Krise, 1946.

Hinton High where Krise played "Hilo March" on the Hawaiian guitar while Rene accompanied him. Although he was capable of rapid movements and was a fairly fast runner in high school, young Krise acquired the nickname Speedy because of his slow mannerisms and a hesitation in his speech patterns. After graduation from high school in 1940, he went to Beckley, West Virginia, which was somewhat of an area center of country music, being the location of radio station WJLS which featured quite a bit of live string band music. For the first year or so at WJLS, he used an all metal Hawaiian guitar, not having obtained a Dobro as yet. His father had previously bought him an electric model, but he never used it on radio or records. At a time when many were switching to the more modern instruments, Krise preferred the older acoustical sound. After a time, he found and bought a broken Dobro for five dollars. Following some extensive repair work it was ready to be played.

There were several country musicians of note who played on WJLS. Skeets and Dixie Lee (Molly O'Day) Williamson, along with both Johnnie and Walter Bailes had been there, but seem to have moved on by the time of Krise's arrival. However, Mel Steele and Blue-Eyed Jeannie were around and so, too, were Little Jimmy Dickens and the Lilly Brothers. In 1941, Lynn Davis and his Forty-Niners with Dixie Lee as featured vocalist, who was now married to Lynn Davis, did a show for Dr. Pepper. Krise first worked with the Davises during that summer. When they left he also worked with the Lilly Brothers, Dickens, Walter Bailes, and the other WJLS artists.

Krise then formed a band known as the Blue Ribbon Boys which included Ed "Rattlesnake" Hogan on bass fiddle and the Barber Brothers, Roy and Carl, on mandolin and guitar. Sometimes the Lilly Brothers and Dickens also worked with them. After a couple of years Krise was drafted into the service and remained in military life until 1946. While in the service he was married to Frieda Pettry whom he had met at Beckley. During Krise's long lifetime they had four children, ten grandchildren, and seventeen great-grandchildren, and a great-great grandchild. Shortly after his release from the service, he was summoned to WNOX by Lynn Davis and went to work for the Cumberland Mountain Folks.

At the time Skeets Williamson recalled that Krise was proficient on both Dobro and electric steel, but Davis indicated he preferred the former and so Krise almost always played the Dobro. The Cumberland Mountain Folks were one of the most popular acts at WNOX and Krise was kept busy with radio work and personal appearances for two years. At the time Krise, his wife, and children lived in an apartment which had once been part of a funeral home and knowing that tended to make him a little nervous. Like other groups, the Cumberland Mountain Folks enjoyed a little fun now and then at the expense of others in the band. Krise recalled one night when he was being dropped off in front of the house, Davis managed to delay him at the car long enough for Mac Wiseman to hide in the bushes and suddenly leap out with a scream giving him a good scare. Such was life with the Cumberland Mountain Folks.

Krise did two record sessions with O'Day and Davis, the first at Chicago in December 1946, where eight sides were cut including the classic "Tramp on the Street." A year later he went to Nashville and did ten more numbers with them including "Matthew 24" and "At the First Fall of Snow." The Davis' had left WNOX and were in semi-retirement in Wheelwright, Kentucky. Krise was then working for another artist, but they got him to do the session with them and again made excellent use of his talents.

When Molly O'Day left WNOX in August 1947, Krise remained in Knoxville working with various groups as a sideman and also had his own group for a while. One person that he worked with most was Archie Campbell. Best remembered today as a comedian on *Hee Haw* and the *Grand Ole Opry*, Campbell spent many of his earlier years in Knoxville, both at WNOX on the *Mid-Day Merry-Go-Round* and at WROL on the *Country Playhouse* and the *Dinner Bell Show* which he headed for a time. He was probably best known for his comic role of Grandpappy and his group consisting of Krise and Red Kirk was called the Oldtimers. Campbell also recorded on Mercury where Krise did at least one session with him including one song of which Krise co-authored, entitled "No One Ran to Meet Me." Like the Cumberland Mountain Folks, Campbell's band had a lot of fun. Krise remembered coming home from a show one night when he and Red Kirk got into a heated argument about which one could run the fastest. Campbell decided they could best settle the dispute with a foot race on the highway then and there. Krise won the race in spite of the widespread reputation for slowness.

When the Oldtimers moved to WROL, Krise went along while still associated with Campbell and formed his own group known as Speedy Krise and the New River Gang which included Southpaw Thacker, a left-handed guitar player. This band soon dissolved and Krise and Fred Smith formed a duet called the Arkansas Travelers. He and Smith did both comedy and sang duets on Knoxville's NBC outlet. Smith, of course, became well known in later years for similar comedy and duet work with Red Rector on the *Cas Walker Farm and Home* television show.

After a while Krise and Smith came back to WNOX to work with Jack Shelton and his Greene County Boys. Shelton had considerable prior experience with such groups as Wade Mainer and the Sons of the Mountaineers and Carl Story's Rambling Mountaineers.

Benny Sims, who was one of Flatt and Scruggs' early fiddlers and recorded with them on Mercury including the lead vocal work on their classic "Salty Dog Blues," also worked with the group. Only the lack of a banjo kept his band from being one of the area's premier bluegrass bands. Krise and Smith continued to work as a singing and comedy team while with the Greene County Boys. Krise also played Dobro on a couple of Mercury record sessions split between the team of Bonnie Lou and Buster Moore and WLAC artist Mac Odell. His work was especially notable on Bonnie Moore's vocal of "Teardrops Falling in the Snow" and Odell's "Red Ball Rocket Train."

It was during these years after Krise left the Molly O'Day group that Krise began to take an interest in songwriting and over a three or four year period wrote a number of songs which were recorded on major labels, primarily by artists of Knoxville background. These included Carl Smith and Mac Wiseman. Speedy Krise also recorded on Capitol with Carl Butler.

These were the two sessions which seemingly introduced the Dobro to bluegrass. Six of the twelve sides recorded were songs which Krise had written. The others who helped on the first session were Tater Tate, fiddle; Hoke Jenkins, banjo; and Jake Tullock, bass. Perhaps the best known of the four sides cut on November 1, 1950, was "White Rose"/"Heartbreak Express," the latter which was written by Krise. "A Plastic Heart" was another song of Krise's recorded at that session. A little later Roy Acuff recorded the song on Columbia and it became something of a country hit. In 1974, Acuff recorded the song again and it was released on his *Back to the Country* album.

On January 23, 1951, Carl Butler did his second session on Capitol with Speedy Krise and Jake Tullock again present. Johnny Whisnant and Art Wooten played banjo and fiddle, respectively, with Smokey White assisting on guitar. Four of the eight songs done had been penned by George Krise, "String Of Empties," "You Plus Me," "No Trespassing," and "Our Last Rendezvous." Luckily, these recordings, after being out of print for decades, were re-released on Carl Butler's *A Blue Million Tears* Bear Family disc.

Mac Wiseman was another bluegrass artist who recorded songs written by Krise. "Georgia Waltz," "You're Sweeter than Honey," and "Goin' Like Wildfire" were all good songs, the latter being also covered in the popular music field by Frankie Laine and Jo Stafford, who were near the top of their class in the days before the advent of rock and roll. Acuff-Rose published most of Krise's compositions and he came to have very high regard for Fred Rose and the aid he gave to young writers. Some of Krise's other numbers were recorded by Carl Smith, Don Gibson, Ray Smith, and Randy Hughes.

As Knoxville began to slip somewhat as a country music center in the 1950s due in part to Nashville's draining off many of their newer stars while some of the older ones either retired or drifted into obscurity with changing styles, the Green County Boys broke up. About 1954, Krise moved back to

West Virginia. For about two years he worked at WOAY in Oak Hill with Billie Jean and Red Lydick and the Dixie Drifters on both radio and television. On the show Krise played Dobro and also did some solo vocals. He remained with the Dixie Drifters until they left the station. Then he followed the path of many of his fellow Mountain Staters and moved to the industrial city of Akron, Ohio. There he left the music business and lived in Akron from the late 1950s and played but little in those years. He still owned the Dobro that he played on record sessions, radio, and personal appearances. Retired on disability from 1973, he nonetheless maintained considerable interest in the older styles of country music and had many pleasant memories of the days he spent with the Lilly Brothers, Tater Tate, Carl Butler, Molly O'Day, and other greats and near greats of the world of bluegrass and traditional country music.

From the mid-1970s, Krise began to play again with friends and neighbors in the Akron area, especially two brothers named George and Glenn Lehman. He attended some bluegrass festivals where he often did guest spots on a Dobro instrumental. He renewed acquaintance with Lynn Davis and Molly O'Day and while they had a few home jam sessions, they never fulfilled Krise's hope that they could record together again. With musical support from the Lehmans, he recorded a series of cassettes which demonstrated that he still had the touch on the instrument. He also demonstrated himself to be a competent vocalist.

In his last years Speedy and Frieda Krise moved to Suffolk, Virginia, where one of their daughters resided and he won increasing respect as a bluegrass and Dobro pioneer. When he died on June 9, 2011, his obituary in the Portsmouth *Virginian Pilot* termed him "a country music icon." Two days after his Virginia funeral, George Edward Krise was laid to rest in Hinton, West Virginia, not many miles from where many of his fellow mountaineer musicians had initiated history-making musical careers at WJLS in Beckley.

SELECTED RECORDINGS

In later years Speedy Krise recorded a number of cassette tapes under his own name, but his best work can be found on his recordings with others especially Molly O'Day (see BCD 15565) and Carl Butler (see BCD 16118). He also recorded on Mercury sessions with Bonnie Lou and Buster, Archie Campbell, and Mac Odell.

✂ Curley Lambert

1930–1982

Curley Lambert had one of the longer careers as a sideman in the formative decades of bluegrass music. Known mostly as a mandolin picker, he worked the road and/or recorded extensively with such figures as Bill Clifton, Charlie Moore, Chief Powhatan (Floyd Atkins), Lester Flatt and Earl Scruggs, Bill and Mary Reid, the Masters Family, the Goins Brothers, but most especially the Stanley Brothers with whom he did three tours of duty and a fourth brief one with Ralph Stanley. When working with the Goins group, Melvin almost invariably introduced the mandolin player as one of the evergreens of the music. The term, of course, referred to the long experience of his balding band member. A review of the career of Lambert indicates that he was indeed one of the more durable and influential, but nonetheless uncredited, sidemen in over three decades of bluegrass history.

Born Richard Edward Lambert at Brodnax, Virginia, on June 13, 1930, Curley Lambert came from a family which included a lot of singers but few pickers. His father played banjo a little bit and several of his mother's relatives sang with considerable skill. In addition to these local influences, a number of radio artists significantly impressed Lambert including Bill Monroe of WSM's *Grand Old Opry* and Luke Beaucom of the Tobacco Tags at WPTF in Raleigh, North Carolina. Needless to say, he favored the mandolin although he also learned to play guitar and bass fiddle.

By the mid-1940s, Lambert had gained considerable local experience as a musician playing with area amateurs. At sixteen, he was working on the farm one day plowing with a mule when a friend, Dwight Moody who became a fiddler of some renown in his own right, excitedly ran up telling that he had gotten them a job as musicians in a theater tour featuring Al "Fuzzy" St. John, the noted comical sidekick of western films. As Lambert recalled, he left the mule and plow in the field and took off to pursue his

The Goins Brothers Band, 1977. *From left:* Melvin Goins, Curley Lambert, Conley Goins, Buddy Griffin, Ray Goins.

show business career. Later he returned home, but in 1949, he began a long vocation with a few interruptions as a sideman which continued throughout his music career. Going to Durham, North Carolina, Lambert played a four-string electric mandolin in a country band headed by Tommy Little, a brother-in-law of Dwight Moody. Within a year, however, he returned to the more conventional eight-string acoustical instrument when he joined Bill and Mary Reid's Melody Mountaineers.

By the end of 1950, military service intervened and Curley entered the U. S. Army. Actually, the young Virginian continued to pick and sing during much of his time in uniform, organizing a group known as Curley Lambert and the Blue Ridge Mountain Boys. This band featured mandolin, fiddle, and guitar instrumentation and relied on a heavy fare of Johnny and Jack numbers.

After completing his army stint, Lambert returned to his job with Bill and Mary Reid. The Melody Mountaineers straddled the fence between bluegrass and country. Their band included Lester Woody, a fine fiddler who had worked with the Stanley Brothers and Burk Barbour, former fiddler with Molly O'Day and others; and Jim Eanes, who worked with the Reids at one time. Pioneering in live television in the Piedmont region, the Reids starred in a thrice-weekly show at Lynchburg, Virginia. One of those influenced by this now nearly forgotten group was Eddie Adcock. Lambert cut three record sessions with Bill and Mary Reid—two on Columbia and one on Starday. The styling of the recordings ranged from the honky-tonk country sound of the early 1950s to straight bluegrass. Lambert's instrumentation may be heard prominently on two numbers, "In My Heart I Love You Yet" and "Get Down on Your Knees and Pray," both of which demonstrate that his skills had already reached a high degree of competence.

While working with the Reids, Lambert also played occasionally with Bill Clifton and between 1953 and 1958, he recorded five sessions with Clifton's Dixie Mountain Boys on Blue Ridge, Mercury, and Starday. Lambert played mandolin on about twenty-five issued Clifton recordings and helped out with tenor or baritone vocals on a few. Among the well-known songs that Lambert helped Clifton put on wax are "Living the Right Life Now," "Flower Blooming in the Wildwood," and the first cut of "Little White Washed Chimney."

In October 1955, Lambert went to work as a sideman for the Stanley Brothers at WCYB in Bristol, replacing Jimmy Williams. He remained with the group off-and-on for a good part of the next decade. When first joining the Clinch Mountain Boys, Lambert received a $50 weekly salary and played daily radio shows and anywhere from five to seven personal appearances in the Bristol listening area to earn his money. At that time, the band included Ralph Mayo on fiddle in addition to Carter, Ralph, and Curley. In subsequent years, others who were part of the Clinch Mountain Boys simultaneously with Lambert included Chubby Anthony, Art Stamper, Bill Napier, and George Shuffler.

During his years with the Stanleys, Lambert participated in several recording sessions on the Mercury, Starday, and King labels. Well-known numbers from the Mercury days beginning in December 1955 which featured his work were "Big Tilda," "Cry from the Cross" and "Let Me Walk Lord By Your Side." On one session, Lambert played bass and Bill Napier played mandolin. Of the many numbers cut on Starday, one song in particular stands out, "Rank Stranger." Lambert believed—and no doubt rightly so—that the mandolin work on that mournful hymn represents his best work. The greater number of songs Lambert cut with the Stanleys appeared on Syd Nathan's King label, a number of which featured him on lead guitar rather than his more familiar mandolin.

Lambert's first two stints with the Stanleys occurred when they were headquartered at Bristol. After the first sojourn which lasted about a year, Lambert went back to the Richmond area and played locally for several months before returning to the Clinch Mountain Boys. His second stay with the band ended at the close of 1958 when Josh Graves called to tell him that Lester Flatt and Earl Scruggs needed a mandolin player and tenor singer to replace Curly Seckler. That led to Lambert's joining the Foggy Mountain Boys. During his stay with the nation's most popular bluegrass band at the time, Lambert participated in one recording session, that of January 23, 1959, when he helped make "Crying My Heart Out Over You" and "Ground Speed." Since Lambert had sung baritone for so long with the Stanleys, he failed to readjust to tenor singing again and terminated his work with Flatt and Scruggs on friendly terms.

After the short tenure with Flatt and Scruggs, Lambert decided to leave the music business and returned to Lynchburg where he worked in a mental hospital until 1960 when he rejoined the Stanley Brothers who had by that time switched their base of operations to Live Oak, Florida. The Clinch Mountain Boys worked a series of television shows for Jim Walter Homes in Jacksonville, Tampa, Tallahassee, Orlando, and Fort Myers and continued to record with King and do some personal appearances. The several albums which Lambert helped the Stanleys cut on King included the *Folk Concert* album recorded in the spring of 1963. Beginning with the University of Chicago Folk Festival in 1961, a portion of which subsequently appeared on the Folkways album, *Friends of Old Time Music*—on which Carter jokingly made Curley redo his mandolin break on "Rabbit in the Log"—this group of Clinch Mountain Boys appeared at quite a number of college folk concerts.

Leaving the Stanley Brothers later in 1963, Lambert joined Charlie Moore, Bill Napier and the Dixie Partners on their daily television show at WJHG-TV Panama City, Florida. Ralph Mayo constituted the fourth member of the band at that time. As the station's signal covered an area of limited population—largely swamp land and the Gulf of Mexico—the band did not play a great number of show dates although they did receive a salary from the show at the station. Commercials were performed as an integral part of the program. Since a food company sponsored the Dixie Partners, a refrigerator full of their products adorned the studio. Lambert recalled that one night the band got hungry and raided the ice box, eating the stage props. He stayed with the group about three months.

After leaving the Dixie Partners, Lambert joined the Masters Family and worked with them for about eight months. This gospel group had been quite influential several years before, introducing to records such important songs as "When the Wagon Was New" and "Cry from the Cross." Members of the Lewis Family rank the Masters Family as among their chief inspirations. Although not a bluegrass band, the Masters' featured an old-time singing style and often included a mandolin in their instrumentation. James Carson of the great James and Martha duet team, spent some time with the group, but by the end of the 1950s the original Masters Family had disbanded. The group which Lambert joined consisted of only John and Lucille Masters in addition to himself and represented an attempt to revive the band. John always referred to Lambert as "Brother Richard Lambert." They played churches plus a lot of show dates with Jim and Jesse. Generally, however, their comeback was not a success and eventually Lambert returned to play a fourth and brief stint with the Stanley Brothers. His last session with the Stanleys was the gospel album in 1965 for Alex Campbell's Cabin Creek Records. In all, including both studio recordings and material released from live shows, Lambert appeared on more than 250 Stanley Brothers numbers.

Lambert stayed out of the music business for several years except for playing a few months with Ralph Stanley in the spring of 1967 and helping on a few of Ralph's early recordings on King and Jalyn. During this time, he worked again as an attendant at a mental hospital in Richmond and even sold his musical instruments. Finally in 1971, he began to get active again locally, working with Chief Powhatan (a.k.a. Floyd Atkins) and his Bluegrass Braves, a combo which included Craig Wingfield on Dobro. The following year, he played some show dates with Charlie Moore and early in 1973 became a regular member of the Dixie Partners again after nearly a ten-year absence from the Moore band.

Lambert played about two years with the Dixie Partners during which time they appeared at quite a number of festivals. They also appeared several times on the *WWVA Jamboree*. Charlie Moore, a fine bluegrass vocalist with a good feel for traditional and older country material, had a style which blended with Lambert's mandolin work. Together with Ben Green, Butch Robbins, Johnny Dacus, Terry Baucom, Henry Dockery, and others, Charlie Moore's Dixie Partners played some high quality bluegrass. This group recorded extensively on the Old Homestead label and some of their best music is preserved on the album *A Tribute to Clyde Moody* and On *a High Mountain*. They also backed Bob Smallwood, a Michigan deejay at that time, on an album.

Lambert left Charlie Moore at the close of the 1974 festival season and except for playing a few dates with Bob Goff and the Bluegrass Buddies did little until joining the Goins Brothers in March 1975. Lambert and Melvin Goins had been close friends since the two had been part of the Ralph Stanley band back in 1967. Together with Ray Goins on banjo and Buddy Griffin, a former WWVA *Jamboree* staff musician on fiddle, Lambert's mandolin helped to give the Goins Brothers band an excellent instrumental quality. The atmosphere with the Goins' was also relatively comfortable and relaxed as bluegrass bands go and Lambert enjoyed working with them more than with any other combination in which he had played. Buddy Griffin's good natured humor and the increased tightness of a well-rounded five-piece band gave the Goins Brothers band one of the most delightful stage shows on the road and Lambert obviously felt quite at home with the group. He played mandolin on the last three of the Goins Brothers' Rebel albums.

With the close of the 1975 festival season, Melvin and Ray Goins played a heavy schedule of school shows in Eastern Kentucky and surrounding areas. The elementary school shows included comedy skits as well as music and Lambert and Conley Goins participated in costumed roles. The band hoped to cut an instrumental album to feature Ray, Curley and Buddy, the latter being adept on banjo and autoharp in addition to being an excellent fiddler. However, once the recording became reality the focus changed to its being a Curley Lambert album *Bluegrass Evergreen* released on Old Homestead which featured a number of mandolin tunes with plenty of fiddle and banjo support. Lambert even sang lead on numbers: "Why Don't You Tell Me So" and the Merle Haggard song, "Swinging Doors."

By 1978, Lambert returned to Charlie Moore's Dixie Partners who played more shows closer to his Richmond home base and recorded two albums with him, one on Leather and his last Old Homestead album *Cotton Farmer* which came out after Moore's death. Moore's health was in decline at the time as his longtime problems with alcohol were catching up with him. Curley played with Moore on his last show in late November 1979 at the Mountaineer Opry House in Milton, West Virginia, after which the Dixie Partners headed for another show date in Baltimore. Moore was unable to play and entered a hospital and as they say came out feet first. Lambert's own health was not good and he pretty much retired from music. The old "Bluegrass Evergreen" passed away on October 22, 1982, looking much older than his fifty-two years.

As an important sideman, Curley Lambert labored as a significant figure in bluegrass for more than thirty years. From his early work with the Reids and Bill Clifton to several noteworthy years with the Stanley Brothers and later efforts with Charlie Moore, and the Goins Brothers, his mandolin and vocal work have been important although generally unheralded. Together with several other bluegrass evergreens, Lambert more than paid his dues.

SELECTED RECORDINGS

Curley Lambert: Bluegrass Evergreen. Old Homestead LP OHS 90072, 1978. Mostly instrumental album with support by the Goins Brothers and band.

Curley Lambert also recorded with Bill and Mary Reid, the Stanley Brothers, Bill Clifton, Lester Flatt and Earl Scruggs, the Goins Brothers, Chief Powhatan [Floyd Atkins], Charlie Moore, and perhaps others.

✐ Joe Meadows

1934–2003

Joe Meadows ranks among the more prominent fiddlers who have made contributions to bluegrass music, particularly during the 1950s and the 1970s. In the 1960s he took a long vacation from music, but during his two active periods he established himself as an influential and significant sideman with the Stanley Brothers, the Goins Brothers, Buddy Starcher, and Larry Sparks. As a member of Jim and Jesse's Virginia Boys, Meadows took his fiddle playing to the *Grand Ole Opry*. In 1983, he settled in the Washington, D. C., area where he worked—and likely fiddled—in the office of Senator Robert Byrd as well as on the local scene before his death at age sixty-eight.

Born Ralph Meadows at Basin, West Virginia, on December 31, 1934, Meadows grew up listening to old-time string music. He spent most of his boyhood in nearby Camp Creek. Both communities were located in Mercer County. His mother picked the guitar with considerable skill and taught all of her nine sons to play that instrument. His father and both grandfathers fiddled, but he never took a formal lesson from any of them. He did not actually take much interest in the fiddle until he was fourteen when he first learned on his own.

Once Meadows began to study fiddle, he received much of his teaching from the radio. At nearby WHIS Bluefield such groups as the Lonesome Pine Fiddlers with Curly Ray Cline, Rex and Eleanor Parker, and Fairly Holden with Wayne Tilford on fiddle all made an impression on Meadows. Somewhat farther away at WCYB Bristol, the Stanley Brothers band usually featured a fiddle. Most significant of all, the sounds of Howdy Forrester, Benny Martin, and Chubby Wise, all noted on the Nashville scene, influenced Meadows and his stylings.

The Goins Brothers Band, 1973. From left: Joe Meadows, Melvin Goins, Ray Goins, Harley Gabbard, George Portz.

Meadows did his first professional work with a group at WGEH Princeton, West Virginia, called the Whispering Strings. This band played a type of music akin to western swing and did a lot of square dances during the six months Meadows worked with them. He then moved to WHIS in Bluefield, West Virginia, and fiddled with Rex and Eleanor Parker for a few months. In August 1953, Meadows teamed up with the youthful Melvin and Ray Goins. The boys had a daily radio show at WHIS and resided in the Drake Hotel. Financial success eluded the youths and they often had to cook their meager food in their hotel room on an electric hot plate contrary to house rules. Melvin Goins humorously recalled one embarrassing incident when he tried to convince the maid that the smoke she smelled was coming from the street at a time the fumes were pouring from a dresser drawer where they were futilely concealing the hot plate!

Meadows played with the Goins Brothers until November 1953 when the band fragmented. Melvin and Ray Goins then joined the Lonesome Pine

Fiddlers. Meadows, on a strong recommendation from Curly Ray Cline, went to Bristol and became one of the Stanley Brothers' Clinch Mountain Boys. At the time Meadows joined Ralph and Carter's group, the Stanley's had achieved wide acceptance from their daily appearances on WCYB's *Farm and Fun Time.* They had also begun to record for Mercury Records. In the couple of years that Meadows played with the band he participated in some of the Stanleys' more memorable Mercury sessions doing twenty songs with them beginning in May 1954. His fiddling is, of course, most prominent on such instrumental showpieces as "Hard Times" and "Orange Blossom Special." It can also be heard on such classic songs as "Nobody's Love Is like Mine," "Harbor of Love," and "Baby Girl" as well as several sacred numbers. Meadows also played lead guitar on a few Stanley recordings.

Meadows also fiddled on the Stanleys' very untraditional Mercury arrangement of "Blue Moon of Kentucky." As Meadows recalled the event, Bill Monroe himself visited the Stanleys when they were in Nashville to record. He played a tape of the newly recorded Elvis Presley arrangement and encouraged the Stanley Brothers to work out a rendition based on the new styling. This is exactly what they did with their then musicians Charlie Cline on lead guitar, Bill Lowe on mandolin, and Meadows on fiddle.

It was also during his Stanley years that Meadows took the name Joe. The Stanleys thought it somewhat confusing to have two persons named Ralph in the group. His mother had previously used Joe as an unofficial middle name anyway although only the name Ralph appeared on his birth certificate. When Meadows left the Stanley Brothers, he returned to West Virginia where he and banjo picker Billy Pack worked briefly with the Lilly Brothers. Everett and Bea Lilly returned home from Boston for a short time and worked out of WOAY in Oak Hill, West Virginia. Then Joe received a call from Jim McReynolds in Wheeling. As a result, he moved to WWVA and joined the Virginia Boys.

At the time Jim and Jesse McReynolds worked at the Wheeling *Jamboree,* Hylo Brown also worked with the group as a sort of double act. In addition to McReynolds, the band also included Don McHan on banjo and Dave Sutherland on bass. George France played banjo part the time and Chick Stripling did some comedy. After two or three months at Wheeling, the group moved to Live Oak, Florida, and worked on the *Suwanee River Jamboree.*

Following this first stint with the Virginia Boys, Meadows went to WSM's *Grand Ole Opry* and Bill Monroe's Blue Grass Boys. This year, 1957, was not a prosperous time for Monroe but, as always, Meadows enjoyed the music. Joe Stuart played banjo at the time and Bessie Lee Mauldin bass. The band went through three lead singers, Carl Vanover, Enos Johnson, and another fellow whose name Meadows had forgotten.

After six months with Monroe, Meadows came back to West Virginia briefly prior to joining forces with Bill and Mary Reid in Lynchburg, Virginia. This now nearly forgotten duo played a variety of country and bluegrass music and had earlier recorded for Columbia. During Joe's stay with the Melody Mountaineers, Swanson Walker played banjo and Curly Garne played electric guitar in addition to the Reids on guitar and bass, respectively. Somewhat later Curley Lambert rejoined on mandolin and the band did a session on Starday. For Meadows, these recordings represented something of a high point in his early career because Benny Martin twin-fiddled with him on the session.

Meadows next worked as a sideman at WSVA Harrisonburg, Virginia, doing both radio and television work with Buddy Starcher. The latter was a straight country musician whose career in radio extended back into the late 1920s although he never made any records until 1946. Starcher's radio career took him over much of the country, but he had a particularly strong following in West Virginia and the Shenandoah Valley. During an earlier sojourn in Harrisonburg in the early forties, Starcher gave Mac Wiseman some of his earliest professional work and Wiseman in turn had recorded two Starcher songs—"I'll Still Write Your Name in the Sand" and "Fire in My Heart"—on his early Dot sessions.

Starcher's group at Harrisonburg included his wife Mary Ann, a one-time singing cowgirl at WLS, and Herman Yarbrough, an electric steel player. The latter also doubled in the comedy role of "Roscoe Swerps," a zany character who wore Bermuda shorts and a baseball cap twisted sideways. Early in 1960, the Starcher band moved to WCHS-TV in Charleston, West Virginia. They soon established themselves as an especially popular group on an early morning show and added more musicians to the band.

They recorded several sides on the Starday and Nashville labels, some of which featured Meadows on fiddle.

After a time, Joe left Starcher and returned to the Princeton area. A couple of years later he returned for about six months and then departed again. Mary Ann Starcher recalled that his devotion to his fiddle music was about the deepest she had seen. Joe, in turn regarded the congenial Buddy as "a fine fellow to work for." This experience in Charleston proved to be Meadows's last professional playing for about a decade during which time he earned his living in construction.

In 1972, Meadows played on stage with the Goins Brothers at their Lake Stephens Festival. Early in 1973, he decided to record a fiddle album after some years of virtual retirement. This recording appeared on the Bluegras label and also featured Buddy Griffin on banjo, George Ward on guitar, and Rob Mashburn on bass. The album included such tunes as "Candy Gal," "Cruel Willie," "The Shawnee," "Katy Hill," and "Rutland's Reel." This effort served as a vehicle for Joe's active reentry into bluegrass.

Melvin and Ray Goins then contacted him about helping them do their Jessup album, *Tribute to the Lonesome Pine Fiddlers*. They journeyed to Jackson, Michigan, on February 2 and the next day recorded what became their finest recorded effort up to that time. Melvin Goins also talked Jessup into doing a fiddle album featuring Meadows. This album included such tunes as "Lee Highway Blues," "Eighth of January," and "Black Hawk Waltz." Harley Gabbard and Leslie Sturgill on Dobro and bass, respectively, also worked on those sessions. On the trip South, Meadows decided to join the Goins Brothers as regular fiddler.

Meadows soon proved he still had all of his skills and perhaps a few new ones as well. His talented fiddle added considerably to the Goins sound throughout the festival season of 1973. It also led to him fiddling with a number of others of like quality on MCA's magnificent live *Beanblossom* album that June. Meadows subsequently recorded two more albums with Melvin and Ray Goins on Jessup—their *God Bless Her, She's My Mother* gospel effort in August and an additional album in December from which only the title song, "Bluegrass Blues," has been released as one side of a single. The entire effort eventually came out on a Plantation cassette. A year after he left the Goins Brothers, Meadows returned long enough to play fiddle on the session that resulted in the brothers' first Rebel album.

Early in 1974, Joe played fiddle with Larry Sparks and his Lonesome Ramblers with Wendy Miller on mandolin, Art Wydner on bass, along with first Tim Maynard and then Dave Evans on banjo. They helped Sparks cut his *Where the Sweet Waters Flow* and *Lonesome Sound* albums on Old Homestead, his *Footsteps of Tradition* album on King Bluegrass, and the remainder of Sparks' last Pine Tree album. Meadows also cut his third fiddle album, *Portrait of a Fiddler*, on Old Homestead with the aid of Sparks, Miller, Evans, and Wydner. The album generally received favorable reviews and included several standards as well as lesser-known tunes like "Oklahoma Redbird," Curly Herdman's "Stony Creek," and Kenny Sidle's "Wally's Tune."

Then in June 1974, Meadows rejoined Jim and Jesse McReynold's Virginia Boys and found his most enduring job as a sideman lasting five years. The McReynolds played one of the most active festival schedules in addition to their frequent *Grand Ole Opry* appearances. Having worked with the group previously, Joe was well-acquainted with their style and personalities. He worked on three albums for Jim and Jesse's Old Dominion label, *Jesus Is the Key to the Kingdom, Songs of Our Country*, and *Palace of Song*. He also participated in their successful 1975 tour of Japan and the joint Towa-Old Dominion two album record set, *Live in Japan*. Another effort with the Virginia Boys consisted of an album of banjo tunes featuring Tim Ellis, their new banjo picker.

Meadows also continued to record on his own. In September 1976 he made a second album on Old Homestead entitled *West Virginia Fiddler* which included several lesser-known and original tunes. This album featured several assisting musicians of which Mike Lilly and Wendy Miller on banjo and mandolin, respectively, were most noted. Somewhat later, Joe recorded a twin fiddle album with Buddy Griffin. The latter, another West Virginian, earned a name as one of the better fiddlers on the contemporary scene. Griffin acknowledges a considerable debt to Meadows in his own stylings. The album itself included some lead guitar work by both Meadows and Griffin. For the most part it featured lesser-known tunes like the title number *Two O' Clock in the Morning* and even an arrangement of Irving Berlin's "Waltz of a Dream Come True" with Griffin on fiddle and Meadows on guitar. Griffin says that before his work with Meadows, his own main interest was banjo. Afterward, he became more serious with the fiddle.

In addition to his recording and continued work with Jim and Jesse, Joe initiated his own fiddler's convention. In 1976 and 1977 he staged the contest near Princeton, West Virginia. Mark O'Connor emerged as the champion the first year and Ohioan Kenny Sidle took the title in 1977. In 1978, Meadows relocated the convention to Point Pleasant, West Virginia, where the facilities were better but the gate receipts were not. After that Joe gave up as a sponsor of fiddle contests. Before leaving the McReynolds, Meadows did a fiddle album with instrumental support from Jesse McReynolds, Tim Ellis, Vic Jordan, Joe Stuart, Charlie Collins, and Keith McReynolds entitled *Super Fiddle*. Recorded in Jack Linneman's Hilltop studio, many critics considered it his finest effort.

In 1983, Meadows relocated to the greater Washington, D. C., area, another well-known hotbed of bluegrass, where he worked in the office of Senator Robert Byrd, who was a well-known fiddler. According to rumor, Meadows and Fiddlin' Bob often twin fiddled in their spare moments. Joe also did some work on the local club scene with various groups and recorded a compact disc, *Mountains, Rivers, and Meadows,* for the Patuxent label in 1998. This allowed him to remain active as a fiddler until his death on February 8, 2003.

Through his work with the Stanley Brothers, Jim and Jesse, and other notable groups, Joe Meadows demonstrated himself as one of the more important bluegrass fiddlers. One thing seems certain, few have demonstrated more devotion to their art or worked harder to play their best than Ralph "Joe" Meadows of Mercer County, West Virginia. His recorded legacy is more than enough to demonstrate his skill.

SELECTED RECORDINGS

Joe Meadows: Mountains, Rivers and Meadows. Patuxent CD-036, 1998.

Joe Meadows also recorded six instrumental long play albums in the 1970s. He also did sessions with the Stanley Brothers, Bill and Mary Reid, Buddy Starcher, the Goins Brothers, Larry Sparks, Bill Emerson and Pete Gobel, and Jim and Jesse.

~ Natchee the Indian (Lester Storer)

1913–1970

In the annals of traditional fiddlers, especially in the decade of the Great Depression, the name of Natchee the Indian is often mentioned. While actual facts about Natchee remained elusive until the 1970s, he seemed to take on the stuff of legend. When concrete information began to surface, the legend persisted. Another enigma comes from Natchee's being unrecorded, unlike such contemporaries as Clark Kessinger, Curly Fox, Clayton McMichen, and Arthur Smith. The following is a compendium of some four decades of data, gleaned by myself and other researchers including the late Charles K. Wolfe.

Natchee was born Lester Vernon Storer probably on December 26, 1913, near the community of Louden, Bratton Township in Adams County, Ohio. It is not far from the Serpent Mound Memorial and the larger town of Peebles. His parents were George and Anna Sprinkles Storer. Natchee claimed this birth date in an August 1945 article in *The National Hillbilly News*. In the same article he also gave his birthplace as the San Carlos Apache Reservation in Arizona and said he was three-quarters Osage Apache. While the birth date is probably correct, the remainder is pure fiction. According to niece Sue Storer Rapp, daughter of Natchee's brother John Earl Storer, Natchee's great-grandmother was a full-blooded Shawnee orphaned as a child in West Virginia and adopted by a white family that came to Ohio. This would make him one-eighth Native American.

Storer grew up, like his contemporaries, learning farm work, but presumably not learning to like it. Researcher Richard Matteson found the Storer family living in Bratton Township in 1920, but in 1930 Storer and his brother as well as their mother Anna lived in Springfield, Clark County, Ohio. Natchee learned to play fiddle and guitar and he and his older brother had a band near Springfield. Niece Sue Rapp reported that in those days

From left: Natchee the Indian, "Little Montana" (Evalina Stallard), Indian Bill (James William Stallard), WSAZ, Huntington, WV, 1944.

musical groups needed a gimmick and Storer who had some Indian features let his hair grow and his mother made him an Indian costume. He became acquainted with Lloyd Copas, another Adams County native from Blue Creek, who ultimately became famous as Cowboy Copas. The latter had gained experience with a local string band, Fred Evans and the Hen-Cacklers. Copas and Lester Storer played around the area including radio station WNBD in Mt. Orab (later WPAY, Portsmouth) and radio stations in Cincinnati and Covington, Kentucky.

Sometime, probably about 1932 or 1933, and in Cincinnati, Storer and Copas met a man named Larry Sunbrock who could best be described as a big-time promoter. A writer for *True Magazine* once termed him "The Greatest Cowboy Con-Man." Sunbrock staged a number of much publicized fiddle contests around the country. Along the way, he invented an enhanced resume for his new cohorts. Although Copas and Storer may have earlier played "cowboy and Indian," the respective Oklahoma and Arizona Apache origins seem to have been Sunbrock inventions. Copas's biographer John Roger Simon supplied that information and considerable anecdotal data gathered from Copas kin and older folks in Adams and Scioto counties who knew both men in the thirties.

Sunbrock staged his contests coast to coast, but the three best documented ones took place in October 1936 at Akron, Ohio—a city loaded with West Virginia migrants—and in Charleston, West Virginia, in November 1936 and October 1937. Contestants at one or both Charleston competitions included the already legendary Clark Kessinger; Robert "Georgia Slim" Rutland, a Kessinger protégé then working for Buddy Starcher; Ralph Hamrick of the Hamrick Brothers and at that time a member of Al Hendershot's Dixie Ramblers; Charles "Big Foot" Keaton of Ashland, Kentucky, described as the "sixteen year old Wonder Fiddler;" and in 1936, Bob Atcher, best known in later years in Chicago as the "Dean of Cowboy Singers," but then serving a short stint at Charleston's WCHS.

There were also band and yodeling competitions. The best-known figure in the yodeling contest and the 1935 champ was Charleston's own Dixie Songbird Billy Cox, a widely recorded figure who often performed in the Jimmie Rodgers mode. Bands included Natchee's Tribe, undoubtedly including Copas; Kessinger's Butter Crust Bakers, named for his radio sponsor; Clayton McMichen and the Georgia Wildcats,1936 only; most of the other WCHS groups; and such forgotten bands as the Cabin Creek Wildcats. Kessinger had apparently been the 1935 winner and the later contests were billed as showdowns between Kessinger and Natchee.

Other competitions around the country included such well-known fiddlers of the era as Bert Layne, Clayton McMichen, Hugh Farr, Curly Fox, Eck Robertson, Red Herron, and Fiddlin' Arthur Smith of WSM and the *Opry*. According to Fox, most of the contests were "fixed" at least within certain limits, subject to audience applause, and the well-known contestants got paid equally. Nonetheless, McMichen hated to lose, especially to whom he referred to as the "damn Indian." Still, McMichen's daughter told Richard Matteson that Sunbrock always paid him, otherwise Clayton, known for his temper, would have killed him. Natchee, it was said, only knew about ten tunes including "Listen to the Mocking Bird" which was almost always a crowd pleaser and usually banned in modern contests along with "Orange Blossom Special."

About 1940, Natchee and Copas went their separate ways although they may have reunited at times. Copas worked at WSAZ with Jake Taylor and the Railsplitters taking a new nickname, the "Gold Star Ranger." Eventually, he replaced Eddy Arnold as vocalist with Pee Wee King's Golden West Cowboys and then as a *Grand Ole Opry* star. "Cope" had many hit records on King and Starday before his death in a 1963 plane crash.

Natchee alternated during the war years as a solo act in Cincinnati and working with other musical groups sometimes at West Virginia radio stations such as WCHS, WMMN (briefly) and WSAZ. Associates included Bill (1914–1981) and Evalina Stallard (1918–1980) who were usually known as "Indian Bill" and "Little Montana." Sometimes Arthur "Arizona Rusty" Gabbard (1918–1990) also worked with them. The Stallards, like Copas and Natchee, had also served musical apprenticeships at WPAY Portsmouth.

By mid-1945 when he was featured in *The National Hillbilly News*, Natchee was working at WSAZ with Bobby Cook and the Texas Saddle Pals. Cook, a Parkersburg, West Virginia, native, often worked with Red Watkins and Glen Ferguson. However, a note in the January 25, 1947 *Billboard* noted that Natchee and Banjo Murphy [McCleese] were again associated with Larry Sunbrock. This connection may have endured as late as 1950. Larry Sunbrock eventually settled in the Orlando, Florida, area, operated race tracks, and had periodic encounters with the IRS.

From that point onward Natchee the Indian slowly drifted into obscurity. During some of that time, he was likely musically associated with Bill Stallard who was known as Billy Starr after he and Evalina split. Gene McKnight, who was a regular on the WSAZ-TV *Saturday Night Jamboree*, recalled seeing him in the 1950s highly intoxicated. According to Juanita McMichen Lynch, he once showed up at Bert Layne's house in similar shape. Alcohol and heavy smoking apparently took a toll on his health.

Then in the summer of 1970, Natchee the Indian came back into public view. It seems that in the course of his life, he had married twice. The first to a woman named Nada (last name forgotten) and second to Elaine Goff Dye (sometimes called Naomi). The latter couple had a son Natchee Thomas Storer in 1941, but divorced soon afterwards and Elaine Storer took the son back to her West Virginia hometown and later to California where the boy grew up having been told that his father was dead.

Through a complicated set of circumstances, Tom Storer learned that his father was still alive. *Cincinnati Enquirer* reporter Peggy Lane wrote a feature story about Natchee after he was arrested and in the drunk tank. As a result a well-to-do man named David Silver bought Natchee a plane ticket to San Francisco where father and son were reunited. The joy was shortlived as Natchee's health had deteriorated. He had emphysema as well as heart and throat problems. In the closing weeks of his life, Tom Storer did preserve a little of his father's fiddling. First there was the novelty train tune "One-Eleven Special," obviously learned from Curly Fox who in turn had learned it from his mentor James McCarroll who had recorded it on Columbia in 1929. There was also an original song called "Too Many Tears" that John Roger Simon placed on a companion compact disc *Musical Associates of Cowboy Copas* to his book *Cowboy Copas and the Golden Age of Country Music* (Jesse Stuart Foundation, 2008).

Spending his last days in comfort, Lester Vernon Storer passed away on December 23, 1970. He was laid to rest in the Santa Clara Cemetery in California. Natchee the Indian was a virtual legend among fiddle music fans in West Virginia, Ohio, Kentucky, and elsewhere.

SELECTED RECORDINGS

Natchee the Indian made no commercial recordings, and if he made any radio transcriptions they have not yet surfaced. In the weeks prior to his death, he made two numbers on home recordings; one a fiddle tune and one with a vocal. They appeared on the compact disc *Musical Associates of Cowboy Copas* that accompanied John Roger Simon's book *Cowboy Copas and the Golden Age of Country Music*. Ashland, KE: Jesse Stuart Foundation, 2008.

↶ Red Rector

1929–1990

The mandolin became a part of bluegrass at basically the same moment as Bill Monroe which is to say, in the beginning. Other bands which took on elements of bluegrass also began to include innovative mandolin pickers. Among them was a young North Carolinian named William Eugene "Red" Rector whose style developed over thirty years into one of the most tasteful and original in the music. Throughout his long career as a sideman, in record sessions, and as a radio/television solo and duet artist, Red Rector's name became a household word among his thousands of admirers.

Born in Marshall, Madison County, North Carolina, on December 15, 1929, young Red Rector—like many other noted musicians—grew up in an atmosphere of music. His mother played piano and organ, and his father once sang in a quartet. However, it was the radio groups on WWNC in nearby Asheville such as the Morris Brothers and Wade Mainer and the Sons of the Mountaineers that attracted young Rector's attention. At about age ten, Rector saw his first live show at the local grammar school when Wiley, Zeke and George Morris together with Steve Ledford and Hoke Jenkins gave a performance. Rector first played guitar, but developed a great interest in the mandolin after hearing the Monroe Brothers' recording of "New River Train." About 1942, Rector heard Bill Monroe at a tent show in Asheville and "really went wild over the mandolin." Bill Monroe cautioned Rector about playing with a stiff wrist and the youth took the advice of the acknowledged expert.

Shortly afterwards, Rector and some other area youngsters began playing a fifteen minute show on WISE in Asheville with Jimmy Lunsford on fiddle and Dempsey Cothran and W. J. Waddell on guitars. As a result of his mandolin work on this show, Wade Mainer hired Rector to go to New York with him to appear in a radio drama for BBC, *The Chisholm Trail*, in

Red Rector, late 1940s.
Courtesy of John Morris.

1943. In addition to Wade and Red, J. E. Mainer and Fred Smith also made
the trip. In New York, they were joined by the Coon Creek Girls who were
Lily, Rosie and Minnie Ledford, as well as several urban folk performers
such as Burl Ives, Woody Guthrie, Cisco Houston, Lee Hays, and Sonny
Terry. Rector primarily helped furnish background music, but also got to
do some vocal work on cowboy songs. After a week or so of practice, they
did the show.

Red returned to Asheville with a little bigger name than before and continued on WISE. Soon, however, he and Jimmy Lunsford got the chance
to move over to the larger station, WWNC and the popular *Western North
Carolina Farm Hour*. Here Rector played guitar in a group known as Oscar
Turner and the Farm Boys which included another pair of pioneers in

bluegrass, Carl and J. P. Sauceman. He also began to play more often with Fred Smith whom he had known for years, but had seldom worked with musically because of Red being six years younger. He and Smith then associated with a group known as the Blue Ridge Hillbillies headed by comedian Tommy "Snowball" Millard. Red Smiley and the Saucemans worked in the band. Smith, Smiley, Rector, and Howard Thompson also went to WJHL in Johnson City and worked with Zeke Morris. When they came back to Asheville early in 1946, Red received a call from Ray Atkins in Raleigh who asked him to join Johnny Wright and Jack Anglin's Tennessee Hillbillies at WPTF. A guaranteed salary of $35.00 weekly sounded good to Rector and he immediately accepted.

By this time—although only sixteen—Red had acquired considerable musical experience. He also began to realize the necessity of developing a more original style. Although greatly admiring Bill Monroe, he worked to perfect his own manner of mandolin playing. Like others with unique styles, however, Red did borrow and acknowledged the influence of Paul Buskirk as being quite important. Buskirk, who had an extensive career in radio that stretched from his native West Virginia to Texas, developed expertise on a variety of instruments including the Dobro, fiddle, and tenor banjo. He recorded instrumental albums on the Stoneway label in the mid-1970s and recorded with Willie Nelson; he also influenced the mandolin work of others. Unlike most pickers, Rector usually played an A-4 mandolin and never used a support strap which seemed remarkable.

When Rector went to Raleigh and joined Johnny and Jack, their group included Paul Warren of later Flatt and Scruggs fame on fiddle; Buster Moore on banjo; Ray Atkins on Dobro, and Johnny's wife Kitty Wells (Muriel Deason Wright), as featured vocalist. Although their string of hits on Victor did not come until several years later, the Tennessee Hillbillies were nonetheless a popular radio and personal appearance band. After ten months at Raleigh, Johnny and Jack received the chance to join WSM. Red, however, decided not to go to the *Opry* and instead joined Charlie Monroe and the Kentucky Pardners at WNOX in Knoxville.

Charlie Monroe enjoyed a very high popularity rating in an area extending from North Carolina to Eastern Kentucky. After a couple of months, on November 7, 1947, the Kentucky Pardners went to New York and cut twelve sides on RCA Victor—Red's first recording session. The sides cut that day included some of Monroe's more popular numbers such as "Walking With You In My Dreams," "When the Angels Carry Me Home," "End of Memory Lane" and "Shenandoah Waltz." Other band members included Rex Henderson, Lavelle Coy, and Buddy Osborne. Later, Monroe and the boys moved to WVOK in Birmingham where they became one of the first acts on a newly opened station.

In the summer of 1948, Monroe took a long vacation and after a brief period of inactivity, Rector and Fred Smith went to work as a duet with Carl Story and the Rambling Mountaineers replacing the Johnson Brothers. Claude Boone and Cotton Galyon rounded out the group at that time. Rector stayed with the Rambling Mountaineers for about seven years and recorded several sessions on Mercury and Columbia. They recorded a lot of gospel quartet numbers and also such secular songs as "Have You Come to Say Goodbye?" and "Love and Wealth," the latter featuring Red's lead vocal.

After a time, the Carl Story group left WNOX and went on to Bristol and Atlanta for short stints and then spent three highly successful years at WAYS Charlotte where they started the *Tar Heel Barn Dance*. Ray Atkins, who had previously worked with Johnny and Jack at WPTF when Red did, played with the Rambling Mountaineers during much of this period following the departure of Galyon and Smith. Rector worked with the band until 1955 when they returned to Knoxville.

These years covered the last part of the great age of live country music on radio. Nightly, the Rambling Mountaineers played school houses, court houses, or theaters to packed audiences. Few artists carried their easily breakable seventy-eight rpm records on show dates, but made considerable extra cash selling souvenir pictures and song books.

While employed with Carl Story, Rector took advantage of two additional opportunities to do session work. The first came on February 1, 1949, when he journeyed to Atlanta and cut eight more sides with Charlie Monroe on Victor including "Rosa Lee McFall," "Red Rocking Chair," and "Time Clock of Life." The second occurred in Charlotte in 1953 when Red worked on Don Reno's and Red Smiley's second King session together with his boy-hood friend Jimmy Lunsford on fiddle, and also Tommy Faile and Nelson Benton. The twelve songs included "Talk of the Town," "Springtime in Dear Old Dixie" and such instrumental classics as "Choking the Strings" and "Tennessee Breakdown."

When Carl Story returned to Knoxville, Rector left the Rambling Mountaineers and teamed up as a duet with Fred Smith. Smith had worked with a variety of other Knoxville artists like Archie Campbell, Speedy Krise, and Jack Shelton in the years since leaving Story. They worked together for about three years adding comedy routines to their act. Then in 1958, the *Mid-Day Merry-Go-Round* was terminated and Rector went to work for Martha White Flour's second unit as part of Hylo Brown's Timberliners. Brown at that time worked a series of television shows in Jackson and Tupelo, Mississippi, and Jackson, Tennessee. After a few months, they traded places with Flatt and Scruggs and then worked on five stations in the Appalachian region. The band also included Tater Tate, Jim Smoak, and Joe Phillips. Together, they cut twenty numbers on Capitol which included some of the most classic bluegrass numbers ever recorded. In addition to the Hylo Brown album which was largely made up of traditional songs, they cut eight original songs released as singles including "Shuffle of My Feet," "Thunderclouds of Love," and "I've Waited As Long As I Can." Rector left the group about a month before it broke up when he got the opportunity to go back to Knoxville and work with Fred Smith again—this time on daily television—for Cas Walker, the Knoxville supermarket owner.

The Cas Walker *Farm and Home Show* on early morning television served as Rector's mainstay until 1983. During much of the sixties, he did not play out a great deal although he did guest on the *Opry* a few times and played some personal appearances. He also worked on some Nashville record sessions including a Tommy Jackson fiddle album on Dot and Walter Hensley's Capitol effort, *The Five String Banjo Today*. An outstanding album which featured both Rector's vocal and instrumental work was *Grandpa Jones Remembers the Brown's Ferry Four* with Merle Travis and Grandpa recreating their original roles in the legendary gospel quartet with Rector and Ramona Jones replacing the Delmore Brothers.

In the next few years, Rector worked a lot of festivals as a solo act giving examples of his virtuosity on the mandolin both in the workshops and concerts. He played some festivals with Fred Smith, his television partner, doing both duet numbers and comedy routines. They also appeared on some country package shows.

Red's work on the Cas Walker show fitted him with a variety of country and bluegrass personalities. In addition to Rector and Fred Smith, the show included banjoist Larry Mathis, Danny Bailey of the once famous brother team, and Claude Boone, a country music veteran who worked with both Cliff Carlisle and Carl Story. Prior to finishing high school in 1964, country superstar Dolly Parton worked on the show. A later addition, Lee "Honey" Wild who once constituted half of the famous blackface comedy team of Jamup and Honey worked on the show until he died in 1982.

Rector also expanded his recording activities. In 1969, he and Fred Smith did an album for County Records with the aid of Bill Chambers and Kenny Baker on banjo and fiddle respectively. The LP consisted of nine old-time country duet numbers such as the old Molly O'Day-Lynn Davis number, "This Is the End," "One Little Word," and "Are There Tears Behind Your Smile?" plus three outstanding instrumentals featuring Rector and Kenny Baker.

In the early 1970s, Rector did his first solo album on Old Homestead with seven ballads and seven instrumentals. On this recording, he received able backup from Doug Green, Vic Jordan, and Buck and Cheryl White. Buck White, an outstanding mandolinist in his own right, played lead guitar except on "Flop Eared Mule" and "Red Wing" on which Red did the guitar work. This was the first time in a quarter century of recording that he had played anything except mandolin on a session. He also recorded an all instrumental album for Old Homestead, *Appaloosa*, with support from Vasser Clements, Jack Hicks, and Buck and Cheryl White which was released in 1975.

Rector also extended his session work as a guest artist. He again recorded with Carl Story on both Jessup and Atteiram. He also helped Rual Yarbrough, Bill Clifton, Ramona Jones, and Wade Hill. Since by this time the Cas Walker program was usually videotaped in two weekly sessions—three at one time and two another—Rector could play out more distantly from Knoxville.

Although continuing to work on the Cas Walker show, Rector began to work personal appearances with other groups more frequently. He and his wife of over forty years, Ernestine, more commonly known as "Parker" (her maiden name) reared four children. After all four reached adulthood, Rector accepted opportunities to play even farther from Knoxville. In 1974, he worked with Bill Clifton on his festival appearances and also worked often with Yarbrough and Joe Stuart. In February 1975, Red spent a month in England and various Western Europe countries giving concerts with Clifton and recording with him. He spent the summer playing numerous festivals—either as a solo act or with various bands.

In fact Rector made several tours abroad with Clifton and further inspired his creative talents for new tunes such as "Crossing the Moors" in northern England and "Salzburg Stomp" in Austria. Back home he recorded two additional albums in 1978 and 1980 for the Revonah label with help from Tater Tate, Vic Jordan, Tom McKinney, and Doug Green. These contained a mixture of instrumentals and vocals. Always creative with his picking, Red also made an album with guitar wizard Norman Blake and a twin mandolin album with Jethro Burns, another old friend from Knoxville radio days who was once part of the renowned comedy team of Homer and Jethro. Rector spent much of the summer of 1982 entertaining visitors at the Knoxville World's Fair at the Stokely-Van Camp Pavilion along with other East Tennessee musical stalwarts such as Danny Bailey and Claude Boone.

As a guest musician Rector worked with banjo picker Don Stover on an album and another with the Alabama bluegrass twosome of Rual Yarbrough and Joe Stuart, both former Blue Grass Boys. In May 1990, Rector and Bill Clifton planned another European tour in the fall and spent much of the Memorial Day weekend practicing previously unrecorded material for a live album to be cut for the Strictly Country label in the Netherlands. Returning to Knoxville on May 30, 1990, while mowing his lawn, Red suffered a fatal heart attack. Bill Clifton, who like Rector loved the old-time country duets, found himself so emotionally upset by his favorite vocal partner's death that he virtually stopped singing for a time.

In forty-five years with country and bluegrass music, Red Rector achieved status as a prominent, creative, and influential figure. His original mandolin work in the pioneer days of bluegrass with such persons as Charlie Monroe, Carl Story, Hylo Brown, and Reno and Smiley helped to put the music on a solid foundation and later high quality efforts assisted in its steadily increasing popularity. Among mandolinists, only Bill Monroe and perhaps one or two others have contributed more to bluegrass music.

SELECTED RECORDINGS

Red and Fred: Songs from the Heart of the Country. County CD 721, 1969. Compact disc
   reissue of classic album.
Red Rector and Bill Clifton: Alive! Elf CD 104, 2001. Taken from 1976 concerts in England.

Red Rector also recorded four long play albums—two on Old Homestead and two on
Revonah—all out of print. His many recordings with Carl Story are in the aforementioned
BCD 16839 and with Charlie Monroe on BCD 16808. Red's Monument album with Grandpa
Jones is included in *Grandpa Jones: Everybody's Grandpa.* Bear Family BCD 15788, 1997,
and with Bill Clifton on *Bill Clifton: Around the World to Poor Valley.* Bear Family BCD
16425, 2001. Red Rector also recorded with Don Reno and Red Smiley, Hylo Brown, Rual
Yarbrough and Joe Stuart, Tater Tate, Jethro Burns, Don Stover, and perhaps others.

⤳ Clarence "Tater" Tate

1931–2007

Tater Tate ranks among the most noted fiddlers in bluegrass music. For more than fifty years he established a reputation as a top musician on fiddle and as a competent sideman on other instruments. In mid-career he led the Shenandoah Cutups for several years. As a band member Tate worked, toured and recorded with most of the premier pioneer bluegrass groups and appeared on the leading radio barn dance programs and regional morning television outlets. In his declining years, Tater taught fiddle for the East Tennessee State University bluegrass program.

Among bluegrass musicians, fiddlers have frequently achieved special attention. At a number of festivals in the 1970s, fiddlers such as Tex Logan, Chubby Wise, and Howdy Forrester made guest appearances and occasionally several fiddlers performed at once on stage. Not even the banjo—bluegrass music's most distinctive instrument—was thusly featured. The prominent place accorded the fiddler at that time may be considered all the more unusual when one recalls that many bands did not even carry one.

Bluegrass music was never short of outstanding fiddlers. From the early days when Art Wooten, Benny Martin, and Leslie Keith served as outstanding sidemen to later times when Kenny Baker, Curly Ray Cline, and Byron Berline were widely acclaimed, musicians who adeptly played the country violin have never really been scarce. However, if one were to ask what bluegrass fiddler had recorded most frequently and played most consistently, the name Tater Tate might likely be considered. Over more than a half century as a professional musician, Tate had begun his first major recordings as a teenager.

Like numerous other bluegrass artists, Clarence E. Tate came from a musical family and a musical area. As the youngest in a family of nine—six of whom played instruments—and a native of southwest Virginia, Gate City

The Shenandoah Cutups, 1973. *Top row from left:* Tom McKinney, John Palmer, Clarence "Tater" Tate. *Front row from left:* Herschel Sizemore, Wesley Golding.

in Scott County, young Tate received a steady diet of music from the time of his birth on February 4, 1931. By age four, he was showing interest in the guitar and a few years later made his radio debut.

At the time, the older members of the Tate family were performing on WKPT, Kingsport, Tennessee, as the Cumberland Mountaineers. Young Clarence received his first professional experience with the group playing guitar and also ukulele, an instrument perhaps more attuned to his physical size in those years. His early performances were limited to local activities: the radio, a Saturday night barn dance in Kingsport and from July 1946, the Saturday morning *Barrel O'Fun* show on WBEJ, Elizabethton, Tennessee. As the older members of the family grew up, they lost interest in playing music professionally and the Cumberland Mountaineers ceased to exist.

Clarence continued his interest in music and added the mandolin to the list of instruments he played while working on the family farm and at a sawmill. But by age sixteen he was ready to leave home for a musical career. In 1947, he teamed up with the Moore Brothers of Nickelsville, Virginia, and they went to Knoxville and WNOX's *Mid-Day Merry-Go-Round*. In less than three weeks, however, he was quickly back home as the Moore Brothers had not found the city to their liking.

Returning home and to the job at his uncle's sawmill, Tate soon came under the influence of Lester Flatt and Earl Scruggs and the Foggy Mountain Boys who were just beginning their career at WCYB's *Farm and Fun Time*. Jim Shumate played fiddle and his styling appealed to young Tate and it became his primary instrument.

The year that saw the launching of the Foggy Mountain Boys—1948—was perhaps the key date in the musical development of Tater Tate. In Kingsport, he helped form a country group named the Ridge Runners which also included Jim Smith who played many years with Carl Smith, and the Haynes Brothers, a.k.a. Walter and Jack. While playing on the *Broad Street Furniture Show* on WKPT, the Ridge Runners were hired by Archie Campbell to entertain at political rallies for Roy Acuff's gubernatorial campaign in the region.

The year or so that Tate spent with Archie Campbell might be considered as the equivalent to a college education in the field of country and bluegrass music. The Knoxville of the late 1940s was literally swarming with both experienced and up-coming musicians that included Carl Smith, Carl Butler, Joe Stuart, Bill and Cliff Carlisle, Archie Campbell, Johnny Whisnant, Speedy Krise, the Bailey Brothers, the Sauceman Brothers, and Tater Tate among others. Radio WNOX and WROL and somewhat later television programs including the *Tennessee Barn Dance, Mid-Day Merry-Go-Round*, and daily programs sponsored by Cas Walker, the supermarket owner, where musicians could not only display their talents, but also trade songs, learn techniques, and gain knowledge from one another. It was also in Knoxville that the young fiddler received the nickname "Tater" from Cas Walker, the name which he would thereafter be known. In Tate's opinion, that 1948–1950 period he spent in Knoxville was his most valued musical experience in terms of development.

Archie Campbell's *Dinner Bell* show on WROL included a number of acts like that of Carl and J. P. Sauceman with whom Tate played fiddle along with Wiley Birchfield on banjo. This was Tater's first exclusive experience in bluegrass music and when the Saucemans moved to WCYB and *Farm and Fun Time,* Tate went with them. About this time, he did his first recording session with Carl and J. P. on Rich-R-Tone and also made some transcriptions in Bristol. On November 1, 1950, he was back at WROL where he fiddled on four songs backing Carl Butler on his first Capitol session, marking Tater's first work on a major label.

By the end of the year, Tate joined the Bailey Brothers and their Happy Valley Boys which also included Hoke Jenkins on banjo and Jake Tullock on bass. They moved to WPTF Raleigh, but Tater soon found himself drafted into the Marine Corps. Released after several weeks, he rejoined the Happy Valley Boys in June who had relocated to WWVA Wheeling and the *World's Original Jamboree.* The Baileys were tremendously successful, drawing large crowds throughout Pennsylvania and adjacent states. Danny Bailey eventually returned to Knoxville, but Charlie Bailey kept a band together and continued to play the area. In June 1954, Tate was again conscripted, this time into the Army. At the time, Tate and Charlie Bailey were making a stay at CKCW Moncton, New Brunswick, a frequent multi-week stop for *Jamboree* acts on extended Canadian tours. During that sojourn with the Baileys, Tate recorded eight sides with the brothers on the Canary label and later fiddled on their two reunion albums for Rounder in the 1970s. He also gained the acquaintance of Buddy Spicher, an aspiring teenage fiddler protégé then playing with Dusty Owens who later became a noted session musician in Nashville. Tate did a country recording session with Mabelle Seiger for the X label, an RCA subsidiary.

While Tate was out of the professional scene for a couple of years, he was not entirely out of music. He spent much of his service career in the Canal Zone where he organized a band that played in NCO clubs. Coming out of the U. S. Army, he intended to drop out of music. Instead he almost immediately received a call from Joe Stuart on behalf of Bill Monroe who needed a fiddler to replace Bobby Hicks who was bound for military service. This proved to be a short stay of seven months as the low pay, competition from emerging rock and roll, and recurring migraine headaches soon led him to rejoin the Bailey Brothers in Knoxville. This tenure also proved to be brief as the Baileys soon dissolved, but Tater did go back to Nashville in February 1957 to record a session on Mercury with Carl Story and the Rambling Mountaineers that included a pair of classics, the instrumental

"Mocking Banjo" and the sacred "Light at the River." Over the next several years, Tate often made additional recordings with Story and the Rambling Mountaineers.

After a brief hiatus from music, Tater went to work as fiddler with Hylo Brown and the Timberliners. Brown had been a featured vocalist with Flatt and Scruggs who was given his own band under sponsorship of Martha White Mills. The Timberliners worked a television circuit based in Jackson, Tennessee; Tupelo, Mississippi; and Jackson, Mississippi, along with the *Louisiana Hayride* in Shreveport. After several months, they exchanged places with the Foggy Mountain Boys and did the Chattanooga and Knoxville, Tennessee, and Bluefield, Huntington, and Clarksburg, West Virginia, circuit, and also the WWVA *Jamboree*. In addition to Tate on fiddle, the band included Red Rector, mandolin; Jim Smoak, banjo and Flapjack Phillips, bass. The twenty numbers this band recorded for Capitol in August 1958, especially the album *Hylo Brown*, is considered some of the best traditional bluegrass ever made. The use of videotape and the syndication of the Flatt and Scruggs program on television stations ended this phase of bluegrass history and Rector left the band and returned to Knoxville. However, Tate and Smoak remained for several more months. One LP and one CD from a respective radio program and a show at New River Ranch featuring the Timberliners from this period have subsequently been released.

Tater departed from Hylo Brown's band largely because his family back in Gate City, Virginia, needed him to be closer home. Accordingly, he went to work for Bonnie Lou and Buster Moore who had a daily morning television program at WJHL in nearby Johnson City, Tennessee, during which time he made some recordings with them. In 1963, he worked again with Carl Sauceman in Alabama and then for a few months with Jimmy Martin and the Sunny Mountain Boys. Working one Decca session with Martin that September, Tater played on four numbers including the truck driving classic "Widow Maker" and a pair of instrumentals that featured essentially his fiddling along with the legendary J. D. Crowe on banjo. Not long afterward, Tate returned to Knoxville and the friendly confines of Cas Walker's morning programs on WBIR-TV and personal appearances and recording with Carl Story's Rambling Mountaineers, an aggregation that also included the Brewster Brothers and Claude Boone.

Remaining in Knoxville through the summer of 1965, Tate turned down a job with Jim and Jesse, but soon accepted an offer to join Red Smiley's Bluegrass Cutups. Moving to Roanoke in October 1965, the Virginia city would be his home for the next twelve years, nearly four with Smiley's band and then for eight as leader of the successor group after Smiley retired, the Shenandoah Cutups. In the first portion of that era, the Cutups in addition to morning television worked at WWVA's *Jamboree, U. S. A.,* formerly the *World's Original Jamboree,* about once a month. Red Smiley also had a weekly program at WOAY-TV in Oak Hill, West Virginia, where they did one live show a month and taped the other three.

Tate's days with Red Smiley not only proved to be musically productive, but also led to a great deal of time in recording studios. The Bluegrass Cutups had four long-play album releases in the United States, one on Rimrock and three on Rural Rhythm. A fifth Smiley album came out on Seven Seas, a Japanese label, featuring Tate's fiddling that has never been released in the United States. Sadly by this time, most bluegrass music had been relegated to the specialty record labels.

Tate also made his first recordings under his own name, cutting one fiddle album for Rimrock and three for Rural Rhythm, the latter two being waltzes that included overdubbed piano. In addition, the Cutups served as a virtual house band for Rural Rhythm's other bluegrass artists, working on two albums for Jim Eanes and one each for Lee Moore, Hylo Brown, Shot Jackson, and J. E. Mainer, the latter providing the venerable old-timer with more of a bluegrass sound on that session.

When WBDJ-TV terminated Smiley's *Top O' the Morning* program in April 1969, Red Smiley in declining health chose to retire, but the band continued. Tate, John Palmer, and Billy Edwards recruited Herschel Sizemore, a quality mandolin picker from Alabama and changed the band to the Shenandoah Cutups. Brief associations with Jim Eanes and Cliff Waldron as guitarist and lead vocalist proved temporary. Tate became leader, Palmer handled the business, and Edwards played banjo and primarily sang lead. With some additions and changes, this foursome constituted the nucleus of the Cutups although Tater more often than not played the guitar rather than fiddle. Retaining their Wheeling *Jamboree* affiliation, Mac Wiseman managed to get them bookings in Pennsylvania as long as he remained at WWVA. With bluegrass festivals in the ascendency, the band thrived for several years although most of them also held part-time day jobs. During the Cutups decade of activity, they made nine albums with Tate playing on eight of them, five on Revonah, and one each for County, Rebel, and Major. In addition, they served as a band for Mac Wiseman on two albums and one for Curly Seckler, best known as Lester Flatt's favorite tenor singer.

In the spring of 1977, Paul Warren, the longtime fiddler with Lester Flatt began to experience serious health problems and Tate went to work with the Nashville Grass, becoming a regular member that August. Although, Flatt's physical condition was also deteriorating, the band continued as long as was possible. Tater cut three CMH albums with Flatt: the double disc, *Live at the Pilot Mountain Bluegrass Festival, Picking Time,* and the instrumental *Lester Flatt's Nashville Grass.* Flatt was able to play rhythm guitar on only part of the project, but a highlight was Tate's fiddling on "Peacock Rag," one of his signature tunes.

After Lester Flatt's death in September 1979, the Nashville Grass continued under the leadership of Curly Seckler, Tate did one album for them and they backed him on a fifth fiddle album, *The Fiddler and His Lady,* released in 1981 on the Revonah label. Tater also fiddled on two albums in 1978 and 1980, with his old Knoxville pal Red Rector. By the time his last fiddle album was released, Tate had switched his primary employment to Wilma Lee Cooper and her Clinch Mountain Clan. Cooper had been a friend of Tater's since their WWVA days of the early fifties and they worked well together doing the Rebel album *White Rose,* but when Wilma put Mike Lattimore in charge of the band Tate gave his notice and worked a short time with Carl Story until he rejoined Bill Monroe's Blue Grass Boys in mid-1984.

Tater Tate's second service with Bill Monroe lasted until March 1996, as long as the aging Father of Bluegrass was able to play; that period found infirmity catching up with him. Tater toured with the Bluegrass Boys in the United States and Canada as well as a Japanese trip and playing the *Opry.* Tate worked on most of Monroe's MCA recording sessions, which included over fifty masters, but actually played bass fiddle and sang bass more than he fiddled. His fiddling with Monroe was most prominent on his 1989 live at the *Opry* and the 1990 studio effort that followed it.

Tater Tate's own career was winding down by this time, but he still did some session work, most notably on traditional country star Patty Loveless's acclaimed *Mountain Soul* project of 2001, when he played bass on five cuts, sang bass on another, and twin-fiddled with Deanie Richardson on one. He also worked on additional numbers with Curly Seckler. In 2002 Tate was inducted into the Virginia Music Hall of Fame, a tribute to his long service in bluegrass music. Retiring from musical touring and recording, he moved to Jonesborough, Tennessee, and spent his latter days teaching bluegrass fiddle in the East Tennessee State University bluegrass program, passing away on October 17, 2007. Clarence E. "Tater" Tate left a legacy as being a key figure in some the best bluegrass bands ever assembled.

SELECTED RECORDINGS

Clarence "Tater" Tate: 20 Bluegrass Fiddle Classics. Rural Rhythm RUR 402, 2011. Reissue of 1960s Rural Rhythm recordings, mostly from Rural Rhythm 193.

Tater Tate recorded three long play albums for Rural Rhythm, and one each for Rimrock and Revonah, all now out of print. His work as one of Bill Monroe's Blue Grass Boys is on *Bill Monroe: My Last Days on Earth*. Bear Family BCD 16637, 2007. Tater Tate also recorded with the Sauceman Brothers, Carl Butler, the Bailey Brothers, Mabelle Seiger, Gloria Belle Flickinger, Red Smiley, Carl Story, Curly Seckler, the Shenandoah Cutups, Lee Moore, J. E. Mainer, Jim Eanes, Red Rector, Hylo Brown, Wilma Lee Cooper, Shot Jackson, Jim and Jesse, Lester Flatt, Patty Loveless, Mac Wiseman, and perhaps others.

↪ Chubby Wise

1915–1996

Although bluegrass music has produced a number of old-time fiddle players who have influenced the art, the name of Chubby Wise must rank as one of the most significant. If one accepts that bluegrass originated with Bill Monroe's band of the middle 1940s which pulled together all of the proper instruments and vocal stylings, then Wise like Monroe, Lester Flatt, Earl Scruggs, and Cedric Rainwater were surely present at the creation. Unfortunately, Wise never fronted great bands of his own, but remained a sideman and featured solo artist. While never obscure, this relegated him to a background position as a member of that milestone bluegrass band. However, Chubby Wise's career as a country and bluegrass fiddler is most certainly a significant one that deserves attention in its own right.

Born in Lake City, Columbia County, Florida, on October 2, 1915, as Robert Russell Wise, Chubby first learned music from his father, a local fiddler of some renown. He learned a few banjo chords around age of six so he could back up his dad. A little later, he fell in love with Riley Puckett's guitar styling and took up that instrument. While Wise developed skill as a guitar picker, he never really equaled the ability of his blind idol.

Wise's interest in the fiddle did not develop until his early teens when he heard and met Bryan Purcell, a Florida champion. Wise then set about mastering the fiddle. Drawing his major inspiration from Purcell, but also from such professionals as Curly Fox, Clayton McMichen, and Fiddlin' Arthur Smith, Wise soon developed into a highly skilled fiddler.

By the time Chubby reached adulthood, he lived in Jacksonville with his wife and infant daughter and drove a cab by day and fiddled in clubs, bars, and dances by evening. One of his best friends, another young Florida fiddler named Ervin Rouse, also played in some of the same places. One night at about 2:00 a.m., the two friends decided to go down to the railway station

Chubby Wise.

and see the Seaboard Air Line's brand new Orange Blossom Special which proved to be the most magnificent train the duo had ever encountered. Returning to Wise's apartment to eat, Rouse suggested that they compose a fiddle tune with train sounds and call it "Orange Blossom Special." Wise recalled that they put the instrumental part together in about forty-five minutes. Later Rouse, with some possible help from his brothers Earl and Gordon, added a full set of lyrics and secured a copyright for it in his name, without Wise's objection. In another version, Claude Casey, at the time leader of a swing band in the Carolinas, offered the opinion that Rouse was actually teaching Wise the tune that he had composed earlier. Certainly earlier recordings of it had been done by Tommy Magness with Roy Hall's Blue Ridge Entertainers and Lawrence Wiseman with Walter Hurdt and his Singing Cowboys. Somewhat later in June 1939, the Rouse Brothers recorded the song on Bluebird and although the original recording did not achieve hit status, it attracted enough attention that others such as Bill

Monroe and Fiddlin' Arthur Smith picked it up and helped make the tune one of the all-time country and bluegrass instrumental favorites. Now the ultimate origins of the tune are lost in faulty memories of long-deceased persons who had told the truth as they saw it.

Leaving Jacksonville in the winter of 1937–38, Wise went to Gainesville where he secured a steady job fiddling with the Jubilee Hillbillies. This group constituted one of the few professional country bands in the state of Florida and managed to keep pretty busy with their radio work, personal appearances, and dances. The Florida fans liked a wide variety of music and the Jubilee Hillbillies repertoire covered a wide range. Wise recalled playing all kinds of material from traditional hoedowns and then current Bob Wills and other western swing tunes to popular numbers like Hoagy Carmichael's "Stardust." In fact, Wise developed some of the stylings in that period which have appeared on some of his Stoneway albums.

The original Jubilee Hillbillies fragmented as a group not long after Pearl Harbor and the American entry into World War II. Some members went into defense work while others entered military service. Wise attempted to keep the group together for a while, but gave up when he received the opportunity to join Bill Monroe and the Blue Grass Boys at WSM on a trial basis. Wise had not played much of the mountain-styled fiddle of such previous Monroe sidemen like Tommy Magness and Art Wooten and some doubt existed as to whether Wise could adapt his western swing-influenced fiddle to the Monroe sound. For a time, Monroe carried other fiddlers such as Floyd Ethridge and Carl Story, but eventually Wise made the grade. He gave Monroe a great deal of the credit for helping him convert to the proper sound and recalled that Monroe spent hours helping Wise produce the style that the Blue Grass Boys needed. Chubby had also listened often to his predecessor which proved to be quite helpful.

When Wise joined the group in 1942, the band consisted of Monroe, Clyde Moody, and Cousin Wilbur Wesbrooks. By the end of 1945, the band included Lester Flatt, Earl Scruggs, and Howard Watts a.k.a. Cedric Rainwater. Wise felt that this latter group produced a somewhat different sound, what we call bluegrass today although it was not such a noticeable change at the time, but a more evolutionary shift. In Chubby's opinion, the sound became more rounded out, particularly with the addition of Flatt and Scruggs. Contrary to some views, Wise believed that Scruggs played a phenomenal banjo at the time he came with the Blue Grass Boys.

Bill Monroe and the Blue Grass Boys constituted an extremely popular band during the period and Chubby was quite busy. The group played numerous personals and did an early morning radio show and a *Noontime Neighbors* show in addition to the *Opry*. Wise played on all of Monroe's Columbia record sessions during 1945–1949. Occasionally, he also recorded with other artists including Hank Williams, Red Foley, Wally Fowler, Denver Darling, and Clyde Moody. It was with Moody that Chubby composed the hit song "Shenandoah Waltz" with Moody writing the lyrics and Wise the music.

In January 1948, Wise left the Blue Grass Boys and with Clyde Moody went to WARL in Arlington, Virginia, to work for Connie B. Gay. Moody headed a group called the Radio Ranchmen which in addition to Wise included Joe and Buddy Wheeler. After a year, they went to Durham, North Carolina, but Chubby soon became dissatisfied and returned to the Washington, D. C., area. In the fall of 1949, he rejoined Bill Monroe. Although his second stint as a Blue Grass Boy lasted only a few months, it did permit him the chance to appear on Monroe's final Columbia session of October 22, 1949, along with Mac Wiseman, Rudy Lyle, and Jack Thompson.

Leaving Bill Monroe for the last time early in 1950, Wise moved to Detroit and played briefly with the York Brothers. He then spent a brief spell with Lester Flatt and Earl Scruggs based at WVRK in Versailles, Kentucky, and at Lexington's *Kentucky Barn Dance*. Although his tenure with the Foggy Mountain Boys lasted only a few months, he did participate in one Columbia session with them, recording six tunes including "Jimmy Brown, the Newsboy" and the classic duet of "I've Lost You" by Lester and Everett Lilly. Following this, he returned to the Washington, D. C., area and played a lot of local club dates. Others doing the same thing at the time included Roy Clark and Jimmy Dean.

In 1954, Chubby Wise returned to Nashville and the *Opry* again. This time, he went as a fiddler with one of the most popular groups on the country scene—Hank Snow and the Rainbow Ranch Boys. Except for an eighteen-month period, 1963–1965, he spent sixteen years with Snow, leaving in March 1970.

In many respects, the years with the Hank Snow troupe represented the high point of Wise's career as a sideman. The band toured extensively throughout the United States and some fifteen other countries as well. Chubby always got to do one instrumental number on each show—invariably the "Orange Blossom Special"—and got quite a thrill delighting audiences as far from his native Florida as London, England, and Hong Kong.

During these years with a name country group, Wise did not totally absent himself from bluegrass music as he participated in sessions for Mac Wiseman on Capitol and Red Allen and Hylo Brown on Starday. He also played considerable fiddle on a Rainbow Ranch Boys album on Starday and did an album of fiddle tunes on a budget label. He participated in some country recording sessions, especially those with his boss Hank Snow, but also twin fiddled on the "Corrine, Corrina" cut on the extremely popular *Fightin' Side of Me* album of Merle Haggard's recorded live in Philadelphia.

In the eighteen-month interval that Wise did not perform with Snow during the early to mid-sixties also saw him again active in bluegrass. He made one tour with the Stanley Brothers. Chubby recorded an album with Hazel and Alice and made some recordings with Red Allen and Frank Wakefield.

In the fall of 1969, Wise made some country fiddle recordings for Stoneway Records of Houston, Texas. The tunes received an unexpectedly enthusiastic reception in the Lone Star State and demands for appearances for him in that region followed. Chubby hesitated, torn between the security of a steady job with Hank Snow and the chance of striking out as a solo artist. Although he had enjoyed steady work in Nashville, he had never really done that well financially and had been able to raise his family only with his wife's help, working as a nurse. Finally the two decided to try Texas.

It had been the Stoneway recording of the old Bob Wills tune "Maiden's Prayer" which provided the impetus for Wise's new career as a solo fiddle act. In Texas and elsewhere, the recording had created a demand for his playing at a variety of locations including dances, clubs and rodeos. Eventually, Chubby's wife, Rossi, became his booking agent and for the next several years managed to keep him quite active. Each summer he played at several festivals and thus made the best of both the revival of western swing and the resurgence of bluegrass. He managed to sneak in a few bluegrass recording sessions here and there, such as the one with Charlie Moore on Wango which produced "Legend of the Rebel Soldier," and an album on the Round label of California with Frank Wakefield, Don Reno, and others. However, most of his later efforts on record were on the Stoneway label on which he had more than twenty albums released. While most of the albums had been with a light country backing of more interest to the western swing or middle-of-the-road fan, a few were more in the bluegrass vein or with Howdy Forrester, another veteran Nashville fiddler who appealed to both bluegrass and western swing fans.

Wise continued this pattern for the remainder of his life as an active musician although bouts with ill health sometimes sidelined him for weeks at a time. In 1984, he returned to Florida with intentions of retiring, but continued fiddling as long his physical condition permitted. In the 1990s he recorded two compact discs of fiddle music for Pinecastle. *Wise in Nashville* and *An American Original*, neither with bluegrass backing, demonstrated that he still had the touch. Wise died several weeks after his eightieth birthday on January 6, 1996.

In retrospect, one may recognize that as the fiddler with Bill Monroe's band during the formative years of bluegrass is alone enough to make the name of Chubby Wise remembered. However, other contributions may also be noted. He possibly helped Ervin Rouse compose "Orange Blossom Special" which must certainly rank as the most original fiddle tune of the twentieth century. He also spent fifty years as one of the more durable sidemen and featured fiddlers in bluegrass and country music.

SELECTED RECORDINGS

Chubby Wise: In Nashville. Pinecastle PRC 1031, 1994.
Chubby Wise: An American Legend. Pinecastle PRC 1041, 1995.

Chubby Wise's recordings with Bill Monroe are on *Bill Monroe: Blue Moon of Kentucky* Bear Family BCD 16399, 2002, and *The Essential Bill Monroe.* Columbia CK 52748, 1996. His country recordings with Hank Snow are on *Hank Snow: The Singing Ranger, Vol. 2.* Bear Family BCD 15476, 1990; *Hank Snow: The Thesaurus Transcriptions.* Bear Family BCD 15488, 1991; and *Hank Snow: The Singing Ranger, Vol. 3.* Bear Family BCD 15502, 1992.

Chubby Wise recorded a fiddle album on Starday with Hank Snow's Rainbow Ranch Boys in 1961 (SLP 154) and some twenty-one long play fiddle albums on the Texas-based Stoneway label during the 1970s and early 1980s (two of them twin fiddle albums with Howard Forrester) that are all out of print. He also recorded with Red Allen, Hylo Brown, Lester Flatt and Earl Scruggs, Hazel and Alice, Charlie Moore, Don Reno, and Mac Wiseman.

PART THREE

Husband and Wife Duets

Husband and wife duets gained tremendous popularity from the mid-1930s beginning with the team of Lulu Belle and Scotty Wiseman. This duo starred on the *National Barn Dance*—and later the *Midwestern Hayride*—made recordings, and even headlined motion pictures. They soon inspired others. While all but one of the couples profiled here fit closer to the traditional country mold, three had strong bluegrass overtones, one exclusively bluegrass.

James Roberts and Irene Amburgey married late in 1939 and soon became well-known by their stage names as James and Martha Carson. They attracted widespread fame from their spirited mandolin-guitar work on Atlanta and later Knoxville radio, rendering and rearranging gospel quartet numbers for two vocalists. First on White Church and then Capitol Records, their music spread to a national audience before their bitter split in 1951 after which Martha became a solo gospel singer while James continued in music, but outside the limelight.

Wilma Lee and Stoney Cooper also made their name in the days of radio at a variety of stations, chiefly at WWVA for a decade, ending in 1957, before they relocated to WSM and the *Grand Ole Opry*. Their repertoire was almost evenly split between sacred and secular songs. Some of their music could be described as virtual bluegrass, and after Stoney's passing in 1977, Wilma Lee's was almost totally bluegrass until she was felled by illness in 2000.

Molly O'Day, the stage name for Lois LaVerne Williamson, and Lynn Davis married in 1941 and split their recordings almost evenly between harmony duets and O'Day's solo vocals. The resonator guitar work by George "Speedy" Krise enhanced the instrumentation of their early Columbia recordings. Most of their best-known songs typified by "Tramp on the Street," "At the First Fall of Snow," "Matthew Twenty-Four," and "Poor Ellen Smith" all became bluegrass standards. After 1951, the Davises did only evangelistic work although they recorded a pair of long-play albums in the 1960s.

Like Lynn and Molly, Bonnie Lou and Buster Moore gained their greatest following in East Tennessee via radio and television in Knoxville and Johnson City. Their music straddled the fence between bluegrass and country. In later years, they worked nightly during the tourist season in Pigeon Forge, Tennessee, where thousands of tourists became acquainted with their tasteful brand of traditional and near-traditional music.

With the exception of a few songs that made use of a Scruggs-style banjo, Doc and Chickie Williams a.k.a. Andrew and Wanda Smik were strictly a traditional country team best known for their long association with WWVA radio and its long-running Saturday night *Jamboree*. They played a large number of older songs and many numbers written for their style. Their half century and more careers made them favorites with those who favored traditional styles throughout the rural northeast and southeastern Canada.

Finally, Joe and Stacy Isaacs play bluegrass totally although their duet is of fairly recent vintage. Joe, however, had been around much longer as a banjo picking sideman and as co-leader of the family award-winning bluegrass gospel group, The Isaacs. Of their duets, most notably their rendition of numbers like the George Jones-Melba Montgomery country classic, "We Must Have Been out of Our Minds," are as good as any ever sung. Meanwhile, the husband-wife tradition in bluegrass continues strong with such quality teams as Darin and Brooke Aldrich, Jim and Valerie Gabehart, and Kenny and Amanda Smith.

✂ James and Martha Carson

1918–2007 and 1921–2004

Commercial country gospel music came into its own during the decade of the forties. In the 1920s, such quartet groups as Smith's Sacred Singers, the Stamps Quartet, and the Vaughn Quartet had numerous sacred releases in the old-time tune catalogs. In the 1930s, however, secular duets like the Monroe Brothers and the Blue Sky Boys, with their mandolin instrumentation and harmony vocals, gave an exciting new dimension to the many gospel songs within their repertoires. The transition from brother teams to a male-female duo seemed complete with the union of James and Martha Carson in 1939.

The elder half of this legendary duet was born James William Roberts near Richmond, Kentucky, on February 10, 1918. His father Philip Roberts soon gained local fame and world renown as "Fiddlin' Doc" Roberts. Lovers of old-time fiddle music for the decade from 1925 went to record stores and Sears Roebuck catalogs to order their favorite fiddle tunes on disc by either Roberts or the Fiddlin' Doc Roberts Trio. The personnel of the latter included Doc's guitarist and vocalist Asa Martin from nearby Irvine and young James who made his first recordings at age ten.

While Doc Roberts is best remembered for his fiddle virtuosity, the trio under the name Martin and Roberts also recorded many vocals of old-time songs that are nearly as memorable. Asa Martin sang lead and played rhythm guitar while Doc Roberts picked a lead mandolin, and young James Roberts sang tenor harmony and also strummed guitar or mandolin. Thus, at the age of ten, James Roberts began a career as a recording artist that eventually placed his music on virtually every major record label. The trio recorded dozens of such well-known songs as "Little Box of Pine on the 7:29," "Dixie Home," "Lilly Dale," "East-Bound Train," and "Knoxville Girl" with Asa Martin and his father between 1928 and 1934. Young James

James and
Martha Carson,
WSB, Atlanta,
late 1940s.

Roberts did a few solo vocals, including such songs as "Duval County Blues" and "String Bean Mama" performed in a style much influenced by Cliff Carlisle and Jimmie Rodgers.

Like other pre-adolescent boys, James had a rather high-pitched voice in those days and recalled being a little embarrassed when folks used to ask Asa Martin the identity of the little girl who sang with him on records. The Doc Roberts Trio made no more recordings after 1934, but Doc and James had earlier gone off to Iowa to try their hand at radio for several months broadcasting for Georgie Porgie Breakfast Food. Doc preferred farm life in

Madison County, Kentucky, and young James, restless for a more adventurous life, enlisted in the U. S. Navy in November 1937. He spent some time as a crew member of the U. S. S. Mississippi, but a spinal injury cut his career short and led to his Navy discharge in 1939. Returning to Kentucky, he went to radio station WLAP in Lexington and joined Asa Martin and his Morning Roundup Gang.

A trio called the Sunshine Sisters was among the other acts affiliated with the *Morning Roundup*. Irene, Opal, and Bertha Amburgey had come from Neon, Kentucky, in mountainous Letcher County. Irene, who would subsequently become famous as Martha Carson, had been born on May 19, 1921. As a child she learned to play guitar and also to read shape notes, a skill that became quite useful in later years. She began displaying singing talent at age six and also learned to play the old-fashioned pump organ. Sisters Bertha and Opal developed their instrumental talents on fiddle and banjo, respectively. James had not been at WLAP long before he and Irene were married and he and the three sisters went to WHIS Bluefield, West Virginia, where they worked with a man named Joe Woods who had an aggregation of musicians known as the Pioneer Boys or the Pioneer Gang. James and Irene sang duets using mandolin and guitar accompaniment while the latter performed in a string band with her sisters in a style then being popularized by the Coon Creek Girls of Renfro Valley fame. In addition to daily radio programming, the musicians who worked for Woods played numerous shows and dances in the many coal camps of the WHIS listening area. James, who had learned a lot about mandolin picking from his father, learned even more from studying the techniques of young Paul Buskirk, already an acknowledged master of the instrument.

By the summer of 1940, James and Irene Roberts and her sisters had returned to Kentucky where they worked for John Lair at his developing *Renfro Valley Barn Dance* complex. The Amburgey Sisters became part of the Coon Creek Girls, being teamed with Lily May Ledford. Violet and Daisy had gone to Texas while Rosie was expecting a baby. James worked at a variety of non-musical chores such as helping park cars, but longed to get back into action.

His opportunity came that fall when Lair decided to send Aunt Ida Harper and the Amburgey girls to station WSB Atlanta where they became Aunt Hattie and the Hoot Owl Holler Girls. The sisters received new first names of Mattie, Martha, and Minnie. While James and Martha sang duets out on the road, *The Atlanta Constitution*, parent company of WSB, had a policy which prohibited husbands and wives from being employed at the station. Hank Penny, the leader of the Radio Cowboys band and a man with a flair for public relations, began referring to James as James Carson, a boy they had found tapping turpentine trees in South Georgia. A few months later when WSB changed their policy and permitted spouses to work at the station the duo became known as James and Martha Carson, a stage surname that would last much longer than either their duet or their marriage.

Although WSB had a popular daytime country show during the thirties dubbed the *Cross Roads Follies*, their night-time jamboree, the *WSB Barn Dance*, did not come into its own until the 1940s. James and Martha Carson became and remained one of the most popular and durable acts on the program. Known as the Barn Dance Sweethearts, the duet had an extremely loyal and popular following in Georgia and adjacent states. James Carson later recalled that several *Grand Ole Opry* stars told him that they could never draw as good a crowd if they were booked anywhere close to where James and Martha had been scheduled to appear.

One might ask what techniques this husband-wife mandolin-guitar duet used that made their gospel songs so appealing to their thousands of fans. Martha Carson's ability to read shape notes became highly useful. From that beginning, they worked up duet arrangements of songs in the Stamps-Baxter hymnals that had generally been designed for quartets. They added a few songs of their own such as "Man of Galilee," "Budded on Earth to Bloom in Heaven," and "When He Heard My Plea." Now and then they would throw in a secular song or James Carson would pick a fiddle tune on the mandolin to put a little more zip into their show. His mandolin dexterity coupled with Martha Carson's good looks and strong stage presence gave their duet an appreciated charismatic quality.

Although the Carsons built up their huge following during the World War II years, those same war-time conditions put some limitations on their musical activities. Gasoline rationing curtailed their travel to show dates and the shortages of shellac limited recording activities. Good treatment from the management at WSB allowed them to prosper and being based in a large growing city gave them more availability to live audiences than country acts in less favorable locales had.

Following the war, the Barn Dance Sweethearts finally got the opportunity to record. RCA Victor and some other companies had often held field sessions in Atlanta from 1923 on and RCA continued the practice after World War II ended. James Carson had been recruited by Victor to play mandolin on a session for Judie and Julie—the Jones Sisters—and someone suggested to A and R man Steve Sholes that he should sign James and Martha Carson to a Victor contract. Sholes reportedly shrugged off the advice by dismissing the duo as "a hopped-up Blue Sky Boys." Given the problems that the Blue Sky Boys experienced with Sholes, one might conclude that he was more attuned to the newer forms of country music than to the more traditional forms of the art.

As a result, James and Martha Carson recorded instead for the Kansas City–based White Church label (the firm also had a secular label, Red Barn). They had eight sides released, six of them in a three-record album set. These numbers dating from about 1946 probably represent the duo's finest work on record. The songs included a classic duet rendition of the quartet number "He Will Set Your Fields on Fire" and also a version of Buford Abner's "I Ain't Got Time." They also did some of their more memorable originals such as "The Man of Galilee," "When He Heard My Plea," "There's an Open Door Waiting for Me," and the spiritual-like "Got a Little Light (and I'm Gonna Let It Shine)." James Carson's original song "Budded on Earth to Bloom in Heaven" came from a tombstone inscription in a family cemetery near Richmond, Kentucky, where he had an infant sister buried. Country music historian Bill C. Malone considered the number among his personal favorites.

Another song recorded for White Church went on to become a bluegrass gospel standard, "The Sweetest Gift (A Mother's Smile)." J. B. Coates, a Mississippi gospel songwriter and singing school teacher, composed the number. The earliest versions on record seemed to have been the Carsons rendition and that of the Bailey Brothers which came out about the same time. The Blue Sky Boys recorded it for RCA Victor in 1949 and more recent versions on disc have featured the Seldom Scene as well as the Judds, Linda Ronstadt, and Emmylou Harris.

The next year saw few recordings being made anywhere because of the Petrillo ban of the American Federation of Musicians. However, not long after the ban terminated, Capitol Records signed the Barn Dance Sweethearts to a contract. The Carsons did their initial session for Capitol in the studios of the cross-town radio station WGST on March 31, 1949. The six numbers included re-cuts of the previously recorded "I Ain't Got Time" and "Budded on Earth." Other highlights from these sessions are the Cleavant Derricks classic, "When God Dips His Pen of Love in My Heart" and the J. B. Coates-Eugene Wright song, "I'll Shout and Shine." Carson added some especially fine mandolin licks to this spirited number which many connoisseurs of the music consider their finest effort. "Living in the Promised Land" and a rare temperance ballad from the 1870s entitled "Don't Sell Him Another Drink," collected by Vance Randolph in 1942 as "Don't Sell Him Any More Rum" rounded out the session.

Some four and one-half months later, the Carsons had another visit with Capitol in Atlanta. Ken Nelson added some background singers and handclappers to the recording which had the effect of diluting the musical purity while adding to the all-night gospel sing atmosphere. The extras included Tennessee and Smitty, the Smith Brothers, and various members of the Carroll Family. The only record released from the session, "Looking for a City" and "King Jesus (Spoke to Me)" proved to be one of their most popular. Two additional songs, "When Mother Read the Bible" and "Where Could I Go," remained in the Capitol vaults.

On December 4, 1949, the Barn Dance Sweethearts did their third session of the year. Ken Nelson continued the practice of using background singers and handclapping. The first released songs paired the old favorite "When I Reach that City on the Hill" with "Crossing over Jordan." A second disc featured "Heaven's Jubilee" backed by "Filled with Glory Divine." By the time James and Martha Carson concluded their third recording experience with Capitol, the Atlanta phase of their careers had about ended. The nine years spent at WSB and the *Barn Dance* had been professionally good to them. They had built up a huge following of listeners who had bought their sponsor's products, wrote thousands of fan letters, bought their records, and even named pets and children for them. In Jacksonville, Florida, a slightly older couple, John and Lucille Masters, the Dixie Sweethearts, managed to win considerable acclaim for themselves as a James and Martha-styled act before adding son Owen to the group and calling themselves the Masters Family. The Barn Dance Sweethearts had not only been the most popular act on the *WSB Barn Dance* and the daily *Barn Dance Party* programs, but on their own weekday show for the Vick Chemical Company. But as James recalled, the situation changed when WSB acquired a new station manager who began to complain that things were not right if a bunch of untrained hillbillies could make more money than he could. Within a few months, WSB ceased to be a leading station for country music acts that began an exodus to other airwave locales.

The *WSB Barn Dance* did not fold until 1952, but the Carsons left at the beginning of 1950. The February 18, 1950, issue of *Billboard* reported that James and Martha had "recently" moved to WNOX, Knoxville. With its popular daily *Mid-Day Merry-Go Round* and Saturday night *Tennessee Barn Dance* this 10,000-watt East Tennessee station had a roster of traditional country music stars that placed among the half-dozen best in the nation. James and Martha Carson fit well into the WNOX format and established themselves almost immediately. On June 18, 1950, the Barn Dance Sweethearts did a fifth session for Capitol, recording six additional numbers. One song from this date entitled "I Feel like Shouting" remains unreleased. Apparently it had been intended to be coupled with a recut version of "Got a Little Light," but for some reason it was not. In addition to the latter, new arrangements of "Man of Galilee" and "He Will Set Your Fields on Fire" appeared on this session as well as "We Will Rise and Shine" and the perennial favorite by Albert Brumley, "I'll Fly Away."

Back in Knoxville, the Carson marriage was unraveling. Although neither of the Carsons said much for publication on the subject, stress and tension had apparently been building for some time. By the time of their final session for Capitol on October 23, 1950, the pair had already separated. Five songs comprised their last professional effort. These included a song by the new singing and writing sensation Hank Williams, "I'm Gonna Sing, Sing, Sing," along with "Shining City," "I Ain't Gonna Sin No More," and "Lay Your Burden at His Feet." One song, "Salvation Has Been Brought Down," was coupled with "Got a Little Light" from the earlier session to become the final James and Martha Carson record release on September 17, 1951.

By that time, James Carson Roberts had been gone from Knoxville for many months. Late in 1950, he went to Wheeling, West Virginia, where he worked with Wilma Lee and Stoney Cooper's Clinch Mountain Clan. He accompanied them to Nashville where on December 18, 1950, he helped them to do a record session. Wilma Lee, Stoney, and James sang a trio on

"Mother's Prayers" and "Faded Love" while Carson also played mandolin on "The Golden Rocket" and "The Ghost Train." Shortly after this Nashville recording venture, Carson became a member of the staff band at WWVA. Meanwhile back in Knoxville, Martha Carson continued in show business working with Bill Carlisle and her sister and brother-in-law Mattie O'Neill a.k.a. Opal and Salty Holmes. She and Carlisle did a single record for Rich-R-Tone. Unlike James Carson, she had to bear some of the criticism and anger of local fans in a rural-dominated society where divorces were still uncommon. About this time, she wrote the song, "Satisfied," considering it a piece of divinely inspired comfort in a time of sorrow.

Although Martha Carson continued the liaison with Capitol records that the Barn Dance Sweethearts had initiated in 1949, she had trouble persuading them to let her do solo work. Fred Rose, much impressed with "Satisfied," finally talked Nelson into allowing her to record as a single artist. In the meantime, Martha Carson did some session work as a part of the Carlisles, the work representing some of her lesser-known musical activity. Yet she was the female vocalist in a trio that cut four sessions on Mercury Records. The vocalists consisting of Bill and Cliff Carlisle together with Martha Carson who cut one of the best-known Carlisle songs: "Too Old to Cut the Mustard." And then Martha and Bill Carlisle along with Martha and Roy Sneed did the vocal work on their biggest hit, "No Help Wanted."

After Martha recorded "Satisfied" solo for Capitol in November 1951, she gained increasing recognition as an individual performer. As a result, she moved to Nashville and became a member of the *Grand Ole Opry*. Continuing to record for Capitol, she did more than two dozen songs for them including "I'm Gonna Walk and Talk with My Lord," "Old Blind Barnabas," "Crying Holy Unto the Lord," "Fear Not," and "There's a Higher Power." The songs mostly fit into a pattern of up-tempo spirituals and spiritual-like numbers that had been established with "Satisfied."

Although Martha Carson vowed to never again record as a duet act, she did do some recording with her sisters—as Mattie, Marthie, and Minnie on King in 1951 and as the Amber Sisters on Capitol in 1952 and 1953. Some numbers tended to be in a more contemporary country vein while others had more of the old-time sound reminiscent of the Coon Creek Girls that originally brought the Amburgey Sisters to commercial prominence. Opal had gone on to some fame in country music circles first as Mattie O'Neill and then as Jean Chapel while Bertha married Ducky Woodruff of Bluebird Record's Woodruff Brothers and retired from music. In this period Martha toured with many of the contemporary *Opry* acts including Faron Young, Little Jimmy Dickens, and Ferlin Husky. She also met and toured some with a young Elvis Presley. Some years later, the rock and roll superstar told some of the Jordanaires that Martha Carson was a major inspiration upon his own act.

Martha Carson remarried to a musical booker and promoter named Xavier Cosse. The couple subsequently had two sons, Rene Paul and Andre Michael. About this time a fad hit the pop music world for what became known as "religioso" or pop semi-gospel music in the vein of Stuart Hamblen's "This Ole House." Martha signed with RCA Victor and both Cosse and Steve Sholes believed that the strong-voiced lady singer could score well with this potential market. As a result, her Victor sessions were conducted in Hollywood and New York with a big band and vocal chorus accompaniment. Although many of the songs seemed similar to those cut for Capitol, the arrangements showed that Victor aimed them toward what would later be termed the crossover market. A few numbers such as "Dixieland Roll" and "Music Drives Me Crazy (Especially Rock and Roll)" had virtually nothing in common with gospel music except the dynamic Martha Carson style of delivery.

Not long after Martha Carson moved to Nashville, James Carson left Knoxville and went to Wheeling, West Virginia. He spent nearly two years at WWVA working as part of the staff band that took the name Country Harmony Boys. Other members of this group included Roy Scott, Will Carver, Gene Jenkins, and Monte Blake. As he later wrote, "I played guitar, mandolin, and bass fiddle, whichever was needed on the program." While in West Virginia Carson married Pearl Arman. They had two children, Anna Marie and Phillip. At one time or another, he worked show dates with Hawkshaw Hawkins, Roy Scott, and most of the other *World's Original Jamboree* acts.

Upon returning to Knoxville, James Carson went to work with the Cas Walker Entertainers on radio, television, and various promotional activities advertising the Cas Walker Supermarkets. He worked on the Walker shows for several years during which time he played mandolin on a couple of 1954 record sessions for Cousin Ezra Cline's Lonesome Pine Fiddlers on

RCA Victor Records. More significantly for his own career as a singer and writer, he did three sessions with the Masters Family on Columbia Records in March and October 1954, and on April 30, 1956. Johnny Masters had throat problems on the first sessions and James Carson had the lead vocals. They did a new arrangement of "When He Heard My Plea" and also some of Carson's newer originals such as "It Takes a Lot of Lovin' to Get to Heaven," "Coming to Carry Me Home," "Everlasting Joy," and "I Wasn't There (But I Wish I Could Have Been)." The latter two as compositions probably rank in quality with some of the best numbers from the James and Martha Carson days or with Martha Carson's original songs. James Carson also wrote a gospel song which the Webster Brothers recorded entitled "That Great Eternal Singing" and a secular lyric entitled "Let's Go Bunny Huggin'" which Sonny James cut on Capitol and aimed at the teenage market.

By 1958, Martha Carson and her husband had returned to Nashville and her more familiar base in country-gospel music. During the time she spent in New York, she had the opportunity to be on some network television programs including those of Steve Allen, Ray Bolger, and Arlene Francis. She also appeared in some big supper clubs where she typically brought down the house with her rousing arrangement of "Swing Down Chariots." Still she felt more at home with a more traditional country audience. She already had a reputation and a following as an established country entertainer and the folks who had enjoyed her songs like "Satisfied" and "I'm Gonna Walk and Talk With My Lord" appreciated her dynamic spiritual numbers as much as ever.

Martha Carson recorded a single for Cadence in 1959 and another one for Dot in 1961. Martha did long play albums for Sims and Scripture during the early sixties. RCA Camden kept some of her Victor material in print for several years and Capitol released albums of her earlier singles. Her Gusto album release *Martha Carson's Greatest Gospel Hits* appeared in 1978. Slowly, she began to attain a well-deserved status as a near legendary figure in country and gospel music.

From the early 1960s, James Carson moved out of an active music career into other occupations including piano tuning and service station management. By the early seventies, he had returned to Lexington, Kentucky, although he still made periodic visits to musical friends in the Atlanta and

Knoxville areas. Scholars sought his knowledge of the early days of recorded music because of his connections with Doc Roberts and Asa Martin as well as his own varying experiences in radio. He appeared at an occasional folk festival at Berea College and elsewhere. In 1982, James and his neighbor Esco Hankins played with other Knoxville country music personalities at the World's Fair. In 1984, he toured the Netherlands with the Dutch musical duo A. G. and Kate and saw an EP release of some of his earlier recordings entitled *Historic Tracks* on the European Strictly Country label. About that time, a limited collector's edition of twenty of their classic duets called *James and Martha: Early Gospel Greats* appeared on the ACM label.

In 1986, the prestigious Bear Family label in Germany released an album of Martha's Victor material from the mid-fifties. Entitled *Martha Carson Explodes,* it gave younger country music fans an opportunity to appreciate the dynamism Martha put into her music during her heyday. The album contained sixteen numbers.

Although James and Martha never reconciled, time eventually caught up with both of them as well as their spouses. Pearl Arman Roberts died after suffering several months from a brain tumor. James married a third time as an octogenarian, before dying on June 21, 2007. Xavier Cosse died in November 1990. Allegedly leaving Martha "drowning in debt," reportedly with the aid of her elder son "she survived the sea of red ink." Following a bout of ill health, she died in Nashville on December 16, 2004.

In 1985, both James and Martha were inducted into the Atlanta Country Music Hall of Fame. Many later generations of musicians including the Lewis Family have remarked of the influence of the Barn Dance Sweethearts. Those with a broad perspective in country music ranked them with the Blue Sky Boys, the Louvin Brothers, and the Monroe Brothers as one of the great country duet acts of all time and with Lulubelle and Scotty as one of the great male-female duets. The British Archive of Country Music in 2006 and 2007 released two compact discs containing their duets as well as some of Martha's solo numbers (and inadvertently a Masters Family song). Their niche in the annals of country and gospel music history would seem secure. In retrospect, one can say that although their marriage did not endure, their music has stood the test of time.

SELECTED RECORDINGS

James Roberts and Martha Carson: I'm Gonna Let It Shine. BACM CD D 161, 2006.
Martha Carson featuring James Roberts: I'll Shout and Shine. BACM CD D 204, 2007.
  Contains the four remaining James and Martha duets, one by the Masters Family (as
  the Dixie Sweethearts), and the rest solo numbers by Martha.

James Roberts (a.k.a. James Carson) also recorded with Asa Martin, the Fiddling Doc
Roberts Trio, Wilma Lee and Stoney Cooper, the Lonesome Pine Fiddlers, the Masters
Family, the Jones Sisters, and under his own name. Martha also recorded with her sisters
as Minnie, Mattie, and Martha, and as the Amber Sisters in addition to under her own
name and with the Carlisles.

✂ Wilma Lee and Stoney Cooper

1921–2011 and 1918–1977

One of the most influential and significant traditional country music duos with a repertoire containing generous amounts of sacred and sentimental inspirational material along with traditional secular songs was the husband-wife team of Wilma Lee and Stoney Cooper. From the time of their marriage in 1941 until the latter's death in 1977, the pair slowly and surely—via radio, records and show-dates—carved their niche in the annals of music. Along the way they helped to immortalize such songs as "Thirty Pieces of Silver," "Legend of the Dogwood Tree," "Walking My Lord up Calvary Hill," "Each Season Changes You," and "Sunny Side of the Mountain." Following her husband's passing, Wilma Lee Cooper continued along the same musical trail that she and Stoney had earlier blazed together.

Their story began in Randolph County, West Virginia, a large mountainous region in the northern part of a state known for its rugged terrain. At the turn of the twentieth century, this county served as residence for two nationally known political figures. Senator Henry Gassaway Davis ran as the Democratic candidate for Vice President in 1904 and incidentally owned the original estate known as Graceland. His son-in-law, Republican Senator Stephen Elkins, authored significant pieces of progressive legislation. Not long after the sun had set on the careers of these two statesmen a pair of musicians who would make their marks in another field of history were born in Randolph County.

Dale Troy Cooper was born in Harman on October 16, 1918. A high ridge of mountains separated Harman from the remainder of Randolph County. The Cooper family furnished a variety of teachers and local officeholders to the village and also a musician or two. Dale Cooper's oldest brother had been a country fiddler who played for local square dances. The younger sibling learned to play guitar and clawhammer banjo, but he, too, favored the

Wilma Lee and Stoney
Cooper, WSM, Nashville,
Grand Ole Opry, 1958.

fiddle, receiving inspiration both from his brother and via radio from the
Grand Ole Opry favorite Fiddlin' Arthur Smith.

Meanwhile, some forty miles away in the upper Tygart River community
of Valley Head, another person had entered the world who would become
a significant musician. Wilma Leigh Leary had been born on February 7,
1921, to Jacob and Lola Ware Leary. Later the Learys had two more daughters, Geraldine a.k.a. Jerry and Peggy. Gospel music played an important
role in the Leary household and the entire family learned to sing from the
paperback shape-note hymnals sold by such firms as Winsett, Rodeheaver,
Stamps-Baxter, and James D. Vaughn. Lola Leary played the pump organ
and taught Wilma that instrument, too. However, her father later bought
Wilma a mail-order guitar from the Chicago School of Music.

When the family began to play at church-related events and other social
gatherings, the guitar was their only accompaniment. In a sense, their music and style developed somewhat similar to, but independent of, the Chuck
Wagon Gang whose recordings and radio broadcasts from Fort Worth,

Texas, had not yet penetrated the Tygart Valley. At first the Learys sang only for the satisfaction of themselves and their neighbors. In 1938, they won a local talent contest and, subsequently, represented West Virginia at the National Folk Festival. The girls began to sing more than just gospel songs. It has seldom been noted that their most significant Library of Congress recording was "Old Black Mountain Trail," probably learned from a 1935 Patsy Montana recording. At any rate, the Leary Family became radio entertainers at station WSVA in Harrisonburg, Virginia.

As the Learys shifted their musical base from the family parlor to the outside world, Fiddlin' Dale Cooper made his initial entry into the world of entertainment. Finishing high school in the spring of 1937, he joined a band known as Rusty Hiser and the Green Valley Boys at WMMN in Fairmont, West Virginia. Although the band did not exactly make a commercial success, young Cooper gained a great deal of experience on the fiddle and also learned vocal parts. When the group switched their base of operation from Fairmont to Lynchburg, Virginia, their financial situation went from marginal to awful and by the spring of 1938, they disbanded and Cooper returned to Harman where he farmed with his dad and brother.

That fall Dale received a postcard from Jacob Leary offering him a job with the band. He and his brother went to Seneca Caverns to see the family play. Offered ten dollars a week plus room and board, Cooper took the position. From their radio home at Harrisonburg, Virginia, the Leary Family worked personal appearances up and down the Shenandoah Valley and adjacent portions of eastern West Virginia. In addition to the family quintets, sisters' trio, and fiddle tunes, Wilma Lee Leary began doing duet numbers with the young fiddler who by this time had acquired the nickname Stoney. Known as "The Singing Pals," the couple became quite popular in the Harrisonburg listening area. At first they did primarily secular songs, leaving the sacred numbers for the entire group. The Singing Pals also pursued courtship, romance, and marriage in 1941. Music and courtship did not occupy all of Wilma Lee's time, however, since she also managed to complete high school and attend Davis and Elkins College (named for the aforementioned politicians as well as the city) in Elkins, West Virginia. This ranked her among the better-educated country musicians of her generation.

In 1941, the Leary Family relocated to WWVA Wheeling. The following March, Wilma Lee Cooper gave birth to daughter Carol Lee and for a time the couple stopped performing. Stoney Cooper went to work for a soft drink distributor. After a few months, however, the pair obtained a new radio job at KMMJ Grand Island, Nebraska, where they did several daily programs, alternating shows with another couple, Ben and Jessie Mae Norman, for whom Stoney sometimes played fiddle. Wilma Lee did typing to help earn a few extra dollars. Later the Leary Family also came to Grand Island and the entire group worked together again, moving to WIBC Indianapolis in the summer of 1943.

Just before the end of that year, the Coopers accepted an offer to bring their duet to WJJD Chicago as a replacement for Bob Atcher and Bonnie Blue Eyes. With their early morning *Breakfast Time* program and the early evening *Suppertime Frolic*, the duo had one of the largest potential audiences in the entire Midwest. The Cooper tenure proved to be brief. A labor dispute led to a strike. This forced Stoney to find work at a defense plant in Gary, Indiana, and WJJD eventually decided to phase out live talent in favor of phonograph records, a trend which later hit most stations for a somewhat different reason, namely the impact of television. This overall situation led the young couple back to West Virginia and the locale where Stoney had pioneered his radio musicianship, WMMN Fairmont.

Their Indianapolis-Chicago experience, albeit brief, made a noteworthy impact upon their style. The immense popularity of Roy Acuff at the *Grand Ole Opry* opened the door for strong voiced lady singers who could sing the type of sacred and sentimental mountain stylings associated with the King of Country Music. Meanwhile Cooper learned to play a National steel guitar to provide appropriate instrumentation along with vocal harmony. Somewhat unknown to the Coopers at that time, a young lady from Pike County, Kentucky, performing at WHAS Louisville experienced a somewhat similar circumstance. Known as Molly O' Day, she performed such songs as "Tramp on the Street" and "Matthew Twenty-Four." Sharing in part a common audience, radio listeners requested these songs and others from both singers and both repertoires. As a result, such numbers as "Tramp on the Street" became linked with both Wilma Lee Cooper and Molly O'Day. The fact that they sounded somewhat similar and both could do numbers with clawhammer banjo further linked them. Oddly enough, the two vocalists who shared style and songs never formally met although they eventually became friends via correspondence.

In Fairmont, the Coopers won quick acceptance since radio fans in that part of West Virginia had some prior acquaintance with them. They also began to add a band to their entourage. Abner Cole, a bass player from Mannington, and Floyd Kirkpatrick, a steel player from Chicago, constituted the sidemen. Somewhat later an additional vocalist named Yodeling Joe Lambert, who did some songs in a different style, became a fifth member of the group. When the territory around Fairmont had been played out, Wilma Lee and Stoney Cooper relocated to station KLCN Blytheville, Arkansas. Lambert continued with them for a brief time and Cole for a longer period.

Not too long after the Coopers arrived in Arkansas they attracted another band member who remained with them off and on for many years. Bill Carver of Grenada, Mississippi, joined them alternating on mandolin and either Dobro or electric steel. Johnny Johnson, who worked for many years as a sideman with the Coopers, Flatt and Scruggs, and other groups, first worked with them in Blytheville, too. Subsequently, he was married to Wilma Lee's sister Jerry. Carol Lee also began to occasionally perform with her parents who called their group the Blues Chasers in those days.

In March 1947, the Cooper family moved to WWNC Asheville, North Carolina. This station was more hemmed in by mountains and covered less territory than Stoney had hoped. As a result, their stay in "wonderful Western North Carolina" was briefer than they had anticipated. Nonetheless, they met Jim Stanton of the small Rich-R-Tone record company and encountered their first opportunity to make discs. The initial sessions conducted in the WWNC studios that summer included four gospel titles among the ten released sides (two sides remained unreleased until 2007). They were Bill Monroe's "Wicked Path of Sin," Roy Acuff's "This World Can't Stand Long," "Tramp on the Street," and "Matthew Twenty-Four." In the case of the latter lyrics, Wilma Lee Cooper's recording was made before Molly O'Day's Columbia version. "Tramp on the Street" made the greater impact and Jim Stanton later recalled that it ranked with the Stanley Brothers' "Little Glass of Wine" as his label's biggest seller. Secular songs cut at the two sessions included Victorian sentimental numbers such as "The Little Rosewood Casket," "Two Little Orphans," and "Girl in the Blue Velvet Band."

However, by the time any of the Rich-R-Tone material had been released, Wilma Lee and Stoney found another position, this one back at the now

50,000 watt WWVA in Wheeling. For the next decade the *World's Original Jamboree* was their home. With their band, the Clinch Mountain Clan, they attained a wide following via the daily programs and Saturday night *Jamboree* through the rural northeast USA and Canada. With a sound built around the acoustical instrumentation that had worked well for Roy Acuff, the Coopers even received recognition from the Harvard Library of Music where a committee named them "the most authentic mountain singing group in America."

Most of their fans, however, came not from the academic ranks, but from rural and working class folks who traditionally constituted the backbone of country music audiences. Their recordings also attracted the attention of Fred Rose who had sufficient connections with Art Satherley to get them a contract with Columbia Records. However, the musician's union had imposed a ban through most of 1948 so no sessions could be arranged until April 8, 1949, when the Clinch Mountain Clan journeyed to the now legendary Castle Studio in Nashville's Tulane Hotel. Over two days they cut eight numbers, half sacred and half secular. Mac Odell's "Thirty Pieces of Silver" comprised the main number that would become an all-time favorite. The most memorable secular numbers, "No One Now," "Willy Roy, the Crippled Boy," "Moonlight on West Virginia," and "On the Banks of the River" had inspirational undertones. In addition to Ab Cole on bass and Bill Carver on Dobro, Blaine Stewart, a fine mandolin picker from New Martinsville, West Virginia, helped fill out their fine acoustical sound.

This pattern resumed in later sessions for Columbia. In May 1950, they did the classic "Legend of the Dogwood Tree," the chorus of which had been written by fellow *Jamboree* artist Juanita Moore of Lee and Juanita and an original sacred cut of their own, "The Message Came Special," plus the lovely mother song "The White Rose." That December they revived a World War II song which featured a trio with James Carson singing the third part and playing mandolin on "Mother's Prayer," a sacred mother-war lyric that had earlier been recorded by Eddy Arnold. Other numbers featured an electric lead guitar played by Gene Jenkins. Their May session also proved to be the first of several that featured Tex Logan on fiddle. The latter, a Texas boy who eventuallly obtained a Ph.D. from the Massachusetts Institute of Technology, played a super hillbilly fiddle, and composed the bluegrass holiday classic, "Christmas Time's a Comin'." Other 1950 Columbia offerings from the Coopers included covers of other country hits such as "Faded Love" and "The Golden Rocket." Another number, "The Ghost Train," had been written by Uncle Jim O'Neal who later became the founder and owner of Rural Rhythm Records.

By 1951, they had acquired a new Dobro-mandolin player, Josh Graves, who went on to become one of the most famous sidemen ever as a result of the many years he spent picking the "Old Hound Dog" for Lester Flatt and Earl Scruggs. Wilma Lee told an interesting story about how Graves had not had much experience out of the country when he first joined the Clinch Mountain Clan and experienced a little culture shock one day when the group stopped to eat at an Italian restaurant in Fairmont. Stoney remarked that the spaghetti sauce did not come up to its usual standard that day. Graves leaned over and said "Mr. Stoney, I think their bread is a little bit stale, too," having never encountered this type of bread before.

From 1951 onward, Wilma Lee and Stoney Cooper recorded somewhat less gospel material than before, but still managed to do a couple of sacred sides per year starting with "I'm Taking My Audition (to Sing Up in the Sky)" and "Walking My Lord Up Calvary Hill." The former song came from the regionally legendary radio trio of Cap, Andy and Flip whom they had known in Fairmont and the second a new composition by Ruby Moody, a Knoxville, Tennessee, nurse. The latter perhaps became their most re-quested number and one which they subsequently recorded again in 1958 and 1973. Originally they did the chorus as a straight harmony duet, but at some point altered the arrangement so that Stoney "lined out" the chorus in a commercialized form of an "old-time" Baptist practice. This made this particular story-song of the crucifixion one of the most appealing in the entire genre.

Three of the more memorable secular Cooper songs from 1951 rank as outstanding. The first "Stoney (Are You Mad at Your Gal)" reversed the roles in the 1946 Cousin Emmy song "Ruby (Are You Mad at Your Man)." The second atypical for their style, "West Virginia Polka," had been writ-ten for them by the Louvin Brothers and had lasting appeal. Finally, a cover version of a song initially popularized by *Jamboree* favorites Big Slim McAuliffe and then Hawkshaw Hawkins, "Sunnyside of the Mountain," was a memorable arrangement featuring Tex Logan and Stoney Cooper playing outstanding twin fiddles.

Later Columbia recordings by Wilma Lee and Stoney did not have the impact of their earlier numbers. Sacred songs did all right typified by "Are You Walking and Talking for the Lord" and "You Can't Take It with You" were adequate, but songs like "Bamboozled" and "Don't Play that Song (on the Juke Box Tonight)" were better forgotten. Stoney Cooper became interested in looking for a new record label.

In 1955, the Clinch Mountain Clan switched recording allegiance to Hickory, a new label established by Acuff-Rose who sandwiched the event between song folios published for the label. The initial sessions that year included some of their best numbers, "Each Season Changes You," a revival of the Bailes Brothers' "I Want to Be Loved," and "I've Been Cheated Too." A little later, they remade "Tramp on the Street" and the new arrangement of "Walking My Lord Up Calvary Hill" with Stoney lining out the chorus. By this time an element of bluegrass via the banjo of Johnny Clark and also a touch of more modern country via an electric lead guitar often played by Chet Atkins began being heard on their discs.

As a result, on January 12, 1957, they received an invitation to join the *Grand Ole Opry*, becoming members on February 1, 1957. The early years in Nashville ushered in an era when Wilma Lee and Stoney Cooper made their biggest impact on the national country music scene. Three songs—"Come Walk with Me," "Big Midnight Special," and "There's a Big Wheel"—all became major country hits and led to appearances on network television. Although not a gospel song as such, "There's a Big Wheel" carried a religious message of sorts and their live shows featured a great deal of sacred material. Daughter Carol Lee Cooper, by now a teenager, worked with them in this era until her 1958 marriage to Jimmy Snow, singer-guitarist and son of Hank Snow. They recorded a number of gospel albums during the years of their marriage. George McCormick became a regular fixture with the Clinch Mountain Clan in those years.

The country music industry increasingly focused on the album market in the early 1960s and Wilma Lee and Stoney Cooper found more opportunities to do more sacred songs. The album *Family Favorites* cut in December 1961 and March 1962 included re-cuts not only of "Matthew Twenty-Four," "Legend of the Dogwood Tree," and "Thirty Pieces of Silver," but also covers of six semi-sacred tearjerker lyrics previously associated with the then retired Molly O'Day, all in the Acuff-Rose catalog. In a single session on

January 29, 1963, the Coopers did their first all gospel album *Songs of Inspiration* which Hickory released a couple of months later. With the exception of a remake of "This World Can't Stand Long," none of the material had been done by the duo before. It ranged from old standards like "The Wayworn Traveler" to Louvin Brother songs such as "Keep Your Eyes on Jesus." Unfortunately, this album was not as well distributed as some of the earlier Hickory material and became the last gospel music they cut for nearly a decade with the exception of a 1964 rendition of "This Train" which constituted one side of their last Hickory single.

In 1965, Wilma Lee and Stoney Cooper signed with Decca, remaining on that label for the rest of the decade. Most of these sessions tried reconciling their mountain style to the Nashville Sound. There were no gospel cuts and only one old classic tearjerker among them, "A Hero's Death." A couple of heart songs from the forties came off mildly successful as did the recitation "History Repeats Itself." A newer topical song "Three Widows," about the Kennedy assassination, did not really click. One can also say in defense of the Decca sessions that some of them coincided with Stoney not being in the best of health. He had a heart attack in early 1963 and wasn't up to par for several years. During Stoney Cooper's initial convalescence, both Coopers became closely acquainted with the more tender-hearted side of Hawkshaw Hawkins, a friend since their days in Wheeling. The lanky honkytonk singer helped nurse his old buddy back to health, even preparing chicken soup for him. It saddened them very much when Hawkins died in a March 1963 airplane crash.

When Wilma Lee and Stoney Cooper had another opportunity to record in the early seventies, they immediately did two gospel albums. In October 1972, they cut an LP for Skylite billed as a tribute to Roy Acuff although only the title song "The Great Speckled Bird" could really be identified with him. The other ten songs varied from archaic standards such as "Amazing Grace" to bluegrass classics such as "I'm Using My Bible for a Roadmap" to the then brand new "Me and Jesus" by Tom T. Hall. The second album, cut fourteen months later, consisted primarily of new versions of earlier favorites, but a few had not been done by the couple before such as "Give Me the Roses While I Live" and Molly O'Day's "I'm Going Home on the Morning Train." Released on Gusto's Power Pak label under the title *Walking My Lord Up Calvary's Hill*, this album received wide distribution and gave many younger fans their first opportunity to hear the near legendary duo in action.

In the mid-1970s they did a Carter Family tribute album for Gusto which contained three gospel cuts—"Keep on the Firing Line," "On the Rock Where Moses Stood," and "God Gave Noah the Rainbow Sign." For good measure they also included a pair of mother songs, "Hello Central Give Me Heaven" and "Picture on the Wall." Signing with Rounder Records gave them a chance to record authentic oldies and they made the best of it, doing sixteen numbers which were sufficient for one and a half albums. These included four old-time gospel pieces. Wilma Lee had learned "I'm a Private in the Army of the Lord" during their brief stay at Chicago and they performed "He Will Set Your Fields on Fire" as part of the Leary Family although Stoney had known versions of the song going back to his childhood at the Church of the Brethren in Harman. The other two numbers came from the early radio days in West Virginia as "Star-Lit Heaven" originated with Cap, Andy, and Flip and "Heaven Express" with Cowboy Loye Pack. Doc Williams had also performed it at WWVA.

All this time Wilma Lee and Stoney Cooper remained active on the *Grand Ole Opry* and also on the road as much as Stoney's health permitted. Bill Carver came back after a long absence and worked with them again. George McCormick remained with them off and on, too, appearing on most record sessions as did daughter Carol Lee. Stoney continued to have periodic heart problems and entered the hospital again on February 4, 1977, remaining there until his death on March 22.

Wilma Lee decided to continue on by herself keeping a band together generally built around banjo, Dobro and fiddle. Sidemen included top-notch fiddlers like Woody Paul, Tater Tate, and Zeke Dawson; banjoists such as Marty Lanham and Mike Lattimore; and folks like Gene Wooten and Tim Graves, a nephew of Buck Graves, on dobro. She maintained a sound somewhat similar to that of the Clinch Mountain Clan in their vintage years albeit perhaps a little more bluegrass flavored. Jerry Johnson had also rejoined her sister's act, adding comedy to the show. As Howdy Forrester remarked one night at the *Opry*, "Wilma Lee, you still have the sound" which he contended was built primarily around her strong lead voice. Wilma Lee Cooper finished the second Rounder album that included one new sacred song, "Far Beyond the Starry Sky." Her 1979 album for Leather contained "A

Daisy a Day;" her 1981 Rebel effort included "Honey in the Rock" and a new arrangement of the sentimental mother song, "The White Rose" originally cut in 1950 which served as the title cut.

Wilma Lee Cooper and the Clinch Mountain Clan continued to appear regularly on the *Grand Ole Opry* and worked the road as well, particularly at bluegrass festivals during the summer months. In later years she was given the title "First Lady of Bluegrass Music." She continued with only slightly diminished activity until she suffered a career-ending stroke on the *Opry* stage in 2001. Nonetheless, made of the tough fiber that has long characterized Appalachian women, Wilma Lee lived for another decade, dying on September 13, 2011, at the age of ninety. Meanwhile in 2007, Bear Family Records released a box-set *Big Midnight Special* that contained the Coopers' entire Rich-R-Tone, Columbia, and Hickory catalog.

Despite her near-legendary status as a vocal interpreter of mountain, sacred, and country heart songs, Wilma Lee remained a sincere down-home, unassuming person. Like her contemporaries Molly O'Day and Rose Maddox, Wilma Lee Cooper rose to prominence as part of a family-oriented musical group on the strength of an unusually powerful voice with a deep ring of sincerity in it that possessed an ability to reach the human heart. Cowboy Copas, who did a pretty decent job on songs like "The Purple Robe," once told Stoney Cooper that no number he had ever heard could really penetrate the inner soul as much as their rendition of "Walking My Lord Up Calvary Hill." Stoney told "Cope" that he had a similar reaction when they recorded it. It was this characteristic that made them and their music so significant to those who appreciate the traditional sounds. As Tony Russell wrote about Wilma Lee in a perceptive obituary, "in both her professionalism and the integrity of her music she stoutly represented the role women had fought to achieve in country music during her lifetime."

SELECTED RECORDINGS

Wilma Lee and Stoney Cooper: Big Midnight Special. Bear Family BCD 16751, 2007. Contains all the Rich-R-Tone, Columbia, and Hickory recordings.
Wilma Lee Cooper: Classic Country Favorites. Rebel REB CD 1122, 1990. Recordings made after Stoney died.

ᴖ Joe and Stacy Isaacs

1947– and 1969–

Joe Isaacs has been playing bluegrass music for fifty years. From the mid-1960s when he started picking the banjo in the clubs of southwest Ohio to the seventies when he turned to bluegrass gospel which eventually evolved into the widely acclaimed family group, The Isaacs, Joe Isaacs has been a significant presence. For the past eighteen years, he has kept a lower profile and traveled less, but still writes quality songs and makes fine music often with musical partner and wife Stacy.

Joe Isaacs was born in Jackson County, Kentucky, on January 24, 1947. Joe was the youngest in a family of seventeen, three of whom died in infancy or early childhood. The Reverend Godfrey Isaacs and his wife Bessie Isaacs lived the old-fashioned way in a log cabin he had built without electricity, running water, indoor plumbing, or a telephone. Rev. Isaacs supplemented his meager income from preaching with farming and blacksmith work. Their transportation was provided by a jolt-wagon. While this manner of lifestyle was becoming obsolete even in the mountains, Joe Isaacs's parents practiced it until their respective deaths in 1985 and 1987. Their simple faith and plain living provided Joe with inspiration for many of his original songs. His daughter, Sonya Isaacs, has placed a touching tribute to her grandparents on The Isaacs website. Joe reports that his oldest living sister Edna occupies the old homestead and lives in the same manner by choice although he says that she had a fine modern home when she lived in Ohio.

Isaacs's fond memories of his youth did not include much cash as what money he could earn through such labor as picking blackberries went for necessities like shoes. While the household contained a wind-up phonograph—termed a Victrola or gramophone—with some old country records, money for items like a musical instrument was beyond his means. Joe learned the

Joe and Stacy
Isaacs, 2011. *Photo
by Vicki Miller.*

basics that much of his generation in that time and place absorbed—what
was termed the "Three R's: readin' 'ritin' and the road to Ohio."

Jackson County is not far from U. S. Highway 25, the Dixie Highway,
later paralleled by Interstate 75. Numerous young people from the hills and
mountains of Eastern Kentucky traveled it, migrating to seek employment.
A byproduct of this trek was enriching the musical culture of southwest
Ohio that could scarcely have been imagined when these journeys com-
menced during the Great Depression and continued for over a half-century.
In 1964, young Joe Isaacs became a part of it, going to Lebanon, Ohio. He
worked in construction and also in a garage.

With some of his earnings, Joe initially purchased a Sears-Roebuck guitar, and then a Sonny Osborne model Vega five-string banjo. He learned a

few basic chords from another aspiring teenage musician, Larry Sparks. Isaacs took to music and the strings as they say "like a duck takes to water." Within a month he was playing in a band. Young musicians were numerous in the area. In addition to Isaacs and Sparks, they included Roy Lee Centers and Fred Spencer who performed together as the Lee Brothers, Lloyd Hensley, Buck Parker, and Lee Allen. Older pickers included Noah Crase and Jack Lynch among others. Red Allen and Frank Wakefield were in and out of the area and the Osborne Brothers had recently left for the *Grand Ole Opry*. On WPFB in Middletown, Paul Mullins spun the discs of Isaacs's favorites, the Stanley Brothers, and other notable bluegrass bands and traditional country acts such as the Louvin Brothers. Bluegrass was played in the club scene in nearby cities such as Cincinnati, Dayton, Hamilton, and Middletown. For those who preferred the sacred to the secular, J. D. Jarvis, Tommy Crank, and Zeke Hoskins & the Country Gospel Aires could be heard in local churches. Both types could mix and mingle in locales like Chautauqua Park in Franklin where Joe first met Carter Stanley in 1965.

The off-and-on, in-and-out team of Red Allen and Frank Wakefield also frequented the Dayton area. In February 1967, the latter recruited Isaacs to come to New York City and become one of the Greenbriar Boys. This first sojourn to the Big Apple lasted only two months, in part because Wakefield soon took off in pursuit of other activity although they did play a six-week engagement at Gerde's Folk City in Greenwich Village. Later Isaacs went back again to New York where he remained until September 1968. The new band in New York, sometimes styled themselves the Lonesome Drifters, included Kevin Smythe on bass, Sandy Rothman on banjo, Artie Rose on resonator guitar, and young Fred Bartenstein on guitar. Joe says that teenager Bartenstein played as good a rhythm guitar as anyone in New York at that time. They made some recordings, minus Rose and Rothman, belatedly released some years later on Old Homestead that also included Frank Wakefield on mandolin and Richard Green on fiddle. Included was Isaacs's first song composition, "Loving Sweethearts" later retitled "Strollin' in the Moonlight." Bartenstein has written that Isaacs seemed very lonely in New York City, thinking often of his family and friends in Ohio and Kentucky. However, he did meet and subsequently marry Lily Fishman, an urban folksinger, during his time there.

Back in Ohio, Isaacs renewed his acquaintance with Larry Sparks, who had been working with Ralph Stanley and was also in the process of forming his Lonesome Ramblers band. Joe worked briefly with Stanley, but mostly in the Sparks band as a banjo picker on the first two albums on Pine Tree Records. He also cut a single "Bottle of Brandy"/"Mantle of Green" under his own name on the same Hamilton, Ohio–based label. In his early days as a vocalist, Isaacs mastered a singing style formally known as *tremulo* where at certain points in a lyric, his voice will quiver as though fearful or nervous. He said he developed it naturally and only does it when he feels a certain way, usually when a certain emotion in the song calls for it.

On December 22, 1970, Joe's brother Delmer Isaacs met his death in an automobile crash while returning from one of Joe's performances. The young picker felt much emotional pain and soon afterward both he and his wife had conversion experiences and turned their musical interests toward sacred song. Together with mandolin picker LeRoy Ramsey, they started a group called the Calvary Mountain Boys. They turned out a pair of albums, one on Pine Tree and another on Old Homestead. Both releases included several of Joes Isaacs's originals, most notably the song and recitation, "Memories of Delmer," being a tribute to his late brother. Joe worked some shows in Ohio and Kentucky with Carl Story, but opted not to go with him full time as he was trying to get his own band organized.

With Lily Isaacs and soon their three children taking a more active role in the group, they took the name Sacred Bluegrass. Slowly but surely they took on increasing stature in both the bluegrass and Southern gospel fields. As with the Calvary Mountain Boys, a number of Joe Isaacs's originals could be found on three Old Homestead LPs and a couple of other custom albums, many concerning either their conversion experiences or nostalgia for the old home and respect for parents. One song in particular, originally called "I Reached Up and Touched Jesus" from the *Lord Light My Way* album (OHS 70051) from 1981, has become a standard under the name "I Pressed through the Crowd." Numerous recordings of it have been made, recently by Dale Ann Bradley on her *Somewhere South of Crazy* compact disc. The song was nominated. but did not win the IBMA gospel song of the year in 2012.

With the passing of time and the inclusion of the children—Ben, Sonya, and Rebecca—Joe and Lily's band became simply known as The Isaacs. They received much acclaim from the late 1980s onward, recorded many compact discs, and continue on today. Taking their music abroad, The Isaacs hosted seven Holy Land tours in conjunction with Kash Amburgy.

Touring Egypt and Jordan gave Joe Isaacs a familiarity with Christian sites in varied Middle East locales. A visit to the Garden Tomb was a very emotional experience which inspired him to write one of his best compositions, "The Garden Tomb."

Recordings especially notable to bluegrass fans included *Ralph Stanley and Joe Isaacs: A Gospel Gathering* in 1995 on Freeland which combined the entire Isaacs group with Ralph Stanley and the Clinch Mountain Boys. The project received a Grammy nomination. Every member did not appear on all the songs, avoiding over-production, but instead various members of both groups participated in differing combinations. Joe contributed three original songs and The Isaacs alone paid tribute to Stanley with his own "Jacob's Vision" as the finale. Shelton Feazell sang bass on several songs. In 1996, Isaacs did an album of standard bluegrass gospel numbers, *Heartfelt Pickin' and Singin'* with a number of guest vocalists including Charlie Louvin, Ralph Stanley, and Porter Wagoner. The achievements of The Isaacs until then were chronicled in *Bluegrass Unlimited* (December 1997).

Near the end of the 1990s, Joe was feeling burned out. His and Lily's marriage was coming unglued which led to what Joe Isaacs called a "devastating divorce." Furthermore, three back operations had taken a toll on his health. Joe bought a piece of land near Berea, Kentucky, close to his boyhood home and for a year or so was inactive. Occasionally he filled in with Vince Combs and the Shade Tree Bluegrass or some other band.

Joe Isaacs's initial emergence from his self-imposed exile came with his *From a Cabin . . . to a Mansion* album in 2000 which was essentially a sacred tribute to his parents and deceased siblings. The entire project consisted of his compositions, some dating back to 1978, but most were written much later. By this time, Isaacs had developed a habit of dating lyrics he composed and the newest one containing a date was September 8, 1999. He had instrumental support from such friends as Don Rigsby, Kenny and Amanda Smith, Charlie Collins, and, of course, his three children who were counted among the best on their instruments of choice. Isaacs considers this disc to be his proudest effort. In addition to the title cut, the parent-tribute theme runs strong in "Share Croppers Wages," "Have a Happy Mother's Day" and "I Miss Their Smiling Faces."

In December 2000, the RFD satellite network and the *Cumberland Highlanders* program were launched. At the urging of former Blue Grass

Boy Wayne Lewis, Joe joined the cast. Soon he made the acquaintance of Stacy York, a traditional-styled bluegrass vocalist. Born in Indianapolis, Indiana, of Kentucky parentage on May 7, 1969, Stacy McKinney began singing in churches and on radio at age six with their family gospel group. Four years later her father became ill and the family returned to Kentucky, settling in Bandy near Somerset. Stacy grew up with bluegrass and gospel music, especially attracted to the Stanley Brothers and to Bill Monroe, Lester Flatt and Earl Scruggs, and Hazel Dickens, among girl singers. After high school, Stacy married Larry York and settled in nearby Eubank, Kentucky. They had two sons, Jonas and Jordan, now young adults. They had a little band called Bluegrass Mountain in which Stacy played guitar and Larry the bass. The Yorks eventually divorced. After being a guest on the *Cumberland Highlanders* a few times, Stacy York joined the regular cast as a vocalist. Joe Isaacs and Stacy York soon found that their voices blended quite well and added a few duets to their repertoire. In the meantime, Joe continued to have health problems and had heart surgery in September 2002.

In 2003 while recovering from this operation, Joe Isaacs recorded *Dreaming of Home for* MME Records. For the first time since leaving Larry Sparks in 1970, he did a collection of secular songs. In addition to Ben and Sonya Isaacs, Rhonda Vincent sang with Joe on "The Weary Heart You Stole Away." York joined in on the chorus of several numbers and she and Isaacs rendered a memorable duet on "We Must Have Been Out of Our Minds," the old George Jones-Melba Montgomery favorite from 1963. Although Joe did not keep a regular band during this period, there was some membership continuity in Mountain Bluegrass, especially Curnie Lee Wilson on lead guitar. The latter was a son of the elder of the Wilson Brothers, Russell and Curnie, a bluegrass gospel team who had cut several albums in the 1970s, two of which *We'll Work Till Jesus Comes* and *Sacred Songs in the Stanley Tradition,* had featured Isaacs on banjo.

While distant travel did not characterize Joe's appearances in this period, he did make two trips to Australia as a result of a chance meeting with some Aussies at the Station Inn in 2004. They worked a festival at Harrietville, Victoria. The first included himself, Wayne Lewis, Aaron Till, and Scot Shipley. In 2005, a second sojourn took Isaacs, York, Lonnie Hopper, and Danny Jones—formerly with the Bluegrass Alliance, Bill Monroe, and the Goins Brothers—where they worked with an Australian group, the Hardrive

Bluegrass Band. As Isaacs recalls it was a good experience, paid their expenses, and provided a nice vacation, but the journey was so exhausting, he does not think he would want to go again.

In 2005, Joe assembled a cast of family singers and musicians at Tom T. and Dixie Hall's for a collection of songs that became *The Joe Isaacs Family Reunion* on Blue Circle Records. All of Isaacs's children took part as did such notable pickers as Butch Robbins, Don Rigsby, and Mike Feagan. Stella Parton and Alecia Nugent helped on the chorus of several songs and Lily Isaacs joined in on one. Ben, Sonya, and Rebecca helped throughout. Joe sang lead on all songs but one, "Get in the Boat," which featured Stacy York on lead. All the songs came from the fertile imagination of Tom T. and Dixie Hall except for "Paul's Ministry" which Joe attributes to the powerful Virginia-Kentucky gospel singer Brother Claude Ely (1922–1977) of "There Ain't No Grave Gonna Hold My Body Down" renown.

Blue Circle Records also released Stacy York's solo album *Kentucky in the Rain* in 2007 which illustrated her musical debt to the Stanley Brothers—five numbers as well as three strong new songs by Tom T. and Dixie Hall. Joe Isaacs played banjo throughout and sang lead on the Onie Wheeler composition "Go Home," a modern temperance song popularized by Lester Flatt and Earl Scruggs. Ben, Sonya, and Rebecca Isaacs along with Curnie Lee Wilson all provided solid instrumental and vocal support.

Another Isaacs release, *Stacy & Joe: Mountain Bluegrass* from 2009 included three Stanley songs, three Monroe songs including Stacy's spirited rendition of "Muleskinner Blues" reminiscent of Dolly Parton's 1970 hit, and a pair of new Tom T. and Dixie Hall numbers. The album is rounded out with Joe's oldest original, "Strollin' in the Moonlight," and a new number, "Old Kentucky Hills," co-written by Stacy and Joe. Stalwart musicians like Butch Robbins, Danny Jones, and Terry Eldridge loaned instrumental support.

On June 7, 2010, Joe and Stacy, having been a musical team for some years, became a married couple. In addition to her work with Isaacs and on the Cumberland Highlander's program, Stacy had been a part of the Hazel Holler Girls, an all-female band, led by bass player Michelle Wallace of Morehead, Kentucky. This band has been around since 2003 and has two compact discs on their resume, but Stacy who sings lead and plays rhythm guitar appears only on their second release, *Kentucky Grass*. Her singing is highlighted on such songs as the Stanley classic "God Gave You to Me," "Mining Camp Blues," and the traditional favorite "Shady Grove."

Joe and Stacy Isaacs did not play much in 2013 and 2014, as Joe had some recurring health problems as well as the illness and subsequent death of some family members. Nonetheless, by later summer of 2015, he felt sufficiently recovered for Stacy and him to return to the studio where they did another parent tribute album *Happy Father's Day Daddy: In Memory of Mom and Dad*, with the help of Ben and Sonya as well as John Rigsby and Wayne Lewis. The pair played at Rosine, Kentucky, in September 2015. He looked forward to an Isaacs family reunion at the 2016 SPGMA gathering.

Joe and Stacy continue to demonstrate a solid traditional duet sound based on both having been deeply influenced by the Stanley Brothers. Unlike the much-traveled The Isaacs who are still taking their unique music to the broader world, Joe Isaacs seems content to play shows in Kentucky and adjacent states and spend more time near his home with Stacy and his trained beagle dog Miss Dixie, named for Tom T. Hall's wife, who can not only hunt rabbits but can count to ten. He had a homecoming on Red Lick Road in 2009, 2010, and 2011. He has a good relationship with his children who can usually be counted on to help at recording sessions. Joe continues to write songs—son-in-law John Bowman had a quality CD *Songs of Joe Isaacs* in 2011. He has material for a new sacred album that is ready for the studio. For a man who since 1964 has taken his music to much of the outside world, Joe and Stacy Isaacs are content in their Kentucky homeland.

SELECTED RECORDINGS

Joe Isaacs: Dreaming of Home. MME 70039, 2003. With Stacy on duet numbers.
Stacy York: Kentucky in the Rain. Blue Circle BCR 009, 2007. With Joe on banjo and duet numbers.
Stacy & Joe: Mountain Bluegrass. Little Cabin LCR-101 CD, 2009.
Joe and Stacy Isaacs: Happy Father's Day Daddy. Little Cabin LCR 102, 2015.

Joe Isaacs also recorded under his own name and with all recordings by The Isaacs—including one with Ralph Stanley—prior to 1999.

∽ Bonnie Lou and Buster Moore

1927– and 1920–1996

The East Tennessee area possesses a musical heritage where hard-core country music and bluegrass can overlap rather easily. The Sauceman Brothers, Carl and Pearl Butler, Carl Story and the Rambling Mountaineers, Molly O'Day and the Cumberland Mountain Folks, Curly King and the Tennessee Hilltoppers constitute a partial list of groups that have at various times exemplified this commercial tradition. One of the most persisting duos to carry on this duet musical style has been the husband and wife team of Bonnie Lou and Buster Moore whose careers spanned five decades.

Hubert R. "Buster" Moore was born in Bybee, Cocke County, Tennessee, on October 28, 1920. He weighed ten pounds at birth and acquired the nickname Buster almost from infancy although he soon outgrew his heaviness. As a teenager, he listened to the radio from Greenville, South Carolina, and especially liked hearing the Monroe Brothers as well as J. E and Wade Mainer on various North Carolina stations. Later he listened to Carl Story and the Rambling Mountaineers, a band which he eventually joined. He also heard the *Mid-Day Merry-Go-Round* on WNOX and Cas Walker programs on other Knoxville stations. The early Monroe influence seemed most profound on Moore for although he eventually learned to play several instruments, he favored the mandolin. Moore wanted to quit farm work and school to become a road musician, but his father persuaded him to stay at home until he graduated from Newport High School in 1939.

Although his family seemed reluctant, Buster remained determined to get into radio. By this time he and some friends had formed a little mountain string band known as the Cocke County Ramblers. He did a guest spot on a Cas Walker show at WROL. A bit later he wrote to Lowell Blanchard at WNOX and as a result also appeared on the *Mid-Day Merry-Go-Round*. Since the other band members did not want to leave home, Moore realized

Bonnie Lou and Buster Moore, mid-1960s.

he would have to go on his own. One day he met another aspiring young musician, Eddie Hill of Etowah, Tennessee. They formed a group and tried to get a regular spot on either WNOX or one of the Cas Walker shows. By then, Buster had moved to Knoxville and worked in a grocery store. They recruited steel player Tommy Covington and fiddler Billy Lamb from Madisonville, Tennessee, and called themselves Smilin' Eddie, Bashful

Buster and the Mountain Boys. Hill, who later became known for his radio salesmanship, finally persuaded Lowell Blanchard to give them time for both an early morning show and a spot on the *Mid-Day Merry-Go-Round*. Fortunately, the Chattanooga Medicine Company, manufacturers of Black Draught laxative, decided to sponsor them and also put their morning show on WDAD Chattanooga. Blanchard booked them in schools and at other locations. This situation continued for several months and the Mountain Boys did pretty well until the advent of World War II. Between the military draft and defense plant work, numerous bands broke up and remaining musicians shifted around adapting to the changing conditions. Moore wound up in Asheville working at WWNC with Carl Story and the Rambling Mountaineers. Finally both he and Jack Shelton received their notices and they, too, entered the army.

During his brief stay in Asheville, Moore met a girl named Margaret Bell. Born on June 4, 1927, she, too, had an interest in music. Wade Mainer later recalled that as children both she and her brother Lloyd Bell had been guests on WWNC's *Farm Hour* program. Margaret Bell and Buster Moore became friends, corresponded during the war although Moore contended that the romance did not get serious until later. Buster's career did not totally lapse during his time in the army because he organized a band there. Also after winning a talent show for servicemen, he appeared on a network show with Bing Crosby.

After receiving an early discharge from the service in 1945, Buster returned to Asheville where the Rambling Mountaineers regrouped and reinstituted their show at WWNC. Story aspired to get on at WNOX so Buster called Lowell Blanchard and soon he returned to Knoxville with Story, Dud Watson, and Claude Boone. As it turned out, however, his stay with the Rambling Mountaineers became exceedingly brief because Moore soon received an opportunity to form his own band at WROL, also in Knoxville. Known as the Dixie Pardners, Buster's band members all attained some degree of musical distinction. Ray Atkins, then only eighteen, became known for his Dobro and steel work as well as his Donald Duck imitations. Wiley Morris had already acquired a reputation as half of the Morris Brothers duet. Willie Brewster, then primarily a fiddler, later played with his brothers. Panhandle Pete, famous for his one-man band act, played bass for the group. The Dixie Pardners did three shows daily over WROL for the Cas Walker Supermarkets.

The Dixie Pardners had a versatile act. Moore sang duets with both Brewster and Morris who also did duets together. Buster also performed an occasional duet with Ray Atkins, Moore, Morris, and Brewster sang trios, and all four did quartets. Pete had his one-man band feature. In retrospect, it seems regrettable that this group never had the opportunity to record.

One day in late spring 1945 Buster received a phone call. Margaret Bell and her brother Lloyd had come over from Asheville to see about getting a radio job, she having just finished high school. Although no openings existed at that time, it did initiate a more serious romance. Buster began traveling to Asheville on the days that the band did not work, and on August 18, 1945, the couple was married. In the beginning neither Margaret nor Buster Moore had any plans that she would continue in music.

Twice a week the Dixie Pardners played at a government recreation hall in Oak Ridge, Tennessee. One night Wiley Morris became ill with what turned out to be appendicitis while playing this show. With Morris being hospitalized for several days, Buster needed a quick replacement. Since he and his wife had sung duets around home, she filled in for Morris and quickly gained popularity with radio listeners. As a result, she remained in the group permanently taking the stage name Bonnie Lou. Buster Moore remarked that the Dixie Pardners act did much better with her singing.

After several months, the Dixie Pardners had pretty well played out the territory in East Tennessee and moved elsewhere. Since most of the band chose to remain in Knoxville, Buster recruited Lloyd Bell and Don Reno and they relocated to Greenville, South Carolina. Things did not go particularly well there and the Moores moved back to Asheville. Buster hoped he could get a spot at WPTF Raleigh as he had heard that Johnny and Jack planned to leave and he aspired to take their place. As it turned out, the Tennessee Mountain Boys did not depart all that quickly so Bonnie Lou and Buster took a position at the other Raleigh station, WRAL. Reorganizing the Dixie Pardners, they secured the services of Art Wooten on fiddle along with Carl Butler and Lloyd Bell. The latter worked almost constantly with Bonnie Lou and Buster except for a period of time when he played with Carl Story's Rambling Mountaineers.

Finally, Johnny and Jack departed and station manager Graham Pointer gave Buster their place at WPTF as planned earlier. For several months they did well with show dates in eastern North Carolina and also began playing Saturday nights on the *Old Dominion Barn Dance* on WRVA Richmond.

However, when Lowell Blanchard called a Moore relative asking him to return to WNOX, they found the appeal for home territory irresistible. Back in Knoxville, they began to have misgivings. Charlie Monroe insisted that they drop the name "Pardners" since it resembled his own Kentucky Pardners too closely. Afterward, they were just known as Bonnie Lou and Buster. Moore recalled that at the first show date Blanchard booked for them in some mountain village, their car looked almost larger than the schoolhouse. Wooten and Butler both decided to go back to North Carolina, but eventually everything worked out. They got Willie Brewster back on fiddle and Ray Atkins returned to Knoxville from Louisiana. The Moores remained in Knoxville this second time for eighteen months. During this period, Bonnie Lou and Buster signed with Mercury Records and subsequently split two sessions with Mac Odell. They recorded the latter's newly composed "Wolves In Sheep's Clothing," the Carter Family's "Lonesome Day," a gospel song, "Meet Me Jesus," and Mac McCarty's new composition "Teardrops Falling in The Snow." Unfortunately for Bonnie Lou Moore, Columbia rushed Molly O'Day's rendition of the latter song onto the market so her Mercury disc did not have much impact. But with Speedy Krise on Dobro, Bonnie Lou's recording showed that she could handle this type of song virtually as well as the now legendary O'Day or Wilma Lee Cooper. Those same Mercury sessions also produced Mac Odell's classic "Red Ball Rocket Train" which featured Krise on Dobro and the Moores' furnishing rhythm on mandolin and guitar. Mercury released the disc under the name Bonnie Lou which has led to some confusion with the Bonnie Lou, born Mary Kath, who recorded for King Records and had a long association with Cincinnati radio and television.

When the Moores played out the Knoxville market the second time, they went to Memphis where Eddie Hill had become established since leaving East Tennessee. Bonnie Lou and Buster worked there on a mid-day program with Lightning Chance on bass, Tony Cianciola on accordion, and Paul Buskirk on mandolin. Moore continued to play mandolin on a hymn time show where only he, Bonnie Lou, Hill, and Chance were present. After about a year the entire group got hired to go to KRLD Dallas and the *Big D Jamboree*. As the time came for departure from Memphis, however, practically everyone got cold feet. Some wished to stay in Memphis, others interested themselves in Nashville. The Moores decided to get out of entertainment and returned to Knoxville.

Buster Moore accepted an offer from a friend and got into store management training with J. C. Penney. He remained in the store between two and
three months, but could not get show business out of his blood. When the
manager of WSVA Harrisonburg, Virginia, called to tell them that Jolly Joe
Parrish and Zag Pennell were leaving there for Knoxville he asked if he and
Bonnie Lou would be interested in a position on the Harrisonburg station.
Moore thought for a few days and decided to accept.

They took a new name—Bonnie Lou, Buster, and the Tennessee Sweethearts. Things went very well for them for eleven months and they even
purchased a new Buick with the proceeds from songbook sales. Then a
new owner took over the station and gave everyone a thirty-day notice.
They worked a few dates in Virginia with Carl Story and the Rambling
Mountaineers. Both groups decided to go to WCYB Bristol, Virginia/
Tennessee since the Stanley Brothers and some other acts were in the
process of leaving. As events developed, Story's band remained there but
only briefly because he received a better offer in Charlotte, North Carolina.
Homer Harris, a vocalist who had a trained horse named Stardust, joined
forces with them for personal appearances. At Honaker, Virginia, Stardust
attracted a large crowd just to see the horse ascend a staircase to an upstairs
auditorium. A year and a half at WCYB proved to be prosperous ones for
the Moores and Harris.

By this time, competition from television began to loom on the horizon.
The threat extended close when WJHL Johnson City made plans to open
a television station. They offered the Moores a job and Buster accepted.
The people at Bristol expressed unhappiness at being abandoned for the
new innovation and must have chuckled when the WJHL tower collapsed
the day before the station opened. Carl Story helped the Moores keep their
band on the road by booking show dates for them.

Finally on October 26, 1953, WJHL-TV opened and Bonnie Lou and
Buster got in on the ground floor. Originally, they had a half-hour early
evening show three days a week, but later switched to a daily early morning
routine. For a time Bonnie Lou Moore also did weather reports and had a
home economics-type cooking show. Homer Harris also continued working
with them until 1958.

Television, Moore said, opened a whole new audience to their music.
On appearance dates they suddenly found many upper middle class and
professional people, who had hitherto ignored radio hillbillies, flocking to

their shows. In addition to Lloyd Bell and Homer Harris, the Moores usually kept a couple of band members, typically a fiddler and an electric steel
player, their one concession to modernization. Benny Sims, L. E. White,
and Tater Tate worked as their fiddle player at various times while Walter
Haynes served several years as their steel man.

Towards the later 1950s they recorded again, doing a gospel album on
the Waterfall label. Buster Moore's mandolin and the electric steel carried
the bulk of the instrumentation. The Moores and Lloyd Bell performed
a variety of good traditional vocal arrangements on such songs as "Rank
Stranger," "Daniel Prayed," and "When Our Lord Shall Come Again."

The Moores remained at WJHL-TV for nine years although towards the
end they gave up their daily shows in exchange for live weekly programs on
a series of stations including ones in Asheville, North Carolina; Bluefield,
West Virginia; Columbia, South Carolina; Nashville, Chattanooga, and
Knoxville, Tennessee; as well as Johnson City. Sponsored by a building firm,
this arrangement led directly into their later *Jim Walter Jubilee* syndicated
shows for Jim Walter Homes. Beginning in 1963, this show continued as a
weekly program on many stations throughout a wide area somewhat concentrated in the Appalachian South. By the 1980s, WATE-TV in Knoxville
served as the flagship station for the syndicated program.

Beginning in 1972, Bonnie Lou and Buster inaugurated another operation which proved not only successful but was considerably less tiring than
the extensive travel required of many musicians. That year they began the
"Smoky Mountain Hayride" from the Coliseum at Pigeon Forge, Tennessee,
near Gatlinburg. There they ran a bluegrass and country show nightly
from April 1 through mid-November. At times, such musicians of interest
to bluegrass fans as Red Rector, Fred Smith, and David West—all veterans
of the *Cas Walker Farm and Home Hour*—worked on these shows. Dobro
players included Monroe Queener and Darrell Henry. From 1974, Don
McHan, known for his writing and playing with both Carl Sauceman and
Jim and Jesse, was a regular on their live shows as well as their television
program. In addition, Buster continued to do his longtime comedy creation
Humphammer. You could also see clog dancing and hear performances by
such mainstream country vocalists as Louie Roberts, son of Hank Snow's
steel guitarist Kayton Roberts.

In 1970, Bonnie Lou and Buster appeared in the major Hollywood film
Walk in the Spring Rain, starring Ingrid Bergman and Anthony Quinn.

Many of the scenes took place in Gatlinburg, one of which featured some music played by the Moores and old-time fiddler James McCarroll who had been with the Roane County Ramblers and recorded for Columbia.

The group recorded a couple of albums on the Angel label. Many of the bluegrass songs were rather standard fare such as "Rocky Top" and "Roll in My Sweet Baby's Arms." This derived from the simple fact that their audiences at the Coliseum tended to be representative of the general public rather than the veteran bluegrass festival fan of a dozen years' experience. In 1988, Bonnie Lou and Buster with Lloyd Bell recorded another ten songs, *Gospel '88*, released only on cassette.

Bonnie Lou and Buster Moore continued their warm weather daily programs at the "Smoky Mountain Hayride" at the Pigeon Forge Coliseum into the 1990s. But age began to take a toll. Buster died on January 13, 1996. Bonnie Lou retired. She and her brother Lloyd Bell, who died in 2014, did make an appearance at Owensboro, Kentucky, receiving recognition as "Pioneers of Bluegrass" a few years ago.

Through more than fifty years of show business on Buster's part and nearly fifty for Bonnie Lou, they exemplified some of the best traditions of country and bluegrass music. Coming out of an East Tennessee and Western North Carolina heritage, both made significant contributions in perpetuating the music of their mountain backgrounds. Through their radio, television, and live shows they always gave their best. Known and respected by their fellow musicians as serious dedicated professionals, they were also known for their friendly, open, and honest dealings with both musicians and fans.

SELECTED RECORDINGS

Bonnie Lou and Buster's four Mercury recordings have been out of print for some six decades. Typical albums from their "Smoky Mountain Hayride" days in Pigeon Forge, Tennessee, are:

Bonnie Lou & Buster Sing Country Bluegrass & Gospel. Angel LP 577177, 1977.
Bonnie Lou & Buster Sing Gospel. Angel LP 33582, 1982.

⚓ Molly O'Day and Lynn Davis

1923–1987 and 1914–1998

During the decade of the 1940s, the woman who made the most significant impact on the traditional country music world was an attractive young lady from McVeigh, Kentucky, whose name was LaVerne Davis. Most of her songs were either sad songs about the tragedy of human life or of a sacred nature. Both were performed with a feeling of depth and sincerity that has been seldom equaled. Some were vocal solos while others were duets with her husband who was a talented artist in his own right. Their music was not bluegrass, but was of a traditionally oriented style which like that of Roy Acuff, the Louvin Brothers, the Bailes Brothers, and similar performers of the period had a profound influence upon bluegrass. While LaVerne Davis may not ring a bell with many persons, the name Molly O'Day by which she was professionally known, will bring pleasant recollections to those whose musical interests range deeper than the current sounds from Nashville.

The future Molly O'Day began life as Lois LaVerne Williamson in Pike County, Kentucky, on July 9, 1923. Her father was a coal miner and the family lived at McVeigh, some thirteen miles west of Williamson, West Virginia. This community has been accurately described as "way back in the sticks" and opportunities for public entertainment were few. Various members of the Williamson family played old-time music on the fiddle and banjo for fun and in the early 1930s, the distant radio stations of WLS and WSM brought a more commercial sound to the ears of the mountain youth. Young LaVerne preferred the Chicago station perhaps because it featured more girl singers while her brother Cecil a.k.a. Skeets, who was three years older, preferred the *Grand Ole Opry*, probably because they had more fiddlers.

Among the girl singers who flourished on the *National Barn Dance* of the era were Lulu Belle Wiseman, Louise Massey, Patsy Montana, Lily May Ledford, and the Girls of the Golden West—Millie and Dolly Good. The

Molly O'Day
and Lynn
Davis, WHAS,
Louisville, 1943.

yodeling cowgirl image was dominant on the scene and the future Molly
O'Day, though hundreds of miles from the wide-open spaces of the West,
absorbed this influence although Lulu Belle had always been her personal
favorite. Soon she learned to play guitar while brothers Skeets was on the
fiddle and Duke was on the banjo. Together they spent many hours practicing and developing their vocal and instrumental talents. Sometimes they
played to entertain neighbors or provided the music for local dances.

Early in 1939, Skeets Williamson left the Kentucky hills and went to
Charleston, West Virginia, to stay with an older sister. Soon he joined the
band of Ervin Staggs on WCHS where he teamed with young Johnnie
Bailes. Together they became known as Fiddlin' Skeets and Smilin' John,
the Happy Valley Boys. The proud brother naturally told of his singing sister

and soon wrote back home and asked her to join the group as girl vocalist. So in the summer of 1939, LaVerne Williamson went to WCHS and became Mountain Fern. In her early professional days she sang the comedy songs of Lulu Belle, the yodeling songs of Patsy Montana, and the blues numbers of Texas Ruby. That fall they left Charleston and played on a small station nearer home at WBTH in Williamson and later at WJLS in Beckley where Mountain Fern became Dixie Lee. After Skeets and Johnnie dissolved as a team in the fall of 1940, Dixie Lee wrote to Lynn Davis, an established radio artist with a group at WHIS in Bluefield, seeking a job as girl vocalist.

Leonard "Lynn" Davis was born near Paintsville in Johnson County, Kentucky, on December 15, 1914. Both his father and an uncle played old-time music and Lynn Davis learned to play guitar and banjo. Later the family moved to Wheelwright, Kentucky. About 1932, he and friend Guy Ferrell went to WSAZ in Huntington, West Virginia, and got a Saturday morning show as Guy and Lynn, the Mountaineer Twins. Lynn Davis played lead guitar and Ferrell on rhythm. They tended to favor the style of the Delmore Brothers who were then gaining a wide audience on the *Grand Ole Opry*. Enjoying their newfound fame as radio performers, the boys also got a Saturday afternoon show on WCHS. Sometimes they went out and played shows with the more established artists at Charleston. Later they went to WHIS Bluefield.

At Bluefield, Ferrell decided to quit and return home, but Davis joined Shorty Fincher's group. Leaving West Virginia, they went to Virginia for a time and also played in Pennsylvania. Late in 1936, Lynn returned to Bluefield where he organized a group called the Forty-Niners. The band included Jimmy Barker, "Georgia" Brown, Buddy Grimsley, Gordon Jennings, and a pair of yodeling cowgirls from Reading, Pennsylvania—Sue and Ann Mason. For a time the group also included the Stepp Brothers— Esland a.k.a. Zeke and Esmond—another Delmore sounding duo. In this period, Davis wrote a few songs for Asher Sizemore including "Don't Wait Till Mother's Hair Has Turned to Silver" and "Sunlit Mountain Home" that the famous father and son team of Asher and Little Jimmy used for a theme song at one time.

About 1939, the Forty-Niners left Bluefield for WPTF in Raleigh, North Carolina, and then went to KVOO in Tulsa, Oklahoma, where they worked on the *Saddle Mountain Roundup*. Other acts working out of Tulsa at the time included Bob Wills and his Texas Playboys, Georgia Slim and Howdy Forrester, Ray Whitley, Fred Rose, and Texas Ruby and Curley Fox. They also played in Texas where one of the yodeling cowgirls was married. When the Forty-Niners returned to Bluefield in the summer of 1940, the other young woman left the band and returned to Pennsylvania. Thus, the Lynn Davis group was left without a girl singer. When Dixie Lee applied for the vocalist job with the Forty-Niners, she was already a longtime admirer of the group, being especially impressed with Davis's rendition of the new Bob Wills hit, "San Antonio Rose." She and, for a time, Skeets joined the band. Soon Dixie Lee and Lynn's admiration became romantic and on April 5, 1941 the two became man and wife. At this time the yodeling cowgirl was still dominant in Dixie's style, but as time passed she developed her own unique style which one scholar has described as a female equivalent of Roy Acuff.

In the summer of 1941, the Forty-Niners moved to WJLS in Beckley where they were sponsored by Dr. Pepper. That September they left the mountains and went to Birmingham, Alabama, for a year where they filled a spot vacated by the Delmore Brothers. Here they played on WAPI and their show went out over a regional network that included stations in Nashville, Memphis; Jackson, Mississippi; and Montgomery, Mobile, Tuscaloosa, Alabama. They played live shows in the area and originated their broadcast live from various stations on the circuit. In Montgomery they made the acquaintance of a tall, gangly young man named Hank Williams who had a radio show there and hired him to advertise and play on the package shows that Lynn promoted in that area. In a few years this friendship proved to be significant for both the Davises and Williams.

The young Williams from Montgomery wrote a lot of his own material. One song that he sang, but did not write was a sacred number he had picked up indirectly from Grady and Hazel Cole called "Tramp on the Street." When first hearing it performed on a show, Dixie Lee thought it the most moving song she had heard and asked him to teach her the words. A little later, Williams who had a drinking problem and had been hitherto unable to have any of his material published, offered to sell Davis a hundred songs for twenty-five dollars. Although first accepting the deal, Lynn had some second thoughts that buying the songs at so cheap a price would be unethical and backed out, suggesting that he keep working on his own to get the songs published.

In the summer of 1942, the Davises went to Kentucky where they played an hour and forty-five minutes daily on the *Early Morning Frolic* at WHAS in Louisville, a 50,000 watt station and on Saturday nights at the *Renfro Valley Barn Dance* which was aired over the CBS network. Soon after their arrival in Louisville, WHAS artist Clayton McMichen told them that there was another performer in the area known as Dixie Lee and suggested that a different name might be used to avoid confusion. Admiring the name of Milly Wayne who had sung on WWVA, she decided to alter that slightly to Molly for a first name. Undecided whether to use Knight or Day for a possible surname, she finally settled on the latter giving it an Irish touch. Although it took a little getting used to, John Lair introduced her as Molly O'Day and then turned around saying, "What are you going to sing, Dixie?" The name soon caught on with the public and became much more of a household word among country fans than Dixie Lee had ever been. In later years, even her parents began calling her Molly.

While they were at Louisville, the noted temperance evangelist Sam Morris lectured and preached on WHAS. One of O'Day's most popular numbers at that time was "The Drunken Driver," an old song she had learned from an act at Bluefield, the Hamid Sisters. Lynn recalled that she once received 4,000 requests on a single day for the song. Reverend Morris also appreciated the number and based the text of a sermon on the song O'Day was making so popular.

For a year and a half, Lynn and Molly worked on the *Early Morning Frolic* and *Renfro Valley Barn Dance*. Wartime shortages of rubber and gasoline held down the number of tourists who came to the "Valley Where Time Stands Still," but their radio audience grew in size and crowds were good at their live shows. The artists at Renfro Valley and WHAS usually worked in units or groups. Those who frequently worked with the Davises included either the Turner Brothers (Red and Lige), Fiddlin' Red Herron, Randy Barnett, or Slim Miller as well as the Holden Brothers (Fairley and Jack), or Lonnie Glosson, the legendary harmonica player among others. From Glosson, Molly learned another sacred song which the public came to identify with her and has been recorded by several bluegrass artists, the millennial hymn "Matthew Twenty-four."

Their radio work at Louisville was also heard by a vast overseas audience. For instance, it was not uncommon for them to receive mail from the

Pacific Theater. One day an aide to General Douglas MacArthur dropped by the station while on a visit to Fort Knox to tell them that the General was a regular listener to their performances on the *Early Morning Frolic* as he had his evening meal at his headquarters in Australia.

Leaving Kentucky in early 1944, Lynn and Molly went to a station where they had played some years before, WJLS in Beckley, West Virginia. Here they again formed a group which included Everett and Bea Lilly, two of the most traditionally oriented performers in bluegrass music history. They played with Dobro player George "Speedy" Krise and Fiddlin' Burk Barbour who would also play with them at a later date. After several months in the West Virginia hills the couple headed for the wide open spaces.

For a three or four month period, the duo worked at KRLD in Dallas. During this time they recorded some material for the Sellers Transcription Company in Fort Worth, presumably for use on the border stations. Over a hundred numbers were transcribed. According to Molly, practically every song in their performing repertoire was included.

In June 1945, Davis and O'Day took their talents to Knoxville and WNOX's popular *Mid-Day Merry-Go-Round*. The Lilly Brothers came down from Clear Creek and rejoined the Cumberland Mountain Folks. Burk Barbour played fiddle and Johnny Harper did comedy and played bass. Somewhat later, Mac Wiseman joined the group as a featured vocalist; Speedy Krise played Dobro after his service discharge. Skeets Williamson was reunited with his sister on stage after his discharge from the Navy in August 1946.

The end of World War II resulted among other things in a return to increased recording activity. Fred Rose, now of Acuff-Rose and an old friend of Lynn's from their days in Oklahoma, vacationed in Gatlinburg, Tennessee, in the summer of 1946 and heard Molly sing "Tramp on the Street" over WNOX. He contacted the duo and offered to see Art Satherley about getting them a contract with Columbia records. Accordingly, they went to Chicago on December 16, 1946, and cut their first session. Williamson, Krise, and O'Day and Davis as well as Mac Wiseman on bass, comprised the Cumberland Mountain Folks on those historic recordings. "Tramp on the Street" unsurprisingly was their first recording and first release. Hank Williams had been sending Molly songs for some time; "Six More Miles" and "When God Comes and Gathers His Jewels" were two of his numbers cut then as was O'Day's longtime radio hit, "The Drunken Driver." Three

Roy Acuff numbers, "Beneath that Lonely Mound of Clay," "Tear-Stained Letter," and "Put My Rubber Doll Away," never recorded by Acuff, and Fred Rose's "Black Sheep Returned to the Fold" were recorded as duets with Lynn. Their record releases usually tended to be a balance of duets and solo numbers by Molly although there was a slight dominance of the latter.

When their first recordings were released in July 1947, they were well received especially "Tramp on the Street." Lynn and Molly continued to play on WNOX until September when they left radio briefly. Lynn operated a grocery store in Wheelwright, Kentucky, for a time. O'Day began to have second thoughts about show business and thought she should get out of music as it was too worldly. As Lynn explained it, in theological terms she sang herself under conviction. However, a coal strike caused the store to lose money and economic necessity forced them to return to radio. In December 1947 while still in Wheelwright with the help of Speedy Krise and Carl Smith, who were still in Knoxville, they did a session in Nashville for Columbia. "Matthew Twenty-four" and "At the First Fall of Snow" constituted the best songs from the collection.

They then returned to radio at WBIG Greensboro, North Carolina, where Charlie Monroe had done well. In April 1949, they again recorded for Columbia. Harmonica playing fiddler James "Slim" Martin gave this session a somewhat unique sound with his harp work on songs like "On the Evening Train" and twin-fiddling with Skeets Williamson on "Mother's Gone but Not Forgotten." However, the most memorable numbers were "Teardrops Falling in the Snow," a song composed by E. C. "Mac" McCarty, a forest ranger from Whitley City, Kentucky, concerning the arrival of the body of a fallen soldier at a train station, and "Poor Ellen Smith," a North Carolina murder ballad on which Molly played a lively clawhammer banjo. The duets "With You on My Mind" and "This Is the End" were the nearest things to honky-tonk songs the pair ever recorded.

Soon they were back in Knoxville on the *Dinner Bell Show* at WROL, a rival of WNOX and the *Mid-Day Merry-Go-Round*. Other performers there at the time included Flatt and Scruggs, Archie Campbell, Carl Butler, and Carl Smith. The latter had worked with the Cumberland Mountain Folks for a time playing bass and being featured on some vocals. He participated on their 1947 recording session for Columbia as a bass player. After leaving WROL, they went to WVLK in Versailles, Kentucky, where they did their last radio work as active performers. In February 1950, both Lynn and Molly underwent religious conversions in Huntington, West Virginia. Henceforth, Church of God evangelism dominated their lives.

The pair did two final sessions for Columbia in 1950 and 1951, recording exclusively sacred material except for one memorable tear-jerker, "Don't Sell Daddy Any More Whiskey." This mournful ballad recounting the plea of a young child to a rum seller became one of her best-remembered songs. Originally written and recorded on London by Mattie O'Neill a.k.a. Mattie Holmes, sister of Martha Carson, the song was sent to Molly and Lynn by Fred Rose and when Columbia released Molly's record they had dubbed a crying baby in the background. While this sound effect may have increased the drama of the scene portrayed in the song, it brought complaints from some of Molly's fans who thought it distracted from her vocal. One angry listener was reported to have called Wayne Raney, the noted deejay at WCKY in Cincinnati, Ohio, and complained, "I wish you'd make that young'n' be quiet so I can hear that woman sing." Other songs at these final Columbia efforts included "If You See My Savior," "It's Different Now," and "Traveling the Highway Home."

In the fall of 1952, Molly was stricken with tuberculosis and as a result of an operation the following February, had a portion of her lung removed. Recovery was slow and left her with less energy than before. Lynn became a licensed minister in the Church of God, which has headquarters in Cleveland, Tennessee, and Molly assisted him in his work as a clergyman, sometimes with singing and testimony. To many her voice had actually improved over the years. In the early 1960s, they operated the Molly O'Day Music Center, a gospel record store in Williamson, West Virginia. For their later years, however, they lived in the Huntington, West Virginia, area where Lynn worked for an investment firm and preached for revivals as time, health, and circumstances permitted. Outside of church work, Molly tended to shun the limelight and avoided most contacts with the entertainment world.

Twice in the 1960s, Davis and O'Day recorded again. The first about 1961 was on the Rem label and subsequently was reissued by Starday, Pine Mountain, and Old Homestead. It was recorded at their home in Chesapeake, Ohio, and featured a good bit of Molly's banjo work on a dozen gospel numbers. In 1968, they made a gospel album for GRS, an

Ohio-based label owned by Reverend Ray Anderson, himself a former country and bluegrass musician of note. This album entitled *The Heart and Soul of Molly O'Day* was also recorded primarily at home with four numbers being cut in the GRS studio at Richmond Dale, Ohio. It later became available again by Queen City Albums and then Old Homestead. Although O'Day herself was somewhat critical of the recording quality, her many fans generally were highly pleased.

In 1974, Lynn and Molly started a little radio project on WEMM-FM, a Christian station in Huntington, West Virginia, which received considerable attention. Each afternoon from a makeshift studio in their home, they did an hour-long show in which they played country gospel—mostly of the bluegrass or traditional variety—interspersed with a friendly down-home style conversation and an inspirational story each day by Molly. Although their mail was not quite as voluminous as it was in the golden age of radio, they received more than 1,000 letters in the first five weeks the show was on the air. Many came from people who remembered them from an earlier era. This was somewhat of a surprise to the couple who thought their performances of twenty-five years earlier had been forgotten. An example of the loyalty and interest of their new audience can be illustrated when an elderly man from about fifty miles away brought them some rhubarb after they had mentioned in casual conversation on their show that they had not eaten any rhubarb in a long time.

Davis and O'Day never made any more recordings, but they continued to do their radio program, *Hymns from the Hills*, at WEMM regularly. As time went by Molly's health began to fail and Lynn often did the program alone. To use one of her own favorite phrases, she "went home to be with the Lord" on December 5, 1987.

Lynn, somewhat less reclusive than Molly, continued to do the program by himself until the day he died, December 18, 2000. He continued to preach as a guest evangelist whenever requested and even attended a couple of old-timer reunions at WNOX Knoxville. He also had the satisfaction of seeing his and Molly's entire recorded work released on compact disc via Bear Family Records in Germany and Old Homestead Records in Michigan.

Although neither Davis nor O'Day ever played bluegrass music as such, their style and songs have had considerable impact on bluegrass musicians.

Songs like "Six More Miles," "Matthew Twenty-four," "Tramp on the Street," and "Teardrops Falling in the Snow" have been recorded by several blue- grass groups. Some of their other songs have also appeared in the repertoire of bluegrass artists. Wilma Lee Cooper, Jeannie West, Rose Maddox, and Rose Lee Maphis exhibited a strong Molly O'Day influence among the more tradition-oriented country singers. Although girl singers are less common in the bluegrass world, those who are conspicuous owe O'Day a debt similar to the one that many tenor singers do to Bill Monroe. Gloria Belle worked with Jimmy Martin and Charlie Monroe and borrowed both songs and style from O'Day. Polly and Janis Lewis as well as Lillie Mae Whitaker also owe a debt to Molly. In bluegrass and traditional country and gospel music, O'Day's musical influence continues strong.

SELECTED RECORDINGS

Molly O'Day and the Cumberland Mountain Folks. Bear Family BCD 15565, 1992. Two com- pact disc collection that contains all of their 1946–1951 Columbia numbers.
The Soul of Molly O'Day, Vols. 1 and 2 Old Homestead OH CD, 312, 313, 1998. All of their recordings from 1961 on the REM and GRS labels.

✄ Doc and Chickie Williams

1914–2011 and 1919–2007

The husband-wife team of Doc and Chickie Williams formed an atypical twosome in the annals of traditional country music. Doc grew up mostly in small town Pennsylvania and came from an East European ethnic background. Nonetheless, he managed to absorb the prevalent country styles of the 1930s while retaining an ethnic flavor. Chickie, his wife, came from a mixed German and Scots-Irish heritage. She was best described by folk music scholar D. K. Wilgus as a "sweet singer." From their longtime base at WWVA radio in Wheeling, they entertained their legion of fans, chiefly in the northeast quadrant of the United States and adjacent parts of Canada. In later years they became known as "Country Music's Royal Couple." In retrospect, an even more accurate phrase might have been "country music's unique couple."

Before Doc Williams existed there was Andrew John Smik Jr. He was born to immigrant parents in Cleveland, Ohio, on June 26, 1914. Doc Williams called himself "the only hillbilly who ever came out of Cleveland," and he was surely one of the few country musicians of Slovak origins. Williams's father and mother had both been born in what is now Slovakia, but in those days the region was part of the Hungarian kingdom in the Hapsburg Empire. The elder Andrew Smik came to America at the age of twenty while his mother, Susie Parobeck, came at age twelve. The couple eventually married and had five children. Williams's younger brother Milo—known professionally as Cy, shortened from "Cyclone" Williams—worked with Doc as a fiddler and occasional duet vocal partner for some two decades.

When Doc Williams was two, his parents relocated to the small community of Tarrtown in the coalfields near Kittanning in Armstrong County, Pennsylvania. Coal camps offered an unusual mixture of rural and urban and the Cleveland boy soon learned something of country living and

The Border Riders, 1947. *From left:* Cy Williams, Chickie Williams, Marion Martin, and Doc Williams. *Courtesy of the Williams Family.*

Appalachian music. His dad played several musical instruments, preferring the traditional fiddle tunes of East Central Europe. Doc Williams's playing eventually came to reflect a mixture of traditional American country music as it was commercially evolving in the late 1920s, with a touch of East European ethnic stylings. The latter mirrored his own background as well as the tastes of audiences in northern West Virginia, eastern Ohio, and western Pennsylvania.

Oddly enough, Doc Williams's first musical instrument was the cornet. From there he went to the accordion, the harmonica, and finally the guitar.

The latter was favored by Jack and Jerry Foy, his earliest country radio influences, and by Jimmie Rodgers whose recordings had considerable impact on Doc Williams from about 1928. Cy Williams learned to play fiddle from their father and the two brothers worked square dances around Kittanning.

Aside from this, Doc Williams gained his first performing experience back in Cleveland, where he periodically went to live with his grandmother. He and neighbor Joe Stoetzer teamed up to play beer gardens. Williams played guitar and harmonica while Stoetzer played a kazoo with an attached horn and also the mandolin. Both sang and together they called themselves the Mississippi Clowns. They auditioned for radio and went on a show called *The Barn Busters* at WJAY in Cleveland, hosted by Morey Amsterdam of later television fame via *The Dick Van Dyke Show*. The Clowns appeared on this program once a week for about six months. They then found themselves absorbed into a larger unit called the Kansas Clodhoppers led by Doc McCaulley, a fiddler from Belington, West Virginia.

About 1935, Doc Williams returned to Pennsylvania when his dad asked him to help support the family by working with him in the coal mines. It was not long, however, until he returned to radio, teaming up with his brother Cy on fiddle and a Nelsonville, Ohio, mandolin player named Curley Sims. With the addition of a bass fiddle, this band took the name Allegheny Ramblers and worked at radio station KQV in Pittsburgh. Doc described their sound as almost "bluegrass at the time, but we didn't know it."

Pittsburgh was no center of hillbilly culture, but the Steel City's varied population did support some early country musicians. Among them were Jack and Jerry Foy, and a band called the Tennessee Ramblers that had been put together by West Virginians Dick Hartman and Harry Blair. The Tennessee Ramblers later included Cecil Campbell, the group's eventual leader, and a West Virginia vocalist Harry McAuliffe, whom Hartman gave the sobriquet "Big Slim, the Lone Cowboy." When Doc Williams arrived on Pittsburgh radio, the Tennessee Ramblers had moved on to Rochester, New York. McAuliffe, however, remained to play a role not only in Doc Williams's career, but also at WWVA. Williams's Allegheny Ramblers soon became the band for girl singer Billie Walker and took the new name Texas Longhorns. At the end of 1936, Walker took an opportunity to go to WWL in New Orleans; the Williams brothers, Sims, and McAuliffe chose to remain at KQV. By this time, the four were known as the Cherokee Hillbillies and were also being carried on two other local stations. It was about this time that young Andy Smik became Doc Williams. He had already been called "Doc," as had his father before him, both being health food advocates, and people had always tended to confuse Smik with Smith. Billie Walker had suggested Williams, since it was a common last name not likely to be confused with Smith. An autographed picture from about 1936 bears the signatures "Cowboy Doc" and "Fiddlin' Cyclone."

In May 1937, Doc Williams and his group changed places with performer Tex Harrison a.k.a. Joe Ray. Harrison came to Pittsburgh and Williams went to WWVA in Wheeling. This was when Williams's band took the name Border Riders. The group now consisted of Doc and Cy Williams as well as Curley and two new members. One newcomer, show business veteran Rawhide Fincher, was a twenty-six-year-old Alabama native who had worked at times with his brother Shorty Fincher and as part of the duo of Rawhide and Sue. In 1934 they had recorded for OKeh and also made transcriptions for Crazy Water Crystals as the Crazy Hillbillies. The other was the not quite eighteen-year-old Mary Calvas, a Davis, West Virginia, native of Italian background known as "Sunflower" She soon married Cy Williams and worked for several years as the band's female vocalist.

The Border Riders achieved almost instant popularity at WWVA and in 1938 were the station's most popular act. Each Saturday night they performed on the *World's Original Jamboree* as it was then called. Broadcast from the Wheeling Market Auditorium before a crowd of 1,200 or more people, the program had been a favorite since its inauguration before a live audience on January 7, 1933. The Border Riders also performed on a daily show from the WWVA studio in the Hawley Building. Each day they greeted their listeners with a theme song that Doc Williams had recomposed from "Riding Down that Old Texas Trail:"

> We are the happy Border Riders, Who ride down that old border trail.
> We are here to bring you cheer, And to sing you songs so dear
> That will tell you of that old border trail.
> Ridin' down that old border trail.

In addition to their radio broadcasts, Doc and the band began playing show dates almost nightly in nearby parts of Ohio, Pennsylvania, and West

Virginia. Since all their programs were done live in the studio, they could never go farther than a hundred miles or so from the station and get back in time for the next broadcast. Most of their stage shows were sponsored by community organizations, fund-raising concerts in the schools, theaters, and public auditoriums of small to medium-sized towns.

In December 1937, Rawhide Fincher was injured at a fire in his apartment and missed several weeks of shows. Doc brought Big Slim McAuliffe to Wheeling to help out. McAuliffe remained at WWVA and became one of the all-time *Jamboree* favorites. Soon after returning, Fincher left to join his brother Shorty Fincher who brought his Prairie Pals to WWVA. Doc Williams, a firm believer in keeping a comedian in his show, hired Froggie Cortez in his place. A native of Pennsylvania, bass-player Cortez sang old country comedy songs like "Courtin' in the Rain" and added a trained monkey named Jo-Jo to the usual bucolic humor of the country clown. The music of the Border Riders continued to be built around the fiddle and mandolin, and Doc's solid rhythm guitar and vocal leads, with other members singing on certain numbers. This band remained together until 1942 when the war brought changes.

During this period, the Border Riders usually took several weeks off in the summer. On one occasion, Doc and Cortez went to Texas and California. Snapshots from their adventure show a pair of fun-loving country boys enjoying themselves, somewhat awestruck by actually experiencing the West they sang about. The Texas border, ranches, horses, cowboys, and the wide-open spaces made an impression later conveyed to fans via their souvenir booklets.

Williams courted and married the one true love of his life during those early years at WWVA. Jessie Wanda "Chickie" Crupe was a West Virginian, born in Bethany on February 13, 1919. Her father, Fred Crupe, was a renowned old-time fiddler. He had been contacted to record for Columbia, but death intervened and the family moved to Washington County, Pennsylvania, where Chickie finished high school in 1938. She had once written a fan letter to Doc when he was still at KQV, but he never got it because it was erroneously addressed to Buck Williams. The two met at a dance in Washington County and following a pleasant courtship were married on October 9, 1939. The first of their three daughters, Barbara Diane ("Peeper") arrived on December 22, 1940. Madeline Dawn ("Poochie") came on April 11, 1943, and finally Karen Dolores ("Punkin") on June 10, 1944. From an early age, each of the girls all performed on special occasions with the Border Riders although only Karen ever made any real efforts at a career in music.

In addition to a wife and mother of his three daughters and a post-World War II singing partner whose popularity matched his own, Doc also obtained what became one of his signature songs. Chickie's maternal grandfather Amos Riggle taught Doc an old ballad "My Old Brown Coat and Me." The song related the story of a young man who wore an old brown coat and was rejected by a high-strung girl named Mary Braid; she marries a lawyer's son who then became a pirate while her failed suitor gains happiness and prosperity. Although untraced, the song seems likely to have been of British or New England origin and a fragment gathered in the Ozarks by Vance Randolph in 1940 about the same time that Williams learned it indicated that the lyrics were once widespread if uncommon. He also learned other songs from Grandpa Riggle, but that was the only one he recorded at his first session in 1947.

The year after Doc and Chickie Wiliams' marriage, the Border Riders turned their summer vacation into a work break. With their first child on the way and some of the band members also with increased family responsibilities, the musicians worked at WREC—again with Billie Walker—in Memphis. On the way home, Doc received an offer from WSM, home of the *Grand Ole Opry* in Nashville. He had sent his wife back to Wheeling early and was driving his band and their families through Tennessee when he stopped to see Harry Stone, the most powerful behind-the-scenes figure at the *Opry*. After hearing the Border Riders, the WSM manager offered them a daily show and an *Opry* spot. Williams, thinking more of his expectant wife in Wheeling and the other band members' squalling babies in the car, asked Stone for a rain check. He never followed up on this offer.

To place this missed opportunity in better perspective, remember that Nashville had not yet attained its status as Music City USA. Doc Williams and the Border Riders might have become as famous as Roy Acuff, Bill Monroe, Pee Wee King, or Ernest Tubb. On the other hand, they might have stayed awhile and then moved on as did folks like Fiddlin' Arthur Smith, Asher Sizemore, Zeke Clements, and the Milo Twins. Nashville's reputation soon received such boosts as the Republic film *Grand Ole Opry* and an NBC slot for the half-hour segment sponsored by Prince Albert Tobacco. In 1940 Wheeling ranked only a little below Nashville in music prestige. In fact, at about the same time WWVA officials passed up a chance for the *Jamboree* to go on the NBC Blue Network.

Back in Wheeling, the Border Riders continued as they had. The *Jamboree*, daily radio programs, and almost nightly live shows kept the Williams brothers, Calvas, Sims, and Cortez busy. The group first sold photos and a little souvenir scrapbook over the air, and about April 1940 they came out with a more elaborate *Doc Williams Border Riders Family Album* that included 39 pictures and 14 songs. They were not making phonograph records, but neither had any other WWVA acts since the Hugh and Shug's Radio Pals session for Decca in July 1937. Among the WSM acts, only Acuff and Monroe were recording at the time. After Christmas 1940, Chickie Williams stayed home with little Peeper and Doc indulged his spare moments in a fascination with aviation. He learned to pilot planes and later even managed an airport for a time.

After Pearl Harbor, the world of country music went through many changes. Gasoline rationing curtailed personal appearances and also reduced the number of fans who came to Wheeling to see the *World's Original Jamboree*. Many musicians entered the armed forces or were called into defense work. At the same time, people depended as much or even more upon radio for entertainment and the popularity of country music increased a great deal. Performances tended to be confined to the studios and from December 1942 until July 1946, the WWVA *Jamboree* was not broadcast before live stage audiences. The musicians who remained with the station were disproportionately women and got more opportunities to sing over the air than ever before.

The effects of the war came gradually for Williams. The service took Cortez and Sims and eventually only Doc and his brother were left. Chickie Williams was singing with them more often by this point. In 1943, Cy entered the military and Doc acquired other musicians. Marion Martin a.k.a. Marion Keyoski, the blind accordionist, had his first association with the Border Riders during this period. So, too, did steel guitarist Tex King.

It was during the war that Williams began to put together the guitar instruction course which became one of his trademarks. With financial help from the WWVA management, he succeeded in getting his *Simplified by*

Ear System of Guitar Chords printed in June 1943. The 42-page booklet proved an instant success as a mail-order item. By 2004, it had sold more than 200,000 copies. The course went through six printings by the end of 1944 and in those months when travel was limited, it provided a major source of income.

By early 1945, Williams began producing transcribed radio programs for airplay in various sections of the country. He bought time on other stations, sent off the large disc recordings, and made some profit. In the latter part of 1944, Doc along with Chickie and Tex King left Wheeling and went to WFMD in Frederick, Maryland. This station had excellent facilities for cutting transcriptions and it was here that many of the early programs advertising the guitar course were made. Doc recalled that when not playing live from the studio, he and Chickie and King would be in the transcription room recording programs for broadcast elsewhere. In later years, Wheeling Records released three cassette tapes from these and later programs. Other entertainers at WFMD included Mac Wiseman and folk singer Ed McCurdy.

The Frederick period came to a sudden end in early 1945 when Andrew J. Smik Jr., found himself drafted into the U. S. Navy. Williams had registered for the Selective Service while living in Memphis in the summer of 1940. Despite one bad eye, he memorized the eye charts and got into Navy flight school. The weakness soon became apparent so he was discharged on April 12, 1945. President Franklin Roosevelt died the same day and the final Allied victory was less than five months away.

When the war was over, Williams returned to Wheeling. Still much under the influence of the romance of aviation, he operated an airport at nearby Martin's Ferry, Ohio, with a friend and also organized a contracting firm, the Cook and Smik Company. An article in the July-August 1945 *National Hillbilly News* reported that "Doc isn't doing any broadcasting in person," but had transcriptions on a station in North Carolina and one in Ohio. Soon he added two more North Carolina stations. Doc remembered one Sunday afternoon at the airport when an old fan pleaded with him to get back into live music on a regular basis. By then he had already resumed solo appearances on the Saturday night studio-based *Jamboree*. A little later, he got his band back together for three-a-week daytime shows at WWVA as well.

Late in 1945, Doc Williams and his reassembled Border Riders gave a show in Newcomerstown, Ohio. That happened to be the residence of

Mountain Broadcast and Prairie Recorder columnist Mary Jean Shurtz, who reported that Williams "really packed them in." Her review of the concert provides a glimpse of the Border Riders in their prime:

> What an act! Flannels Miller . . . is just about the cutest thing. . . . Flannels plays the fiddle, banjo, bass, guitar and almost any musical instrument in the old time band. . . . Then there's Doc's wife, sweet little Chickie. She's called the Girl with the Lullaby Voice. . . . Chickie plays bass, and is one swell radio personality. The next Border Rider is Curley Sims. . . . Curley is doing quite a bit of comedy . . . along with the rest of his entertaining features. Now we come to that fellow every WWVA listener has admired . . . for years—Doc Williams! . . . Congratulations, Doc, for working at it until you have the Border Riders where they belong—at the top of the world in old time musical entertainment.

Flannels Miller fiddled for the Border Riders until Cy Williams returned from the service. Froggie Cortez and Sunflower had gone off to New Castle, Pennsylvania, to work with Curley Miller's Ploughboys since Cy Williams's and Calvas's marriage had become a casualty of the war. Cy was back with the Border Riders by 1946 and a later article by Mary Jean Shurtz praised his fiddling on "Orange Blossom Special" and his singing on the recent Spade Cooley hit, "Shame on You." Cy continued to work with his brother until October 1956, when he left show business for a job with the U. S. Post Office.

Doc Williams hired William Henry Godwin, an old-time vaudeville performer, to replace Froggie Cortez as comedian. A native of Georgia, by way of Texas, Godwin had recorded for Columbia in 1929 as Shorty Godwin. By the time he came to West Virginia in 1938 with Mack Jeffers and his Fiddlin' Farmers, Godwin had developed his comic character, "Hiram Hayseed." Specializing in novelty fiddling, dancing, comedy and singing, he remained a Border Rider from 1946 until his death in 1959. When Curley Sims left in 1947, Marion Martin renewed what became perhaps the longest association of any musician with Doc Williams outside his own family. If the Sims mandolin had been the outstanding feature of the Border Riders sound in the earlier years, Marion's accordion provided the main characteristic for the next quarter-century. The three Williams daughters often performed, too, especially during the summers when they were not in school.

Doc Williams made his first record in 1947. The WWVA management had not encouraged phonograph recording by their artists earlier, and Doc had not concerned himself much with this aspect of entertainment. But the increasing importance of records for radio airplay made the post-war situation different. Chickie had come into her own following Sunflower's exodus, and Doc decided to feature her on record as well. Both did their initial recording in Cleveland in December. Chickie's first release was "Beyond the Sunset," a single with "Bright Red Horizon" on the flip side. The sacred "Beyond the Sunset" included a recitation of the Rosey Rosewell, long-time Pittsburgh Pirate radio broadcaster, poem, "Should You Go First," and was the hit of the session. The sentimental performance spread the lovely twenty-eight-year-old brunette's fame far and wide.

Other numbers from that first session also had some impact. Doc's original "Willy Roy (the Crippled Boy)" a ballad about a little boy with a terminal illness, went on to become a bluegrass standard although Wilma Lee and Stoney Cooper's 1949 recording would have more influence than Williams's own. "Silver Bell," an old song about an Indian maid by Percy Weinruch, became one of Doc's best-known numbers while "Merry Maiden Polka" showcased the sound that made Doc Williams and Marion Martin popular with ethnic audiences.

This 1947 recording session was a promising beginning for Williams's new enterprise, the Wheeling Record Company. Between them, Doc and Chickie Williams had more than 200 masters for the label which released singles and long-play albums and eventually cassettes and compact discs into 1994. Wheeling Records never had any million sellers or adequate distribution, but it still has records in print and ultimately much of its catalog remained available on cassette for years. In the meantime, the Williamses passed up a chance to record for Mercury in 1949.

While the pair sometimes recorded songs associated with other contemporary country artists, they concentrated on songs uniquely theirs or written by others especially for them. Chickie Williams's songs in this category included "Wintertime in Maine," "World's Meanest Mother," "He Said He Had a Friend," and the sacred "'Neath the Old Olive Tree." In all, the "Girl with the Lullaby Voice" turned out five separate albums. Oddly enough, although Doc and Chickie Williams were a team, they only did one album of duets in 1965.

Doc's repertoire included songs written or designed for him such as "The Little Red Wheelchair," "Daddy's Little Angel," "Tonawanda Rose," and one of his last numbers, "Super Lotto Blues," which described the pitfalls associated with winning the lottery. Some of his other notable numbers included a New England folk song "Nell of Narragansett Bay," another number from the Cowboy Loye songbook "Heaven Express," and 1930s country offerings typified by "Lonesome Valley Sally."

Both Doc and Chickie filled out their albums with old songs from the earlier days of country music such as "Hills of Roane County," "Mary of the Wild Moor," "Where the Silvery Colorado Wends Its Way," and "The Cat Came Back." In 1967, the Williams family added a sacred album to their offerings, and since they were popular in Canada, they did a few songs from North of the Border. Many of their Wheeling releases appeared on the Quality label in Canada.

From 1947 through 1949, Doc Williams operated a summer country music park at Musselman's Grove near Altoona, Pennsylvania. Parks of this nature with weekend afternoon family entertainment had become quite popular through the tri-state area, especially in the Keystone State. Jake Taylor's Radio Ranch near Grafton was West Virginia's best-known park. Williams and his group played often with big-name talent from Hollywood such as singing cowboys Tex Ritter and Jimmy Wakely. Doc promoted Chicago *National Barn Dance* stars like Lulu Belle and Scotty, and such *Opry* heroes as Roy Acuff, Bill Monroe, and Ernest Tubb. *Jamboree* performers like Big Slim McAuliffe and Hank Snow also appeared at Musselman's Grove.

By 1950, the Williamses and the Border Riders were doing far better than most country acts. Few performers enjoyed much security at the time. One contemporary recalled that when he came to WWVA in late 1950, folks said Doc Williams was the only entertainer at the station prosperous enough to pay cash for a suit of clothes. Doc hardly felt rich, however. In 1950, he finally let the WWVA management excuse him from broadcasts long enough to do more road shows. He said he had only "eighty-seven dollars in the bank" when he left for an extended tour in the East and Canada. On this and later trips he drew good crowds in eastern Pennsylvania, upstate New York, rural New England, Ontario, Quebec and the Maritime provinces. Williams's several tours of Newfoundland proved especially rewarding. WWVA had been a powerful 50,000-watt station since October 1942, and its artists found that they had an eager audience waiting in eastern Canada. Daily live shows began to be phased out during the 1950s, but WWVA entertainers now could play personal appearances in a much larger hinterland.

Doc left WWVA a second time in the fall of 1956, buying a thirty-seven per cent interest in radio station WMOD in Moundsville. One-time *Jamboree* artist Jake Taylor was the other principal owner. Brother Cy Williams had remarried and quit music. His replacement, Buddy Spicher, later left to go with Johnnie and Jack and Kitty Wells in Nashville. Doc Williams decided to get off the road for a while. He did fifty-five minutes of deejay work daily and spent most of his remaining time in the business end of things. He did not play at the *Jamboree* because WMOD gave WWVA a lot of competition for the daytime audience. He did not play many live shows either, but did do a three-month television stint at WTRF in Wheeling.

By 1958, Doc had sold his interest in WMOD and returned to his true calling. His love for music, for the *Jamboree*, and for performing proved stronger than the attraction of radio as a business. During this WMOD interlude, Williams did his first Nashville record session on October 8, 1956, with Chet Atkins among the accompanying musicians. The results were not especially satisfying and he did not return to Nashville to record until 1963.

For another twenty years, Doc Williams and the Border Riders remained on the road much of the time, entertaining at school auditoriums, parks, clubs, fairs, and other such locales. Doc branched out into live television, hosting a very successful show for two years at WJAC in Johnstown, Pennsylvania, and earlier at WFBG Altoona. The Williams girls grew up and went to college. Peeper and Poochie obtained degrees from the University of Pittsburgh and West Virginia, respectively. Punkin attended Shepherd State College for a couple of years before pursuing a musical career as Karen McKenzie. Paul Cohen, who had produced Patsy Cline's hit recordings, chose McKenzie as a replacement after Cline's tragic death in 1963. Cohen produced McKenzie's session for ABC Paramount Records, but then his own death intervened and the releases never went anywhere. Nonetheless, Karen remained a fine contemporary country singer who recorded for the Wheeling label. Her oldest son, Andy McKenzie served in the West Virginia State Senate and later as mayor of Wheeling.

After Hiram Hayseed died in 1959, Smokey Pleacher worked for more than a decade as Border Rider comedian until his own death in 1971.

Pleacher and Marion Martin recorded a pair of albums for Wheeling Records. During the 1960s, Pleacher and Martin became as well-known as Cy Williams and Shorty Godwin had been earlier. Other sidemen came and went during those later years with Dean McNett, Curt Dillie, Gary Boggs, Fred Johnson, Jack Jackson Rube Shaffer, and Bill Barton among the more memorable. Sometimes older WWVA figures like Toby Stroud, Roy Scott, and the armless musician Ray Myers worked tours with Doc Williams.

By 1966, Doc Williams played the Saturday night show now known as *Jamboree USA* only about once a month. Much of the rest of the time, the Doc Williams Show remained on the road. Crowds mostly were large and the Border Riders continued to please their fans. But with the increasing conformity in musical styles associated with the bland Nashville Sound, Doc and Chickie Williams found themselves the survivors of a vanishing breed. Still, Doc recalled the middle and late 1960s as among the most lucrative times of his career.

The 1970s proved to be a time of transition. At the beginning Doc and Chickie continued as before, but then their careers began to wind down. They eased away from constant touring and began playing only now and then. The couple made two tours of the British Isles and during the second one in November 1976, they recorded an album in Harrogate entitled *Full Circle*. Most of the songs had not been recorded by them before including "A Flower from the Fields of West Virginia," a song somewhat rewritten from an amalgam of "Flower Blooming in the Wildwood" and "A Flower from the Fields of Alabama." By the end of the decade, their *Jamboree* appearances were down to one or two per year and sometimes then for old-timer reunions or other special occasions. Although Doc and Chickie had connections with the *Jamboree* as solid as Roy Acuff or Minnie Pearl had with the *Grand Ole Opry,* the Wheeling management never seemed to appreciate them in the same way, often favoring some special guest from Nashville. The local management never had the continuity of that at WSM and perhaps that was a reason. Williams, for his part, became increasingly a spokesman for regional distinctiveness and the endangered notion of country music as clean family entertainment. He became a critic of modern complex and expensive recording arrangements which together with emphasis on the Top-40 formats by country radio stations, forced many musicians far younger than himself into near obscurity.

Williams also opened his Country Store across the street from WWVA's Capitol Music Hall in 1977. Stocked with a good selection of Wheeling and music souvenirs, western clothes, and traditional country recordings and publications, the store became a gathering spot for the music's traditionalists and long-term *Jamboree USA* fans. Daughter Peeper managed the store and her parents were often seen helping serve the customers who crowded in on Saturdays. Sometimes the widows of deceased WWVA comedians Hiram Hayseed and Smiley Sutter a.k.a. Crazy Elmer helped out in the store, too. The store remained a popular spot for *Jamboree* fans for more than two decades.

Doc and Chickie still played several show dates yearly through the 1980s. From 1979 until 1984, he organized a yearly reunion concert which featured his own family, former Border Riders, and West Virginia show business veterans like Lee Moore, Blaine Smith, Curley Miller, Bonnie Baldwin, and Roy Scott. Beginning in 1974, the Williamses and their band taped several programs for the public television station in Morgantown. One that featured an in-depth interview by folklorist Carl Fleischhauer later was aired on 200 Public Broadcasting System stations nationally. In 1982 a crew from the British Broadcasting Corporation came to call, filming Doc Williams for an overseas special on West Virginia music. In August 1985, he and his wife appeared on the *Jamboree* with Grandpa Jones and the Sunshine Boys. In February 1986, the couple headed a group of *Jamboree* veterans in a show that included such old favorites as Shirley Barker and Lloyd Carter, as well as younger performers like Jimmy Stephens and Junior Norman. In 1983, Doc was probably the major symbol of continuity when *Jamboree USA* celebrated its 50th anniversary as a live radio barn dance.

Although Chickie became more content in semi-retirement, Doc remained interested in playing, although his appearances were increasingly few and far between. A big special *Jamboree USA* at the Capitol Music Hall on May 19, 1987, honored Doc Williams's fifty-years on the program. He was honored as a Distinguished West Virginian, as West Virginia's Country Music Ambassador by Arch Moore during his first term as governor, and as a 1984 inductee of the Wheeling Hall of Fame, along with opera singer Eleanor Steber. Doc more than made his mark on the state's musical history and in 2009 was inducted into the West Virginia Music Hall of Fame in Charleston. Along with other West Virginia figures who favored older forms of country music such as Wilma Lee Cooper, Little Jimmy Dickens, and Buddy Starcher, Doc and Chickie Williams were living reminders of the Mountain State's contributions to the music.

The couple did their last show together on May 1, 1998. Earlier that year they had made their last trip to Canada. Then on September 14 of that year, Chickie had a crippling stroke that left her paralyzed on her right side. Doc did not play much after that although he and Little John Graham, a veteran radio performer from the early days, had a memorable jam session at Davis and Elkins College in 1999, which was captured on videocassette.

Doc also began to have visual problems caused by macular degeneration. Although he never became totally blind, his eyesight was very limited. However, his mind remained clear and strong. He organized a collection of compact discs for reissue of his and Chickie's earlier recordings—four volumes of ninety-four songs as well as the family's sacred album from 1967 and thirty-one cuts from their radio transcriptions. In addition, the Williams's daughters did a sacred disc of their own. Doc also began making a series of autobiographical tapes that were transcribed and assembled by Peeper in 2006 into book form as *Doc Williams: Looking Back,* a 176–page volume of text and photos which is still in print more than a decade later. Both Doc and Chickie Williams outlived *Jamboree USA,* which terminated in 2005. But time marched on. Cy Williams, retired from music for fifty years, died in the spring of 2006 and Chickie Williams died on November 18, 2007. Doc Williams lived on until January 31, 2011, having outlived most of his contemporaries, his and his wife's musical legacy secure. Daughters Barbara, Madeline, and Karen continue to honor their parents, maintain a website, and are always helpful to fans and researchers who fondly recall the days of the Border Riders.

SELECTED RECORDINGS

Doc Williams and the Border Riders. Four volumes. Wheeling WR 505, 606, 707, 808, 2000–2004. Original recordings of both Doc and Chickie Williams from 1947 to 1972.
The Doc Williams Family Sacred Album. Wheeling CD WR 505–6. Sacred songs from 1967 featuring Doc, Chickie, and their daughters.

PART FOUR

Brother Duets

One of the new phenomena that came out of old-time country music in the Great Depression and attained wide popularity were the harmony duets comprised of two brothers. The Alabama team of Alton and Rabon Delmore initiated this trend with their first Columbia recording in 1931. They followed with weekly appearances on the *Grand Ole Opry* and a whole string of Bluebird discs that extended from 1933 until 1940. The brothers continued cutting material for other labels until Rabon Delmore died in 1952.

The Delmore popularity soon sparked a wave of other duet acts beginning with Bill and Joe, the Callahan Brothers of western North Carolina, in 1934. J. E. and Wade Mainer, who also hailed from the same area of the Tar Heel state, started recording in 1935 after attaining radio popularity in Charlotte. They usually used a larger band and did not sing together. Within a year, they split into separate bands and banjo picking Wade Mainer sang duets with Zeke Morris and later with others. Fiddler J. E. Mainer often used duets in his band, but did not sing in them himself. Zeke Morris somewhat later formed a duet with his brother Wiley and a third Morris brother who worked as half of the duet within J. E. Mainer's Mountaineers. With the exception of the Callahans who held contracts with the American Record Corporation and later Decca, the others were all heard on Victor's budget depression label Bluebird.

Both the Delmores and Callahans had used their own guitar accompaniment. But in 1936 the guitar-mandolin instrumentation of Bill and Charlie, the Monroe Brothers, featured high harmonies and a spirited mandolin lead that introduced a second duet style. By the end of 1938, the Monroe brothers had gone their separate ways with Bill going on to become the Father of Bluegrass. Charlie carved out his own unique musical style which was an amalgam of old-time music, the 1940s newer traditional country, and elements of what would soon emerge as bluegrass. The other new acts in the studio, the Blue Sky Boys—Bill and Earl Bolick—featured a more subdued mandolin-guitar sound with smooth but tight harmony. Nonetheless, many of their songs found their way into bluegrass repertoires. Other brother teams of the 1930s that influenced the development of bluegrass to varying degrees included those of the Anglins, Carlisles, Dixons, and Sheltons in addition to the aforementioned Morris Brothers.

Although the peak popularity of these duets came in the later 1930s, most continued to thrive into the immediate years following World War II. Some new ones entered into the musical limelight including the Stanley Brothers from Virginia, the Bailes Brothers from West Virginia, the Louvin Brothers from Alabama, and Mel and Stan Hankinson—the Kentucky Twins. Both the Bailes and the Louvins contributed many original songs that found their way into bluegrass while The Kentucky Twins toured extensively as a featured act with Bill Monroe during their three years in Nashville.

Four duos from the later 1940s ultimately evolved into full-fledged bluegrass bands. The Lilly Brothers started as a straight duet act on various West Virginia radio stations, but with the addition of banjo picker Don Stover and fiddler Tex Logan they introduced bluegrass music to New England. Roughly a decade younger, the Goins Brothers—also from the southern West Virginia coalfields—after some radio work in Bluefield, became part of the Lonesome Pine Fiddlers off and on for a number of years. They formed the Goins Brothers in 1969 and remained an active group for nearly three more decades. Jim and Jesse McReynolds, brothers from the Virginia mountains, became members of the *Grand Ole Opry* after years of struggle as did the somewhat younger duo of Bob and Sonny, the Osborne Brothers. The latter soon added a third non-family member and performed more often as a vocal trio.

With the exceptions of Jesse McReynolds and Bobby Osborne who remained active in 2017, members of the pioneer brother duets of old-time and early bluegrass music have passed into history. Still the tradition remains and newer teams have come along. Some of those in the bluegrass mainstream today include the Crowe Brothers from Georgia, the Gibson Brothers from New York, and the Spinney Brothers from Nova Scotia. Even the ethnic German, Swiss-born, North Carolina migrant Kruger Brothers fit at least partially into this broad picture.

✄ The Bailes Brothers

Kyle, 1915–1996
John, 1918–1989
Walter, 1920–2000
Homer, 1922–2013

Many who have written about country music history have often referred to the 1930s as the era of the brother teams and duets. While a great number of brother groups flourished in that period there were a goodly number in other time periods, too. For instance, one can examine the development in the 1940s and find the presence of several such groups that are quite noteworthy. Among them was a set of brothers whose popularity extended from their native West Virginia hills to Nashville's Ryman Auditorium and to the cotton fields of northern Louisiana's Red River Valley. These were the Bailes Brothers—Kyle, Johnnie, Walter, and Homer. Their songs and styles had a lasting effect on bluegrass and traditional country music.

Homer Abraham Bailes was a carpenter and preacher who practiced both his trades in Kanawha County, West Virginia. Homer Bailes and his wife, Nannie Ellen Butler, had four sons. She also had children from a previous marriage. Although the family's background and outlook were rooted in the middle class, even at best their economic condition could be described as poor. Going to church and singing at home were among their few comforts. Homer and Ellen's four boys were Kyle Otis, born May 7, 1915; John Jacob, born June 24, 1918; Walter Butler, born January 17, 1920; and Homer Vernon, born May 8, 1922.

In 1925, Homer Bailes died leaving his family to get along the best they could. Things were already tough, but after that with no man at the head of the household just before the Great Depression soon hitting the entire nation they became a great deal worse. Ellen Butler Bailes took in washing

Bailes Brothers: Homer Bailes, Walter Bailes, Johnnie Bailes, Kyle Bailes.
KWKH, Shreveport, 1947.

and ironing and did all kinds of work in order to make ends meet. Even then success came in small packages; she kept the family alive and together, but at times food was pretty scarce, never abundant and more than once the family went to bed hungry. She did manage to buy the boys a guitar for $2.95, paying for it in payments of fifty cents a week. Many years later Walter Bailes saluted his mother's efforts to raise the family in the song "Give Mother My Crown" which Lester Flatt and Earl Scruggs made into a bluegrass classic.

The first real musician in the family was an elder half-brother named Jennings "Flash" Thomas who worked as a rodeo performer and carnival musician. Thomas came home in the early 1930s after several years of wandering and made quite an impression on his younger half-brothers. For a time he and Kyle Bailes sang on radio together. The major influence on the Bailes Brothers's later vocal stylings included a background in sacred singing, their musical half-brother together with what they heard on record and local radio acts like Billy Cox, Hank and Slim Newman, the Holden Brothers, Cowboy Copas and Natchee the Indian, T. Texas Tyler and Harmie Smith as well as Cap, Andy, and Flip.

The spring that Johnnie Bailes graduated from the eighth grade saw a flood destroy the crop on the little farm which the family rented and as a result they decided to move into the city of Charleston fourteen miles away where Johnnie could find some work and help keep Walter and Homer in school. The boys continued to sing at home and in church where they sometimes performed as a group and were known as the Hymn Singers. Johnnie began to aspire to a career as a professional musician and about 1933 worked for several months in the Charleston area with a medicine show group known as Doc Grayfeathers and his Cowboys that also included Robert "Georgia Slim" Rutland on fiddle, Jack Carter on guitar, and Pee Wee Stripling. Johnnie Bailes also played and sang in a talent contest and won first prize singing "Wabash Cannonball" which he had learned from an old Carter Family record.

One of Johnnie's best friends at the time was young Woodrow "Red" Sovine and the two decided to form a duet. After playing locally for several months in everything from churches to honky tonks, they got a job in radio with Jim Pike and his Carolina Tar Heels in the latter part of 1937 on WCHS. At the time they were known as Smiley and Red, the Singing Sailors. In 1938, they moved to Wheeling and played at WWVA for a few months. Although they performed well, times were still hard and they found the going tough. Sovine decided to go home and get married and the duo hitchhiked back to Charleston.

Back at WCHS, Johnnie joined up with Ervin Staggs and his Radio Ramblers which also included Ervin's wife Wilma. At this time Staggs and Johnnie composed the song "Pale Horse and His Rider" which the Bailes Brothers never recorded, but was recorded in later years by Carl Sauceman, Roy Acuff, Hank Williams, and Red Smiley among others. Soon Skeets Williamson joined the group on fiddle and in the summer of 1939, Williamson's sister Molly O'Day also joined them. That fall Johnnie and Skeets went to WBTH in Williamson and then to WJLS in Beckley as Johnnie Bailes and the Happy Valley Folks where Molly O'Day, Cowboy Jack Morris, and Little Jimmy Dickens, whom Johnnie billed as the "Singing Midget," made up the group.

In the meantime Walter Bailes had gotten out of school and entered the music business. He and his older brother Kyle had worked as the Bailes Brothers at WPAR in Parkersburg, West Virginia, and he also had a group at WCHS. Since Johnnie Bailes's band seemed to be doing better at Beckley, Walter and his group also came to WJLS. According to Skeets, he and Johnnie did well enough at Beckley to eat three meals a day—hot dogs with slaw for breakfast, hot dogs with mustard for lunch, and hot dogs with chili for supper. Occasionally they had ketchup on the hot dogs when they wanted a little variety.

Late in 1940, Walter Bailes and his group went back to Charleston and Johnnie Bailes and the Happy Valley Folks went to WHIS in Bluefield and worked briefly for Joe Woods before they broke up and went their separate ways. Johnnie, too, went back to Charleston where he and Walter formed the Bailes Brothers as a duo and went to work at WCHS. Since they never were able to do very well playing shows in the Charleston area, both brothers labored in the Kelly Ax factory in addition to their pickin' and singin' over the airways. From time to time, their brothers Kyle and Homer also worked with them. For a few months in the winter of 1941–42, Johnnie and Walter went to WAPI in Birmingham, Alabama, where they worked with Molly O'Day and Lynn Davis, but then they returned to West Virginia. Finally, they decided to leave Charleston and go where they thought they might become successful.

With a $19.95 guitar bought on credit, Johnnie and Walter Bailes went to WSAZ in Huntington, West Virginia. Things started to go well for them. They became quite popular in the station's three-state listening area which included Eastern Kentucky and southeastern Ohio. They started a show called the *Tri-State Jamboree*. Fiddlin' Arthur Smith, formerly of the *Grand Ole Opry*, worked with them, and they also acquired a bass player and vocalist, Evelyn Thomas, known as "Little Evy" or "Evy Lou." Del Heck, a fiddle player from Huntington, joined the group and a husband and wife team, Charles and Honey Miller, worked with them some, the former being a steel guitar player. This was during World War II and the brothers expected to be drafted into the service, but as matters turned out only Homer passed the physical. Walter even wrote a song to describe the induction of the three boys into the service called "Boys Don't Let Them Take Away the Bible," but the scene described never took place.

The Bailes Brothers played at WSAZ for about two years and were quite popular there doing three or four quarter-hour shows daily, selling many songbooks, and playing several live shows. In 1944, Roy Acuff played a show in Huntington and became a close friend of Johnnie and Walter. He considered their talents to be of *Grand Ole Opry* caliber and a few months later he was able to persuade George D. Hay and Harry Stone into getting them a spot at WSM. Accordingly, they moved to Nashville that October. Within a few weeks they became members of the *Grand Ole Opry*. Johnnie and Walter also did early morning shows on WSM sponsored by Martha White Flour, along with Milton Estes being among the first groups to advertise the product later made world famous by Lester Flatt and Earl Scruggs.

In addition to Walter and Johnnie Bailes, Little Evy Thomas, and Del Heck, Ernest Ferguson, formerly with Johnnie Wright and Jack Anglin, joined the Bailes band known as the West Virginia Home Folks on mandolin. It was this quintet that went to Chicago in February 1945 and recorded ten sides for Columbia. Included in this session were some of their best original songs like "Dust on the Bible" and "I Want to be Loved." "Down Where the River Bends," written by Jim Anglin, one-time member of the Anglin Twins with his late brother, Jack was not released until 2000, but ranked among their most copied songs. Two other numbers recorded at that session, "Searching for a Soldier's Grave" and "As Long As I Live," have been officially credited to Roy Acuff although it is said that both songs were really also written by Anglin.

"Dust on the Bible" in particular became one of the most popular country sacred songs of the mid-forties. It was a hit for the Blue Sky Boys on Victor the next year and it also did well for Wade Mainer on King. The song has since been recorded many times including bluegrass versions by the Stanley Brothers, the Lewis Family, Charlie Moore, and others. Walter Bailes wrote the lyrics in 1940 getting his inspiration from a sermon he had heard preached in 1937 by Reverend Willard Carney of the Prayer and Faith Tabernacle in Charleston. They had sung it often on their radio shows in earlier years.

Throughout the entire career of the Bailes Brothers they recorded a high percentage of original material—nearly all of it either sacred or heart songs. Walter was the prime composer of the group although some of his songs were written either in collaboration with his wife Frankie or with Johnnie or with Homer. In addition to the songs recorded by the brothers, their material included such classic numbers as "Traveling the Highway Home" and "Higher in My Prayers" recorded by Molly O'Day and "Give Mother My Crown" by Lester Flatt and Earl Scruggs. Carl and Pearl Butler also recorded a lot of Bailes material as did Kitty Wells. In the more than two years that the Bailes brothers worked at the *Grand Ole Opry* they became one of the most popular acts on WSM and are said to have received more mail than any other group there at the time. They put out two excellent *Opry* song books, both of which sold very well. They did have some personnel changes in their band. When Del Heck left, brother Homer joined them on fiddle when he got out of the Army. Charles and Honey Miller who had been with them some at Huntington also worked on the *Opry* with the West Virginia Home Folks for a time. However, they acquired their best-known sideman when Shot Jackson, who played steel guitar, switched over to their group after having played with Cousin Wilbur.

After Jackson joined the band they went to the WSM studios in the latter part of 1946 and cut about twenty sides for King, some of which were never released until 2012. Homer Bailes recalled that Syd Nathan took considerable interest in the session and kept urging Jackson to put a lot of "jelly," as he called it, into his playing, an example of Nathan's role as a blender of southeastern and western swing styles in the recording studio. As on their first Columbia session, Ernest Ferguson was there and Ramona Jones replaced Little Evy on bass fiddle. Among the many sides recorded at this session were "Romans Ten and Nine," "Broken Marriage Vows," "She Has Forgotten," and "Daniel Prayed." Apparently the boys were impatient with Columbia who delayed release of all but one of their 1945 session offerings.

Near the end of 1946, the Bailes Brothers switched their base of operations from WSM and Nashville to KWKH and Shreveport, Louisiana. Dean Upson, who had been commercial manager at WSM and a former member of the Vagabonds, an early *Opry* trio, moved to the Shreveport station and Johnnie and Walter went along taking Homer, Ernest Ferguson, and Shot Jackson. Older brother Kyle played bass fiddle. Although Kyle Bailes did not work with the act for long periods, he did perform some valuable service as manager for a longer tenure. In April 1947 when the Bailes Brothers did their second session for Columbia, the personnel consisted of the four brothers plus Ferguson and Jackson. This time such memorable numbers were recorded as "Whiskey Is the Devil," "Oh So Many Years," and "Ashamed to Own the Blessed Savior."

The Bailes Brothers quickly established themselves as a popular group at KWKH and had so many requests for personal appearances that they had to hire a second unit to fill the demand for their services. Jimmie Osborne, who was later billed as the Kentucky Folk Singer, headed this second group and the brothers secured him a recording contract with King and backed him on his initial session in which he recorded four sides—one of which was a Bailes number entitled "My Heart Echoes" that they later recorded themselves on Columbia. On his own a little later, Osborne recorded many sides for King including the memorable "Death of Little Kathy Fiscus" and several Korean War ballads before his tragic death by suicide in late 1957. Claude King played guitar and Buddy Attaway fiddled and played comedy in this second unit.

In July 1947, Walter Bailes joined the church and was subsequently called into the ministry. Thereafter he seldom appeared with the group although he did play once with them on the *Louisiana Hayride*. Homer Bailes then became co-leader of the band with Johnnie. This caused some change in their vocal arrangements as heretofore Walter had usually sung lead in the duets and Johnnie the tenor part. After that they usually switched parts depending on the song.

When Dean Upson and the Bailes Brothers first came to Shreveport they planned to inaugurate a live country show of major proportions. All during 1947 they continued to play their daily radio shows and heavy personal appearance schedule, but also auditioned talent for their planned live jamboree. In April 1948, the *Louisiana Hayride* was started and Roy Acuff was there as a special guest from WSM and he also originated the Prince Albert Network portion of the *Opry* from Shreveport that night. Probably no other Saturday night live country radio show ever had as spectacular a beginning as did the one that originated from KWKH.

In the meantime, the Bailes Brothers had done their last Columbia session the previous December in Nashville. Johnnie and Homer Bailes, Shot Jackson, Clyde Baum, and Tillman Franks made up the personnel, and the songs included the beautiful and touching "Will the Angels Have a Sweetheart," "Pretty Flowers," and "Has the Devil Got a Mortgage on You." Various combinations of the brothers wrote numerous other songs that were never recorded, but were published in their Acuff-Rose Song Folios. Homer assumed the comedy role. After Kyle quit playing, Franks became bass player.

Through 1948 and most of 1949, the West Virginia Home Folks continued to be among the more popular groups at the *Louisiana Hayride*. During this time the boys played an instrumental role in the early careers of two emerging country superstars. Hank Williams came to Shreveport and began his climb to stardom under the Baileses' tutelage. Homer recalled that the white suit worn by Williams in many early photos was one that had been furnished him by their bass player Franks because the lanky Alabaman lacked suitable stage clothes when he arrived at KWKH. Webb Pierce also got his start on the *Hayride* at the urging of the brothers, and he remained their lifelong friend.

Late in 1949, Johnnie and Homer had some differences. Johnnie Bailes and Dalton Henderson went to KTBS in Shreveport and performed for a time. Homer, like Walter had done earlier, eventually went into the ministry. He received training at Southern Methodist University. After 1950 none of the Bailes Brothers worked in a country music act although Johnnie—playing mandolin—and Walter performed together as a gospel duet from 1952 until 1956 in connection with Walter's evangelistic work. They sang on radio KCRT in Baytown, Texas, and did some more recording for King in 1953, including "Muddy Sea of Sin," "Standing Somewhere in the Shadows," and "Avenue of Prayer." They also made some transcriptions for use on a border station.

After that Walter Bailes remained the most musically active, mostly in connection with his ministry. At various times he recorded on smaller labels such as Sarg, Loyal, White Dove, Starlit, and Old Homestead. He also had a religious program on WSM for which he bought the time. At times he made duet recordings with brothers Homer and Kyle and even Ernest Ferguson, but none re-ignited the Baileses' career as it had thrived in the mid-and-late 1940s.

Kyle Bailes, after working some as a duo with Homer on radio in Arkansas and Ohio, recorded a single with him on Briar Records. He eventually settled in Birmingham, Alabama, where he worked as an air conditioner repairman until he retired in 1982. This gave him more time to play with Walter, mostly in churches, but also at an occasional bluegrass festival. In 1982, they also went on a tour of the Netherlands in conjunction with the Dutch country duo, A. G. and Kate.

From 1969 Homer pastored Methodist churches, most notably in or near Roanoke, Louisiana. In 1972, he and Johnnie recorded an album for Starday Records titled *Gospel Reunion*, but between the use of modern Nashville Sound instrumentation and Starday being in a financial bind at the time it attracted little attention. Only later did the Bailes brothers realize that their fans preferred the kind of musical backing that had made them distinct in the 1940s, namely mandolin, fiddle, and either steel guitar or Dobro.

In June 1956, Johnnie Bailes moved to Swainsboro, Georgia, where he first worked as a deejay at WJAT radio and later as manager after Webb Pierce and Jim Denny bought the station and added more stations in neighboring towns. Johnnie also managed an auditorium which hosted a country show, the Peach State Jamboree. Pierce also helped Johnnie get a contract with Decca Records for which he cut eight sides, none making much of an impact. Johnnie also played an occasional bluegrass festival, most notably the Red River Festival with Homer in Louisiana in 1976 and at Summersville, West Virginia, with Walter and Kyle in 1985. Johnnie retired in 1982 from radio management and remained in Swainsboro.

Much of the failure of the Bailes Brothers to maintain the momentum that had made them so popular in the 1944–1949 era could be credited to an animosity that existed between one another as well as to personal problems that tarnished their on-stage image. Walter Bailes once summed it up in a conversation with WSM deejay Eddie Stubbs as "wine, women, and song." Without going into detail, most longtime observers of the boys would agree with that assessment although the first two were probably dominant. Nonetheless, many of their best songs live on as bluegrass standards.

Finally, on Labor Day weekend 1977, the four brothers got together at Johnnie's home along with older half-sister Minnie Thomas Fisher and made a *Reunion* album for John Morris's Old Homestead label with instrumental support from Ernest Ferguson on mandolin and Arthur Ball on Dobro. Shot Jackson had been scheduled to do the session, but when he failed to make it, Ball, a close friend of Ernest Ferguson, became an able replacement. Two years went by before the album was released, during which time some of the old dissension resurfaced. Walter and Kyle Bailes, Shot Jackson, and Ernest Ferguson played the Vandalia Festival in Charleston in 1979 at which time Minnie made the confidential remark that John Morris must be a very patient man, an understatement to say the least. All four of the brothers appeared together in June 1983 when they were inducted into the Walkway of Stars in Nashville.

Time eventually ended the lives of the Bailes Brothers whose careers had ended years before. Johnnie died in Georgia on December 21, 1989; Kyle in Alabama on March 3, 1996; and Walter in Tennessee on November 27, 2000. Homer Bailes recorded a pair of gospel albums for Old Homestead in the 1980s and was the only surviving brother present when the Bailes Brothers were inducted into the West Virginia Music Hall of Fame on December 14, 2009. Homer died in Louisiana on December 2, 2013. The two instrumentalists who helped define their sound—Shot Jackson died in 1991, with Walter Bailes preaching his funeral; genial, gentlemanly Ernest Ferguson, who got along with all the brothers, outlived them all, passing away in 2014.

The Bailes Brothers were not a bluegrass group. However, like Molly O'Day, Roy Acuff, the Louvin Brothers, and other artists of similar stylings, they had considerable influence on bluegrass music. Their vocals of both secular and sacred material were characterized by an intense feeling of fervor and sincerity which country music historian Bill Malone termed Pentecostal. Many of their songs such as "Dust on the Bible," "Whiskey Is the Devil," "Pretty Flowers," and "Down Where the River Bends" have been recorded by bluegrass artists. Many of the other songs in their repertoire would also adapt well to bluegrass and it seems that more of their material will likely enter bluegrass.

One can only speculate on how successful they might have been if internal dissension and personal problems had been avoided. A testimony to the Bailes Brothers lies in the fact that their entire King and Columbia recordings are in print via Bear Family Records of Germany.

SELECTED RECORDINGS

Bailes Brothers: Oh So Many Years. Bear Family BCD 15973, 2002. All of their 1945–1947 Columbia songs, some previously unissued.

Bailes Brothers: Remember Me. Bear Family BCD 17132, 2012. King sessions from 1946, eight previously unissued.

Bailes Brothers: Standing Somewhere in the Shadows. Bear Family BCD 17133, 2012. King sessions from 1953, plus two by Walter and Frankie, and the Johnnie Bailes Deccas.

The Bailes Brothers: Johnnie and Homer. Old Homestead OH CD 103, 2000. Four radio transcription shows from KWKH in 1949.

ᔖ The Callahan Brothers

Walter "Joe" 1910–1971
Homer "Bill" 1912–2002

The 1930s might well be called the decade of the brother duets in country music. As radio stations became more widespread and ways to hear commercialized rural music got nearer home, the number of groups increased. For some unexplained reason brother groups became especially popular. Primary attention has hitherto focused on the Monroe Brothers, whose music provided the antecedents of bluegrass, and the excellent vocal harmonies of the Blue Sky Boys. Alabama's Delmore Brothers with two guitars came along somewhat earlier. Nonetheless, numerous other brother duets flourished with high popularity and their own styles of doing a song, among them were the Callahan Brothers.

The reason why the Callahans have received less attention than their other North Carolina contemporaries of the 1930s, the Monroes and the Bolicks, seems to be the direction they took both geographically and musically. Bill and Charlie Monroe, after their split, each developed a new style that was anchored in Southeastern and Appalachian music. Bill and Earl Bolick continued to play in the same way throughout their careers. The Callahans, however, shifted their base of operations to Texas in the 1940s and while retaining a strong Appalachian influence in their style made accommodations with the type of music that was more popular in the Southwest.

The mountain communities of Faust and Laurel, North Carolina, in Madison County, provided home for the Callahans in their early years. Walter, the elder brother, was born January 27, 1910, and Homer on March 27, 1912. Music played a significant role in the home as the boys' father Bert Callahan played the organ and also served as a voice teacher in addition to his day job as a grocer and the Laurel postmaster. Their mother, Martha Jane Callahan, also played the organ and sang frequently in the home.

Homer (Bill) and Walter (Joe) Callahan.

Homer Callahan (*left*) and Walter Callahan (*right*). Others unknown; KRLD, Dallas, sometime in the 1940s.

Several of the older ballads later recorded by the brothers were traditional tunes they learned from their parents including "Banks of the Ohio" and "Katie Dear." In addition to their parents' influence, Homer and Walter Callahan also were familiar with the music of other area musicians such as the Carolina Tar Heels and Bascom Lamar Lunsford. As teenagers, the Callahans came to enjoy recordings of artists from outside their home territory such as Riley Puckett, Jimmie Rodgers, and the Skillet Lickers. They got comedy ideas from Emmett Miller, a blackface comedian, and Jack King, a vaudeville comedian who often performed in Asheville.

The Callahans began playing together locally in about 1924. Walter almost always played guitar but his brother, who started out on 5-string banjo, eventually developed proficiency on a wide variety of instruments including the fiddle, mandolin, guitar, ukulele, tenor banjo, harmonica, and bass fiddle. They served out a musical apprenticeship of several years in western North Carolina, playing for area social events and at fiddlers' conventions. Although they evidently won a fair share of fiddlers' contests, Homer stated later that their showmanship and talents as entertainers far exceeded his fiddle skills.

Duet yodeling became an early identifying characteristic of the Callahan Brothers. While the team of Reece Fleming and Respers Townsend preceded them on record and perhaps influenced both their style and their repertory, Homer and Walter certainly carried it to greater heights of popularity. Following a very well-received appearance in which they featured duet yodeling at the Rhododendron Festival in Asheville in 1933, a local furniture dealer contacted W. R. Calaway of the American Record Company. The veteran A&R man made quick arrangements to record the boys. In January 1934 the brothers journeyed to New York and cut fourteen sides on their first session. Among the tunes recorded were "St. Louis Blues" and "She's My Curly Headed Baby." The latter song became the best-known number identified with the Callahans and other artists soon covered it on record including Riley Puckett and J. E. Mainer's Mountaineers. The song was popular enough that the brothers made second and third versions of it in 1935 and 1936 respectively.

The year 1934 also saw the beginning of a long radio career for the brothers. After their first record session they were offered a program on WWNC Asheville sponsored by JFG Coffee; it paid each of them $4.00 per week. That August they went to New York and cut another fifteen sides for ARC. This time their sister Alma Callahan went along and helped them on four numbers which were released under the name the Callahan Family. Although these sides constituted the only numbers recorded by the three Callahans, Homer recalled Alma as being an excellent vocalist. She lived near Asheville for many years. "Little Poplar Log House" became one of the better-known songs recorded at their last 1934 session and was later recorded by the Carter Family. At these first two sessions, the Callahans also recorded some recompositions of Jimmie Rodgers tunes, including "North Carolina Moon" and "T. B. Blues No. 2".

The following year saw the Callahans move their base of operations to station WHAS in Louisville, Kentucky. J. L. Frank, later famous as a *Grand Ole Opry* artist manager and the father-in-law of Pee Wee King, induced them to switch their radio work to the Falls City by paying them as much per day as they received for a week's work in Asheville. They also did another recording session for ARC in New York. This gave them a total of more than forty sides on wax before the Mainers, the Monroes, or the Bolicks ever set foot in a recording studio.

In 1936 the Callahan Brothers, still based in Louisville, did two more sessions in New York. On the latter trip to the studio in December, they took along Shorty Hobbs as a mandolin player. At the time Hobbs, who had earlier recorded with Asa Martin on Gennett and later gained fame as half of the Shorty and Little Eller team at Renfro Valley, worked on WHAS with Frankie Moore and the Log Cabin Boys and Cousin Emmy. Although Homer usually played mandolin on the radio and at personal appearances, they hired an extra mandolin player on their recordings. Hobbs, whose comedy work offstage must have at least equaled his professional efforts, was remembered as being an unusually lighthearted individual on that trip to New York. Homer Callahan recalled one occasion when the little musician went skipping down Broadway and attracted a small crowd of onlookers with the old trick of staring upward towards the sky. Hobbs played with them on fourteen sides including "The End of Memory Lane" and "She Came Rollin' Down the Mountain," a somewhat risqué number. In fact, looking at Callahan recordings, several of their numbers were a little bolder in content than what the Blue Sky Boys or Dixon Brothers might have done.

From Louisville, the Callahans went to WWVA Wheeling for a short stint. Later, in 1937, Walter Callahan decided to give up show business for a time and returned to North Carolina. Homer continued on, going to WLW in Cincinnati. The Ohio city served at the time as the home base of John Lair's *Renfro Valley Barn Dance*. Lair had severed connections with WLS and started his own barn dance in Cincinnati although his later famed complex in Rockcastle County, Kentucky, was not completed until late 1939. Red Foley, Slim Miller, and the Coon Creek Girls worked for Lair and Homer Callahan joined this entourage as mandolin player, singer, and comedian.

Homer worked with this group for about two years in various musical and comedy roles. An especially popular combination was a comedy vocal group known as the Goofus Band which included Homer Callahan, Red Foley, Slim Miller, and Doc Swalley. He was occasionally joined by his brother, and in February 1939 they did a final record session for ARC, by then known as the Columbia Recording Corporation, in Chicago. The Callahan Brothers, together again, went to Springfield, Missouri, before the end of the year where they worked on radio with the Weaver Brothers and Elviry. In 1940, the Callahans shifted briefly to KVOO's *Saddle Mountain Roundup* at Tulsa, where they met Herald Goodman (formerly of the *Grand Old Opry* vocal group, The Vagabonds) and promoter Gus Foster. Together they went to KRLD in Dallas, which remained the main base of operations for the rest of their career.

Gus Foster, with the help of the Callahans, made KRLD a very important country music station and at the same time brought a great number of more Eastern and Southeastern artists and acts to the Southwest. Most important, of course, were the Callahans, but others who came to Dallas for stints of varying lengths were Georgia Slim Rutland and Howdy Forrester, Fairley and Jack Holden, Skeets Williamson, Molly O' Day and Lynn Davis, half of the original the Coon Creek Girls, and the Buskirk Family. Gus Foster's *Texas Roundup* eventually grew into the *Big D Jamboree*, one of the most popular Saturday-night country shows.

When the Callahan Brothers went to Texas, their old Christian names, Homer and Walter, became replaced by the nicknames Bill and Joe respectively. It was under these pseudonyms that they recorded numerous transcriptions for use on the Mexican border stations. It has been suggested that since the Shelton Brothers—Bob and Joe—were already popular in the Southwest, the company wanted the Callahans to have similar-sounding first names although not exactly the same. The names Bill and Joe became so well known that the true names of the Callahan Brothers are almost forgotten today.

In their early months at Dallas, the Callahans worked as the Blue Ridge Mountain Folks with Daisy Lange and Violet Koehler who had, together with Rosie and Lily May Ledford, made up the Coon Creek Girls at WLW. The Ledford sisters remained with John Lair and for a time there were two groups of that name. Koehler later returned to Kentucky and married Custer Ledford, the brother of Rosie and Lily May. Lange lived her later years in Indiana.

The Callahans also recorded in Dallas, doing a session for Decca in 1941. They cut seven sides, one of which has never been issued. Bill shifted to bass fiddle, and harmonica on one song, for this session. Bass was an instrument he played more often in the later years. Young Paul Buskirk, who had recently come to KRLD with his brothers from West Virginia, was featured on mandolin.

During the war years Bill and Joe Callahan did live radio shows at both KRLD and KWFT Wichita Falls. Their transcriptions, most of which were made for the Sellers Company of Fort Worth, were played on the border stations and perhaps other stations as well. They gained great popularity and made numerous personal appearances. They also began to make some accommodations with Southwestern musical styles, incorporating some elements of western swing and honky tonk into their sound. Their shows also included quite a bit of comedy, as did most country acts during the 1940s. Bob Pinson recalled seeing a Callahan show in the mid-1940s and his most vivid memory of the event was a scene from a comedy routine in which Bill Callahan ran across the stage carrying a fire extinguisher. Bill sometimes did comedy with other acts as well. Lynn Davis remembered him working several shows with his and Molly O Day's group in the spring of 1945.

Also in 1945 the Callahans journeyed to Hollywood where they became one of a number of country acts to be featured in musical B westerns. *Springtime in Texas* was a Monogram picture which starred Jimmy Wakely and featured Lee "Lasses" White and the Callahan Brothers. After the picture's release they toured quite a bit with Wakely and the picture did very well. It is possible that the Callahans may have had uncredited parts or were simply extras in other films during their Hollywood sojourn. Bill also began to do session work as a bass fiddle player and through the late 1940s and early 1950s worked on many sessions both in Dallas and on the West Coast, mostly on the Capitol and Columbia labels. Among the artists with whom he did studio work were Jimmy Wakely, Wesley Tuttle, Gene O' Quin, Lefty Frizzell, Ray Price, and Marty Robbins. Probably the best-known recording which featured his work as a sideman was the famous pop-country hit of 1949, "Slippin' Around."

Bill Callahan also took time out from his work with his brother to make an extensive tour of the Eastern states with Ray Whitley in 1946 and 1947 as a comedian. While in Philadelphia during this tour, he recorded two songs on the small Cowboy label. After the tour, he returned to Dallas and KRLD. By this time his children Ronnie and Buddy were sometimes appearing with him and his brother on radio.

The Callahans were becoming old timers on the country scene and new artists seemed to be attracting the attention of the fans by the early 1950s. Among them, young Texan Lefty Frizzell was managed by Bill Callahan for more than a year. In 1951 the brothers made one of their last extensive tours as a part of Frizzell's troupe. That same year the Callahan Brothers did their last recording session for Columbia. By then the instrumentation behind their duets featured the contemporary country sound of the early 1950s.

As the decade passed, the Callahan Brothers as a group gradually dropped out of the musical field. Joe returned to Asheville and entered the grocery business. Bill went to work for an auto parts company, but he still continued to play music as a sideline. He did some country comedy and also played as a sideman in a ballroom dance orchestra.

In the early 1960s, Joe returned to Dallas for a while and the brothers sometimes played together. They appeared often on the Lloyd "Cowboy" Weaver television show and at other places, too. By the end of the decade, Joe Callahan, in ill health, returned to Asheville where he died of cancer on September 10, 1971.

Bill Callahan and his family continued to reside in Dallas. In later years, he made his living as a photographer while continuing as an active country musician—primarily in the Dallas area. He had been connected with a live show, The Texas Jamboree, as both part owner and performer. Comedy work remained his mainstay both onstage and off. Even when taking pictures, he got much delight from getting smiles and laughs from the adults and especially the children who sat before his camera. At one point, he heard that WWVA's *Jamboree, U. S. A.* needed a comedian after the 1980 death of their longtime comic Crazy Elmer, but ultimately stayed in Dallas. He died there on September 12, 2002. While perhaps not as significant as the Bolicks, Delmores, or Monroes, the Callahans did their part and were the outstanding brother duet for the American Record Corporation.

SELECTED RECORDINGS

The Callahan Brothers. Old Homestead OHCD 4031, 2000. Reissues of 1934–1941 singles.
In Memory of the Callahan Brothers. Cattle CCD 267, 2002. More singles from 1934–1941.
More Memories of the Callahan Brothers. Cattle CCD 277. Another twenty of their originals.

✄ The Goins Brothers

Melvin, 1933–2016
Ray, 1936–2007

In the early years of bluegrass, a large number of combinations rather quickly took up the style being popularized by Bill Monroe and his band. While it is true that most of the elements of the bluegrass style had been around for several years and various bands had unconsciously used portions of the emerging sound, after 1945 many made deliberate efforts to emulate the Blue Grass Boys by adapting their own material to the style. Most prominent among these were the Stanley Brothers and after 1948 Lester Flatt and Earl Scruggs. Somewhat less prominent, but nonetheless a long-established group with a distinct style was the Lonesome Pine Fiddlers that bluegrass scholar L. Mayne Smith considered one of the ten major groups when he wrote his pioneering study "An Introduction to Bluegrass" in a 1965 issue of the *Journal of American Folklore*.

Unfortunately for those of us who had become hard-core bluegrass fans only in the late 1960s, the Lonesome Pine Fiddlers no longer existed as a group. They never played any college concerts and disbanded before bluegrass festivals became numerous. Throughout most of their career they played to audiences in the small towns and coal camps of Appalachia. Likewise, their records, although cut primarily on major labels, received fairly limited distribution both in the early 1950s on RCA Victor and a decade later on Starday. Nonetheless, several bluegrass musicians prominent on the later scene worked with that now legendary group. Most notable among these was Curly Ray Cline, a four-decade veteran of Ralph Stanley's Clinch Mountain Boys, who managed to inject his own personality upon the bluegrass public to a greater degree than most other expert sidemen. Although others worked with the Fiddlers, it was through Melvin and Ray, the Goins Brothers, that much of the distinct vocal and instrumental sound of the Lonesome Pine Fiddlers survived to delight the ears of later bluegrass fans.

Melvin (*left*) and
Ray Goins (*right*),
ca. 1971.

Melvin Goins, lead singer, rhythm guitar player, and spokesman for the
Goins Brothers, was born near Bramwell, Mercer County, West Virginia,
on December 30, 1933. Ray Goins was almost exactly two years younger,
his birthdate being January 3, 1936. There were a total of ten children in
the Goins family, most who played or sang old time or country music. Both
of their grandparents played banjo and other relatives played the fiddle.
Although only Melvin and Ray were long-term professional musicians, one
brother, Donnie, played drums for quite some time with country singer Mel
Street. Younger brothers James, Harold, and Conley played bluegrass and
appeared at some shows and festivals with Melvin and Ray.

The Lonesome Pine Fiddlers got their start as a band in 1938, a time
when the Goins Brothers were hardly out of the cradle. The Cline family of
Gilbert, West Virginia, formed the nucleus of the group, the leader being

thirty-two-year-old Ezra Cline on bass. The other members included Lazy Ned Cline, tenor banjo; Curly Ray Cline, fiddle; and Gordon Jennings, guitar. The group got their start in radio as a guest on the Lynn Davis show at WHIS in Bluefield and soon had their own show on the station. Bluefield was fifty miles from the Cline home which meant rising in the wee hours of the morning in order to make it to the studio. During the war, fuel scarcity caused the band to abandon their radio show although those who were available played for dances and local social events around Gilbert. Ned Cline was killed in World War II and younger brother Charlie Cline who played several instruments joined the band. For clarity Curly Ray, Ned, and Charlie Cline were brothers while Ezra Cline was their cousin. Jennings also left the group to play on numerous radio stations around the country before later returning to Bluefield with his own radio show. In 1945, the Fiddlers returned to Bluefield with a daily show for Black Draught. The band's sound, although somewhat traditional in nature, was not what would be called bluegrass. Curly Ray Cline described it as being somewhat akin to the Delmore Brothers.

In November 1949, Bob Osborne, on guitar, and Larry Richardson, on banjo, joined the Lonesome Pine Fiddlers at which time they really emerged with a full bluegrass sound. In March 1950, the Fiddlers made their first recordings for the Cozy label, a small company in Davis, West Virginia, owned by country-gospel musician John Bava. Ezra Cline, Bobby Osborne, Larry Richardson, and Ray Morgan made up the foursome on this session as Curly Ray Cline had temporarily left the band. "Pain in My Heart" and "Lonesome, Sad and Blue" attracted considerable attention and Bava leased the masters to Coral Records while Lester Flatt and Earl Scruggs covered "Pain in My Heart" on Mercury. By all accounts, Osborne and Richardson were a hot act in the area and Cline kept the sound in most of his later bands.

Meanwhile the youthful Goins Brothers were passing into adolescence and absorbing the music played by various kinfolk. On radio they listened to the *Grand Ole Opry* where their favorite performer was Bill Monroe and to such local performers on WHIS as the Lonesome Pine Fiddlers and Rex and Eleanor Parker. From about 1947 on, however, their favorite station was WCYB in Bristol where they could hear the Stanley Brothers, Curly King and the Tennessee Hilltoppers, and, at various times, Charlie Monroe,

Mac Wiseman, and Flatt and Scruggs. The brothers also got to see some of their favorites at Glenwood Park near Princeton where many country and bluegrass artists frequently played on summer Sunday afternoons. Soon they manifested an interest in playing themselves. A relative gave Melvin Goins a guitar and they traded four chickens and a rooster for a banjo. Later their father swapped the banjo in a horse trade and the brothers replaced it by doing a week's hard labor at basement digging. With the proceeds of their toil they purchased a new banjo at a music store in Bluefield. When free from their chores, the boys spent hours practicing in an isolated mountain cabin. In 1950 and 1951, they occasionally guested on Gordon Jennings' radio show on WKOY in Bluefield.

Jimmy Martin came through Bluefield early in 1951 and played briefly with the Fiddlers, but then teamed up with Bobby Osborne while Curly Ray Cline left for greener pastures. Richardson also departed about this time. Ezra Cline recruited two teenagers—Jimmy Williams and Paul Humphrey who called themselves the Williams Brothers. Jimmy Williams soon left leaving Paul with the name Williams which he has retained through his musical career. Ray Goins then joined the band. Meanwhile the Lonesome Pine Fiddlers contracted with RCA Victor, becoming their first bluegrass band. In May and October 1952, the band did their first two sessions on RCA Victor. The band then consisted of Ezra, Ray, and Curly Ray as well as Paul Williams and Rex Parker. "My Brown Eyed Darling" was perhaps their most popular number from their 1952 sessions, being composed by Ezra's daughter Patsy with the assistance of Paul Williams as a tribute to her fiancé Bobby Osborne then in military service.

The Lonesome Pine Fiddlers reorganized somewhat after that. Curly Ray's younger brother Charlie Cline, who had been working with Bill Monroe, replaced Ray Goins on banjo. They moved briefly to WOAY in Oak Hill and then for a longer stint to 50,000-watt WJR in Detroit where Casey Clark had a popular daily show, *The Big Boy Frolics*. This band did a third session for RCA in August that had Cline relative Albert Puntari guesting on mandolin.

Of the six numbers they did, "Dirty Dishes Blues" ranked as most memorable—a song composed by a local Cincinnati musician named Gene Masters. It also included a pair of instrumentals that featured Curly Ray and Charlie Cline. The story goes that the Fiddlers also made some recordings for the

Detroit-based Fortune label, some of them also backing the youthful Davis Sisters although no confirmation or masters have ever surfaced.

Ray Goins, together with older brother Melvin, Joe Meadows, and Bernard Dillon, a distant relative, organized the first Goins Brothers band and also played a daily radio show at WHIS Bluefield. This group played from August to November. It was a struggle trying to make it as a group although Melvin's colorful anecdote about their trying to save money by cooking on a hot plate which they hid in a dresser drawer seems to have been the most memorable moment in this phase of their career.

The struggles of this initial effort of the Goins Brothers ended in November 1953 when Paul Williams entered military service and Charlie Cline opted to rejoin Bill Monroe. Ezra Cline returned to Appalachia and secured a program at WLSI Pikeville, Kentucky. Melvin and Ray leapt at the chance to work for $12.50 a week as their share of the radio job and earned an additional five dollars a day when they played personal appearances.

For the remainder of their existence, the Lonesome Pine Fiddlers continued to be based in Eastern Kentucky. In the heart of Appalachia, it is a land of rugged topography with narrow, crooked roads and numerous small towns, most of which are, or have been, coal camps. More recently it has become known to the outside world as an area of grinding poverty, cultural backwardness, and corporate exploitation. Despite this bleak picture, life in Eastern Kentucky has enjoyed its moments of happiness—perhaps as many, if not more, than more affluent parts of the world. Among other enjoyments the inhabitants of those towns were treated to frequent shows by such groups as the Lonesome Pine Fiddlers. The band's main source of income, however, was derived from a variety of live appearances at both indoor and outdoor theaters, matinee and evening performances in schoolhouses, and the so-called "candy show."

However, that form of entertainment, the candy show, commonly used by the Fiddlers in the fifties no longer flourishes in Appalachia or anywhere else. One might describe the candy show as something like a medicine show only for the consumer with a sweet tooth rather than an ache or pain. Melvin Goins described it thusly:

> It was a free show . . . we would go into these little communities and play
> these little ball parks, fields, close to country grocery stores—any place where

we could find a big place in the road where we could assemble a lot of people for a big free show. We had what they call a candy show and we done [*sic*] free entertainment and sold candy . . . for a quarter a box and gave away gifts and prizes [in the candy box].

The Fiddlers announced the locations of their forthcoming candy shows on their radio programs and also promoted it in the particular community by loudspeaker on the day of the performance. Ezra Cline in 1974 recalled that the crowds were generally large, as many as a thousand persons, and that they sometimes remained for several days in the same location if attendance remained high. The financial rewards, while not great by modern standards, compared favorably with the shows where admission tickets were sold. It was also at these outdoor shows that the Fiddlers first used a sound system, having performed in the early years without the aid of a PA set.

In February and September 1954, the Lonesome Pine Fiddlers did their final two record sessions on RCA Victor. The band's make-up for these sessions was Ezra and Curly Ray Cline and Melvin and Ray Goins, plus James Roberts. Roberts, sometimes known as James Carson, was the son of Doc Roberts, the famous old-time fiddler and pioneer recording artist. A few years earlier, James had recorded gospel duets on the White Church and Capitol labels with his wife, Martha Carson. Four numbers were recorded at each of these RCA Victor sessions. Of these, "Windy Mountain" and "No Curb Service" ranked as most memorable. The session of September 1954 was the last recording by the group until 1961 when they went to Nashville to record for Starday. Most of the Victor recordings were original material, several of which were written by Curly Ray Cline, Paul Williams, or Kessler Cline. The foursome of Ezra and Curly Ray Cline and Melvin and Ray Goins continued to work together as the Lonesome Pine Fiddlers until April 1955 when Ray Goins departed for Flint, Michigan, and a GM plant. Melvin Goins stayed until June 1955 when he also left the group. As replacements, Ezra first hired Udell McPeak and then Billy Edwards. After his return from the service, Paul Williams rejoined the Fiddlers for a brief time before going with Jimmy Martin.

Although this combination made no recordings, they undoubtedly made some excellent music and played a weekly television show at WHIS in Bluefield for Piggly Wiggly Stores as well as their radio work in Pikeville.

Udell McPeak, who died in 2009, possessed a wit and sense of humor virtually unsurpassed among bluegrass musicians. He also played a costumed comedy role of a character named Jasper. During this period Ezra Cline published the *Lonesome Pine Fiddlers Song and Picture Book* which has today become a treasured collector's item.

When Melvin Goins left the Lonesome Pine Fiddlers, he soon got back with his brother Ray who had returned from Michigan and the brothers again formed their own group with their uncle Bernard Dillon and cousin Buck Dillon. From July until November, they played a half-hour daily radio show at WPRT in Prestonsburg, Kentucky. "With winter coming on," as Melvin put it, things "got a little cold and times got hard" and the band dissolved. After working at various odd jobs throughout the winter, the brothers returned to Bluefield in the summer of 1956. Melvin, who had married in June of that year, sought more substantial employment. He found it at WHIS-TV with Cecil Surratt. During the next few years, bluegrass music went through a difficult period because of the impact of rock and roll. Even in Appalachia, traditional country groups found it necessary to make some accommodation, an electric guitar becoming the minimal addition. For the next couple of years until late 1958, the Goins Brothers worked as part of Cecil Surratt's group on his daily afternoon television show and also on Saturday night. Smitty Smith soon joined the entourage on electric guitar. They also worked a Friday evening jamboree on WOAY-TV at Oak Hill and played numerous personal appearances and dances throughout the region. After Billy Edwards left the Lonesome Pine Fiddlers, he came to Bluefield where he was already known through his television appearances with Ezra Cline's band. Billy Edwards's versatile talents were used in a variety of ways until Ray Goins again quit music for a time to work in a furniture factory at Bluefield after which Edwards played banjo.

The Lonesome Pine Fiddlers also changed their style somewhat in response to the times. Through much of the later 1950s, they used electric guitar played by Charlie Cline. Lee Barnett, Charlie's wife, was featured on vocals along with the ever-present Curly Ray and Ezra Cline. During much of 1958, they played a weekly half-hour show at WSAZ-TV in Huntington, West Virginia, along with their radio work at Pikeville.

About 1960 or 1961, Charlie Cline left the Lonesome Pine Fiddlers for the final time and entered the ministry, relocating to Alabama. Shortly afterward,

Melvin and Ray Goins rejoined Ezra Cline's band. The Fiddlers began to record traditional bluegrass again, this time for Starday and had three albums released in the next two years. They did a fourth album with Hylo Brown and he in turn helped out on their last album which was cut at the same session in November 1962. For about fifteen months Ezra and Curly Ray and Melvin and Ray worked at WCYB-TV in Bristol where they had a show on Monday evenings. This foursome remained together until 1964.

By this time the Lonesome Pine Fiddlers were becoming a part-time group. Ezra Cline had already entered the restaurant business in Pikeville some years before and also operated a swimming pool during the summer months. Curly Ray did some work in the mines as did Ray Goins until he acquired a grocery store. The two also helped local artists on occasional recording sessions including Hobo Jack Adkins, the original composer of "No School Bus in Heaven" that was recorded both by the Stanley Brothers and Red Ellis. However, throughout the mid-sixties they continued to play a few school matinees and dances. Kentucky Slim Branham played guitar in this latter period. Guitar picker Landon Messer and banjoist Lowell Varney also would fill in as Fiddlers on occasion.

Melvin Goins on guitar together with Billy Edwards on banjo, Louie Profitt on fiddle, Norman Blake on Dobro, Bill Lowe on bass, and sometimes Ray Goins on banjo worked a lot of package shows at parks, drive-in theaters, and schools. Often they appeared with other name acts such as the Louvin Brothers and the Osborne Brothers. They worked one memorable show with Bill Monroe; at the time one of the Blue Grass Boys, Ed Mayfield, was stricken with what proved to be a fatal illness. The assistance of the Goins Brothers and their band at this time helped to cement Melvin and Ray's lasting friendship with Bill Monroe.

Mostly, however, this group worked with Hylo Brown and Melvin Goins did the booking for Hylo for a couple of years. He also played a comedy character named Hot Rize Charlie. Norman, Billy, and Louie worked on Hylo's last session for Capitol records in late October 1960. Unfortunately, it was not released until 1992.

The Lonesome Pine Fiddlers did not actually disband until 1968 when Ezra Cline retired from his restaurant and moved back to West Virginia. He lived at Baisden, a small community near Gilbert, and worked in the Community Action Program. Not wholly out of music, he sometimes emceed a show in the area or played with local musicians. He kept up with the contemporary bluegrass scene, particularly the activities of the Osborne Brothers as his daughter was married to Bobby at the time. Ezra died on July 11, 1984.

When they left the Lonesome Pine Fiddlers in 1964, Ray Goins dropped out of music for a while except for part-time work with the Fiddlers. Melvin stayed in the business. He worked some as a single, played with Hylo Brown and a few other groups part-time. In January 1966, Melvin booked some shows for the Stanley Brothers and shortly after joined the Clinch Mountain Boys full time. In this period he played rhythm guitar and bass and did comedy as Big Wilbur while also helping out with bookings. After Carter Stanley's death in December 1966, Melvin Goins remained with Ralph Stanley's Clinch Mountain Boys for two and one-half years. He participated in Stanley's early recording sessions on Jalyn and King, playing rhythm guitar and singing bass or baritone. He left Stanley's group to reform the Goins Brothers in May 1969.

While Melvin worked for Ralph Stanley, Ray had been operating a country store near Elkhorn City, Kentucky. One of the Goins Brothers first moves was to record an album on the Rem label entitled *Bluegrass Hits Old and New* with the able assistance of Paul "Moon" Mullins on fiddle and Kentucky Slim Branham on bass. The album was highlighted with four Lonesome Pine Fiddler numbers and a couple of Jim Eanes songs that became Goins standards—"Wiggle Worm Wiggle" and "Your Old Standby." A deejay friend who went on to write several songs for them, Mike Paxton, contributed "Black Lung Blues" which dealt with a hot topic in the coalfields. Harley Gabbard, an Indiana Dobro player, joined the band for most of their shows. A second album recorded in May 1970 on Jack Lynch's Jalyn label titled *Bluegrass Country* included the first bluegrass version of the old Al Dexter country hit "Pistol Packin' Mama" and a new song by Paxton, "Fly Little Bluebird." Gabbard and Dave Sutherland, a former bass player with Jim and Jesse, rounded out the backup which some critics thought was a bit thin. Later Goins recordings did not lack mandolin, fiddle, or both. Meanwhile, as bluegrass festivals began to increase in numbers, the band stayed busy in the warmer months.

For more than twenty years until 1994 the Goins Brothers played a weekly television show at WKYH in Hazard, Kentucky, and in the early 1970s made semi-regular visits to the popular *Sleepy Jeffers Show* at WCHS-TV in Charleston, West Virginia. The elementary school programs sometimes extended into adjacent parts of West Virginia and Ohio. While these paid little, it allowed the boys to maintain a band in the slack season.

The Goins Brothers began recording with the new Jessup label in Jackson, Michigan, in late 1971. The first album *Head of the Holler* featured quite a bit of new material and ironically no Lonesome Pine Fiddler numbers. Mike Paxton contributed the title song and co-wrote four others. Art Stamper of Louisville, Kentucky, a veteran of the Stanley and Osborne bands, fiddled on this session and his presence contributed greatly to the album's musical success. Newcomer Leslie Sturgill played mandolin on this album and veteran bass player Bill Rawlings rounded out the session. Bringing near-legendary sidemen such as Stamper back into the bluegrass fold would not be a unique accomplishment for Melvin Goins as a band-leader as he later repeated the process with such figures as Joe Meadows and Curley Lambert among others. The downside for the Goins Brothers came from the fact that these persons often moved on to other bands that could afford to pay them more.

The brothers did two more albums for Jessup. The first, *A Tribute to the Lonesome Pine Fiddlers*, brought Joe Meadows back into bluegrass music. Meadows had worked with the first Goins band some two decades earlier before going to work with the Stanley Brothers, Bill Monroe, and Buddy Starcher. Meadows also did a fiddle album for Jessup and then went on to work with other bands. The last Jessup album constituted the first Goins sacred effort and made use of the Louvin Brothers favorite *God Bless Her She's My Mother* for a title song. It also included a new standard by J. D. Jarvis, "Six Hours on the Cross," and revived a couple of Lonesome Pine Fiddler gospel songs. A fourth Jessup album *Bluegrass Blues* contained one of the best songs describing the life of Appalachian migrants to Midwestern cities as a title number, but was released only as a single at the time and finally came out on a Plantation cassette in 1984.

In addition to supporting Meadows on a Jessup album, the Goins Brothers Band backed a women's gospel quartet made up of four sisters whose family name was Wood and with a quartet known as the Woodettes. Melvin Goins later married their leader, Willia Wood, and the sisters subsequently made additional albums with instrumental support from the Goins

Brothers. Willia also recorded a solo album, but it was released only on eight-track tape.

With more and more bluegrass festivals springing up, the Goins Brothers tried their hand at promoting them either by themselves or in partnership with others. By and large, the results were mixed. The first took place at Lake Stephens Park near Beckley, West Virginia, in 1971 and ran through 1975. One of the better ones, at Scioto Furnace, Ohio, took place on the farm of R. W. Skeens. The latter, a tireless worker, even built an upper deck in the seating area, making it unique among festival locales. Other good festivals in which Melvin Goins had an interest included Clay City, Kentucky; Prestonsburg, Kentucky; and Round Eyes Park at Painter's Creek, Ohio. Others are better forgotten.

In November 1974, the Goins Brothers signed with Rebel Records which had become a leading company for bluegrass music. Over the next five years, they released four albums—two of them sacred—with some of the best band members they had assembled. Veteran mandolin picker Curley Lambert who had made many recordings with Bill Clifton and the Stanley Brothers, joined the band, usually introduced by Melvin as the "old bluegrass evergreen." Youth were represented by Buddy Griffin, an innovative fiddler who had worked with the *Jamboree, USA* staff band, and the youngest of Melvin's brothers, Conley Goins. Born in 1955, he played bass fiddle and sang such George Jones songs as "He Stopped Loving Her Today" with real sincerity. Conley died in 2010. Dick Freeland sold Rebel Records to David Freeman in 1979 who reduced the label's talent roster, but Melvin Goins did later return to Rebel.

After Griffin and Lambert's departure from the band, Melvin again displayed his skill for recruiting quality band members by bringing back Art Stamper who had preceded Joe Meadows in the group and getting the younger Danny Jones—a veteran of the Bluegrass Alliance and Monroe's Blue Grass Boys—to play mandolin. Dave Skeens, son of R. W. Skeens and brother-in-law of Conley Goins, became the band's bass man. In addition to another high-powered fiddler in Stamper, the combination benefitted immensely from Jones who brought songs from his repertoire that were new to the band. The two albums recorded for Old Homestead in the early 1980s had just a little bit different sound while still immersed in traditional bluegrass. The material included several numbers from the Flatt and Scruggs catalog and new arrangements of two Lonesome Pine Fiddler classics, "Dirty Dishes Blues" and "No Curb Service." In 1988, the Goins Brothers did a sacred album for Lou Ukelson's Vetco label produced by Buddy Griffin who was then working with Katie Laur, but played fiddle on the session.

The next four years ushered in a period in which vinyl albums were becoming out of date but compact discs were not yet in widespread use. So the next four recording projects of the Goins Brothers came out only on cassette. Melvin also added some zip and comedy to the band with three young pickers—Rick May on mandolin, Bill Hamm on bass, and Gerald Evans on fiddle—that he named the "Shedhouse Trio," a term used a decade earlier by a group within Ralph Stanley's Clinch Mountain Boys. The last cassette also included a live recording made at the prestigious University of Chicago Folk Festival in February 1992. The latter, among other achievements, showcased the recording debut of young fiddler Jason Carter who went on to become a stalwart figure in the Del McCoury Band. That same year Melvin Goins received another honor of sorts by becoming the first and perhaps only bluegrass musician to date ever featured on the cover of the *Smithsonian* magazine.

By 1993, the compact disc was clearly ascendant in the record field and the Goins Brothers signed with Hay Holler Records of Blacksburg, Virginia. The band now included in addition to Melvin and Ray, John McNeely who had been on many of the cassettes and had progressed from bus driver to lead guitarist-vocalist; James Price, another quality young fiddler who moved on to Ralph Stanley's Clinch Mountain Boys after a couple of years; and John Keith, a young mandolin picker from Ohio. The songs included the usual number of standards, some never recorded by the band before: "Honky Tonk Blues" and "Lonesome Pine" from the Fiddlers repertoire, a couple of John Keith originals, and a McNeely-Keith collaboration. The album title *Still Goin' Strong* proved rather fleeting within months after the disc's release.

In 1994, Ray Goins, despite being the younger of the two brothers, began to experience heart problems and late in the year had open heart surgery which curtailed his music playing considerably. The *We'll Carry On* album released in 1995 actually featured Ray on only five of the fourteen cuts. Buddy Griffin, back from a sojourn in Branson, Missouri, played banjo on the rest of the album and also played fiddle on others as Price had departed prior to the album's completion. Depending on the song, either John Keith or John McNeely assisted Melvin on the several vocals where Ray did not sing.

Ray Goins returned to the studio in April 1997 for what was to be his musical swan song. An all-gospel disc *Run Satan, Run* featured a couple of guest artists—Larry Sparks on two vocals and Ralph Stanley on four. Two of the best fiddlers in the business, Art Stamper and Buddy Griffin, served as guest instrumentalists. Dale Vanderpool's presence on banjo was a signal that Ray's traveling days with the band were numbered. Thereafter, Ray appeared only on a few occasions, usually either at a bigger festival or closer to home such as Poppy Mountain or at Ralph Stanley's Home Place. He died on July 2, 2007.

Melvin Goins regrouped and continued on, first simply calling his band The Boys, but soon renaming it Windy Mountain from the best known of the numbers he made with the Lonesome Pine Fiddlers in 1954. His first studio effort *Talk to Your Heart* came from a country song that had been one of the first Ray Price songs to attract attention. Melvin again demonstrated his ability to get able sidemen: longtime stalwart John McNeely, Dale Vanderpool, and all-purpose musician John Rigsby who spent the next several years alternating between Melvin Goins's band and the Clinch Mountain Boys. David Bowlin rounded out the group on bass and he, too, became a semi-regular with Windy Mountain over the next several years. Melvin went back to Hay Holler Records and with Jason Hale on bass and otherwise the same personnel did "Talk to Your Heart" again, but the other songs were different including a revival of "Bluegrass Blues" which became the title song.

Although nearing seventy, Melvin never lost an opportunity to promote himself and the music that had supported him through good times and bad. He successfully approached a local Ford dealer in Ashland to sponsor a Sunday morning gospel music program on WSAZ-TV in Huntington called *America's Bluegrass Band*. Built initially around Melvin, Don Rigsby and Ernie Thacker, the several sponsors also released a compact disc of the same name in 2005 and touring bluegrass groups began making appearances. Eventually it seemed the guest bands crowded out the original founder, but for a time the program achieved considerable popularity in the Kentucky–Ohio–West Virginia tri-state region.

Nashville artists and songwriters Tom T. and Dixie Hall, who had written and sung so many country classics in the 1970s, increasingly turned their attention to composing new material for bluegrass artists, and Melvin Goins and Windy Mountain were among them. The Halls even let artists use their studio if they included some of the new items in the vast Hall catalog. Melvin and his entourage made full use of this doing two projects—one on his newly inaugurated Rooster label *Light in the Window Again* and the other on Hall's own Blue Circle Records named for a new Tom T. and Dixie original *Dancin' in the Dirt*. In all, Windy Mountain did five new Hall songs. The veteran writer and aging bluegrass picker seemed to have hit a friendly chord. Tom T. Hall's liner notes on one album reported that as the band prepared to leave, they asked Melvin if he needed anything to which he replied with a classic Melvinism, "I couldn't be happier . . . if I'd a wanted dessert, I'd a et more beans."

In between the two Hall experiences, Melvin and Windy Mountain returned to David Freeman's Rebel Records in 2004 and came out with a new sacred effort *I Wouldn't Miss It* which was credited to "Melvin Goins and Friends," with the latter being Dave Evans, who had briefly worked with Goins in the late seventies; Larry Sparks, who had been a Clinch Mountain Boy along with Melvin in the late sixties; and Paul Williams, who had preceded Melvin as lead vocalist with the Lonesome Pine Fiddlers in 1953. Windy Mountain members were Billy Rose on banjo, John McNeely on guitar, Joe Clark on mandolin, and Danny Cripple on bass and all got some microphone time as well. Except for a pair of new songs by the Halls and one by Clark, the others were standards, but in all, it was a tasteful, well-produced piece of work. Melvin and Windy Mountain also had a couple of discs released from live shows in Ephrata, Pennsylvania, and Milton, West Virginia, in 2005 and 2009 respectively.

As Melvin Goins became one of the senior figures in bluegrass music who went back to the music's first decade, fans and scholars came to recognize that in addition to being a quality picker and singer that he was a marvelous story teller with skills in this area that even he may not have recognized. In most of the stories, he himself was at the center such as his tale of the hidden hot plate in the hotel room at Bluefield in 1953 describing the frugal living he experienced with Curly Ray and Ezra Cline as a Lonesome Pine Fiddler, and his experiences with the Clinch Mountain Boys in 1966 when

Carter Stanley slipped laxatives in Jimmy Martin's drink and Martin shuffled off the stage rapidly singing "Hold Whatcha Got" when he could not hold it any longer!

In his later years some honors came to Melvin Goins and associates. These included the 2009 induction of the Lonesome Pine Fiddlers into the Bluegrass Hall of Honor when Bobby Osborne, Paul Williams, Jimmie Williams, and Melvin Goins were the only surviving members. In 2013, the Goins Brothers entered the West Virginia Music Hall of Fame. Buddy Griffin did the inducting and reported that the octogenarian musician was at his humble best. By 2014, Goins was visibly showing his age as his hearing and vocal quality were in clear decline, but he moved forward as best he could.

Still in declining strength, Melvin Goins continued working local jamborees and festivals into 2016. On July 29, 2016, while playing at a festival in the province of Ontario, he suffered a fatal heart attack. His obituary in the August 5 *Ashland Independent* described him as "very humble, talented, and generous" who "always had a big smile and loved to make people laugh" and "tell stories."

The Goins's repertoire came primarily from three sources: bluegrass standards, new traditionally oriented material by Mike Paxton to Tom T. and Dixie Hall, and from the Lonesome Pine Fiddlers. From the hard days of low pay with the candy shows and the elementary school programs, to college concerts and the big festivals typified by Poppy Mountain, whether as junior members of the Fiddlers, the Goins Brothers, or Melvin leading Windy Mountain, they were in bluegrass for the long haul through thick and thin. Reflecting on their forty-five year career in 1995, bluegrass expert, Bill Vernon, perhaps said it best, "the Goins Brothers have personified the soul of traditional bluegrass music."

SELECTED RECORDINGS

The Goins Brothers at Their Best. Old Homestead OH CD 4058, 2008. Despite the many albums recorded by the duo between 1969 and 1982, some of which were probably among their strongest, this is the earliest ones on compact disc, and comes from two albums cut in the mid-1980s.

The Goins Brothers: Still Going Strong. Hay Holler HHH CD 501, 1993.

The Goins Brothers: We'll Carry On. Hay Holler HHH CD 502, 1995.

Goins Brothers: Run Satan, Run. Hay Holler HH CD 1338, 1997. Buddy Griffin fills in for
    Ray on some cuts.
Melvin Goins and Windy Mountain. Hay Holler HH CD 1346, 1999. Melvin's first solo effort
    after Ray's retirement.
Melvin Goins and Friends: I Wouldn't Miss It. Rebel REB CD 1797, 2004. Friends included
    Dave Evans, Larry Sparks, and Paul Williams.
Melvin Goins: Dancin' in the Dirt. Blue Circle BCR 018, 2008. Melvin's last studio album.

✂ Mel and Stan Hankinson—The Kentucky Twins

Mel, 1922–2000
Stan, 1919–2014

To the younger generation of bluegrass fans, the number of brother duets whose stylings influenced the music's development must seem endless—from Anglin, Bailes, Cope, and Delmore. One can then shift to Andrews, Bolick, Callahan, Dixon, and perhaps move right through the entire alphabet. During the period running from about 1935 to 1955, brother groups were indeed numerous. While some have been more significant than others, to varying degrees the vocal harmonies of all went to the roots of bluegrass. One of these once significant pairs gained a considerable reputation as Mel and Stan Hankinson—the Kentucky Twins. They worked extensively on major radio stations during the later 1940s, recorded on major labels, and toured widely as a featured act with Bill Monroe and his Blue Grass Boys.

Harlan County, Kentucky, served as the birthplace of the Kentucky Twins. Stanford Darwin Hankinson was born there on December 25, 1919, and Melvin William Hankinson on March 23, 1922. Like Jack and Jim Anglin, the Kentucky Twins did not achieve twin status until they were adults and professional musicians. Neither did they remain in Kentucky for long as their coal miner father moved the family to Chambersville, Pennsylvania, about 1925 with the family of ten children in tow.

The Great Depression proved to be tough years for the Hankinson's, but like most other working-class folks they managed to survive through a combination of farm and mine work. After 1933, the Civilian Conservation Corps provided some work, briefly for Mel Hankinson, and two more extended stints for Stan Hankinson in Virginia and New Mexico respectively. At the latter location, Stan assisted a crew of archeologists uncovering primitive Indian relics and other remains at Chaco Canyon National Monument some ninety miles from Gallup, New Mexico. Eventually he returned to

Mel Hankinson (*left*) and Stan Hankinson, WSM, Nashville, 1947.

Pennsylvania and took a job in the mines with his father. Three years later he worked in another mine at Ernest, Pennsylvania.

Stan Hankinson recalled that he began listening to the *Grand Ole Opry* regularly when he was about ten and began to pick and sing at age twelve. Mel Hankinson began to play at about the age of ten. This coincided with a period when the Delmore Brothers started to attain popularity via WSM radio and Bluebird Records and the Hankinsons tended to be much influenced by them. Stan always played rhythm guitar and his brother usually played tenor guitar. However, the latter also displayed skills on mandolin, fiddle, and banjo. For several years the two worked as part-time musicians in the Pennsylvania coalfields. Stan recalled that they often played square dances for two dollars a night. In the meantime, both brothers married and had children.

When World War II came to an end, several new radio stations went into operation, among them WDAD in Indiana, Pennsylvania, where Mel and Stan Hankinson obtained a regular program. They also had a program at WJTN Jamestown, New York. Soon they acquired sufficient popularity that they considered a full-time career in country music. First, they decided to try getting on at WWVA, but as they drove toward that Ohio River industrial center their thoughts turned more toward Nashville.

Like many unknowns in Nashville, the Hankinson boys found themselves in a big, strange town filled with accomplished and aspiring hill-country pickers. A fortunate encounter with Art Satherley of Columbia Records helped provide them with an opening of sorts. Uncle Art, as he was known, assisted the brothers in securing a regular radio spot at KMOX in St. Louis, Missouri, which at that time featured some daily country shows and a Saturday morning program, *Barnyard Follies*, on the CBS network. The job in St. Louis provided them with additional experience and exposure, but not a whole lot of money since KMOX's more established artists tended to retain the most lucrative spots for themselves. By 1947, they decided to try Nashville one more time and then head back to Pennsylvania if unsuccessful. The boys had an original song entitled "Tennessee Gambler," which they hoped would unlock the door of success.

Forced to sell their 1937 Chevrolet for cash, they purchased bus tickets to Nashville via Louisville. Stan Hankinson remembered that FBI agents apparently mistook them for a pair of criminals while they were at the bus depot. However, they made it to Nashville and went to the WSM studio where "Tennessee Gambler" made a highly favorable impression on Bill Monroe. Noted for his reserved nature, Hankinson said Monroe was "not a man to make a big fuss over anything." Nonetheless, it was apparent that "he really got a big kick out of 'Tennessee Gambler'" and had them sing it over several times. Monroe had sufficient influence at WSM that he secured a spot for the young duo on a morning program. Stan recalled that he even threatened to take his about-to-go-to-press new songbook and go to WLAC if they were not hired. In gratitude, the brothers gave Monroe a share in "Tennessee Gambler" which he included in his second song folio, *Bill Monroe's Blue Grass Country Songs*

The brothers immensely enjoyed the three years—roughly 1947 through 1949—they spent at WSM and the *Grand Ole Opry*. In the earlier period they worked most of the time with Bill Monroe's unit. They remembered Lester Flatt, Earl Scruggs, Benny Martin, and Jackie Phelps as among their close associates at that time. The duo also played outfield positions with the now legendary Blue Grass Boys baseball team.

It was also in that first year of 1947 in Nashville that Mel and Stan did their initial recording session with Majestic Records. They cut the four songs with only their own guitars and a bass fiddle in the WSM studios. The first release consisted of "Tennessee Gambler" backed with Roy Hall's old hit of 1940, "Don't Let Your Sweet Love Die." This coupling, Stan believed, was their most popular record and that their rendition of "Don't Let Your Sweet Love Die" kept that song alive in a period when virtually no one else had been doing it. After Mac Wiseman and Reno and Smiley recorded it some years later, the song went on to achieve the standard status it has today. Mel and Stan Hankinson's second Majestic release was a cover of the Monroe hit, "Mother's Only Sleeping" and a less memorable original entitled "Love Me or Leave Me."

The Kentucky Twins hoped that these initial recordings would rejuvenate Art Satherley and Columbia's initial interest in them. However, as Stan remembered it, Columbia moved rather slowly and in the meantime Tex Ritter, who had a liking for their traditionally oriented duet, induced Lee Gillette to sign them to a Capitol contract. They subsequently went on to cut a dozen sides with that firm.

As with the Majestic sides, the Capitol masters were all cut in the WSM studios with only acoustical accompaniment. In addition to their own guitars and a bass fiddle, they had Mac McGar, a highly significant *Grand Ole Opry* mandolin picker, helping out on several of the numbers. The seldom recorded McGar is perhaps best heard on record on Ernest Tubb's Decca cuts of "Warm Red Wine." Songs recorded at the initial session in March 1949 included an early Louvin composition entitled "Whispering Now" and an answer to the Bailes Brothers' hit of 1945 called "I Have Dusted off the Bible" with lyrics that Kyle Bailes had written. Another release featured a pair of their own songs, "I've Lost All" and "I'll Gladly Take You Back Again."

A second Capitol session made in September 1949 resulted in eight additional songs. The numbers included a pair of mother tributes, "Always Remember Your Mother" coupled with "I Dreamed I Saw Mother in Heaven," the latter being among their compositions. "I'd Like to Find a New Friend Everyday" received a great deal of air play and an inspirational number entitled "Tear Stains on the Old Family Bible" attracted considerable attention. Other Capitol releases included Wally Fowler's "Silver Tears," "Carolina," "There's Just One Life to Live," and "Remember Me Love in Your

Prayers." Although several of the songs they cut for Gillette were good ones such as "I'd Like to Find a New Friend," "Tear Stains on the Old Family Bible," their own "I Dreamed I Saw Mother in Heaven," and the Louvin original "Whispering Now," unfortunately none achieved the hit status needed to either propel them to stardom or sustain a lengthy career.

As time passed, the Kentucky Twins found themselves working less with Monroe and more with Ernest Tubb and especially the blackface team of Jamup and Honey. While the Kentucky Twins had plenty of regular work on personal appearance tours, it hardly ranked as an easy living. Those were the days of tent shows in the warm months and schools in the cooler ones. Stan remembered frequently being on the road for two weeks, having about four hours at home with his family on Saturday afternoon, playing the *Opry*, and then taking off quickly to play a Sunday afternoon show in Michigan. Since they did not seem to be getting but about two songs on the *Opry* anyway, and not the best time spots, they looked for possible breaks elsewhere.

About this time, the winter of 1949–1950, Zeb Turner induced the Kentucky Twins along with Grady Martin and a couple of other Nashville musicians to move to KWKH Shreveport, Louisiana. Things did not go well for them at the *Louisiana Hayride* and after a few weeks the Hankinsons returned to Nashville and secured a 5:15 P.M. daily program at WLAC. The so-called studio stars at this Nashville station, such as Mac Odell and Big Jeff Bess, relied more on salaries and songbook sales to sustain them than extensive touring which at least gave them more time with their families. Since Mel and Stan still had Capitol recordings being released and a new songbook for sale to listeners, their six-month stint at WLAC proved to be both lucrative and relatively relaxing. Their songbook illustrated that in addition to songs recently recorded by the brothers that their repertory included numbers from the older duet tradition as the Dixon Brothers original "Two Little Rosebuds" and the Carter Family's "Jimmy Brown, the Newsboy," which was soon to be revived by a Flatt and Scruggs's recording.

Meanwhile, relatives in Pennsylvania kept urging the Hankinsons to re-locate closer to home. As a result, they secured a job at the WWVA *World's Original Jamboree* with Red Belcher and the Kentucky Ridge Runners. Belcher played a respectable old-time banjo and sang a bit, but relied more on his talents as a pitchman—good radio advertising salesman—to sustain him on radio and the skills of better musicians—usually a brother duet—to attract crowds to show dates. Budge and Fudge Mayse, Galen and Melvin Ritchey, and Everett and Bea Lilly had earlier fulfilled this role with Belcher's group when the Kentucky Twins joined forces with the jovial radio veteran.

The Hankinsons stayed with the *World's Original Jamboree* for a year working extensively not only with the Kentucky Ridge Runners, but also with vocalist Hawkshaw Hawkins whose honky-tonk vocals mixed with some older-styled songs was making him into a major figure in country music. They also worked a great deal with the Sunshine Boys, a well-known quartet. However, work at Wheeling also meant more travel and road work again and as the Kentucky Twins grew older their once youthful enthusiasm for show business began to wane. Spending more time at home with their families appealed to them as time passed. Moving to Michigan, they secured factory jobs and relegated themselves to weekend club work for the next couple of years. Various musicians including Hawkins and Merle Travis came through from time to time and the brothers maintained their contacts with show business people.

In 1953, through a friend of the Kentucky Twins' brother Carl Hankinson, they learned that WABI Bangor, Maine, wanted a country duet. The brothers contacted the station and went back to music full-time. For the next three years, Mel and Stan based themselves at WABI radio and also at WABI-TV which was a brand new television channel. Stan was told that he and his brother constituted the first live country television act in the Pine Tree State.

During this era the Kentucky Twins issued a second songbook which they sold over the air and on their show dates. Unlike the earlier book which contained many of the songs the boys had recorded as well as old standard duet tunes, this newer book contained numerous songs popular in the mid-1950s such as "I Don't Hurt Anymore," "Your Cheatin' Heart," and "You Better Not Do That," numbers not generally associated with duet acts. This suggested that even without the rise of rock and roll that many of the traditionally-oriented acts were finding that much of the newer material did not adapt well to recent trends in the business.

Still, business remained good for the Hankinsons during their Bangor years. Many Wheeling *Jamboree* acts like Doc and Chickie Williams and

Wilma Lee and Stoney Cooper appeared on their shows often and they drew good crowds. *Opry* stars also worked the area at times. Maine itself has produced several major hard-core country vocalists over the years such as Lone Pine a.k.a. Harold Breau, Dick Curless, and Gene Hooper, not to mention major bluegrass pickers such as Clarence and Roland White. Despite its northerly and "way Down East" locale, many commentators have talked about the popularity of country music in Maine, so perhaps it is small wonder that the Kentucky Twins prospered there.

From 1956, however, both brothers decided to abandon the business. Mel returned to Pennsylvania and worked in the steel mills, retiring after about a 22-year stint. Stan moved to Chillicothe, Ohio, where he spent eighteen years working primarily in wholesaling and rearing his family of five. In 1975, with coal enjoying an economic renaissance and skilled miners much in demand, he went to work for the Southern Ohio Coal Company whose three large captive mines fueled the huge Gavin Plant at Cheshire, Ohio. Stan retired in 1982 and lived near Wellston, Ohio, until his death on June 8, 2014. He was buried in nearby Hamden, Ohio, where a guitar adorns his tombstone. Mel Hankinson lived in Ambridge, Pennsylvania, passing away on May 10, 2000.

From time to time, the Kentucky Twins got together and did a little picking and singing mostly just for the entertainment of themselves, family, and close friends. They had no regrets about their years in country music and Stan spoke glowingly about his experiences with Roy Acuff, Ernest Tubb, and, most especially, Bill Monroe. At the same time they also had no regrets that they left country music when they did. Still, the broad tradition of harmony duets of which they were once a part survive, chiefly in the sounds of bluegrass, vocal harmony, and to a lesser extent in the sounds of the newer wave of traditionalists.

SELECTED RECORDINGS

Despite recording four numbers for Majestic in 1947, and twelve for Capitol in 1949, none of their material has been reissued as of this publication.

✂ The Lilly Brothers

Mitchell "B" or "Bea," 1921–2005
Everett, 1924–2012

One of the reasons that old-time and bluegrass music attracted a wide audience among urban college youth of the East was the long presence of the Lilly Brothers and Don Stover in the Boston area. Through their nightly appearances at Hillbilly Ranch and their pioneering concerts at the University of Chicago Folk Festival, Harvard University, and other schools in the Northeast, the Lillys were influential in acquainting urban youth with Appalachian vocal and instrumental styles. Because of this long sojourn in New England, the Lillys' career is often considered to have been primarily concentrated in Boston and at Hillbilly Ranch. However, to place the careers of Bea and Everett Lilly in a broader perspective, when they first went to Massachusetts they were not at their beginning, but had already experienced more than a decade as seasoned professionals.

Clear Creek, West Virginia, is a rural community located in Raleigh County, about midway between Charleston and Bluefield. Fifteen miles away is Beckley, the county seat and an important center for live country music on radio during the 1940s. The Lilly family is one of the largest in West Virginia, being descended from Robert Lilly, an associate of Lord Baltimore, who came to Maryland about 1640. The Lilly Reunion held in Flat Top Mountain during the 1930s and 1940s attracted crowds in excess of 75,000, a figure comparable with those at the largest festivals of our own time. Old-time music fans may recall Roy Harvey's recording "The Lilly Reunion," which described the first of these events. A few years later Everett and Bea Lilly were among those who entertained their numerous kinfolk and other visitors.

Emory and Stella Stearns Lilly of Clear Creek were the parents of seven children including Mitchell Burt Lilly called Bea or B from his middle initial, born on December 15, 1921, and Charles Everett Lilly, whose name

Everett Lilly
(*left*) and
Mitchell B. "Bea"
Lilly, WWVA,
Wheeling, West
Virginia, 1948.

was recorded on his birth certificate as Charly Edwin, born on July 1, 1924. Farming was the prime occupation of the Lilly family although coal mines were in the area and both brothers worked for a time in the mines. Church gatherings, prayer meetings, and revivals provided not only spiritual comfort, but one of the few social activities. The isolation of rural life helped to make the local people create their own entertainment. Music was an important part of the local religious scene and it was here that Everett and Bea heard their first music outside the family home. By 1933 when Bea was twelve, he was playing the guitar and both he and his younger brother were singing.

In those early years the public performances of the Lilly Brothers were limited to the Clear Creak vicinity, but nonetheless they managed to make themselves heard. Everett Lilly recalled that on occasion they would go from house to house and sing for one or two families at a time. They also sang at churches and other such local events as weddings and funerals. Their first professional job was at a movie theater in Ameagle, a company town some eight miles from Clear Creek.

By the 1935–1936 period, the Lilly Brothers began to be more influenced by professional groups outside their local area. Although they were already familiar with the better-known country groups such as the Carter Family and Jimmie Rodgers, the appearance of the brother duet groups in the mid-thirties had a more direct impression on their style. The twosomes featuring mandolin and guitar made the deepest impact. Although they initially used two guitars on their recordings, beginning in 1934 Homer and Walter Callahan were the first such group to record extensively. In 1936, both the Monroe Brothers and the Blue Sky Boys also began to record extensively even though the former were already well known for their radio work. Bill and Charlie Monroe undoubtedly had the most direct influence on the development of the Lilly style with livelier vocals and more complex instrumentation, but the Callahans were their early favorites. Everett described the early Monroe music as "get up and go . . . lively" while the subdued approach of the Bolicks was referred to as "livin' room" music. Guitar duet groups such as the Delmores, Dixons, and Sheltons along with string bands like the Mainers had a lesser impact upon the Lilly Brothers' style.

As a result of the popularity of the mandolin-guitar brother duets, Everett took up the mandolin and it always was his major instrument although he was also adept on fiddle and played drop thumb or clawhammer banjo, and on rare occasions the guitar. By about 1939, their radio career began on station WJLS Beckley then in its broadcasting infancy. Shortly after, the Lillys, through the assistance of a neighbor, began playing on the *Old Farm Hour* at WCHS in Charleston. Although this show is only a memory today, both it and daily programs on the same station are among the forgotten great disseminators of early country music. Several important artists and groups either began or spent a major part of their careers in Charleston. Probably the most popular locally was the team of Cap, Andy, and Flip comprised of Warren Caplinger, Andrew Patterson, and William Strickland. Billy Cox, known as the Dixie Songbird, was Charleston based throughout his career and recorded extensively for both the Gennett and Columbia labels. Two of his many compositions that have become standards are "Filipino Baby" and "Sparkling Brown Eyes." The Buskirk Family worked there, too, and so for a time did Buddy Starcher, T. Texas Tyler, Natchee the Indian, and Molly O'Day and Lynn Davis. Frank "Uncle Si" Welling, who had been half of the recording team of Welling and McGhee, was director of the *Old Farm Hour* that was performed before a live audience on Friday night. Despite the tough competition, the Lilly Brothers held their own as a popular act during their sojourn on the show. For a time, they were known as the Lonesome Holler Boys, but throughout their career, they always maintained their identity as the Lilly Brothers even when they were part of another group.

Back in Beckley, WJLS was becoming a more important station on the country scene. The Lilly Brothers also worked there for quite a while with Molly O'Day and Lynn Davis. This was in the period before O'Day had become the living legend of country music that she eventually became through her classic recordings on Columbia. Although O'Day and Davis headed the group, the Lilly Brothers retained their identity by performing part of the show as a brother duet team. Another member of the act was Charles Elza, known as Kentucky Slim, the Little Darling, whom many bluegrass fans will remember for his comedy work with Flatt and Scruggs and Hylo Brown during the middle and late 1950s. The group played almost nightly personal appearances in the mountain communities of southern West Virginia. Everett Lilly recalled the many hours spent in Lynn Davis's 1941 Ford including one time when he dozed off while driving and ran the car over a curb in some small town without even waking the others. Davis and O'Day were also remembered as very nice people with O'Day being a motherly type who kept the boys' clothes and buttons neat before their stage appearances. In addition to their work at WJLS, Everett and Bea also worked for a time at WNOX in Knoxville with Davis and O'Day on the *Mid-Day Merry-Go-Round* and the *Tennessee Barn Dance*. The brothers also worked as a separate act on radio at Beckley. Paul Taylor, an excellent clawhammer banjo player, worked with them much of the time and remained a close friend of Everett's, living near him in Raleigh County in 1974. Later Rattlesnake Hogan, a comedian, was added on bass. Mel Steele, Little Jimmie Dickens, and the Bailes Brothers also worked at WJLS in the early forties. The Lilly

Brothers worked for a brief period on WPAR in Parkersburg, West Virginia. The Lillys and Taylor worked a second time at WNOX in Knoxville with fiddler Burk Barbour. Lonnie Glosson, the legendary harmonica player from Arkansas, worked with them for a time as did George "Speedy" Krise, the well-known Dobro player. The brothers and others often interchanged to form various groups on road shows, one of which was called Burk Barbour and the Smiling Mountain Boys. Another group they worked with for a time was called Speedy Krise and the Blue Ribbon Boys.

While in Knoxville, the brothers were approached by Syd Nathan of King Records, but as he at first proposed using the name of Burk Barbour and His Band on the record, the Lillys refused. Later Nathan told them they could record as the Lilly Brothers. Sadly, they were negligent about contacting him again and passed up the opportunity.

It was indeed unfortunate that the Lillys made no recordings during these early years in radio for it was during those years that their sound reached its full maturity. However, there were many other performers of early country and bluegrass music who went unrecorded despite a wide degree of popularity and excellent musicianship. In many respects, students of early music receive a distorted picture of this period because they are forced to rely on phonograph records, and much less often, transcriptions, for source material. Hundreds of hours of live radio shows—good and bad on stations large and small—are gone forever. As a result the sound of once important artists such as Cowboy Loye Pack will probably never be known except to the fortunate few who heard them. For others, such as the Bailey Brothers, we have only a small part of their careers on record. And for the Lillys, only some of the middle and primarily their later sounds are available on record.

The Lilly Brothers began a phase of their careers which is better known in the spring of 1948. They started to work on the WWVA *Jamboree* in Wheeling, West Virginia. At first they worked with Red Belcher and the Kentucky Ridge Runners, a group which included Tex Logan on fiddle and comedian Crazy Elmer a.k.a. Smilie Sutter on bass. Although Belcher was a clawhammer banjo player of some talent, his major role was as a salesman for the sponsor's product. In this respect he was similar to Byron Parker in Columbia, South Carolina, whose principal musicians were Snuffy Jenkins and Homer Sherill and many years before, Charlie and Bill Monroe. Everett and Bea did most of the performing on Belcher's shows. The group was probably the most popular at WWVA for a time and had three fifteen-minute shows daily ranging from early morning to mid-afternoon. With personal appearances almost nightly and the Saturday night *World's Original Jamboree*, opportunities for sleep were limited. During this period the Lillys received their first opportunity to record. In 1948, Red Belcher, Bea Lilly, and Tex Logan cut two sides as the Kentucky Ridgerunners that were issued on the Page label, a small Pennsylvania firm. Everett absented himself from the session, believing that the brothers should record only under their own name. Later in the same year, the Lillys had a session of their own on Page records which produced one single. However, no material was ever issued from a session on the Cozy label. The Page recordings, including those with Belcher, later appeared on a Rounder anthology, but the Cozy masters have yet to surface.

Mac Martin of Pittsburgh became a devotee of the Lilly's music during their years in Wheeling. He recalled that the brothers lived with their families in an apartment building on Wheeling Island that housed several *Jamboree* families including that of Sunflower a.k.a. Mary Calvas and Marion Martin, the blind accordion player, both part of the Doc Williams entourage. In those days the *Jamboree* originated in the Virginia Theater rather than the later day Capital Theater (1969–2005), but the daily shows were done in studios located in the Hawley Building.

It was during this period that Tex Logan's song "Christmas Time's A Comin'" was introduced on radio by the group. A couple of years later, Logan gave the song to Bill Monroe who recorded it in October 1951. It has since become a standard bluegrass Christmas song. Belcher paid each of the brothers a salary of sixty dollars per week which covered both their radio work and all personal appearances. The Lillys received no other compensation except what little they derived from the sale of their pictures and some travel expenses as they furnished transportation for their own group and many of the other *Jamboree* performers in their fifteen-passenger stretch bus. Belcher evidently believed he was overpaying the boys and in 1950 a financial dispute transpired in which Bea and Everett were offered a choice between a ten-dollar weekly wage cut or being replaced by Mel and Stan, the Kentucky Twins. The Lillys chose neither alternative and decided to quit. Although offered their own radio show and the opportunity to tour extensively with Hawkshaw Hawkins, they decided instead to leave Wheeling.

From WWVA they went to WMMN at Fairmont where Everett served as program director supervising the shows of the various live acts that appeared on the station in addition to their own daily show. However, the policy at Fairmont for road shows called for all the performers to work together in a package arrangement. According to Everett Lilly this meant there were too many entertainers and as a result the financial pie had to be cut into extremely thin slices. Unable to make much money on personal appearances, the Lilly Brothers soon quit and returned to Clear Creek.

Later in 1950 after a short rest, Everett joined Lester Flatt and Earl Scruggs playing mandolin and singing tenor. At the time the Foggy Mountain Boys were playing daily radio shows on WVLK at Versailles, Kentucky, and Saturday nights at the *Kentucky Barn Dance* in Lexington. Flatt and Scruggs had attempted to get Everett in their band on previous occasions without success. During this period Bea Lilly returned to West Virginia and worked in Beckley.

While Everett worked with the Foggy Mountain Boys, he participated in their second and third Columbia sessions in Nashville in May and October 1951, respectively. Among the songs recorded were "Over the Hills to the Poorhouse," a recomposition by him and Flatt of an 1874 poem. He had gotten some lyrics from his mother. Flatt and Scruggs later made a second recording of the song for their *Hard Travelin'* album and its continued popularity was illustrated by its being the title song of the third Lester Flatt-Mac Wiseman album. The Foggy Mountain Boys at the time also included Chubby Wise on fiddle and Jody Rainwater on bass. After a while Wise left and Howdy Forrester played fiddle on the last Columbia session. The Foggy Mountain Boys moved to WDBJ in Roanoke after leaving the central Kentucky area. In early 1952, they switched places with the Bailey Brothers, moving to WPTF in Raleigh.

Later that year Tex Logan—who had been in Boston with Frank and Pete, the Lane Brothers—stopped off in Raleigh and soon Everett decided to go to Boston with Tex. Bea Lilly and Don Stover, a young banjo picker from Raleigh County, joined the group and the four became known as the Confederate Mountaineers. The band worked daily on radio station WCOP. Transcribed material from these shows has been released on a Rounder compact disc. The group played on numerous other country shows in the Boston area, helping to sell bluegrass to New England audiences. The group later played regularly at clubs, first the Plaza, then the Mohawk, and finally a long sojourn at Hillbilly Ranch where their nightly appearances made them a legend in their own lifetime.

Logan left Boston in 1956, breaking up the original group. Herb Hooven from North Carolina played fiddle much of the time, but for brief periods Canadian Dave Miller, Scotty Stoneman, and former Lilly Brothers fiddler Chubby Anthony were the band's fiddlers. Don Stover left Boston for brief periods, first to go with Buzz Busby and the Bayou Boys about 1955, second with Bill Monroe in 1957, and last in 1966 with Bill Harrell and the Virginians. During these times Joe Val, primarily a mandolin player, played banjo as did Bob French. Tom Heathwood, a good friend of the Lillys who also wrote about their career, often played bass or guitar with them. In later years some of Everett Lilly's children, Everett Alan, Tennis, La Verne, and the late Jiles Lilly worked with the group occasionally as did Bea Lilly's son, Monty. Everett Alan Lilly also played with the Charles River Valley Boys. From time to time, various well-known performers in the country, folk, or bluegrass field came to Hillbilly Ranch to watch and perhaps do a few numbers with the Lilly Brothers. During an eight-month period in 1958–59, Everett Lilly returned to Lester Flatt and Earl Scruggs, working with them on the *Grand Ole Opry* and their string of daily television shows. However, he always preferred working with his brother and their own group and despite his good relationship with Flatt and Sruggs soon returned to Boston.

By the end of the decade, the Lilly Brothers had attracted a solid following in New England which was beginning to include numerous college youth. With the growth of the interest in folk music on campus, the Lillys became part of the urban folk revival and helped to pioneer bluegrass concerts in colleges, particularly in the New England area, but also in more distant locations such as New York's Carnegie Hall and the University of Chicago Folk Festival. Everett believed these efforts constituted the Lilly Brothers' most significant contribution to their chosen musical field.

The Lillys received more opportunities to record during the Boston years. In 1956 and 1957, they recorded eleven numbers for the Event label of Westbrook, Maine. Four sides were released as singles shortly afterward and in 1970 Dave Freeman issued all of the songs on a County album. In 1961, they recorded an album for Folkways and somewhat later two additional albums for Prestige International, one of which featured the Lilly Brothers only on singing and instrumentation with no fiddle or banjo. Both were later reissued by Rounder. Some years later a taped live show made in this period at Hillbilly Ranch was issued on a Japanese album. In 1996, a second live recording from Hillbilly Ranch came out on the Hay Holler label. During Everett's second sojourn with the Foggy Mountain Boys in 1958, four cuts by Bea Lilly and Don Stover were issued on the Folkways album *Mountain Music Bluegrass Style.*

The tragic death of Everett's son Jiles on January 17, 1970, in an auto accident resulted in the end of the Boston phase of the Lilly Brothers career. The incident made a deep emotional impact on Everett and his family who, with the exception of three of his grown children, decided to return to West Virginia. A memorable family concert was given at John Hancock Hall on February 14, 1970, and in April the Lillys moved back to Clear Creek. For several months the Lilly Brothers stopped performing and for a time it was doubtful if Everett Lilly would ever play again. In the fall of 1970, however, they began a thirteen-week series of television shows on WOAY in Oak Hill, West Virginia. Bea had also returned to West Virginia for a time, but went back to Boston after a few weeks.

Beginning in 1971, the Lilly Brothers began to appear at a few bluegrass festivals and in succeeding summers broadened the number of their festival appearances. Don Stover and Tex Logan worked with them on most of the festivals as well as various Lilly children. Everett's ten-year old son, Mark, worked on all their appearances in 1973 and showed considerable promise as an entertainer. In March 1973, the Lilly Brothers also recorded a gospel album for County, their first recording since their three albums on Folkways and Prestige International during the height of the urban folk revival.

Certainly one of the highlights of the Lilly Brothers entire career came in September 1973 when they toured Japan with Don Stover and Everett Alan Lilly, giving three concerts and recording three albums during the week they were there. The albums were eventually released on the Japanese label Towa. In one concert they played with Robert and Jerry Tainaka, the Smokey Rangers, long-time friends of the Lilly family and two of Japan's more accomplished bluegrass performers. The Lillys went over so well that they subsequently made two more trips to the Land of the Rising Sun.

In their song repertoire the Lillys always stuck close to traditional old-time and bluegrass material although many of their numbers were among the lesser-known old songs rather than the well-worn standards. Two such examples were Bert Layne's "The Forgotten Soldier Boy," a topical ballad alluding to the bonus march of unemployed World War I veterans in 1932, and Wade Mainer's "That Star Belongs to Me" which is a child's lament to a father killed in World War II. Neither brother had been a notable composer although Everett's working of "Over the Hills to the Poorhouse" with Lester Flatt and his own "Southern Skies" and "What Are They Doing in Heaven" illustrated that he had some talent along that line. Bea Lilly's composing talents are displayed in his work as the prime writer of "They Tell Me Your Love Is Like a Flower," originally cut by Flatt and Scruggs in 1956 and now a much-recorded standard.

For several years from the mid-1970s, the Lilly Brothers seldom played more than two or three shows yearly. In 1979 they were the subjects of a documentary film, *True Facts in a Country Song,* which premiered at the Culture Center in Charleston, West Virginia, followed by a Lilly Brothers concert that found a warm audience. Bea remained in Boston as did Don Stover while Everett lived in Clear Creek, drove a school bus, and fashioned a band that included Billy Pack on banjo and his maturing younger sons, Charlie, Mark, and Daniel.

Everett Lilly's family band took the name Everett Lilly and Clear Creek Crossing which at times included some non-family members. Their repertoire and style used elements of both country and bluegrass. They made several cassette and compact disc recordings including *It Is Almost Heaven, I Have Found the Way,* and *Savanna's not in Georgia* which were marketed in the home territory of central West Virginia. Charlie Lilly formed his own band and made some cassette recordings and also worked out of Nashville. After Everett retired from his school bus job, he and Bea began to play over a wider area taking the name Lilly Mountaineers. In 2002, the Lilly Brothers and Don Stover, who had died in 1996, were inducted into the Bluegrass Hall of Honor in Owensboro which increased the brothers' appeal as an act. However, by this time Bea was showing his age and could do little more than stand on stage and play rhythm guitar. Everett, Daniel and Mark carried the load. Bea Lilly passed away on September 18, 2005.

A few weeks before Bea's death, Charlie Lilly and Bill Wolfenbarger, a self-described "honorary Lilly," set out to produce a new compact disc

Everett Lilly & Everybody and Their Brother. Many of the more noted bluegrass musicians including Jason Carter, Rob and Ronnie McCoury, Mike Bub, Rhonda Vincent, and Marty Stuart loaned their talents to supporting Everett Lilly and his boys including country star Billy Walker for whom Charlie Lilly worked as a band member. It was a fitting tribute to one of bluegrass music's most durable and unsung heroes. A couple of bonus tracks included vocal numbers that had Bea Lilly helping on one song and a Charlie Lilly solo. The liner notes quoted Marty Stuart who termed Everett Lilly, "God's favorite mandolin player."

Although Everett had his share of honors in old age, tragedy continued to stalk the family. On May 21, 2006, Billy Walker, his wife, and band members Charlie Lilly and Danny Patton all died in an Alabama auto crash while returning from a show. Everett continued to play with Mark and Daniel until shortly before his own death on May 8, 2012. At his finest, he displayed the best characteristics of Appalachian people. As a person, he was a tower of strength in a moral, physical, and musical way. Together, the Lilly Brothers exemplified the best in traditional and bluegrass music.

SELECTED RECORDINGS

The Lilly Brothers and Don Stover: On the Radio, 1952–1953. Rounder 1109, 2002. From radio transcriptions made for WCOP Boston.

The Lilly Brothers and Don Stover: Early Recordings. Rebel REB CD 1688, 1991. Material initially recorded for the Event label in 1956 and 1957.

The Lilly Brothers and Don Stover: Live at Hillbilly Ranch. Hay Holler HH CD 1333, 1996. Taken from a July 1967 live show.

The Lilly Brothers and Don Stover: What Will I Leave Behind. Rebel REB CD 1788, 2003. Reissue of a 1973 sacred album.

Everett Lilly also recorded with Lester Flatt and Earl Scruggs, as well as with Clear Creek Crossing, a band that included his younger sons.

✂ J. E. and Wade Mainer

J. E., 1898–1971
Wade, 1907–2011

In the decade that preceded the development of bluegrass music, the group that probably did the most to provide the connecting link between the old-time string bands of country music's first decade and the pioneer bluegrass bands of the late 1940s was a number of Carolina musicians headed by two brothers named Mainer. Sometimes together and sometimes separately, the Mainers through their recordings, radio work, and personal appearances did much to preserve mountain string music while simultaneously pointing in the direction of bluegrass. Their fiddle, banjo, and vocal work contributed much to the sound of country music. In addition both Mainers had long careers and remained musically active until their deaths which in the case of J. E. was 1971 while Wade, after a few relatively quiet years, rejuvenated musically in his old age becoming one the longest-lived figures in American musical history, dying at age 104 in 2011.

The Mainers were a large mountain family living in Buncombe County, North Carolina. Two musicians of fame were born into the clan of eight children. The older, Joseph Emmett, known as J. E., was born on July 20, 1898, while the younger brother, Wade, arrived on April 21, 1907. Two years later, the family moved to Union, South Carolina, where J. E. went to work in a cotton mill. Afterward, they lived near Weaverville, North Carolina. Scraping a living from the mountain soil was difficult for the family so J. E. left home at twelve years of age to live in Knoxville and work in the mills. As a result, Wade who was little more than an infant never really knew his brother very well until both were grown. Unlike some family musical groups, the Mainer boys did not grow up picking and singing together.

In the next several years, J. E. Mainer worked in textile mills in various locations. In 1922, he came to Concord, North Carolina, met the girl he married, went to work in the mills, and settled down there. He later

Wade Mainer (*behind fence*) and J. E. Mainer, unknown date but probably the late 1940s. *Courtesy of John Morris.*

worked as a musician in many locations, but Concord remained home to J. E. for the remainder of his life. Although William Mainer, family patriarch, played a little banjo, brother-in-law Roscoe Banks provided the major musical inspiration for the boys. A left-handed fiddler of local renown, Banks played for local square dances and J.E. who had learned to play banjo at age nine helped to provide back up during those periods when he came home from the mills to work on the farm. Wade Mainer also got his early musical training playing the banjo behind his brother-in-law's fiddle. It was at this time that Wade developed the two-finger banjo style for which he became famous. He worked at Banks's sawmill for much of his youth. They also played at the sawmill with other local musicians on evenings and whenever they had a few spare moments from their labors.

Records also provided musical inspiration for the Mainers. Wade recalled Doc Walsh's Carolina Tar Heels, Charlie Poole's North Carolina Ramblers, Gid Tanner's Skillet Lickers, Grayson and Whitter, and, of course, Jimmie Rodgers and the Carter Family as being among his favorite artists in the late 1920s. Although the boys often heard live music at square dances and fiddlers conventions, they never met any of the recorded old timers until they met Riley Puckett in the Victor studios several years later.

After J. E. married and settled down in Concord, Wade decided to leave a fifty cents-a-day job at the sawmill and move in with his older brother. He, too, went to work at the yarn mill and in their spare time the two finally got to know each other well and began to seriously play music together. J .E. had become more interested in the fiddle by this time and Wade played banjo behind him. On J. E.'s day off, he often drove back to Asheville to play with Roscoe Banks and improved his fiddle work.

After a while the Mainer boys accepted invitations to play at corn shuckings and other local social events. As their playing improved, J. E. and Wade entered fiddler's contests and did quite well. Fisher Hendley, an old-time musician of some renown himself, sponsored or ran many of the contests. Wade remembered that they seldom came in lower than second. Throughout the years J. E. won many contests. Soon three other musicians joined up with them and the Mainer's Mountaineers came into being: Daddy John Love, a guitar player and singer of blues and yodel songs who lived in Concord, as well as Lester and Howard Lay, a brother duet. In addition to their appearances at the conventions, they occasionally played

Saturday nights on the *Wayside Program* at the small radio station WSOC in Gastonia, North Carolina.

It was this group that J. W. Fincher, president of Crazy Water Crystals, heard about and in 1934 hired to play on radio under his company's sponsorship. The group then became J. E. Mainer's Crazy Mountaineers at WBT in Charlotte, North Carolina. They played Saturday nights on the *Crazy Barn Dance* with other area artists employed by Crazy Water Crystals such as the Dixon Brothers, the Tobacco Tags, Fisher Hendley, Johnson County Ramblers, and Dick Hartman. Although Fincher paid the Mountaineers a small salary, he collected the receipts from their personal appearances.

Having met with considerable success at Charlotte, Crazy Water Crystals decided to move the Mountaineers to WWL in New Orleans. However, their fans in the Carolinas began requesting their return. They stayed in Louisiana about three months and then came to WWNC, Asheville for a short stint prior to coming back to WBT. Upon their return to Charlotte, they received a raise and now had two daily radio shows in addition to the *Crazy Barn Dance*.

In the meantime, the Lay Brothers had left the Mountaineers and Zeke Morris joined the band. It was this foursome of Love, Morris, and the two Mainers that cut their first recordings on August 6, 1935, in Atlanta, Georgia. Wade Mainer recalled that the Mountaineers took no audition to record. The RCA distributor in Charlotte asked the boys if they would be interested in making records on the Bluebird label. When they agreed, he made the arrangements.

Fourteen sides were cut at the initial session including their biggest hit, "Maple on the Hill." This song was an old popular number written some forty years earlier by Gussie Davis, an African-American lyricist. Previous old-time artists such as Vernon Dalhart, Tom Darby and Jimmie Tarlton, and Frank Welling and John McGhee had recorded it, but the Mainer arrangement, somewhat different from the others with Wade and Zeke's duet, really caught on and became one of the biggest country hits of the mid-thirties. The Mainer version of "Maple on the Hill" entered bluegrass via recordings of the Country Pardners and the Stanley Brothers among others and has become a true standard in the field.

Three of the remaining songs recorded in Atlanta were "New Curly Headed Baby," "Take Me in the Lifeboat" and "Ship Sailing Now." Also featured was

Daddy John Love's blues vocals. Morris did a solo on "This World Is Not My Home" and the remaining songs featured various combinations of all or part of the band on the vocal work. Although the Mountaineers did no instrumentals, J.E. Mainer's hard-driving fiddle was prominent on much of the session with the exception of Love and Morris's solos. Oddly enough, although the foursome that recorded together in Atlanta constituted the best-known Mainer's Mountaineers grouping with John Love, it was the only session on which the four appeared together.

By the time of the February 1936 sessions held in Charlotte, recording personnel for the Mainers' had undergone considerable change. Daddy John Love recorded as a solo vocalist completely independent of his former associates. Wade Mainer and Zeke recorded as a duet with their own banjo, harmonica, and guitar accompaniment with Wade doing the banjo and harmonica work. The recordings issued under the name, J. E. Mainer's Mountaineers, featured the personable leader with backing by Howard Bumgardner, Clarence Todd, and Ollie Bunn. The latter two constituted top-notch fiddlers in their own right who subsequently recorded with Daddy John Love's string band, the Dixie Reelers. Together, the two Mainers groups cut twenty sides including the fiddle numbers "New Lost Train Blues" and "Number 111" and ten duets by Wade and Zeke.

In the spring of 1936, Crazy Water Crystals moved the Mountaineers to Raleigh and station WPTF. The band now consisted of the Mainer brothers, Morris, and young Boyd Carpenter known as the Hillbilly Kid, who played guitar and harmonica. The front page of WPTF's newspaper *On the Air* carried their picture and an accompanying feature article claimed that the group had so many followers that "not a day passes when the studio is not jammed with fans who have driven into town to see and hear their favorites on the air." As at WBT, they performed on daily shows and a Saturday Night *Crazy Barn Dance*.

In June 1936, they returned to Charlotte and did another Bluebird session. This time, the brothers and Morris recorded together again with some instrumental assistance from some other musicians: Harold Christy and Beacham Blackweller on guitars as well as Junior Misenheimer on banjo. Together, they did twelve numbers including J. E. Mainer's version of Blind Alfred Reed's "Why Do You Bob Your Hair Girls" and "Watermelon on the Vine" with the brothers and Morris all on the vocals. Wade and Zeke did six more. On one number, "Cradle Days," Norwood Tew, the song's composer, did the vocal. Tew, who was known as the "Old Lefthander," also cut four sides as a solo vocalist at those same Charlotte sessions.

Not long afterward, the brothers split. Unlike most musical separations, this one seemed to have been more the result of a fuss with the sponsor than of internal dissension. Wade and Zeke, already unhappy with the policy of Crazy Water Crystals' keeping the money the Mountaineers made from show dates, had a dispute with J. W. Fincher's son, Hubert, over being late for a radio program. They decided to quit, but remained at the station with a show of their own. Graham Pointer, station manager at WPTF, secured a show and a new sponsor for the boys at an increased salary and allowed them to keep all their personal appearance proceeds. J.E. remained with Crazy Water Crystals out of a sense of loyalty to the company. Forming a new Crazy Mountaineers band, he continued at WPTF. Although now separate, he and his brother remained on friendly terms.

Wade and Zeke continued to work as a banjo-guitar duet at Raleigh. Somewhat later, they added a fiddler Homer Sherrill to the group. He later spent many years with Snuffy Jenkins at WIS, Columbia, South Carolina. This threesome recorded eight sides for Bluebird in October 1936 including the memorable nonsense song, "Hop Along Peter." For a brief time Wade left the band and Wiley Morris joined. Later when Wade came back, the four played together. Wade and Zeke recorded their February session by themselves, having been reduced to duet status again. At this session Wade recorded "Train that Carried My Girl From Town" with slide guitar in the style of Frank Hutchison.

When Wade and his new band with Bucky and Buddy Banks, the Smiling Rangers, played a show at Spruce Pine, North Carolina, a fiddler approached Wade and Zeke asking if he could do a couple of numbers with them. They liked his style and asked him to join them. The fiddler, Steve Ledford, who had previously recorded for American Record Company with his own Carolina Ramblers String Band, remained with Wade for about three years. He helped create much of the Wade Mainer band styling of the later 1930s that came very near to being bluegrass. The August 1937 session which featured Mainer, Morris, and Ledford illustrated this very well. On numbers like "Little Pal" where there is prominent fiddle and banjo work combined with Wade and Zeke's vocal harmony, it certainly approached bluegrass music. To be sure, Wade's two-finger banjo work is more primitive than the Scruggs' style and Ledford's fiddle is not like that of Chubby Wise. Nonetheless, their recordings demonstrated that the Mainers took old-time music a long way in the direction that culminated in the Bill Monroe sound of the mid-forties. At this same session, Wade helped to get his young nephews Robert and Morris Banks a.k.a. Buck and Buddy on record. He billed them as Wade Mainer and the Little Smiling Rangers. They assisted on eight sides, being featured on four vocals by themselves and assisting Wade on three others.

The Smiling Rangers worked around central North Carolina. Morris had quit and so Wade was only working with Buck and Buddy Banks, Ivan Overcash, and Steve Ledford. Then Zeke joined back up again and Mainer, Morris, and Ledford went to Columbia, South Carolina. While there, Zeke quit again. Wade decided to go to Marion, North Carolina, to talk to Jay Hugh Hall who had worked once before with him briefly about going to work for him again. Hall suggested that Wade also hire his friend, Clyde Moody, which he did and took them to Columbia. However, Wade felt that Byron Parker more or less had WIS sewed up and that he had talked the station manager into getting rid of Wade and his group when they became competition to him. So Wade left and went back to WPTF.

During 1938 the band now known as the Sons of the Mountaineers did two sessions on Bluebird, recording ten and fourteen numbers each time. Wade's fiancée, Julia Brown, was featured on one song, "Where Romance Calls." One number, "Mitchell Blues," constituted an instrumental adaptation of Narmour and Smith's "Carroll County Blues" with Steve Ledford's fiddle and Wade's banjo backing containing many elements of bluegrass. Some numbers recorded at these sessions were done with neither fiddle nor banjo.

In 1939, the group did two more Bluebird sessions, recording ten songs each time. "Sparkling Blue Eyes," recorded in February, probably constituted the most popular number that Mainer's band did on Bluebird. Billy Cox, the song's composer, and Cliff Hobbs had recorded the song the previous year and it became one of the country hits of the late 1930s, also being covered by Cliff Carlisle and Cliff Bruner on Decca. Only the Mainer rendition, however, proved popular enough to warrant a number two version. The August 1939 session also witnessed the final guest on Wade's recordings when a Reverend Bradley helped the Sons of the Mountaineers sing four songs including "What a Wonderful Savior Is He" and "Why Not Make

Heaven Your Home." Although Wade recalled Bradley, Tony Russell's discography credits Dan Hornsby with no mention of Bradley as assisting on the session.

In the meantime, the Sons of the Mountaineers moved to WWNC Asheville where they initiated the *Farm Hour*. Wade had contract troubles with Victor in the spring of 1940 and sat out the February session although his band cut six sides with Hall, Moody, and Ledford as the Happy-Go-Lucky-Boys. At least one record was issued as Steve Ledford's Mountaineers. Shortly afterward this band broke up. Ledford went out on his own for a while and Hall and Moody worked briefly for J. E. Mainer. Hall and Ledford then joined Roy Hall's Blue Ridge Entertainers. Clyde Moody went on to join Bill Monroe and later became a solo performer. Wade Mainer, in turn, organized a new band.

The 1939 edition of the Sons of the Mountaineers included Howard Dixon on Hawaiian guitar, formerly of the Dixon Brothers, and Walter "Tiny" Dodson on fiddle and comedy. However, Dixon and Dodson never recorded with Wade Mainer. The Shelton Brothers, Jack and Curley, rounded out the group. They continued to work on the *Farm Hour* on WWNC and played personals. Their live shows were generally held in schoolhouses, but they sometimes played outdoor shows in ballparks during the summer. At times the band had as much as $200 to divide among them after a successful night. On other occasions, their profits might be much smaller. Generally, however, Wade Mainer and his group proved to be a popular drawing card. Sometimes J. E. Mainer came over and played with them and the two brothers would be briefly reunited.

After many years in the Carolinas, Wade went to Tennessee in the winter of 1940–41 taking the Sheltons with him. Going to Knoxville, he worked at Lowell Blanchard's *Mid-Day Merry-Go Round* on WNOX. He also appeared occasionally on the local NBC station WROL. In September 1941, they cut their last Bluebird session in Atlanta, recording eight songs of which the banjo song "Old Reuben" and the Mainer version of Roy Acuff's "Precious Jewel" are probably best known.

About this time, Wade lost a probable opportunity to become a member of the *Grand Ole Opry*. George D. Hay gave Mainer a call asking him to be a temporary replacement for an absentee act. Although Lowell Blanchard temporarily approved things, he changed his mind at the last minute evidently fearing the move might be permanent. After the coming of World War II, Wade decided to give up active pursuit of his career. He returned to Asheville where he owned a small farm and left radio and travel for a time. Later, however, he returned to a more strenuous schedule.

When Wade Mainer and Zeke Morris went on their own at Raleigh in 1936, J. E. formed a new group and continued to work for Crazy Water Crystals. When the show terminated, J. E. went back to Concord and farmed briefly. However, he soon put another band together consisting of George Morris and Leonard Stokes on guitar and mandolin, respectively, together with Snuffy Jenkins on banjo. Like Wade's group of the same period, this combination came very close to bluegrass.

The Mountaineers went into radio again at Charlotte, later moving to Spartanburg and Columbia. In August 1937, they cut twelve sides for Bluebird. Eight of the numbers featured Morris and Stokes doing duets while J. E. and Snuffy seem not to have played. The last four sides featured the full group with Snuffy's three-finger-banjo style being quite audible and the entire band sounding very similar to bluegrass on "Don't Go Out Tonight," "Don't Get Trouble in Your Mind," and "Kiss Me Cindy." One of George Morris and Leonard Stoke's duets, "We Can't Be Darlings Anymore," later became one of the early classics of bluegrass as rendered by Lester Flatt and Curly Seckler.

J. E. Mainer's Mountaineers then went to Spartanburg, South Carolina, and WSPA. After about four months, J. W. Fincher put them back to work for Crazy Water Crystals at WIS in Columbia for quite some time. In the six-month period from October 1937 to March 1938, the Mountaineers drew 8,305 pieces of mail "without benefit of contests or free offers." This indicated something of their popularity and rated them as the station's "biggest mail puller."

While at WIS, the Mountaineers did twelve more numbers for Bluebird most of which were guitar-mandolin vocal duets. If Mainer and Jenkins were present, they are inaudible on the recordings. Then J.E. started to get the idea that "they began to want him [Byron Parker] to take over." So in Wade's words, "J. E. pulled out" and went back to Concord. The band remaining in Columbia first took the name Byron Parker's Mountaineers and subsequently the WIS Hillbillies, enjoying a long career in the South Carolina capital.

J. E. did his last Bluebird session in February 1939 with the guitar backing of Clyde Moody and Jay Hugh Hall as part of Wade's band as J. E. Mainer apparently had no group at the time. J. E. vocalized on the amusing "Drunkard's Hiccoughs" and performed two fiddle tunes, "Concord Rag" and "Country Blues." It was during this period that he also did some work with Wade at WWNC.

In 1940, J. E. Mainer got back into the business again on a regular basis when he picked up Hall and Moody who had recently left his brother's band. Together they went to WAPI Birmingham and played for a time and then returned to North Carolina playing in Greensboro with another new band comprised of Price Sanders, Mitchell Parker, and Gurney Thomas. Then J. E. retired again for a brief period leaving the band to carry on alone.

A few weeks later in the fall of 1940, J. E. Mainer accepted an offer to go to Texas and play shows on the Border Stations sponsored by Kolorbak, a patented hair darkener for those who thought they were prematurely gray. Accordingly, he again picked up Price Sanders and Mitchell Parker along with his nephews Buck and Buddy Banks and headed for the wide open spaces. The Mountaineers worked about seven months doing live shows and cutting transcriptions. The Carter Family also worked there at the same time. The next year J. E. took the group to St. Louis and worked for a year at KMOX.

The sojourn in Missouri marked one of J. E. Mainer's last long periods of an extended absence from home doing radio work. Henceforth, his musical activity, except for recording, remained largely confined to the Carolinas until the Folk Revival of the early sixties created a renewal of interest in J. E. Mainer's brand of old-time music. However, he continued to entertain locally.

During much of World War II, Wade Mainer remained out of music. He had bought a little farm near Asheville and alternated farm work with some long earned relaxation. However, in 1942, Alan Lomax contacted him and had him along with Tiny Dodson and Jack Shelton go to Washington, D. C., to play for President and Mrs. Franklin D. Roosevelt. Wade recalled telling Dodson when he first saw the White House, "that sure would have held a lot of hay." His most vivid recollection of the event came when he spilled some ice cream on the First Lady's dress. Fortunately, she did not seem to mind and helped to put the mountaineer, who was embarrassed, at ease.

Another time Lomax got Wade to go to New York City to participate in the BBC production of *The Chisholm Trail*. He took J. E. and two area youngsters with him who later became famous to the bluegrass world as Red Rector and Fred Smith. They were joined there by Lily, Rosie and Minnie Ledford, the Coon Creek Girls from Renfro Valley, and such now legendary urban folk performers as Woody Guthrie, Cisco Houston, and Blind Sonny Terry. They all spent a week together rehearsing and transcribing the production.

Early in 1947, Wade recorded the first of four sessions for King Records in Cincinnati, Ohio. J. E. had done a session for this new company a few weeks earlier. Wade's band at the time consisted of Red Wilson on fiddle, Arville Freeman on mandolin, and Ned Smathers on guitar. On Wade's cover of two Bailes Brothers' recordings, Jethro Burns played mandolin instead of Freeman. On two numbers, Freeman did the lead vocals while Wade took a rest. Ten of the twelve numbers were soon released, but the two featuring Freeman were held back for nearly forty years. In retrospect, the most interesting cut may have been Wade's original "I'm Glad I'm on the Inside Looking Out," a sacred number with a touch of humor which was later covered by country artists as diverse as Cowboy Copas and Hank Snow.

The immediate aftermath of World War II resulted in the founding of numerous new radio stations that soon began to crowd the airwaves. Many of these stations had limited signals and were daytime stations only. Wade got back into radio in September 1947 at WBBO Forest City, North Carolina, as a single doing two shows daily—one for Tru-Pak Aspirin and the other for Acme Tractors. Somewhat later, he got a band together and went to the station at Mount Airy, North Carolina. Subsequently, he again went to Asheville and to WWNC. During this time Wade's band changed personnel frequently. He likely found out the hard way that post-war radio was not what it had been earlier. Although WWNC undoubtedly still had some drawing power and the Mount Airy station eventually made history, the business was changing.

Wade did not go back to King again until March 17, 1951, when he did a session in Charlotte. Some interesting topical gospel numbers such as "God's Radio Phone" and "Little Book" along with a cut of the old Doc Walsh song "Courtin' in the Rain" that remained unissued until 2006 were among the eight songs done at this time. Willie Carver played steel guitar and Wiley

Morris on guitar and baritone vocals were band members. The third session back in Cincinnati on November 19, 1951, featured Troy Brammer on banjo, Marion Hall on guitar, and Lloyd Burge on mandolin. For the most part Wade played guitar and Brammer's three-finger banjo gave the recordings a more bluegrass sound. The old chestnut that went back to 1899, "The Girl I Left in Sunny Tennessee," was the outstanding cut among the six numbers. A World War II song, "That Star Belongs to Me," later became a favorite in the repertoire of the Lilly Brothers. With the exception of a single on the regional Blue Ridge label in 1953, it was Wade Mainer's last studio recording until 1961.

During this time, Wade's style remained about the same as that of his pre-war groups although he believed that he made some accommodation in the direction of the Bill Monroe and Flatt and Scruggs sounds of the period. This seemed to have been a reversal of the pre-war situation when the sounds of the Mainers, the Morrises, the Halls, and other associated musicians obviously made some impact on Monroe, Flatt and Scruggs, Reno, and the other pioneer innovators of bluegrass. Undoubtedly, the bluegrass sound had some effect on recording engineers, for Wade's two-finger banjo received more prominence on King than on the old Bluebirds.

Wade Mainer remained musically active in the Carolinas until 1953 when he "professed religion" and ceased to perform professionally. He gave up banjo playing since it seemed to be "out of line." Agreeing to help an evangelist friend he did, however, sing in church with guitar accompaniment at a revival in Flint, Michigan. At this time, he decided to remain in the North, securing a job at the local General Motors plant. That Christmas, his family joined him and Wade Mainer entered an eight-year period of relative musical inactivity.

Unlike Wade, J. E. Mainer never stopped playing professionally although his career did pass through several phases. One phase began at the end of World War II when the eldest of his children, J. E. Mainer Jr., known as Curley, received his discharge from the service. Twenty-two year old Curley, a lead singer and guitar player, together with his eighteen-year-old brother, Glenn, along with their father made up the nucleus of the Mountaineer band that played on radio at Johnson City, Tennessee. This band also cut twenty-four sides on King in two sessions, nineteen of which subsequently were released. Some vocals featured J. E. Mainer while Curley sang on others. Perhaps the most memorable number, "Run Mountain," featured J. E.'s hard-driving fiddle work and singing. Although the original King singles have long been out of print, sixteen of the numbers remained available during the 1960s on the classic King LP 666, *Good Ol' Mountain Music.*

The Mountaineers did no more recording for another fifteen years, but did continue to play a lot of personal appearances in western Virginia and western North Carolina. Evidently they continued to perform the traditional mountain style that had come to be associated with the Mainer name. In addition to J. E., Curley, and Glenn, the two Mainer daughters Mary and Carolyn played with the group on occasion. Others who were often in and out of the band included Jim Dillon, John Cook, and Floyd and Otis Overcash. The Mountaineer show in addition to music featured blackface comedy skits until they went out of favor.

On June 8, 1961, J .E. Mainer's Mountaineers returned to Cincinnati and the King Studio after a fifteen-year absence from recording. Those musicians present at the session besides J. E. and Glenn Mainer included Dillon and Cook. Although the earlier Mainer bands showed evidence of progressing in the direction of bluegrass, none seemed more so than the 1961 version of the Mountaineers. J. E.'s fiddle work remained more old-time and primitive sounding, but Glenn's banjo work had become totally bluegrass and he contributed two original Scruggs's-style instrumentals—"Glenn's Chimes" and "Country Breakdown." About this time they also recorded four songs on Atlantic for a folk music anthology series.

Although the Mountaineers continued to perform much as before during the 1960s, one important aspect of their careers changed—the urban folk song revival followed by a resurging interest in old-time and bluegrass music widened their audience. During the late 1930s they had ranked among the most important country groups, but changing times in the next two decades had again localized their following.

In 1962, Chris Strachwitz of Arhoolie Records visited J. E. Mainer and the following April recorded him on a label which had some appeal for the folk audience. This led to an appearance at the Berkeley Folk Festival in 1963. Later the band appeared at other folk and bluegrass festivals.

Perhaps no other old-time artist was ever more prepared for a resurgence of interest in his brand of music than Joseph Emmet Mainer. Beginning in July 1967, he recorded a long string of albums on Uncle Jim O'Neil's

Rural Rhythm label. He laboriously wrote personal letters to all old-time music enthusiasts who wrote him, never missing the opportunity to plug his albums, single records, and song books with his quaint phonetic brand of spelling. Besides his recording work for Uncle Jim, he cut an album and several singles on the Blue-Jay label and reissued two albums of vintage material on his own Ball Mountain label. RCA reissued some material in both the USA and Japan on two albums featuring original Mainer material which appeared on the Old Timey label. Although J. E. Mainer died on June 12, 1971, before a scheduled appearance at the Culpepper Bluegrass Festival and before having the proper opportunity to express himself, it is my belief that he enjoyed every minute—and deservedly so—of his return to the musical limelight.

J .E. eventually recorded sixteen separate albums on Rural Rhythm—the others are largely a repackaged mixture of the earlier ones, but the earlier releases in the series were unquestionably the best. Some of the same persons who had recorded on King and Arhoolie such as Curley and Glenn Mainer worked with him and their quality was quite good. Later, quantity seemed to become the chief goal although all of the sessions produced some good music. Among the other musicians who worked with J. E. Mainer on these recordings included Earl and Jerry Cheek, Bill Deaton, and Morris Herbert who eventually came to be featured more than J. E. on the later albums. One album was made with the Red Smiley band from WDBJ in Roanoke—Billy Edwards, Tater Tate, John Palmer, and Gene Burroughs. The latter recalled the session with a great deal of pleasure and said that J. E. Mainer was a happy person who often laughed so much during the session that some numbers required several takes. Evidently it was an occasion enjoyed by all.

While J. E. kept playing to audiences great and small, Wade continued to work at the GM plant in Michigan, taking little interest in music. Eventually, he manifested interest in playing at church functions largely because of the encouragement of Lynn Davis and Molly O'Day whom he had met at a revival. On April 7, 1961, Wade together with his wife Julia, fiddler Ed Bryant, and guitarist Owen Bloodworth, entered the King studios for a final session of twelve songs, one of which was never issued. Except for three numbers, all were sacred and most featured Julia Mainer singing lead. After many years of being out of print, Gusto reissued Wade's entire

King output in a two-compact disc set with liner notes by scholar Richard Spottswood who was in the process of working on a Wade Mainer biography. Towards the end of the 1960s Wade recorded a gospel single on the Knob label which indicated that he, like his older brother, was still capable of producing some fine music.

In the early seventies, he began to be seen and heard a little more often. He recorded an album on the IRMA label that was subsequently rereleased as Old Homestead 90014, and Wade began to make an occasional festival appearance on the gospel portion, including one at Bean Blossom. He also made two albums on the Old Homestead label—one that contained some secular material. Retiring from GM in 1973, Mainer found his otherwise quiet retirement frequently interrupted by requests to play at festivals.

Wade and Julia Mainer kept pretty busy in the remainder of the 1970s and 1980s. They did several albums for John Morris of Old Homestead Records and worked at least as much as the pair of old-timers felt like playing. He delighted audiences playing the banjo behind his back and other tricks similar to what Uncle Dave Macon had done in the 1940 motion picture *Grand Ole Opry* although Mainer was much older than the seventy-year old Macon had been at the time. In those later days he even did a guest spot on the *Opry*

Recognition and honors came to Wade Mainer in those later years. In 1987, he became a recipient of a National Heritage Fellowship and in 1990 a Lifetime Achievement Award from the International Bluegrass Music Association. Since Old Homestead was slow to get into compact discs, John Morris urged Wade and Julia Mainer to do a compact disc for June Appal which they did in March 1991 when they recorded *In the Land of Melody* in Big Stone Gap, Virginia. In October 1992 Mainer did what was apparently his last studio album for Old Homestead, *Carolina Mule*. Eventually, many of the Old Homestead albums came out on compact disc and John Morris did reissues of several of his Bluebird and King recordings as well as a DVD of one of Wade's birthday celebrations. In 2009, two four-CD box sets from JSP Records in the United Kingdom contained the entire Mainer Bluebird 1935–1941 output. He had long hoped to get his life story into print and Stephen Wade and Richard Spottswood came out with *Banjo on the Mountain: Wade Mainer's First Hundred Years* (University Press of Mississippi, 2010). Unsurprisingly, there would not be a second volume as the venerable old-timer passed away on September 12, 2011, at the age of 104. Julia, age 95, passed in 2015.

One cannot study or listen to the music of the Mainers' Mountaineers of the late 1930s without arriving at the conclusion that they provided an important link between old-time mountain music and bluegrass. Some of their recordings displayed these characteristics more than others. Scholars who have traced the origins of bluegrass have focused their attention on brother duets, the development of the three-finger banjo styles in the Carolinas, and the combination of a variety of other instrumental sounds. However, it seems apparent that J. E. and Wade Mainer together with the musicians who played with their various bands made major contributions toward the creation of what has become known as bluegrass music.

SELECTED RECORDINGS

Although there were earlier reissues of Mainer's Mountaineers Bluebird Recordings from the 1935–1941 era, chiefly on County and Old Homestead, both brothers entire early output appeared in 2009 on two four compact disc sets from the United Kingdom:

J. E. Mainer: *The Early Years, 1935–1939.* JSP 77118, 2009.
J. E. Mainer: *The Early Years, 1936–1941.* JSP 77124, 2009.
Wade Mainer: *I'm Not Looking Backward, 1947–1961.* Gusto GT 0957, 2006. Two disc set of Wade Mainer's King Recordings.

In later years both Mainers continued to record extensively, J. E primarily on Rural Rhythm, and Wade mostly on Old Homestead. Only a sampling of this material is listed here:

J. E. Mainer's Mountaineers: *Run Mountain.* Arhoolie CD 456, 1997. Reissue of 1963 long play album.
J. E. Mainer & his Mountaineers: *Old Time Mountain Music.* Rural Rhythm RHY 1032, 2007. Reissue of J. E.'s first two Rural Rhythm albums, first made in the mid-1960s.
Wade Mainer: *From the Maple to the Hill.* Old Homestead OH CD 4000, 1998. Originally a two-album set recorded in 1976.
Wade and Julia Mainer: *In the Land of Melody.* June Appal JA 0065, 1992. The first Mainer album made for compact disc release.
Wade Mainer: *Carolina Mule.* Old Homestead OH CD 90207, 2005. Wade's last studio recording, made when he was just past 85.

PART FIVE

Families
and Groups

Families and groups have played important roles in traditional country music almost from the beginning. The Carter and Stoneman families rose to prominence prior to the Great Depression as well as those with such nearly forgotten surnames as Deal, Smith, and Thrasher, many of whom exclusively recorded sacred songs. This trend continued in the post-World War II field of Southern Gospel with such groups as the Goodmans, the Hemphills, the LeFevres, the Rambos, and the Chuck Wagon Gang, sometimes termed the other Carter Family.

In 1948 the three-person Florida-born Masters family made up of John and Lucille and their teenage son Owen emerged from this complex mixture. Their own instrumentation was dominated by the mandolin, but on recording sessions they supplemented with the mainstream country and western instrumentation of the day using electric lead and steel guitars and sometimes piano, as on their original "Glory Land March." John Masters also composed outstanding songs such as "Cry from the Cross" and lyrics that concerned contemporary Southern religious issues such as "That Little Old Country Church House," which addressed declining attendance in rural congregations, and "They Made a New Bible," which was about the Revised Standard Version translation. The Masters Family prominence lasted for only about a decade, but their influence extended over a much longer period.

Family bands also emerged in bluegrass beginning with an updated Stoneman Family, known as the Bluegrass Champs, in the Washington

D.C., area. Continuing in this manner came the Stevens, Cox, Cochrane, Cockman, and Cherryholmes families among others. Family gospel bluegrass bands included those of Forbes, Marshall, and Sullivan.

Although the Sullivans came first and had a long history, the Lincolnton, Georgia-based Lewis Family easily out-distanced the others. Just as the Masters Family had introduced country-western instrumentation, the Lewis Family achievement consisted of the fusion of Southern gospel trios with the hard driving Scruggs-style banjo and fiddle and mandolin instrumentation. In addition to the group's quality music, they had a highly polished stage presence which included generous doses of comedy by banjoist Little Roy Lewis. In their fifty-seven year history, the Lewis Family left a legacy of over sixty long play albums and compact discs which continues with two successor bands.

Musical groups also emerged early in the evolution of country music with the Hillbillies in the 1925–1928 period. The rise of radio brought other groups into the limelight. At Charlotte's WBT, the Briarhoppers had a long history beginning in 1934 with moderate personnel changes through the years with the most noted being the mandolin-guitar team of Whitey and Hogan (Roy Grant and Arval Hogan) and also longtime fiddler Hank Warren. After their radio show ended, the group became more or less semi-active, but reactivated in 1973 with the above threesome and past band members, bass guitarist-western vocalist Don White, and banjo picker Shannon Grayson, also a veteran of the Carlisles and his own Golden Valley Boys. This quintet played regularly until 1991 when Grayson's health forced his retirement. David Deese replaced him. Dwight Moody later replaced Warren, but the Briarhoppers remained active for several more years.

Kentuckian John Lair came up with several innovations in his long life including creating a radio music jamboree in a true rural setting, albeit somewhat contrived, *The Renfro Valley Barn Dance*. Talent wise, Lair's major creation came in the form of an all-girl, old-time string band. The Coon Creek Girls worked his programs in Cincinnati and Renfro Valley for two decades. While fiddler-banjo picker Lily May Ledford was the central figure, the band was a team effort and an historic moment when they became the first traditional country act to entertain British Royalty at the White House in 1939. In later years, they became an inspiration for all-girl bluegrass bands.

Many bluegrass bands over the years have been of short duration. The band known as Betty Fisher, David Deese and Dixie Bluegrass was different in one respect; the co-leaders already had significant earlier careers in their own right. Fisher became one of the first women to lead a successful band with mostly male members for nine years ending in 1980. Banjo picker David Deese had distinguished himself as a sideman with Bill Monroe, Arthur "Guitar Boogie" Smith, Red Smiley, the Jones Brothers, and the Briarhoppers. Circumstances beyond their control forced them to disband, but they had already earned their niche in music.

✄ The Briarhoppers

Roy "Whitey" Grant, 1916–2010
Arval Hogan, 1911–2003
Shannon Grayson, 1916–1993
Walden "Don White" Whytsell, 1909–2005
Garnet "Hank" Warren, 1909–1997
Dwight Moody, 1929–2013
David Deese, 1941–2011

For a period of more than 15 years, the WBT Briarhoppers constituted one of the most popular regional country music groups in radio. Sponsored by Peruna, this group achieved such a following in the Carolinas and adjacent states that it sometimes became necessary for the band to divide into two units to keep active on the road simultaneously in order to satisfy the demand for personal appearances. In the 1940s the music and songs of the Briarhoppers included elements of old-time string music, harmony duets, western vocals, and bluegrass as well as mainstream country music. After the decline of live radio, the Briarhoppers became relatively inactive, but in the mid-1970s they reactivated and played bluegrass festivals and other Southeast venues. Through a dozen of the Briarhoppers' best years, the team of Whitey Grant and Arval Hogan formed the nucleus of the group; this mandolin-guitar duo sang in a style that had wide appeal during the 1930s and 1940s. Although the Briarhoppers as such made no recordings until the 1970s, individually and with other groups all of them made recordings in the 1930s and afterward. As advancing age took a toll on some members by the 1990s, they added a pair of new musicians and kept playing until the early years of the new century. But time eventually terminated the act entirely.

Hogan, the older and mandolin playing half of the duet, was born in Robbinsville, North Carolina, on July 24, 1911. Four years later the family

Briarhoppers, 1977. *From left:* Hank Warren, Shannon Grayson, Roy "Whitey" Grant, Arval Hogan, Don White.

moved to Andrews, North Carolina, where Hogan's father directed a church choir and taught his three sons to sing at an early age. During the late 1920s, the Hogan Brothers—Clarence, Garland, and Arval—together with a neighbor on fiddle started a local string band. Since all the Hogans played guitar, it was suggested that Arval get a mandolin. At the time, he did not even know what the instrument was, but ordered one from Sears, Roebuck & Company. Subsequently, he learned to play it by listening to a record of "Chinese Breakdown " by the Scottsdale String Band. Thereafter Arval Hogan played mandolin with the group at "square dances, parties, churches, and family gatherings for a long time." In 1936 he left Andrews and went to Gastonia, North Carolina, where he met both his future wife Evelyn and his "life-time music partner," Whitey Grant. Born in Shelby, North Carolina, on April 7, 1916, Grant's interest in music dated from his earliest memories. He recalled urging his parents to buy phonograph records of Vernon Dalhart and other old-time singers. He bought his first guitar at fifteen and had the man he purchased it from draw diagrams showing finger positions for various chords. Church parties and family gatherings provided audiences for Grant's developing talents. In 1932 he met Pauline Chapman, and after they married in 1935, he went to Gastonia to work in a cotton mill. Not long afterward he met Hogan and they were a musical duet "ever since."

The two soon began to play at local venues and from there went on to regular radio appearances. They first broadcast on a regular basis from WSPA in Spartanburg, South Carolina, as featured performers on Scotty the Drifter's program. When radio station WGNC was built in Gastonia, Whitey and Hogan auditioned and got their own daily quarter hour show at 12:45 each afternoon. Sponsored by Efird's Department Store, they were called the Efird Boys. Later, Rustin's Furniture Store became their sponsor and they did their show live from the department store's show window. Although they gained considerable local popularity, the duo did not feel secure enough in their careers as entertainers to give up work at the textile mill. Following the show, they went to the afternoon shift in the twisting department at Firestone, making the fibers that went into automobile tires. Grant contended that the pair was late for the show only once during the radio days at Gastonia and that was because "Hogan was up at the dime store watching a bunch of goldfish, and we forgot we were going to be on the air." "(I'm Riding On) My Savior's Train" served as their radio theme song, and they performed both secular and sacred numbers.

During the stint at WGNC, Whitey and Hogan made their first recordings. The Decca distributor at Charlotte arranged for them to go to New York City in the fall of 1939 where they recorded sixteen numbers on November 8. The most memorable songs included a cover of the Blue Sky Boys' "Sunny Side of Life," one of the earliest recordings of "Turn Your Radio On," (preceding the Bill and Earl Bolick version by nearly a year), the sentimental "Old Log Cabin For Sale," the later bluegrass standard "Gosh I Miss You All the Time," their own "Answer to Budded Roses," and the beautiful but seldom heard "You'll Be My Closest Neighbor." The trip to New York took three or four days and they recalled that they "were treated like kings" and reimbursed for all their expenses when they returned.

Whitey and Hogan remained at Gastonia until September 1941, when they were asked to join the Briarhopper program at WBT Charlotte. Since the Briarhoppers had a show at 4:30 in the afternoon, the duo switched to working the third shift at the mill for six months until they saw how the new job shaped up. Then they "followed music continuously for [many] years" as a full-time occupation.

The Briarhoppers were already an established group at WBT when Whitey and Hogan joined them. The group had originated back in the mid-thirties when the Drug Trade Products Company of Chicago wanted to sponsor a country music program at WBT, so they got some "boys together and started a program but they didn't have a name." One day announcer Charles Crutchfield was out hunting with some fellows. When they jumped a rabbit and one of the hunters said "look at that rabbit jump those briars," Crutchfield hit upon "Briarhoppers" as the name for the band that advertised Peruna. So the Briarhoppers they became, and the Briarhoppers they remained for sixty years. Actually, the Briarhoppers were but one of several country groups sponsored by Peruna around the nation. By 1946, Drug Trade Products Company employed multiple groups and programs including Cap, Andy, and Milt in Charleston; the *Morning Frolic* in Louisville; Cousin Emmy and Her Gang in Atlanta; and the Briarhoppers at Charlotte as well as the Cactus Kids, Uncle Enoch and His Gang, Pete Haley and His Log Cabin Girls, the Bohemian Orchestra, the Bar Nothing Gang, the Haden Family, and the Smiling Hillbillies at other locations. Often, the groups worked under Peruna sponsorship for only six months of the year since Peruna tended to be a popular product only in the winter months when listeners suffered from coughs and colds. In some years, however, the company sponsored the Briarhoppers the entire year. At other times, a band might have to seek another sponsor or other means of employment in the off season.

Although Whitey's and Hogan's dozen years with the group placed them among the more durable members of the Briarhoppers, many other notable musicians worked with the band in their seventeen years or so at WBT. A complete history of all these musicians would run into a lengthy article and outside of those who made up the Briarhopers from the 1970s only a few will be mentioned here. Big Bill Davis played bass fiddle with the band through most of its years at WBT. Davis retired to his High Point, North Carolina, residence, but still played an occasional show with the Briarhoppers when they played near his home in the late 1970s. Davis died a few years later. At times, members of the Tennessee Ramblers had brief associations with the Briarhoppers including Cecil Campbell, Claude Casey, and Harry Blair.

Fred Kirby was another key member of the Briarhoppers during the World War II years. Born at Charlotte on July 19, 1910, Kirby worked with Cliff and Bill Carlisle at various times, led his own band the Carolina Boys, and worked as a solo vocalist. At one time or another, he also recorded on most major labels including Bluebird, Columbia, and Decca as well as lesser-known companies like Gotham and Sonora. Kirby achieved considerable success in the mid 1940s with his song "Atomic Power" which was covered on nine record labels. Kirby also composed "Reveille Time in Heaven" which is one of Mac Wiseman's bluegrass standards. He remained active in Charlotte although no longer associated with the Briarhoppers. Kirby later had a popular children's television program in Charlotte for many years and entertained in summers at the Tweetsie Railroad, a tourist attraction in the Smoky Mountain area at Blowing Rock. He died on April 22, 1996.

Garnet B. Warren, better known as "Fiddlin' Hank," served one of the longest stints with the Briarhoppers. Born at Mount Airy, North Carolina, on April 1, 1909, Warren also became interested in music at an early age and had memories of seeing the early blind recording pioneer Ernest Thompson play on the streets. He learned to read music, and was one of the few traditional performers to do so, and played violin in the high school orchestra. He later learned to play mandolin, tenor banjo, ukulele, and hand saw. He was interested in old-time music, too, so regularly participated in and won contests at fiddlers' conventions in the Mount Airy area prior to organizing a local band known as Warren's Four Aces. In 1931, he was married to Inez Turney and then went on to play fiddle with a professional group—Jack Richie and his Blue Ridge Mountaineers.

Warren then joined Dick Hartman's Tennessee Ramblers, one of the most popular country bands in the Carolinas who played regularly at WBT. Since this group played a lot of uptown and western-styled country music, they are not as well remembered today as bands that clung to the mountain styles. But a Crazy Water Crystals souvenir booklet of the mid-thirties suggests that their popularity probably at least equaled that of Mainer's Mountaineers. Other members of the group at various times included Harry Blair, Kenneth Wolfe, and Cecil Campbell who later became their leader. Hank Warren stayed with the group for about two years, playing on two and perhaps three Bluebird sessions with the band. In 1936, he went to California where the Ramblers made the movie *Ride Ranger Ride* with

Gene Autry. After the film's release, the band toured widely with the picture appearing in theaters.

After leaving the Ramblers, Warren went to WPTF Raleigh where he worked with the Swingbillies, a group led by Charlie Poole Jr. In 1937, he returned to Charlotte and joined the Briarhoppers. Fiddlin' Hank remained with them until 1950. In 1943, he sponsored one of the most unusual contests ever held on radio when he suggested that listeners to the Briarhopper program submit names for his newborn son. Some 10,000 fans sent in names and the proud father selected the name Larry and awarded a ten dollar prize to the winner.

There were also two "Homer" Briarhoppers. One, Homer Drye, a youth who recorded for Bluebird and Decca in the late 1930s and Mercury in the 1940s, continued to use that name although, like Kirby, he had not been a part of the group for many years. Drye spent most of his later career in Raleigh, dying in 1983. Gib Young was a fine guitar player for the group as was Dewey Price. Eleanor Bryan worked as a vocalist for some time and also played guitar.

Another important Briarhopper was Don White who played with the group off and on for several years and could best be described as a western singer despite his Appalachian upbringing. White's real name was Walden Whytsell and he came from West Virginia, being born at Wolf Creek on September 25, 1909. Don White first learned to play guitar from his mother and eventually added bass, mandolin, rhythm and steel guitar. Early entertainment experiences included a stint with Otto Gray's Oklahoma Cowboys. He first came to Charlotte as a musician in 1933 with the Blue Ridge Mountaineers playing at WSOC radio. He later returned to West Virginia, but came back to Charlotte in 1935 as a member of the Crazy Buckle Busters and worked for Crazy Water Crystals at WBT. Later Don switched to the Briarhoppers, remaining with them until 1939. On June 19, 1936, White made his first recordings of three solo numbers—"Mexicali Rose, "Rocking Alone in an Old Rocking Chair," and "What a Friend We Have in Mother." He also did two duets with Fred Kirby, "My Old Saddle Horse Is Missing" and "Play That Waltz Again."

White and Kirby left WBT in 1939 for WLW in Cincinnati. White moved on to KFAB in Lincoln, Nebraska, as a single and in 1941 to WJJD Chicago. In 1942, he rejoined the Briarhoppers at Charlotte. The following year he moved over to the Tennessee Ramblers who then worked on the same program. He remained with them until 1946 during which time the group appeared in three films. The first one, *Swing Your Pardner,* starred Lulu Belle and Scotty as well as Dale Evans; the second, *Sundown Valley,* featured Charles Starrett with Jimmy Wakely; and the third was *O My Darling Clementine* with Roy Acuff, Pappy Cheshire, and Irene Ryan. In 1946, White returned to Chicago and spent the next six years leading the WLS Sage Riders, a popular western music team that included Dolph Hewitt, Red Blanchard, and Ray Klein. When WLS changed ownership in 1952, the Sage Riders disbanded and White returned to Charlotte, his wife's home town. He left the entertainment field for more than twenty years until rejoining the Briarhoppers in the 1970s.

Shannon Grayson was probably the most important member of the Briarhoppers in respect to their relationship to bluegrass music. Grayson was born in Sunshine, North Carolina, on September 30, 1916. This community was only about ten miles from where Snuffy Jenkins grew up and Jenkins influenced Grayson's banjo style. Grayson took an interest in music at an early age as his family owned an organ, and he humorously contended that he almost drove them away with his playing. Later, his father bought him a banjo since Grayson could be sent to the barn with it and rest the ears of the household from listening to his organ music. He also became adept on mandolin, guitar, and bass fiddle.

Grayson played at a number of local entertainments prior to joining the touring group of Art Mix who claimed to be the brother of cowboy film star, Tom Mix. Later Shannon returned home and worked in the textile mills. About 1936, Bill Carlisle approached him about working with his group on radio at Charlotte. Since Carlisle already had a reputation as a radio and recording artist, Grayson thought "that was the greatest thing I had ever heard, to get to work with somebody like Bill Carlisle and be on the radio and play shows and get paid for it too. That was too good to be true!" Grayson played with Bill Carlisle at WBT Charlotte, WWNC Asheville, and WCHS Charleston. He recorded with him on Bluebird the year that he joined him.

After the group worked in the West Virginia capital for some time, Carlisle took them to New York City where he scheduled a Decca recording session. Cliff Carlisle met them there and the brothers recorded both together and separately. That session proved to be one of several that Grayson did with the Carlisle Brothers on Decca and Bluebird. On these recordings, Shannon usually played mandolin, but occasionally used a five-string banjo. Among the many songs recorded by this group included an early version of "Footprints In the Snow," "Two Eyes in Tennessee," and a number called "Are You Going to Leave Me, Lil?" which featured some wild mandolin work and came quite close to bluegrass. Most of this recorded repertoire featured a lot of mandolin along with Cliff Carlisle's resonator guitar.

Following the Decca session on which Grayson played, the Carlisle brothers reunited for radio work and went to WNOX Knoxville. They remained in the East Tennessee city for several years. Shannon stayed with them until 1943, playing on the *Mid-Day-Merry-Go-Round*, early morning radio shows, and hundreds of personal appearances. Of the latter, Grayson recalled the most memorable as being in Harriman, Tennessee, where they worked a show with Bing Crosby. Dixie Lee Crosby, Bing's first wife, called Harriman home and the couple had been slated to attend and entertain as had the Carlisle band. Dixie Lee Crosby developed an illness and failed to appear although Bing Crosby came and the Carlisles ended up providing musical backing for him. Grayson recalled that things worked pretty well with "a bunch of hillbillies" accompanying Hollywood's most popular crooner, and that everyone was congenial.

In 1943, Grayson went to Charlotte and joined the WBT Briarhoppers. He was more or less part of the group from that time on except during those years when he led his own band, the Golden Valley Boys. This combination worked together in the late 1940s and early 1950s doing guest spots on various radio shows while cutting some vintage bluegrass for the King and RCA Victor labels.

The Golden Valley Boys consisted of Grayson playing banjo and singing lead, Dewey Price on guitar and tenor vocal, and Millard Presley doing the mandolin work and baritone singing. Harvey Raborn sang bass in the quartets but played no instrument. A studio bass player was used on their sessions. Tommy Jackson fiddled on some cuts and electric steel was used on part of the Victor recordings. In all, the Golden Valley Boys had four sides issued on King and eight on Victor.

Most of the band's repertoire consisted of sacred material, especially quartets. Shannon did some banjo instrumentals like "Earl's Breakdown" and "Flint Hill Special" and the group performed some secular material like "Work Is All I Hear" and "Roses and Thorns" which they recorded on Victor. Some of the best-known sacred songs included "If You Don't Love Your Neighbor" which Carl Story also recorded, "I Like the Old Time Way," "Since His Sweet Love Rescued Me," "Sunset of Time," "Childhood Dreams," The Secret Weapon," and "Pray the Clouds Away."

Although the Golden Valley Boys had no regular radio show, they managed to keep about as busy with show dates as those groups that did. They appeared regularly on the Briarhopper program. Somewhat later they appeared often on the Arthur Smith television program and other radio shows. Such appearances together with their recordings gave them good drawing power in the Carolinas.

Meanwhile, all during the forties, the Briarhoppers with Fiddlin' Hank and Whitey and Hogan's duets continued to be very popular throughout the decade. During the war years the band participated in bond drives and entertained servicemen while continuing to play regularly in auditoriums, theaters, and schools. Sometimes they were booked on package shows with artists from the *Grand Ole Opry* and other country music radio jamborees. One memorable night they vividly recalled was June 6, 1944—D Day—when they were playing in Norfolk, Virginia, with Ernest Tubb and Pee Wee King's Golden West Cowboys. Over the years, Whitey and Hogan played shows from Georgia to Washington D.C., and Lexington, Kentucky, when they made a guest appearance on the *Kentucky Barn Dance*. For their "outstanding accomplishments in selling [war] bonds," Whitey and Hogan received a citation from U. S. Secretary of the Treasury Henry J. Morganthau.

After World War II, Whitey and Hogan also had the opportunity to make more records. They cut eight songs on the Deluxe label about 1946 or 1947 of which six were issued. Those released included a cover of Molly O'Day's "Tramp on the Street," one of their own compositions entitled "There's a Power Greater than Atomic" (an excellent topical song of the period), and Karl and Harty's old number "I'm Just Here to Get My Baby Out of Jail" together with three lesser-known songs—"You've Had a Change in Your Heart," "Bear Creek Hop," and 'I'm Just A Used to Be."

On Sunday mornings, together with Arthur Smith and the Cracker Jacks, the Tennessee Ramblers, and the Rangers Quartet, Whitey and Hogan were regular features on *Carolina Calling* which went out to a national audience over the CBS network. The Briarhopper program, however, remained their major source of popularity. Whitey and Hogan jokingly contended that the show's appeal stemmed from being broadcast just before *The Lone Ranger* came on the air, and that listeners tuned in to their show so they would not miss the popular network adventure show.

Whitey and Hogan cut more records later in the decade. They had one release on the Cowboy label, both sides of which featured numbers from their songbook. "Jesse James," their most popular tune, was an excellent harmony duet which featured Grayson on bluegrass banjo and Bill Davis on bass. This number, together with Grayson's "If You Don't Love Your Neighbor," was released on Rounder Records' *Early Days of Bluegrass #1*. The other side, their own tune, "I Have Tried but I Have Failed," had a more typical guitar-mandolin sound. The duo also recorded for Sonora records in New York with four sides being released. Hank Warren's fiddle and Bill Davis' bass complemented their own guitar on "Used to Be," a completely different song not to be confused with the Bill Monroe composition of a similar title. In addition to Grant's guitar and Hogan's prominent mandolin, accompaniment on the session included Big Bill Davis, bass; Roy Rector, steel guitar; and Sam Poplin, fiddle. Two numbers have never been released from this session, one of which was "The Bible My Daddy Left for Me." The Deluxe material constitutes what may have been Whitey's and Hogan's best recorded efforts.

In 1947, *Whitey and Hogan's Mountain Memories* song book came off the presses of Bourne Music Publishers of New York. This coincided with their peak period of popularity during which time they appeared not only on the Briarhopper program but also on WBT's *Carolina Hayride* and *Dixie Jamboree*. They did a session for Sonora records that included a cover of the widely popular "Have I Told You Lately That I Love You" by Scotty Wiseman, which did very well, with the reverse being a novelty tune, "Mama I'm Sick." The other Sonora release was "Talking to Mother" and "I'm Longing for My Sweetheart," a pair of good sentimental numbers.

Whitey and Hogan also provided musical backing on record for three other artists. They helped Dewey Price, then a member of the Briarhoppers, do a session for Majestic. Released as Dewey Price and the Blue Ridge Mountain Boys, two of the titles cut have entered bluegrass repertoires although the accompaniment on the records is somewhere between western swing and bluegrass. Leon Rusk's composition "Air Mail Special," originally done as a smooth western swing number, eventually became a bluegrass classic as performed by Jim and Jesse while Vaughn Horton's "Sold Down the River," also recorded by the Blue Sky Boys, finally received a typical Bill Monroe treatment in 1960. Whitey and Hogan also helped Majestic's A and R man, Riley Shepherd, on a session and assisted fellow Briarhopper Fred Kirby on some of his Sonora recordings. In addition, the Blue Sky Boys recorded one of Whitey and Hogan's songs, "I'll Take My Saviour By the Hand," and the Buchanan Brothers did a cover of "There's a Power Greater Than Atomic" on RCA.

The forties, however, proved to be the last full decade of the golden age of radio. The Briarhopper program was terminated in 1951 although Whitey and Hogan continued as regular performers on television until 1953. Gradually, various members of the group went into other occupations. Grayson became a carpenter and cabinetmaker specializing in making bank furnishings and fixtures. Warren became a photographer working for WBT-TV. Whitey and Hogan, faced with remaining in Charlotte where their children were in school, or continuing radio work in a new location, chose to give up show business. As Whitey put it, "Our children at that time could go to school and go to church and not have to cross the streets. . . . so I started driving a city bus here in Charlotte." Somewhat later he entered the postal service becoming a city letter carrier. Hogan entered the restaurant business briefly in West Palm Beach, Florida, but returned to Charlotte and sold insurance until he, too, became a mailman. For some 20 years they played music mostly for their own amusement or occasional local functions.

In August 1973, five members of the Briarhoppers decided to get back together—Whitey Grant, Arval Hogan, Shannon Grayson, Hank Warren, and Don White. The Rounder Records people sought them out in May 1973 to get background data for their *Early Days of Bluegrass* series and afterward they began to play more frequently. Renewed interest in old-time, bluegrass, and their brand of country music together with a general infatuation with nostalgia gave the Briarhoppers a new audience while many of their old fans fondly remembered them.

The Briarhoppers appeared at the Snuffy Jenkins Bluegrass Festival and also at other festivals in the Carolinas. They also played at schools, churches, and senior citizen centers, plus once again on radio and television. Old Homestead records released an album made up of material from their old records, radio transcriptions, and home recordings. Some of the hitherto unreleased numbers available on this record included an excellent rendition of the Bailes' song "Dust On the Bible," the Delmore's "Lonesome Gamblin' Man," and a song foretelling the energy crisis entitled "The Old Grey Mare Is Back Where She Used to Be."

In December 1977, they did a new session for Old Homestead from which two albums were belatedly released. They also recorded for Lamon Records. In all, the Briarhoppers found considerable satisfaction with their rejuvenated careers in traditional country and bluegrass music. Warren, White, and Hogan retired from their day jobs although Grant and Grayson continued to work for a couple more years and then they, too, retired.

The band continued to thrive into the early years of the twenty-first century. They played numerous festivals, but worked in other venues as well. For several years, they did many programs in public schools as part of Folk Arts in the Schools under sponsorship of the North Carolina Arts Council. Some of the largest crowds saw them at the Bob Evans Farm Festival in Rio Grande, Ohio, where they appeared each October from 1979 through 2000. On October 25 and 26, 1985, they participated in another grant-funded program, The Charlotte Country Music Story, which united many of the early radio and recording artists who made Charlotte a base in past decades. From Bill Monroe to Wade Mainer, from the Briarhoppers and Tennessee Ramblers, to Fred Kirby and Joe and Janette Carter, the old-timers gathered and delighted audiences. Of those still living at the time, only the Blue Sky Boys, not on good terms then, were conspicuous by their absence.

Time, however, began to take a toll on the original five who had rejuvenated the Briarhoppers in 1973. Grayson, ironically the youngest, developed Alzheimer's and dropped out in 1991. He died on May 10, 1993 after choosing his successor—David Deese of Salisbury, North Carolina, a veteran of the Blue Grass Boys, the Bluegrass Cutups, and the Jones Brothers' Log Cabin Boys; he worked in the band for the remainder of their days. By 1992, octogenarian Warren often did not feel like playing and Homer "Pappy" Sherrill of the Hired Hands filled in for him on several occasions including the Bob Evans Farm Festival. Warren, too, had selected a permanent replacement, Dwight Moody who had previously worked with Clyde

Moody and his own sons, the Moody Brothers. Like Deese and the Jones Brothers, he was a member of the Oasis Shrine Temple Bluegrass Band. He also owned Lamon Records for which the Briarhoppers had recorded in the 1980s. Warren lingered for four years, dying on December 12, 1997.

The remaining Briarhoppers continued to play anywhere from five to ten shows per month, many of them in schools. On April 23, 2002, they became recipients of the North Carolina Folk Heritage Award. Lamon Records released a new CD to celebrate their honor although somewhat more than half was from previously recorded material. Hogan was weakening and played only a few more shows after that, one of his last being at Bluegrass Thursday Night in York County, South Carolina. He died on September 12, 2003. White held on for another year, dying on March 6, 2005 after a short illness.

Reduced to three members, the Briarhoppers continued on although Whitney was quoted in May 2005 as saying "we don't do a lot of school concerts since Don White died. . . . But we do a few." In those declining days, David Moody sometimes filled in on bass when he was available. In 2006, Cattle Records in Germany released a CD credited to the Carolina Playboys and identified several of the 1946 Briarhoppers as being the personnel although there were some doubts. Grant seemed to confirm that it was indeed several of the Briarhoppers including Dewey Price and Fred Kirby. The original recordings had been released on the Sonora label for which Kirby along with Whitey and Hogan had recorded in that period. At one time David Deese and Dwight Moody had talked of keeping the Briarhopper name alive although Whitey Grant preferred that it be retired after his death. Grant passed on September 17, 2010. The two younger Briarhoppers soon went to their final rewards as well. David Deese died on March 13, 2011 and Dwight Moody passed on July 12, 2013.

Over many decades the various members of the Briarhoppers made notable contributions to old-time, bluegrass, and country music. Whitey and Hogan with their harmony duet and Shannon Grayson with his pioneer bluegrass quartet are particularly exceptional. Fiddlin' Hank Warren and Don White contributed to both old-time and western music. Even those who were Briarhoppers from 1991 and 1993, respectively, made significant contributions to their music of choice. Vestiges of the Briarhoppers remain in current bluegrass musicians in that banjo-playing Kristin Scott Benson of the Grascals is Hogan's granddaughter.

SELECTED RECORDINGS

Although Whitey and Hogan, Shannon Grayson, and Don White all recorded under their own names prior to 1954 (Warren recorded with other groups), none of these have had any recordings released on compact discs. The only Briarhopper items on compact disc from this period are those recorded for Sonora under the name, Carolina Playboys which included Whitey, Hogan, White, Warren and Bill Davis as well as sometime Briarhoppers Fred Kirby, Dewey Price, Claude Casey, and Nat Richardson. All of these were not necessarily present on every number.

The Carolina Playboys Sing and Play Country and Western Classics. Cattle CCD 253, 2006.

Post 1970 Briarhopper recordings on compact disc are:

The Legendary Briarhoppers. Lamon LR 10259, 1996. Contains a mixture by the first
   Briarhopper reformation group, and the latter configuration after Deese and Moody had
   replaced Grayson and Warren.
The WBT Briarhoppers. Lamon LR 10314, 2003. Similar to the above with mostly different
   songs.

Warlick, Thomas and Warlick, Lucy. *The WBT Briarhoppers: Eight Decades of a Bluegrass
   Band Made for Radio.* Jefferson, NC: McFarland & Co., Inc. 2008. A collective biography
   of the group, which includes a quote from Whitey Grant about the Carolina Playboys and
   their Sonora recordings.

✂ The Coon Creek Girls

Charlotte "Rosie" Ledford, 1915–1976
Lily May Ledford, 1917–1985
Esther "Violet" Koehler Ledford, 1916–1973
Evelyn "Daisy" Lange Perry, 1919–2002
Minnie "Black-Eyed Susan" Ledford, 1923–1987

The Coon Creek Girls attained prominence for twenty years from 1937 as America's first all-girl old-time string band. The group originated in the creative mind of radio entrepreneur John Lair and through most of their existence was associated with his *Renfro Valley Barn Dance* programs. The key members were usually fiddler and old-time banjo picker Lily May Ledford and her sisters Rosie Ledford and Black-Eyed Susan Ledford, but at times included others. In later years when more women began playing bluegrass music, many took a degree of influence and inspiration from this historic band, especially those who formed the group known as the New Coon Creek Girls.

Lily May Ledford, the acknowledged leader throughout their heyday, was born in the rugged Red River Gorge area of Powell County, Kentucky, on March 17, 1917, while older sister Rosie was born on August 16, 1915. The much younger Minnie Ledford was born on October 10, 1923. The Ledfords were a large family of eleven children who survived infancy. They rented hillside land and grew mostly corn and sorghum cane. The meager yields were supplemented with vegetables, hunting, fishing, trapping, as well as raising a little livestock and digging ginseng and yellow root for sale or trade. For entertainment, their father Daw White Ledford, played fiddle, banjo, or guitar—when he had one. Soon some of the children took to these instruments as well during their few spare moments from laboring.

In 1929, the family moved several miles downstream to another farm where the land was better, neighbors more numerous, school more acces-

The Coon Creek Girls, 1939. (*From left*): Rosie Ledford, Violet Koehler,
Lily May Ledford, Daisy Lange.

sible, and life somewhat easier. Then Lily May and Rosie Ledford along with
brother Coyen and neighbor Morgan Skidmore formed a string band called
the Red River Ramblers. They became quite popular entering and often
winning contests and entertaining at a variety of social events throughout
Powell County.

In 1935, some Skidmore kinfolk who had moved to Rochester, Indiana,
came to Kentucky for a visit. They liked what they heard and suggested
that the band come back to Indiana with them and audition for WLS radio
in Chicago, home base for the *National Barn Dance* and numerous other
daytime country music shows aimed at rural mid-south and Midwestern
rural audiences. While Lily May Ledford was accepted, the others were not.
John Lair, program director at WLS who had longer range plans of his own,
suggested that she attend another audition which was to be conducted the
following July in Mount Vernon, Kentucky.

The tryouts in Kentucky resulted in Lily May Ledford's signing a five-year management contract in August 1936 with Lair who insisted that she sign with him and not with WLS for reasons that became apparent in the coming months. Within days the nineteen-year-old backwoods girl was on a train to Chicago and soon became a cast member of the *Pine Mountain Merry Makers*, a daily program sponsored by Pinex Cough Syrup, shared with Red Foley and the Girls of the Golden West, Millie and Dolly Good. Lair had her playing banjo more often than fiddle, and he insisted that she maintain a mountain image rather than moving in the direction of western styles that were becoming increasingly dominant among the WLS artists. A little later, on September 19, 1936, Lily May first appeared on the network *National Barn Dance*. The Mountain Gal was on her way, so to speak.

Lily May found near instant popularity with WLS listeners. Soon the station's promotional magazine *Standby* even had a comic strip "Lily May, the Mountain Gal" named for her, likely a first for a girl country musician. The weekly salary of sixty dollars must have seemed fabulous to one reared in a cash deficient depression culture, even though twelve dollars of it went to Lair for his management fee. Plus when she played at a live show, she earned an additional eleven dollars daily. This happened a lot the following summer. She had sufficient funds to pay her own living expenses, buy things for her kin back in Kentucky, and even send a little cash back home. However, it was some time before she earned more money.

Meanwhile, Lair slowly took steps to implement his grand scheme to start a new barn dance program in a true rural setting rather than a simulated one in an urban theater, such as the *National Barn Dance*. The talent roster would be built around those WLS artists as he could interest or those with whom he had management contracts, such as Lily May Ledford. The ultimate locale of this program was Lair's own home area in Rockcastle County, Kentucky. The actual site was adjacent to U. S. Route 25, a.k.a. the Dixie Highway, a major north-south automobile and truck route. Another step in the Lair plan was to initiate his *Renfro Valley Barn Dance* at WLW in Cincinnati, a radio outlet as powerful as WLS, if not more so. For a new act, he proposed an all-girl old-time string band built around Lily May Ledford and her sister Rosie.

While Lily May, the Girls of the Golden West, and Red Foley were almost nightly working the county fair circuit and Saturday *Barn Dance*, John Lair had been auditioning members for the all-girl band and choosing them. Those he picked were Esther Koehler, a Wisconsin girl, born on February 6, 1916 who played mandolin, and Evelyn Lange, an Ohio native who was born on July 7, 1919 and who could play bass and also a decent fiddle. When Lily May and Rosie Ledford came to Cincinnati in September, he introduced them to Koehler and Lange, and they worked well together. He gave the new twosome flower names:, Violet and Daisy, respectively and named the band, the Coon Creek Girls. Lily May went to work on the daily Pinex program and soon secured a half-hour daily show at WCKY, then based across the river in Covington, Kentucky. The women made their debut on the WLW *Renfro Valley Barn Dance* at the Cincinnati Music Hall on October 9, 1937. Whether on their WCKY program or the *Barn Dance*, the Coon Creek Girls were an instant hit with listeners. The program at WCKY was not ordinarily designed to be a live audience show, but fans kept crowding into the studio, hallway, and stairs to see them, often bringing gifts and naming their children and pets after them.

Having more freedom at WCKY, the band used one of their songs, "Flower Blooming in the Wildwood" for a theme, composing a new verse for an intro:

There's a Lilly that is blooming in the wildwood,
A Rose that is blooming there for you,
And a Violet sweet with dew and a Daisy there too,
We are flowers that are blooming there for you.

In May 1938, Lair took the Coon Creek Girls to Chicago where they recorded nine songs for the Vocalion label, only eight were released. The numbers included some of what became their signature tunes, such as "Pretty Polly," "Little Birdie," "Banjo Pickin' Girl" and their theme "Flower Blooming in the Wildwood," minus the personalization. In addition, Aunt Idy Harper, whose real name was Margaret Lillie, and who was formerly with the Weaver Brothers and Elviry vaudeville act that Lair had hired for comedy accompanied them and recorded four songs in her raucous vocal style with the Coon Creek Girls providing instrumental and choral support.

In the fall of 1938, the live stage version of the *Renfro Valley Barn Dance* moved from the Cincinnati Music Hall to the Dayton Municipal

Auditorium. The crowds were as big as ever, but dissension was growing within the ranks of the entertainers. Lair had reduced salaries to the bare minimum, in part to finance construction of the Big Barn and other facilities in Renfro Valley. Some of the musicians believed—not without justification—that they could sell their talents elsewhere for more money. Lily May Ledford had a contract with Lair and while she and her sister did not mind as they would be closer to their Powell County home, Violet Koehler and Daisy Lange, who had no roots in Kentucky, became increasingly disgruntled. Still, the four stayed together for a few more months.

On June 8, 1939, the Coon Creek Girls experienced a career highlight when they performed at the White House for the Roosevelts and the King and Queen of England. Needless to say, the group members were all quite excited at such an opportunity. They performed three songs in their part of the program: "Get Along Home Cindy," "Soldier and the Lady" and "How Many Biscuits Can You Eat." Both Roosevelts and the Queen smiled pleasantly, but King George VI with "a long-faced, dour, dead-pan look, worried Lily May a little." Then she looked down and "caught him patting his foot . . . and I knew we had him!" More relaxing moments took place earlier in a rehearsal room when a man entered calling himself "Cactus Jack" and wished to have a little fiddle jam session. Lily May said he "was pretty good" and she later found out that he was Vice President John Nance Garner. The next morning the band went to a studio and recreated their musical program as a souvenir for the Royals and themselves. Copies of this have long been in circulation, and it is on a Coon Creek Girls compact disc.

Back in Cincinnati, as the day grew nearer when the *Barn Dance* would relocate to Renfro Valley, the unity of the original Coon Creek Girls terminated. Violet Koehler and Daisy Lange left briefly for Tulsa in company with Bill and Joe Callahan before heading to KRLD in Dallas where they became part of *Gus Foster's Texas Roundup*. Lair found temporary replacements in the personage of Lily May and Rosie's kid-sister Minnie Ledford who became Black-Eyed Susan, who had learned bass fiddle and sang in vocal trios. The *Renfro Valley Barn Dance* premiered to a packed house in the newly completed big barn on November 4, 1939, with Lair and Red Foley splitting the emcee chores. Crowds slacked off when winter came and both Foley and Whitey Ford, who each owned a share of the business, began to have second thoughts, sold their shares, and returned to WLS. Cotton

Foley, Red's older brother who had married Rosie Ledford, remained as did Freeman Keyes, an advertising man who secured corporate sponsors for the radio programming. However, for all practical purposes, Lair had total business control of Renfro Valley. Crowds picked up in the spring and the Renfro project became the institution Lair had hoped it would. In addition, WLW executives had decided to initiate their own barn dance program, the *Boone County Jamboree* that was later renamed the *Midwestern Hayride*. Henceforth, Renfro Valley programs were channeled to the CBS network through WHAS in Louisville.

More temporary changes came to the Coon Creek Girls. When Rosie Ledford took family leave and with Black-Eyed Susan Ledford still in high school, the talented Amburgey Sisters—Bertha, Irene, and Opal, more commonly known on stage as Mattie, Martha, and Minnie—filled in for the other two Ledford girls. By fall, Lair who had an interest in the evolving radio barn dance at WSB Atlanta, sent the Amburgeys to the Georgia station where they became the Hoot Owl Holler Girls. Other substitutes over the years included Jo DePew, Betty Callahan, and Inez Coffey. With occasional personnel substitutions, the Coon Creek Girls more or less fixed with the three Ledford girls.

For the next eighteen years life went on for the three Ledfords as the Coon Creek Girls at the *Renfro Valley Barn Dance, the Morning Gatherin'* (from 1943), and other Renfro Valley radio programs. The pay was not very good, but relatively steady. Sometimes Rosie or Lily May would be off for family and maternity leave and temporary replacements filled in for them. Rosie Foley had three children: Lois, Clarence Jr., and Clyde, the latter becoming a Renfro Valley regular in the late 1980s. The Foleys also established a flower shop business in nearby Berea.

Except for a period of time when Black-Eyed Susan Ledford worked in a defense plant during World War II, she held various jobs for Lair including music librarian and helping run the fan-oriented monthly newspaper, *The Renfro Valley Bugle*, to supplement her entertainment income. When the group opted to disband after the 1957 season, Susan Ledford married John Jennings who had been an engineer at the newly opened WRVK radio station. Soon after, the couple moved to Marathon, Florida.

Lily May Ledford married Glen Pennington, a returning World War II veteran who also worked as a Renfro Valley entertainer for a time, but had more of an eye for business and soon owned an auto dealership in Berea and many years later was a part-owner of Renfro Valley. The Penningtons had three children: Bobby, Barbara, and James, known as "J. P." J. P. became leader of the country band Exile which had ten No. 1 hits in the 1980s. Lily May Pennington had a son, Benny Joe Pearson, from an earlier marriage to Kirt Pearson. Although her marriage to Pennington did not endure, Lily May kept the Pennington name and resided in Lexington. In later years, she found herself in demand for folk festivals.

The only other recordings the Coon Creek Girls made during their active career were a couple of singles for Lair's Renfro Valley label and another for Capitol—"I'll Not Worry over You" and "To Heck with the Good Old Days" all in the mid-1950s. At the same Capitol session, they provided background support for then country star Ferlin Husky. Sadly, Renfro Valley Records were poorly distributed and the Capitol ones did little better. "Don't Blame the Children" which featured a social commentary-recitation by Husky on the current wave of juvenile delinquency, did attract some attention.

By 1957, Lily May Pennington believed the Coon Creek Girls to be an anachronism. She said, "There seemed no market at all for our old-fashioned music, and I began to realize that we'd no fans except for a few loyals." Near the end of the season, they were contacted by Sunshine Sue Workman of *Old Dominion Barn Dance* fame about doing some shows on Broadway in New York City. All three girls went and the shows were well received. And as Lily May said, "The audience ate it up!" One person who heard her was a young Ralph Rinzler who later played a major role in rejuvenating the girls and especially Lily May Pennington.

For the next several years, little was heard of the Coon Creek Girls. In 1962 a Renfro Valley Barn Dance group played at the Kentucky State Fair, which included them and Lily May Pennington played it again in 1963, but the second year was not considered a success. A better opportunity came when Ralph Rinzler persuaded them to go to the Newport Folk Festival in 1966. Susan broke her arm, but Rosie and Lily May went over well, especially with the young audience. Following this, all three girls recorded an album for County Records which was gobbled up by their old and new fans. Lily May Pennington and Rosie Foley played at a couple of Renfro Valley Tape Club Reunions joined by Violet who in the intervening years had married their brother Custer Ledford. He had spent a career in the army and moved back to Kentucky. Sadly, Violet Ledford's reunion days with the Coon Creek Girls was short-lived as she was soon diagnosed with a terminal illness and passed away on October 4, 1973.

Folk festival opportunities opened for Lily May and sometimes the others after the Newport experience and the County album. At the behest of Ralph Rinzler, all three Coon Creek Girls worked at a festival in Montreal in 1972 and at the Smithsonian in 1973 where they represented the Commonwealth of Kentucky. Lily May worked a number of folk festivals over the next few years from Toronto to Vancouver and in the Pacific Northwest. She also recorded another album which came out on the Greenhays label in 1983. Meanwhile, Rosie Ledford Foley died on July 24, 1976. With the help of Mike Seeger, Lily May Pennington appeared at numerous college concerts in her later years and in 1979–1980, a National Endowment Grant supported her to do numerous workshops and concerts through sponsorship of the Berea College Appalachian Center. She was increasingly plagued by ill health in those years, but worked as often as she could. In 1980, the same Berea College Appalachian Center published an autobiographical booklet, *Coon Creek Girl*, which was apparently an abridged version of a much longer manuscript. In June 1985, the National Endowment for the Arts announced that she was among the twelve recipients of their annual National Heritage Award which carried a five thousand dollar cash stipend, but sad to say the Banjo Pickin' Girl was in a Lexington hospital and died on July 14, 1985, before she had a chance to enjoy it. Black-Eyed Susan Ledford died in Florida two years later on July 22, 1987. Daisy Lange remained in music for a time after leaving the original Coon Creek Girls and eventually married Wayne Perry and settled in Frankfort, Indiana. She resurfaced in 1989, was subject of a *Bluegrass Unlimited* article, played a few shows, and again vanished from public view, apparently passing away in 2002.

Back in 1979, a group of young women in Renfro Valley organized a bluegrass band and received permission from Lily May Pennington to call their group the New Coon Creek Girls. Led initially by Jan Cummins and then Vicky Simmons, the dynamic group was well received at both the *Barn Dance* and on the festival circuit and helped keep the name and spirit of the first all-girl band alive. Although to those who had fond memories of the originals, it was a bit of a stretch when Simmons made remarks on stage such as "Back in 1937, when we were first organized . . ." when none of those on stage had yet been born in that earlier era when radio could make one famous in their field. The New Coon Creek Girls disbanded after eighteen years, but reassembled in 2014 to raise funds to assist Simmons who had suffered an aneurysm.

While the original Coon Creek Girls had moments of fame and a secure place in history as the first all-girl string band, they never reaped much financial reward that their talents warranted. In later years, Lily May Pennington was somewhat ambivalent in her feelings toward John Lair. While he gave them their start and organized them, his later opposition to major label recording contracts and Renfro Valley's not having anything approaching a star system held back what they might have achieved in other venues.

SELECTED RECORDINGS

The Coon Creek Girls: Early Radio Favorites. Old Homestead OH CD 4142, 2006. Contains all of their 1938 Vocalion recordings, their fifteen-minute program for the King and Queen of England plus some additional items made in the 1940s.

✂ Betty Fisher and David Deese

Betty, 1935–2012
David, 1941–2011

New bluegrass bands coming on the scene became relatively common by the 1990s. Many of these groups also proved to be of short duration, even some of those that had a significance of their own. One of these, Dixie Bluegrass, for example, blended the talents of a longtime veteran sideman, David Deese, with that of one of the first women to lead a bluegrass unit in the 1970s, Betty Fisher. The result seemed to paraphrase a band name once used by Porter Wagoner that many fans might term the right combination. The band endured for barely two years because of circumstances beyond the control of its members, but the achievements of the leaders endured.

Betty Buchanan was born at Crossnore in Avery County, North Carolina, on September 28, 1935. In spring 1942, the family moved to Bakersville in Mitchell County. Music occupied an important place in both household and community. Locally renowned musicians such as fiddler Steve Ledford congregated on the porch or at gatherings and picked with Betty's dad Millard "Buck" Buchanan. Frank Buchanan, another noted bluegrass musician, was among her more distant kin. Buck Buchanan initially steered his daughter toward the mandolin, but she preferred the guitar, so he eventually gave in and bought her one.

As Betty grew older, she and her dad played on local radio and made appearances over a wider region as Betty and Buck. They had offers to go full time with a musical career, but Buck chose to stick with his prospering sawmill business and remain a semi-pro picker. They played one night a week at the Carolina Barn Dance in Spruce Pine and were guests on such noted radio programs as WNOX's *Mid-Day Merry-Go-Round* in Knoxville. Betty Buchanan also dabbled in writing and when Jimmie Skinner visited them he took several of her songs to Acuff-Rose who contracted her. Some were recorded, most notably "Women Beware" by Preston Ward. It never became

The Dixie Bluegrass, 1993. *From left:* Ralph Keller, David Deese, Betty Fisher, Larry Plyler, Glenn Brown.

a hit, but high school student Betty recalled that it kept her in spending money.

After graduation, Betty found work as a secretary and continued playing music with her dad. When she married Jesse Thomas Fisher who was usually known as J. T., the Betty and Buck duo was terminated. For the next several years, Betty Fisher concentrated her efforts on home, family, and children. Living in Walhalla, South Carolina, she confined her musical activities to entertaining friends and neighbors.

Meanwhile, another young Carolina musician was embarking on a musical career of his own. Clonnie David Deese was born near Salisbury, North Carolina, on July 9, 1941, the son of a guitar picker and the grandson of an old-time banjo player. David Deese learned guitar well enough to go on stage at age twelve and took up bluegrass banjo at fifteen. He also played clarinet in the school band.

From age fifteen, Deese played on radio and local television usually with his father. They appeared on shows in Spartanburg, Albemarle, and Mount Airy, but the most interesting place was the *Old/New Dominion Barn Dance* at WRVA Richmond. There the youngster met such notables as Bill Monroe, Mac Wiseman, Chief Powhatan a.k.a. Floyd Atkins, the Louvin Brothers, Don Reno and Red Smiley, and Stonewall Jackson. In the summer of 1958, David gained some invaluable experience playing shows over both Carolinas with the now legendary J. E. Mainer's Mountaineers. By either necessity or choice, J. E. Mainer lived a pretty plain and simple lifestyle. Deese wondered if this would be his fate as a traditional musician.

In late December 1960, Arthur "Guitar Boogie" Smith introduced Deese to a young fiddler, Jimmy Buchanan. After a brief jam session, Smith hired them as regulars for his show as a banjo-fiddle singing duet. Beginning on January 9, 1961, the two initiated their work with Smith which included an hour of early weekday morning television at WBTV, another half-hour on Thursday evening, and a daily radio program as well. During this time, young Deese gained a great deal of experience switching off to play upright bass, six-string bass guitar, and even a bit of snare drum work. The Smith crew worked personal appearances two nights a week all over the Carolinas and sometimes Georgia, Tennessee, and Virginia. Smith also ran a recording studio and band members did some session work now and then.

After nineteen months with the Smith show, David Deese acquired a case of Nashville fever. In July 1962, he journeyed to Music City where Josh Graves helped him get an audition with Wilma Lee and Stoney Cooper who decided they could use him. David went back to Charlotte, gave Smith his notice, and returned to Nashville in two weeks, leaving most of his cash with his college student wife of a year, Barbara. Deese was somewhat shocked to find out the Coopers were out on tour in Missouri and found himself virtually penniless and stuck in a town where he knew almost no one. Fortunately, he ran into Frank Buchanan at the *Grand Ole Opry* who was then playing guitar for Bill Monroe. Tony Ellis had just left the Blue Grass Boys and after a quick audition, David found himself in a station wagon headed for Illinois with the master of the trade. It was not a particularly prosperous time for the band, however; so Deese did not make much money, but he managed to keep eating. After a few months, he felt sufficiently cured of Nashville fever and returned to North Carolina.

Coming back to Salisbury, David went to work for the state as a prison guard. Barbara Deese had finished college and was teaching school and both looked forward to a relatively early retirement. Then in early November 1964, Carlton Haney called informing David that Don Reno and Red Smiley planned to split within the month and also that Smiley wanted him as banjo picker for his Bluegrass Cutups band on the *Top O' the Morning Show* at WDBJ-TV in Roanoke. Thinking that the noted twosome might soon reunite, David initially declined, but Haney asked him to think it over. Deciding to visit Smiley, he reconsidered and accepted. Deese started with Red Smiley's Bluegrass Cutups on the Monday after Thanksgiving. Other original band members included the ever-present John Palmer on bass, Bobby Lester on fiddle, and Gene Burroughs on mandolin and rhythm guitar.

During his tenure with Smiley, David and the whole band stayed busy. Besides their daily morning television show, the Cutups did a weekly television program at WSVA Harrisonburg, Virginia, videotaping every other one. In January 1965, they added another program at WOAY-TV in Oak Hill, West Virginia, where they did one live and three taped shows each month. They also videotaped material for use at WLAC Nashville. Beginning in May 1966, they taped quarter-hour radio programs for airing each week night at WWVA Wheeling and played the *Jamboree* every third week, alternating with Moore and Napier and Mac Wiseman. In addition, they worked quite a few package shows with country acts in Virginia and North Carolina. In August 1965, Bobby Lester left the band. Bonny Beverly filled in as fiddler for two months after which time veteran sideman Tater Tate joined Smiley's outfit as a regular. Deese recorded three different times with the Cutups, but the only material released to date has been the two albums on Rimrock in January 1966, one gospel and the other a Tater Tate fiddle album.

Deese's career with Smiley ended suddenly on July 6, 1966, when he became an employee of the U. S. Department of Defense as a conscripted soldier. He spent three years in the army—the second year in Vietnam and the third in Richmond as a clerk typist at the induction center. This latter assignment afforded him an opportunity to do some banjo picking on the local scene. He enjoyed stints with George Winn's Bluegrass Partners, Ray Lumpkin, and Chief Powhatan's Bluegrass Braves. He cut ten songs on an album released on the Homestead label with Chief Powhatan, being featured on instrumentals "Grandfather's Clock" and "Sun Dance."

Discharged from the army in July 1969, the Deeses and their young daughter Connie returned to Salisbury as Red Smiley had retired from performing a few months earlier. David remained out of music until 1971 when he joined the Jones Brothers who had recently split from Carl Story. Deese went on to spend some twenty-one years as a Log Cabin Boy, playing guitar for the first two and a half years and then moving over to banjo. In this period, the band worked numerous festivals and recorded several albums.

During the 1970s, while traveling the festival circuit, David had met J. T. and Betty Fisher, the latter having rejuvenated her own musical career. Betty had sometimes been asked to perform a song or two at local gatherings during her self-imposed retirement, but it took a visit to the Lavonia, Georgia, bluegrass festival to really light the fire to play regularly again. At this festival, she met some old acquaintances that she knew from the Buck and Betty days such as Jim and Jesse, Joe Stuart, and Bill Monroe and was pleasantly surprised to learn that they remembered her. They also urged her to become active again. According to Don Rhodes, she expressed some interest in forming an all-girl band, but Bill Monroe told her she would likely find it difficult to find the personnel, so Fisher settled for primarily male side people although she did recruit Murphy Hicks, now Murphy Henry, as bass player. Betty Fisher and the Dixie Bluegrass Band made their professional debut at Charlotte, North Carolina, in the fall of 1971. As events developed, Fisher became one of the first females to lead her own band.

Over the next nine years, Betty Fisher and the Dixie Bluegrass Band carved a niche for themselves in the musical world cutting five albums, one each on K-Ark and Playhouse and three on Carl Queen's Atteiram label, playing on several radio and television programs, and appearing at numerous festivals. The latter included virtually all of Roy Martin's operations including Lavonia, Georgia; Lawtey, Florida; and Myrtle Beach, South Carolina, along with various Carlton Haney and Bill Monroe extravaganzas. The group played as far west as Oklahoma and as far north as Ottawa, Ohio.

Acting on the advice of an expert, Betty chose her musicians from the younger generation. Murphy Hicks was her original bass player and when she left to form the duo of Red and Murphy, Fisher's son Tommy replaced her. Tommy Jackson (not the legendary fiddler), Dale Tilley, and Ricky Rakestraw were among her banjo pickers. Danny Smith, Marvin Tuck, Randy Carrier, and Dennis Flowers played mandolin at various times.

Richard Hollis played resonator guitar on her early albums and George Gillis fiddled on one while Dennis Tibbitts played second guitar on her final effort. Band members performed in various vocal capacities on the Dixie Bluegrass Band's recordings and were often featured in lead vocals.

Betty included a few of her original songs on the albums. Perhaps the best was the nostalgic memoir of her childhood, "Carolina Mountain Home," which was the title cut on her first Atteiram album. Band members also contributed some of their own songs such as Dale Tilley's "Sailboat to Heaven" on the gospel album. Two fine Rebe and Rabe duets were revived from the early 1950s, "Two Empty Arms" and "You Didn't Say Goodbye," that ranked among the other outstanding performances by the group on disc. Augusta journalist Don Rhodes also contributed "Bluegrass Music All the Time" to their recorded repertoire.

At the end of the 1970s, J. T. Fisher's work took the family to Houston, and Betty found it difficult to maintain her appearance schedule with most of her band still back east. So, after the August 1980 festival at Ottawa, Ohio, the Dixie Bluegrass Band disbanded. Betty Fisher retired from show business a second time and began enjoying a new role as a grandmother. In 1990, the Fishers returned to South Carolina.

Meanwhile, David Deese who was completing more than twenty years with the Jones Brothers, began to feel he needed a change of pace. He got along well with Bruce and Lee Jones, in addition to his work with the Briarhoppers, but had become enamored with the idea of starting his own group. When he learned that Betty Fisher had come back to Carolina, he aspired to form a band with her. The two families got together for a weekend and decided to form a band. Other recruits to Dixie Bluegrass included bass player Larry Plyler, mandolinist Ralph Keller, and fiddler Glenn Brown. Unlike the old Dixie Bluegrass Band of the 1970s, the ranks of the newer band were filled with veteran pickers. Ralph Keller, the senior member, was a native of Cabarrus County, North Carolina, where he was born on July 24, 1936. Having spent twenty-two years of his life in military service, Keller lacked the professional experience of the others, but had played both guitar and mandolin for his own amusement since his teens. In the early 1970s, he took an interest in bluegrass banjo and became acquainted with Deese while home on leave. Following retirement in 1976, the two continued to pick together in their spare moments and Ralph and family also settled near Salisbury. He began driving a tractor-trailer for UPS and while hanging around and jamming a bit at early practice sessions, the others asked him to join as a full-fledged member.

Two years younger than Keller, fiddler Glenn Brown also had grown up in the Salisbury area, listening to the Briarhoppers on WBT radio and often playing music with young David Deese and his dad. Brown also knew Keller from high school, but had played with him only once before their experience with Dixie Bluegrass. Glenn did play quite a bit with local Carolina groups such as the Country Pets, Pinetucket, and Sassy Grass, working with the latter group with some regularity. He joined Dixie Bluegrass in September 1992, just two days before they went into the studio to record their two albums.

Larry Plyler, the baby of the outfit, actually had the most musical experience other than the leaders. Born on May 24, 1952, he started on guitar at thirteen and bass at twenty-one, being originally inspired by his parents and then by such local pickers as guitarist Heath Baucom, the versatile Junior Harris, and fine fiddler Lawrence Barbee. Plyler worked with a local band out of Marshville, North Carolina, for about nine years. He then spent about four years from 1982 with the Chubby Anthony group, Big Timber, then being managed by Glen Odom and featuring the excellent Tommy Cordell on fiddle. This experience provided Plyler with the opportunity to work several major festivals and make some fine recordings. Larry and his wife Jackie had four children, and he operated a pair of small businesses with his sons that allowed him to take time off whenever musical opportunities arose.

While getting Dixie Bluegrass off the ground, David Deese worked out his commitments with Bruce and Lee Jones. Then Shannon Grayson, longtime banjo picker with the Briarhoppers, experienced problems with Alzheimer's and had to retire. The other Briarhoppers asked Deese to take his place and he became the junior member of this legendary Carolina musical combo. For several weeks, he actually found himself working in three groups until his tenure with the Jones Brothers ended. Afterward, he continued to be a member of both bands, ran his accounting business, and took part in local Masonic activity.

In September 1992, Dixie Bluegrass recorded their only two albums on the Deese label, both released on cassette only. The first, titled *I'm Branching*

Out, included a fine duet version of a neglected Mac Wiseman classic "Are You Coming Back to Me," Plyler's bluegrass rendition of Fats Domino's "I'm Walkin,'" a new arrangement of Fisher's longtime favorite "Carolina Mountain Home," and a snappy adaptation of the Rambling Mountaineer banjo tune from 1957, "Banjolina." The second album, an all-gospel offering entitled *I'm Just a Stranger Here,* was highlighted with Fisher's touching treatment of a Flatt and Scruggs chestnut from 1951, "He Took Your Place." Deese contributed "I Wasn't There (But I Wish I Could Have Been)" that James Carson wrote and recorded during his days with the Masters Family. A pair of Reno and Smiley songs, "The Tree of Life" and "Springtime in Heaven," ranked among other fine numbers on the set along with "Camping in Canaan" and "Take Up Thy Cross."

The Dixie Bluegrass worked a number of dates in 1992 and 1993. They suspended their activity after January 1994 because of a terminal illness which ultimately took the life of J. T. Fisher in mid-1994. Although they did get together for a couple of jam sessions that summer, they never reactivated the group.

Retired from music, Betty Fisher lived for eighteen years in Walhalla, South Carolina. She was diagnosed with cancer in her late seventies and died on July 7, 2012. Murphy Henry included a chapter on her in *Pretty Good for a Girl: Women in Bluegrass* (2013). Fisher deserves to be remembered as one of the first women to lead a bluegrass band.

Her brief early 1990s younger partner, David Deese preceded her in death. He had remained musically active with the Briarhoppers as long as Whitey Grant played, and filled in with other bands including rejuvenating some of the Arthur Smith groups such as Ray and Lois Atkins and Tommy Faile. He was among the leaders in organizing annual reunions of Bill Monroe's Blue Grass Boys. Deese suffered a heart attack in early March 2011 and died on March 13. While his time as a co-leader proved brief, as an outstanding sideman and true gentleman he was one of the best.

SELECTED RECORDINGS

None of the recordings made by Betty Fisher in the 1970s or any of the recordings made by Betty Fisher and David Deese have been reissued as of this publication.

✂ The Lewis Family

James Roy "Pop" Lewis, 1905–2004
Nannie Omega "Miggie" Lewis, 1926–2017
James Wallace Lewis, 1928–2007
Talmadge Lewis, 1934–
Polly Lewis Williamson Copsey, 1937–
Janis Lewis Phillips, 1939–
Roy McArthur Lewis, 1942–
Travis Lewis, 1958–
Lewis Phillips, 1972–

Throughout the last half of the twentieth century, one of the most popular and durable gospel and bluegrass acts on the American scene was a dynamic family group from Lincolnton, Georgia. A common phrase often heard tended to be "even people who don't care for gospel music love the Lewis Family." Although primarily a stage act that had an abundant amount of clean humor in between their complex vocal arrangements, they also chalked up an immense quantity of quality recordings as part of their musical legacy.

The Lewis saga began on September 22, 1905, with the birth of James Roy "Pop" Lewis in Pickens, South Carolina. When the boy, usually known as Roy, reached age five his parents settled in Lincoln County, Georgia, which has since been the family home. Later Roy Lewis became acquainted with Pauline Holloway, a neighbor girl five years his junior. In October 1925, the pair eloped to McCormick, South Carolina, and were married. Roy and Pauline Lewis had eight children with seven growing up to have musical involvement to some degree.

Their first-born child, Nannie Omega (May 22, 1926), nicknamed "Miggie" never married, sang alto in a girl's trio, and as time went by "the old maid" bore the brunt of much of the good natured humor of their youngest

The Lewis Family, ca. 1970. *Top row from left:* "Little" Roy Lewis, Roy "Pop" Lewis, Talmadge Lewis, Wallace Lewis. *Seated from left:* Polly Lewis, Miggie Lewis, Janis Lewis.

son, Little Roy. The oldest boy, James Wallace—born on July 6, 1928 and known by his middle name—played a solid rhythm guitar, composed and sang some solo vocals, and shared emcee chores with Pop, Polly and Little Roy. The second son Esley played bass with the forerunner group, Lewis Brothers, but pretty much retired from music after he entered the U. S. Army in 1951. A third son Mosley died in 1935 at the age of four.

The four younger children all played key roles in the Lewis Family as a musical group. Talmadge who was born on December 11, 1934, and named for a colorful Georgia governor, sang tenor and played mandolin or fiddle depending on the arrangement. He left music in 1972 to devote full-time to his business endeavors, chiefly Talmadge Lewis Motors, a retail automobile and bus outlet. Polly Lewis was born on January 23, 1937, and shared lead singing in the trio with Janis Lewis, who was born on February 13, 1939. Polly shared emcee duties and managed to avoid being thrown off track by Little Roy Lewis most of the time.

Finally, the youngest, Little Roy McArthur Lewis, who was born on February 24, 1942, and became a skilled banjo picker in the Earl Scruggs manner, provided most of the on-stage comedy and humor and also played a solid lead guitar or autoharp whenever the arrangement called for such. It would not be exaggerating to say that without Little Roy, the Lewis Family was an excellent gospel group. But with him, they became virtually unexcelled as an entertaining stage act.

About 1947 Wallace, Esley, and Talmadge formed a group known as the Lewis Brothers that played country songs and square dances at local entertainment in the area around Lincolnton. Esley played bass fiddle and after Little Roy won a banjo contest at age eight, he sometimes joined them. As Pop later said, "the boy was virtually born with a banjo in his hand" to which the child prodigy added, "I sucked that thing for two years." In 1951, Esley left for military duty which was about the time the Lewis Brothers evolved into the Lewis Family. As they recalled, their first public appearance as such came in 1951 when they entertained at a Woodmen of the World supper in Thomson, Georgia. At that show, the family consisted of Pop, Miggie, Wallace, Talmadge, and Little Roy. From that time on they were a gospel group exclusively. Polly and Janis joined a little later. Esley only played a little after returning from the army in 1953.

Like all upcoming groups, the Lewis Family had drawn inspiration from professional music groups in addition to local family influences. Among bluegrass bands, that of Bill Monroe as well as Lester Flatt and Earl Scruggs ranked as most significant. Little Roy Lewis gives almost total credit to Scruggs as an inspiration in his picking. However, a variety of gospel groups influenced their singing styles. Chief among them were the Masters Family and the Chuck Wagon Gang.

The Charlotte-based Johnson Family Singers, the Louvin Brothers, and the WSB Atlanta duet of the forties, James and Martha Carson, also ranked as important and influential. As Lewis Family members explained, they later played numerous shows with Martha Carson after she had gone solo and that her manager-husband Xavier Cosse always presented Little Roy Lewis with a silver dollar. They also retained a warm spot for her ex-husband James Carson with whom Polly Lewis once sang a duet on stage at the Renfro Valley Bluegrass Festival.

The year 1953 proved to be a significant one for the Lewis Family. Until then they had been playing mostly at local events, churches, and occasionally at larger gospel sings headlined by better-known, full-time professional singing groups. Finally, they appeared on some of Wally Fowler's All-Night Singing Conventions. They later expressed gratitude to the Goodman Family for helping them get booked on these programs. In that era, Bibletone Records had become a major force in gospel music, cutting discs for many of the legendary Southern gospel quartets. The family did four songs for them at WJAT radio in Swainsboro early that year, but the company went out of business before any of the sides were released so they came out on 78 rpm on the Sullivan label, a firm owned by Hoyt Sullivan, an area businessman. The first master they made was a number called "Carry On" and credited to "The Musical Lewis Family." That first master was a Wallace and Polly Lewis original with the girls' trio handling vocals. It demonstrated that eleven-year-old Little Roy Lewis had already become a top notch banjo picker. A little later in July, the family did a couple more songs for Hollywood, a King subsidiary, and still later four more songs. These numbers subsequently appeared along with many others on Starday releases. Lance LeRoy, who later became Lester Flatt's manager, recalled listening to the Family in those early days when they appeared at the Beulah Baptist Church near his hometown of Tignall, Georgia. He had already heard about "a little Lewis boy in Lincoln County" who pick[ed] the fire out of a banjo." Seeing and hearing the group confirmed the rumors that led him to attend the event.

The other event that took place in 1953 was the opening of WJBF-TV in Augusta that October. The Lewis's did a guest spot or two on local programs. Steve Manderson, who worked at the station, offered them a program of their own on the noon to 1:00 p.m. slot on Sunday a normally difficult time for television programs. The Family began their show in April 1954; it became successful and ultimately stayed on the air for thirty-eight years. Manderson served as their announcer and did most of the talking in the early years. Hoyt Sullivan, who had initiated their first disc releases, was a key sponsor in the early days. Eventually, after the introduction of videotape, the program was syndicated first on KTVE in El Dorado, Arkansas, and finally on several other stations.

In their early years as a professional group, most members of the Lewis Family held day jobs, primarily in textiles at McCormick Mills in McCormick, South Carolina. Polly described it as "the only place anybody in Lincolnton or McCormick could even get a job." By the early 1960s, however, they felt secure enough in their musical careers that they became full-time entertainers in their chosen field.

In the meantime, the grown Lewis children married and started families of their own. Talmadge married Cornelia LaGroon in 1956, and they became the parents of three sons. Wallace married Betty Jean Butler in 1958 and they had three children. While the others continued living in Lincolnton, Talmadge Lewis as well as Esley Lewis resided in Augusta. Polly married Elzie Williamson in 1960 and they had Sheri and Scott. Sheri, as she grew up, sometimes filled-in with the Family and eventually married Jeff Easter, son of James Easter of the well-known Easter Brothers and the twosome have a quality gospel group of their own. Janis married Earl Phillips and their only child, Lewis Phillips, became a top-notch banjo picker in his own right. Earl Phillips handled much of the business for the Lewis Family. Little Roy remained single until 1986 when he married a Louisiana woman named Bonnie Reeves who had a daughter Kristen by a previous marriage.

In 1958, the Lewis Family began a decade-long affiliation with Starday Records. Initially they did a series of four-song extended play releases. Several of their Sullivan and Hollywood releases appeared on their first album *Singin' Time Down South* (SLP 121) released in 1960. At two sessions in January and July 1961, the Family marked ten years in the business with *Anniversary Celebration* (SLP 161) which also demonstrated a switch away from 45 rpm releases toward long-play albums. Janis, now twenty-two, emerged as a quality solo vocalist with her rendition of Molly O'Day's 1947 hit "Matthew Twenty-Four." She would later shine on such numbers as "Purple Robe" and "Keep on the Sunny Side."

During the sixties the Lewis Family recorded bluegrass gospel material for Starday which on rare occasions had Polly playing the piano on sessions. However, their concert dates were mostly with Southern gospel groups. They shared the stage with other legendary figures in that field as the Blackwood Brothers, the Blue Ridge Quartet, the Florida Boys, the Sunshine Boys, the Speer Family, Wendy Bagwell and the Sunlighters, and the LeFevres. In 1966, they appeared in a motion picture featuring many of these folks and others entitled *Sing a Song for Heaven's Sake*.

The third Starday album *Gospel Special* from 1962 featured the song that became the signature comedy-sacred number for Little Roy Lewis. "Honey in the Rock" had been composed by F. A. Graves in 1895 and seemingly first appeared in print in 1904 in *Soul Winner's Hallelujah Songs*. The African-American Blind Mamie Forehand recorded it in 1927 for Victor followed by the Carter Family a decade later on Decca. Little Roy Lewis's version, adapted by him, featured his playing three invisible instruments including a trombone, making the appropriate sounds with his mouth, jumping high in the air, and pulling on his bright red suspenders. It became a stage show closer and almost always drew encores from the audience. In later years when the Family changed labels, they did the song again and Little Roy continues doing it on stage shows, even after passing the age of seventy.

Meanwhile, their Starday recordings began to pile up. Through 1968, they totaled thirteen long-play albums including a banjo album of sacred songs by Little Roy Lewis. In 1965 they did an album with Starday's other major contractee in the field of bluegrass gospel, Carl Story. Later on, three of their best compilations brought their totals to sixteen, not counting three reissues on Starday's budget label, Nashville. The albums always contained a good mixture of original songs by Wallace or Polly, some classic Albert Brumley compositions, and country gospel hits of earlier years including James and Martha Carson's "The Man of Galilee" and Wilma Lee and Stoney Cooper's "Walking My Lord up Calvary Hill." Although personnel remained constant with the seven principal members throughout the Starday years, there was more than sufficient variety within the Lewis band's arrangements to avoid what one might term sameness.

When Starday went through one of its periodic upheavals, the Lewis Family did an album for a label called Solid Rock, apparently owned by their television announcer Steve Manderson. Titled *Crest Album* because the cover was adorned by the Lewis Welsh coat of arms, this effort has become one of the rarest Lewis releases since most sales were done by themselves at personal appearances. Among the notable songs were covers of the Easter Brothers' "Peter Was a Fireball" and the then current Johnny Cash hit "Daddy Sang Bass." The latter recording started a trend which continued with their next record contract. Soon, however, the Family began a new and longtime association with Canaan Records of Waco, Texas. This firm constituted the Southern gospel division of Word, Incorporated which had become a major force in the field of religious music.

Although the Starday recordings were quite good, the Canaan efforts generally surpassed them in both quality and quantity. Following a practice displayed on the *Crest* recording, new songs written by others were soon covered on both stage shows and long play albums. For instance, when LaVern Tripp of the Blue Ridge Quartet had a major success with his lyric "I Know" which borrowed the tune of an older song, it appeared on their first Canaan album *Sing in Gospel Country*. Dolly Parton's hit "Daddy Was an Old Time Preacher Man" was featured prominently next on *Lewis Country*. Some years later they quickly adopted Christy Lane's "One Day at a Time," Johnny Russell's "Baptism of Jesse Taylor," and John Anderson's "I'm Just an Old Chunk of Coal" into their stylings.

After the first five Canaan albums, Talmadge dropped out of the group to devote full-time to his business endeavors in Augusta. Henceforth, fiddle and mandolin sounds on recordings were furnished by noted Nashville musicians typified by Buddy Spicher on fiddle and by either Jesse McReynolds or Bobby Osborne on mandolin. In 1974, Wallace's son, Travis, who was born December 26, 1958, took over the bass fiddle chores from Pop, who continued to join in the singing and do his solo specialties typified by "Just One Rose Will Do" with an added recitation and Don Reno's "Someone Will Love Me in Heaven." Travis also did a little mandolin work occasionally, but as time went by became known as one of the best bass players in the business. In speaking of Travis Lewis, his aunt Janis told Murphy Henry—historian of women bluegrass artists—"Pop, Polly, and I alternated the bass playing, but when we heard Travis we realized we were not playing as well as we thought we were. The three of us haven't played since." When a piano was heard on recordings, it was usually played by session musician Hargis "Pig" Robbins. New songs by such composers as Paul Craft and Randall Hylton also became a characteristic of the Lewis's Canaan sessions especially the latter's "Hallelujah Turnpike" and "Slippers with Wings" that was co-written with his sister Wanda Dalton. During their sixteen years with Canaan, the Lewis Family turned out twenty-four albums of new recordings including three banjo albums with Little Roy. Toward the end of the Canaan era, the company issued an additional *Best of the Lewis Family* and a *Best of Little Roy Lewis* consisting mostly of previously released material.

Ironically, even though the Lewis Family had always been associated with bluegrass gospel music, when bluegrass festivals first began in 1965 the Family did not play any of them until August 1970 when they played Bill Grant's Festival in Hugo, Oklahoma. A few weeks later they appeared on Carlton Haney's big festival in Camp Springs, North Carolina. From then onward, they became among the most popular acts on the circuit, typically playing fifty or more per year. Lancaster, Pennsylvania, with its large Amish and Mennonite communities, constituted another favorite bluegrass venue where they played often. With the Shindig on Cripple Creek in warm weather, and the Shindig in the Barn in cold weather, they worked a total of eighty-eight times during the years it operated. As Little Roy told Lance LeRoy in 1995, "Any state we play in one time then we'll get asked back."

Shortly after Travis became the initial third generation member to play in the band, the even younger Lewis Phillips, who was born on April 5, 1972, began to make himself known as a child prodigy. Under the tutelage of Little Roy, Lewis began to play banjo at the age of three and appeared on stage when five. He made his recording debut on a live show at Lester Flatt's Pilot Mountain Festival in June 1977 picking "Wildwood Flower." The next year he picked banjo on a CBS Network Special with Carol Burnett's *Carol & Dolly in Nashville*. In the early years on stage he made the song "God's Little People" virtually his own until he outgrew it. By then he also had become a quality lead guitarist.

Another third generation Lewis, Polly's daughter Sheri Williamson, who was born on October 17, 1963, sometimes appeared as a fill-in beginning in 1980, especially in the summers since she became a student at the University of Georgia. In mid-1984, Sheri met Jeff Easter, who was born on March 18, 1960 and was a son of James Easter of the Easter Brothers. In addition to his family group, Jeff had worked with both the Singing Americans and the Gold City Quartet. The blossoming romance culminated in their wedding in Lincolnton on June 18, 1985, shortly after Sheri graduated from college with a degree in marketing. The young couple worked and recorded with the Lewis Family—with Jeff Easter playing harmonica—until 1988 when they went on their own and subsequently made a name for themselves in Southern Gospel Music winning several awards along the way.

Meanwhile in 1986, the Canaan era ended and the Family began recording for Riversong, a division of the Benson Company, which had hitherto been into religious music publishing that had earlier owned the Heart Warming and Impact labels. Over the next decade, eleven Lewis Family albums were released on either Riversong or Benson, including four with twenty songs and one which contained Christmas carols. During those years, recording companies made the transition from vinyl albums to compact discs while still issuing material on cassettes. They also made the first of six video cassettes, with the initial one being made of a concert in Bristol, Tennessee, and a later one exclusively of Christmas music.

As the Lewis Family entered into their fifth decade as professional musicians, some changes in personnel began taking place. Wallace began experiencing serious health problems, eventually diagnosed as Parkinson's disease, and he retired in 1995. Mom Lewis, who did not perform, nearly always traveled with them and looked after their record tables as well as provided what Fred Bartenstein termed support. She increasingly remained at home which usually necessitated Miggie's staying with her. Pop continued to travel until he was past ninety-six, but age ultimately forced his retirement as well. His last appearance on disc came with the *50th Anniversary Celebration* album in 2003 when he made his final recording of "Just One Rose Will Do," a phrase that would later be inscribed on his and Pauline's tombstone. Mom Lewis passed on February 8, 2003, and Pop died on March 23, 2004. Wallace lived on until May 16, 2007. After his death, Gusto Records released a compact disc containing many of his original compositions or lead vocals entitled *The Songs of Wallace Lewis*. Gusto also released a two CD set of the early Lewis Family recordings through 1961, including those sides on Sullivan and Hollywood.

Other changes took place off as well as on stage. Elzie Williamson died on June 12, 1984, at the relatively early age of fifty and Polly subsequently remarried to Leon Copsey who was about a year younger than the late Elzie. In 1992, since they were so busy on the road, the Family dropped their long-running WJBF-TV show after thirty-eight years, but continued doing an annual special. In the mid-1990s, they began recording for Thoroughbred, a division of Daywind Music Group, and the production of quality music on disc continued. In 1996, Lance LeRoy wrote a twenty-four page booklet commemorating their forty- five years as a professional group. LeRoy had considered himself a Lewis fan since he first saw them as a teenager in rural Georgia. In May 2004, Travis Lewis departed from the band after three decades and for the first time the Family hired a musician from outside the family circle, Scot Yarbrough, on bass fiddle.

Another crack in the family circle came in November 2006 when Sheri Easter sent a heartfelt message that her mother Polly had been diagnosed with both Parkinson's disease and Lewy body disease. She continued performing for a time, but as conditions became more acute, her days with the Family were numbered although she still sang some into 2009. "With a heavy heart," Sheri wrote that "while everything inside me wants to scream out that life isn't fair," she still took comfort in the fact that Polly had experienced more than fifty years of success with a musical group. Polly apparently appeared on the final three Lewis Family albums, *Flyin' High* in 2006, *Handpicked* in 2007, and *We Are Family* in 2008. The latter effort, produced by Jeff and Sheri Easter, included not only Jeff and Sheri, but also the Easter Brothers. For the most part it included favorite songs popularized by all three groups. It subsequently won two Dove Awards.

Actually the Lewis Family had been playing less often and more selectively after Polly's health problems had increased. As Little Roy later told bluegrass journalist Penny Parsons, "after going a hundred thousand miles a year, it started slowing down to seventy thousand. The next year it would slow down to fifty thousand. . . ." In essence, the youngest and ever vigorous member of the Family began to see the end of the road approaching for the long-standing group.

Finally in 2009, with age and declining health taking their toll, the original Lewis Family called it quits. They announced their forthcoming retirement on May 24, but worked several dates from June 6 through September 5 with the last being in Dover, Pennsylvania. They also taped their annual television special for Augusta's WJBF on November 7 which was then shown three times in December.

The younger members soon regrouped into a pair of acts. Janis Lewis, Lewis Phillips, and Travis Lewis became the Lewis Tradition. They recorded a compact disc *Precious Memories* in 2010 which included old standards like the title cut, "Softly and Tenderly," "Old Camp Meeting Days," and the Flatt and Scruggs classic "I'm Going to Make Heaven My Home" along with newer songs by such modern composers as the late Randall Hylton, James Elliott, Dick Gaskin, and Jerry Salley. Making their debut on December 10, 2009, at the Larkin Family's Christmas in the Smokies in Pigeon Forge, Tennessee, spokesman Lewis Phillips told longtime Augusta journalist and Lewis Family fan Don Rhodes, "Mama is going to sing some of her most requested songs . . . and I'll do some songs off my [recorded earlier] solo CD, *Empty Fields*." The Lewis Tradition subsequently added Travis's son Jamison Lewis, to their entourage, making him the first fourth generation of the group to go professional. Earl Phillips's illness caused the group to become inactive in 2016. He died on August 1, 2016.

The ever energetic Little Roy Lewis at sixty-seven also had already formed a new group which had played increasing numbers of shows when the Family had not worked, becoming the team of Little Roy and Lizzy. Lizzy was a neighboring teenager for whom Little Roy and Bonnie had assumed legal responsibility in 1999. Elizabeth "Lizzy" Long had a sister Rebekah. Both of the sisters attended Glenville State College in West Virginia under the tutelage of super sideman Buddy Griffin. While the fiddle became Lizzy Long's primary instrument, she also gained expertise on virtually all the other instruments associated with bluegrass as well as the piano. She had often played shows with the Lewis Family over the years especially in the summer.

After leaving West Virginia, Lizzy went to Nashville and did additional college work at Belmont University where she studied arranging and or-chestration. She also won friendships with Music City's bluegrass commu-nity including Buddy Spicher, Mac Wiseman, and both Earl and Louise Scruggs. She had already done an album in Nashville, *Sing a Sad Song*, that had Mac Wiseman as a guest vocalist and demonstrated that she was equally adept in a country music setting. In 2007, Vine Records that the Lewis Family had recorded for in their latter days did an album with Lizzy, Little Roy, and Earl Scruggs titled *Lifetimes*. In 2008 and 2009, she and Little Roy did two more albums *Front Porch Pickin'* and *Breaking Like Dawn*. These efforts were about equally divided between instrumentals and songs featuring Lizzy's vocals. With her instrumental virtuosity, Little Roy, who also had taught her a great deal, once said, "pull a plank off the wall and she'll play it." Session musicians included Clay Hess and Ben Isaacs.

The Little Roy and Lizzy Show with Bonnie Lewis as booking agent and manager began scheduling show dates. They put together a band for 2010 which included Doug Flowers on mandolin and Ricky Rakestraw on guitar. They began a heavy touring schedule not unlike the Lewis Family had worked for much of their careers. Bonnie's efforts prompted Lizzy to write that if it weren't for Bonnie, we "could never have gotten out of the driveway." In 2013, in conjunction with promoter Norman Adams, they began their own blue-grass festival at Elijah Clark State Park near Lincolnton. In essence, it is a reconstituted Lewis Family Festival that had been discontinued after 2009. Their first compact disc, recorded on the Vine label, *Straight from the Heart of Dixie,* included a tasteful mixture of old and new, sacred, and secular numbers. Highlighted new songs included "Mountaintop" and "Sit Down and Cry," the former co-written by Lizzy and the latter from Tom T. and Dixie Hall. She led on three old-time spirituals and also sang a solid version of the Carter Family oldie "My Dixie Darling." A couple of instrumentals rounded it out.

By early 2011 the pair had a new band together that included Al Hoyle of Ellijay, Georgia, on guitar, his sister Lisa on bass, and Nathan Stewart on mandolin. For some reason, although Stewart did not play on their next disc, he went on to become their longest serving sideman. *Tradition with a Twist* came out on Vine in March 2011, and proved to be, if possible, even more polished than the previous one. From an up-tempo rendition of the old favorite "Are You from Dixie" followed by one of Albert Brumley's newer, snappier, and atypical compositions, the album proved quite strong. The same was true for *Lord in the Morning* released in 2012. Stewart was heard more on these releases and also on the nearly all instrumental *Pop Goes the Banjo.* Although the singing featured the band members, most of the instrumentation aside from Lewis, Long, and Stewart came from session pickers including Ben Isaacs, Clay Hess, and Irl Hees. Producer Wayne Haun of Vine Records was also heard on several cuts either playing an un-obtrusive piano or on some vocal refrains.

In 2015, the compact disc offering *Blueberry Pie* tended to be different. Most of the songs were of more recent origin with the possible exception of "Feed the Birds" which came from the 1964 Disney motion picture *Mary Poppins.* A Lizzy Long-Rhonda Vincent duet, "God Is There," subsequently won a Dove Award as the Bluegrass Gospel Song of the Year. Sam Bush was featured prominently on mandolin on both "Communication Breakdown" and "Figueroa Mountain." Little Roy Lewis, maintaining an atypical lower profile, mostly played either banjo or autoharp. Wayne Haun had or shared composer credit on four of the eleven cuts.

Going into the 2016 season the Little Roy and Lizzy Show continued to work a heavy schedule of tours. Their band included Nathan Stewart on mandolin, Tyler Biddix on guitar, and Haley Stiltner on bass. Sometimes an additional musician, Bennett Boswell, traveled with them. On December 9, 2015, Lizzy Long was married to Michael McCombs, a Lincolnton businessman. He is also an avid hunter and sponsors fish frys. In late April a new CD *Good Time Down Home* came out on StowTown Records which featured a guest appearance by Marty Stuart. Unlike the Lewis Family, they are not an all gospel group, but nonetheless do quite a bit of sacred songs. Along with the Lewis Tradition and Jeff and Sheri Easter, all three groups are doing a great deal to keep the sixty-eight-year tradition of the Lewis name prominent in bluegrass and gospel music.

In their long career, the Lewis Family and the two successor groups chalked up an immense recording legacy of over seventy albums and compact discs that is matched only by the Stanley Brothers and Ralph Stanley. When one considers that with Little Roy's comedy, the Family was as much if not more a visual act, their total of all quality music becomes even more impressive. Other family-oriented bluegrass gospel groups have earned their share of acclaim—the Sullivan Family comes to mind—but it is unlikely that any will surpass those folks from Lincolnton, Georgia.

SELECTED RECORDINGS

Lewis Family recordings are so numerous that only an important few will be listed here:

Lewis Family: Born of the Spirit. Starday CD 0953, 2003. All their first forty-six early recordings from 1953 to 1961 with good liner notes by Gary B. Reid are contained here.

The Lewis Family: 20 Country Bluegrass Hymns. Benson 84418-2897, 1992. A good sampling of their music.

The Lewis Family: 50th Anniversary Celebration. Thoroughbred 20412, 2003. Includes new recordings of some their best numbers such as "Hallelujah Turnpike" and "Slippers with Wings."

Lizzy Long & Little Roy Lewis: Straight from the Heart of Dixie. Vine TMS 1358, 2010. First disc by the most active of the Lewis successor bands.

LeRoy, Lance. *The Lewis Family: 45 Years on the Stages of America.* Hendersonville, TN: Dulany Printing, 1996. A good brief history of the group through 1995.

✄ The Masters Family

Johnnie, 1913–1980
Lucille, 1917–2006
Owen, 1935–1997

Back in the early years of bluegrass music, a family gospel group achieved wide popularity in their field. They did not play bluegrass, but did use prominent mandolin instrumentation and featured a good deal of duets and trios with outstanding original gospel songs. This group, the Masters Family, became a major influence both on bluegrass and the broadening field of commercial gospel music. Although the family ceased activity in the mid-1960s, their songs continued to be widely heard.

John Mace Masters was born near Jacksonville, Florida, on May 27, 1913. Originally his last name had been Purdom, but his father died prior to his birth and his mother remarried to P. S. Masters. Known as Johnnie, he eventually had his name legally changed to Masters, but continued to use the name J. M. Purdom on some of his composer credits. His wife, Lucille Masters, appeared on the credits of some of their original songs under her maiden name Lu Ferdon. Johnnie Masters first became interested in music as a child and listened to many of the old mountain songs on records. At the age of twelve Johnnie learned to play guitar and over the next few years, he frequently played square dances and other local functions.

In 1932, he began to play on radio at WJAX Jacksonville. The following year he met Lucille Ferdon at a personal appearance. She had been born in Homerville, Georgia, on September 13, 1917. However, she had lived in Jacksonville since 1918. After a brief courtship, the two married. Eventually, the couple had three children: Johnnie Owen, born February 3, 1935; Evelyn, born April 23, 1936; and Deanna (named for Deanna Durbin), born April 11, 1941. Both Owen and Deanna performed with the Masters Family.

In 1942, Johnnie and Lucille sang on radio together on WPDQ Jacksonville as the Dixie Sweethearts. He played either guitar or mandolin while

From left: John, Lucille, and Owen Masters, probably in the late-fifties. *Courtesy of John Morris.*

she sang harmony. Their style bore some resemblance to that of James and Martha Carson then gaining widespread popularity over WSB in Atlanta. In 1946, the pair moved over to larger station WJHP whose *Dixie Barn Dance Gang* show constituted the most popular program in Jacksonville. From 3:30 to 4:00 p.m. on Tuesday and Thursday afternoons, the Masters' show was broadcast over the Mutual Network. In addition to the Dixie Sweethearts, *Dixie Barn Dance Gang* listeners had the opportunity to hear such other regional favorites as Sleepy Gibbs, Tex Watson, and Pee Wee Jenkins.

In 1947, the Dixie Sweethearts made their first recordings for Jim Stanton's Rich-R-Tone label. The Masters' cut two sides including "Silver in My Mother's Hair" and "Prettiest Wreath of Flowers." Stanton evidently tried to give the impression that the Dixie Sweethearts were James and Martha Carson who used the name Barn Dance Sweethearts. This caused considerable confusion among record collectors. It was made all the more confusing by the fact that Martha Carson and Bill Carlisle did indeed record on Rich-R-Tone at a later date. Nonetheless, John and Lucille Masters were the Dixie Sweethearts on Rich-R-Tone.

John and Lucille Masters had experienced religious conversion in 1946 and from this time on they performed predominantly sacred material. They did a few secular numbers in later years and Johnnie Masters continued to compose love songs as well as religious ones. However, from that time onward they were known as a gospel group.

Twelve-year-old Owen Masters became a regular member and the Dixie Sweethearts became the Masters Family in 1947. Little Deanna also worked with the group and sang on radio from the age of three. At times she sang duets both with Owen and with Lucille, but did not actively participate on recording sessions. The Masters Family made their first recordings early in 1948 on the Mercury label. Their first session took place in Jacksonville where Tiny Greer played bass fiddle and Marvin Phillips played rhythm guitar along with Johnnie's mandolin and Owen's lead guitar. Their first release was "I Found It in Mother's Bible" and "Give Them the Roses Now." Their second release from this first session consisted of two James and Martha Carson songs, "Man of Galilee" and "Somebody Needs Just You," the latter never recorded by the Carsons.

Some months later, the Masters Family did a second Mercury session, this one in Nashville. These recordings also featured strong doses of Johnnie's mandolin and Owen's guitar and three original compositions: "That Little Old Country Church House," "It's All Coming True," which was later covered on Columbia by Lynn Davis and Molly O'Day, and a re-cut of "Wreath of Flowers." The old gospel standard "I Won't Have to Cross Jordan Alone" constituted the fourth song on this session. "Little Old Country Church House" clearly made the biggest impression of all their Mercury recordings and some years later was erroneously included on the Flatt and Scruggs album, Mercury 20542. According to one account, Flatt and Scruggs got so many requests for the number that they eventually learned to do it themselves.

By the time the Masters Family cut their second Mercury session they had made the acquaintance of Fred Rose and Archie Campbell who met them at a personal appearance in Tampa. This meeting eventually led to their move to Knoxville where they worked on the *Dinner Bell* Show led by Campbell at radio station WROL. At this time, they became friends with Lynn Davis and Molly O'Day and with Lester Flatt and Earl Scruggs who also worked on WROL. Their friendship with Fred Rose apparently went a bit deeper than mere business for he had written them at Jacksonville as early as May 18, 1949, telling them how much he enjoyed "talking about things that are in the Bible" and that considering "you folks feel the same way, so I'll make a special effort to see you soon."

After several months in Knoxville, the Masters Family got somewhat homesick for Jacksonville and returned to Florida in the winter of 1949–1950. However, in April 1950, the Masters Family went to Nashville where they appeared on WSM's *Grand Ole Opry* for three months. During this sojourn, Art Satherley and Don Law of Columbia Records signed them to a contract after they had obtained their release from Mercury. Johnnie also contracted his writing talents with Peer-Southern at the behest of Troy Martin. While their stay at WSM proved to be of short duration, it could be classed as a very fruitful one business-wise.

By the time the Masters Family signed their Columbia contract on September 25, 1950, they were back in Knoxville where they had begun a long term employment for Cas Walker, the East Tennessee supermarket magnate. Except for a few months in 1952 when they went to WWVA Wheeling, West Virginia, the Masters Family remained closely connected with Walker until January 1956. Their popularity on the Cas Walker show can best be illustrated by the sales of their first songbook, the profits of which paid for a new automobile.

The initial Masters session with Columbia took place on November 20, 1950, and consisted of songs written or co-written by Johnnie Masters except for Howards Watts's a.k.a. Cedric Rainwater, "I'll Be Going to Heaven Sometime." Lester Flatt and Earl Scruggs recorded the song on Mercury about the same time or a little earlier. The original compositions consisted of "While the Ages Roll On," "Let the Spirit Descend," and "Just a Sinner Saved by Grace." Mandolin and guitar instrumentation predominated on these recordings with Howard Watts—a recent alumni of the Bill Monroe and Flatt and Scruggs bands—likely playing bass fiddle. The Masters Family's second Columbia session on May 8, 1951, resembled the first in instrumentation and featured all original compositions. "Happiness Comes on Spiritual Wings," "This Old World is Rocking in Sin," "Stop Kicking God's Children Around," and "Hand Me Down My Silver Trumpet" comprised the four gospel songs. The latter attained the most popularity and bore close similarity to an old spiritual. The Family also did two original secular songs of considerable interest. The first was "When the Wagon Was New" which Johnnie wrote a few years earlier at Jacksonville. Later recordings of this song by such artists as Sam McGee, Charlie Moore, Jim and Jesse, and Wendy Bagwell have given the song virtual standard status in both the bluegrass and gospel fields. The other song, "From 40 to 65," has been cited as an outstanding piece of social protest about the problems of middle age. The original recording has been re-released in the Library of Congress *Bicentennial* series.

Beginning in early 1952, the sound on Masters Family recordings changed notably. Don Law of Columbia suggested that styles were in transition and wanted more modern instrumentation. As a result, their later Columbia work featured a lot of electric steel guitar, usually played by Don Helms. Their first session with this new sound produced two of their biggest successes. "Cry from the Cross" featured Helms on steel and subsequently received such excellent bluegrass adaptation by the Stanley Brothers and then by Ralph Stanley that younger fans have forgotten it was a Masters' original. Their gospel hit, "Gloryland March," attained enough success to be covered by several artists including Hank Snow on RCA and Wilma Lee and Stoney Cooper on Hickory. Charlie Arnett did the spirited piano work on "Gloryland March." He comprised half of the husband and wife team of Daisy Mae and Old Brother Charlie who recorded several sides of their own on Mercury and Columbia. Daisy Mae also recorded Owen's composition "The Boy across the Street" which could be described as being a few years ahead of its time. The song fit quite well into the teen-love ballad mode that boomed in the early days of rock and roll.

It was during this period of association with the Arnetts that the Masters Family went to WWVA Wheeling. However, they remained there for only a few months. By the fall of 1952 they were back in Knoxville working at WROL and WIVK for Cas Walker who himself was heavily involved in East

Tennessee Republican politics. His musicians often found themselves working at political rallies. The Family worked several times for Congressman Howard Baker Sr., father of the later Tennessee Senator. They also entertained at an appearance headlined by vice presidential candidate Richard Nixon. Lucille recalled that the Californian seemed not to be familiar with their type of music, but listened attentively from the front row to their entire performance and was so impressed that he tried to get Cas Walker to release them to campaign with him throughout the South. Walker chose, however, to retain the Masterses in his employ. In fact, the family worked numerous charity shows for Walker.

Meanwhile Johnnie, Lucille, and Owen continued to record on Columbia. Traditionalists may have found the instrumentation less appealing, but could still appreciate their exciting original material. "They've Made a New Bible" protested against the new Revised Standard Version translation. "Back in the Good Old Days" was another nostalgic look at an earlier day when people evidenced more piety. They did another secular record, "South Bound Passenger Train" and "My Heart's Like a Beggar."

On the last two Columbia sessions in 1954 and 1955, James Carson joined the group for recordings. He had often played shows and radio with them and on one session a bad case of laryngitis prevented Johnnie from singing. The trio on those songs consisted of James, Lucille, and Owen. On one number, "Noah and the Mighty Ark," Johnnie Masters did a recitation while the trio sang behind him. They cut four of James's compositions—"Everlasting Joy," "I Wasn't There," "It Takes a Lot of Lovin' to Get to Heaven," "Waiting the Call," and their particular styling of "Over in the Glory Land." Don Helms, John "Papa" Gordy, a legendary gospel pianist, and bassist Junior Huskey also worked on those sessions. In all, the Masters Family recorded thirty-four sides on Columbia.

On April 1, 1955, Owen suffered severe injuries in an automobile crash. Several months passed before he was fully recovered. In fact, Lucille contended that things never were quite the same again. Young Masters was by this time pretty much grown up and soon had his own family and own life to lead. Nonetheless, he continued to record with his family and worked some personal appearances, too.

Throughout the early 1950s, Johnnie Masters scored several notable successes as a country songwriter. In 1953, he had a top-ten hit with Hank

Snow's "Honeymoon on a Rocket Ship." Carl Smith did quite well with "That's the Kind of Love I'm Lookin' For." Other good Masters' songs included Roy Acuff's "Sixteen Chickens and a Tambourine," Don Gibson's "Walking in the Moonlight" and Johnny and Jack's "Winner of Your Heart."

The Masters Family also attracted something of a foreign following although they never toured outside the United States. Their records sold through such parts of the British Commonwealth as England, Canada, the Gold Coast, and Australia. They treasured requests for autographed pictures from West Africans in Accra and Gold Coast (now Ghana) who heard their records and wrote to them at WROL. Australian country singer Reg Lindsey helped popularize them Down Under and once tried to get them to come to Australia.

In January 1956, the Masters Family left Knoxville and the employ of Cas Walker. Like any other group who finds themselves somewhat confined to a single area, Johnnie, Lucille, and Owen wanted to play personals over more extended territory. Walker had been particularly close to the Masters Family because Johnnie wrote most of his commercials and jingles. Lucille believed that they perhaps contributed more to his business growth than any other act associated with his shows. Walker apparently hated to see them go and wrote a reference letter among other things stating, "anyone interested in reaching the ordinary people, what I mean by this is the working people and farm people, would make no mistake by employing the Masters Family for either radio or television."

In the next few years the Masters Family worked over a wider area based from their old home in Jacksonville. Lucille remembered that they played shows as far west as Missouri and Iowa. For several months in late 1959, they came back to Knoxville and worked with James Carson and for Walker again. A few years later, noted bluegrass mandolinist Curley Lambert worked with them for several months in 1963–64. Lambert who favored a worldlier lifestyle, recalled how Johnnie used to introduce him in churches as Brother Richard Lambert. By this time, Owen rarely worked personals and the group consisted of only Johnnie, Lucille, and Curley. They played a lot of churches and also shows with either Jim and Jesse or the Lewis Family.

In those years, the Masters Family recorded two new albums and had three albums of their earlier material released on Columbia-Harmony. The first album, *Gospel Sing* for Decca in 1961, featured the Masters Family trio singing by Johnnie, Lucille, and Owen and some solo vocals by the latter. An acoustical lead guitar played by Billy Grammar took the main instrumental part. Songs included new arrangements of "Little Old Country Church House," "When the Wagon Was New," and "The Man of Galilee." Newer songs included Johnnie's "Walk around Heaven," "The Great Gilded Hall," and the now bluegrass gospel standard, Betty Sue Perry's "Medals For Mothers." Decca also released the two latter cuts on a single. They recorded such older standards as "Take up Thy Cross," and the Bailes Brothers favorite, "One Way Ticket to the Sky."

The following year, the Masters Family recorded their last album, *The Gloryland March* for Starday. In addition to the title song, this album contained a new version of "Hand Me down My Silver Trumpet" and several of Johnnie's later compositions. Owen recorded a country single at that time with Pete Drake on steel, but Starday never released it, a fate which also befell an earlier solo session on Columbia. The instrumentation tended to be thoroughly modern and is the only Masters Family album that continued to be in print for several years. Unfortunately, it does little to bring out the old-time traditional sound of the earlier Masters Family recordings and live shows. Despite their later recordings and bearing the distinction of being the first gospel group to use modern country instruments on their record sessions, Lucille recalled that they always used only mandolin and guitar on their personal appearances.

From the latter part of 1964, the Masters Family went into musical retirement. Johnnie worked as a deejay and advertising manager for a radio station in Jessup, Georgia, from 1966 through 1968. In later years, he suffered from ill health and had several heart attacks. He and Lucille lived in Jacksonville as did oldest daughter Evelyn. Lucille continued to sing in church. Deanna lived in Longwood, Florida, which is near Orlando. Owen resided in Mt. Juliet, Tennessee, outside Nashville, with his family and worked in the printing business. Active in songwriting, he did not take much time to promote his material. One of his better efforts was "I'm Heaven Bound," which is on the Lewis Family's *Wrapped with Grace and Tied with Love* album. Jimmy Martin recorded a bluegrass Christmas song of Owen's entitled "No Room."

For the most part, the 1970s were less than satisfactory for Johnnie Masters. For a time, he and Lucille went their separate ways. Meanwhile, he saw his songs continuing to attract attention. Ralph Stanley used "Cry from the Cross" as the title cut for his first Rebel album and "When the Wagon Was New" and "Glory Land March" continued to be recorded and sung. By the end of the decade, things were looking upward. He and Lucille got back together and he had thoughts of a comeback. But it was not to be as he died of a heart attack on January 21, 1980.

While Masters Family songs lived on, the original musical family went to their reward. Owen died on March 1, 1997. Lucille lived in Clay, Florida, near the surviving daughters until March 14, 2006, when she died, having outlived her husband by more than twenty-six years. That same year Cattle Records in Germany issued a compact disc containing two dozen of their Mercury and Columbia originals, making their music available for dedicated fans. Whether for their wonderful original songs or being the first sacred group to use standard country instrumentation on their recordings, the Masters Family deserves to be better remembered.

SELECTED RECORDINGS

The Masters Family: Back in the Good Ole Days. Cattle CCD 327, 2006. A collection of four
of their original Mercury songs from 1949 and twenty Columbia recordings from 1950
through 1954.

Further Reading

Artis, Bob. *Bluegrass*. New York: Hawthorn Books, 1975. The first good popular treatment of the music by a member of Mac Martin's Dixie Travelers.

Bartenstein, Fred, ed. *Roots Music in America: Selected Writings of Joe Wilson*. Knoxville: University of Tennessee Press, 2016. A collection of the writings from the late Joe Wilson, founding director of the National Council for the Traditional Arts.

Bartenstein, Fred, Gary Reid, and others. *The Bluegrass Hall of Fame: Inductee Biographies, 1991–2014*. Louisville: Holland Brown Books, 2014.

Berrier, Ralph Jr. *If Trouble Don't Kill Me: A Family's Story of Brotherhood, War, and Bluegrass*. New York: Crown Publishers, 2010. A biography of the Hall Twins who were members of the Blue Ridge Entertainers in the early 1940s. It also contains much material on Roy Hall.

Cohen, Norm. *Folk Music: A Regional Exploration*. Westport, CT: Greenwood Press, 2005. Puts bluegrass within the broader field of folk music.

Green, Douglas B. *Country Roots*. New York: Hawthorn Books, 1976. A good popular treatment of the broader country music field.

Malone, Bill C. *Country Music, U. S. A.* Revised Edition. Austin: University of Texas Press, 1985. The definitive work.

Rosenberg, Neil V. *Bluegrass: A History*. Urbana and Chicago: University of Illinois Press, 1985. The definitive work on the country music subtype.

Smith, Richard D. *Can't You Hear Me Callin': The Life and Music of Bill Monroe*. Boston: Little, Brown and Company. 2003. Biography of the man who developed and named bluegrass.

Tribe, Ivan M. *Country: A Regional Exploration*. Westport, CT: Greenwood Press, 2006. Differs from the other works by taking a regional approach.

Wolfe, Charles K. *Tennessee Strings: The Story of Country Music in Tennessee*. Knoxville: University of Tennessee Press, 1977. Brief survey of a key state in the development of bluegrass.

Index of Names

A. G. and Kate, 193, 256

Acuff, Roy, 16, 32, 41, 51, 61, 66, 133, 137, 199, 208, 253, 255, 289, 326, 370

Adcock, Eddie, 141

Adkins, Hobo Jack, 274

Aldridge, Darin and Brooke, 182

Aldridge, Talton, 13

Allen, Lee, 208

Allen, Red, 30, 111–12, 178, 208

Allison, Joe, 6

Amber Sisters (a.k.a. Amburgey Sisters), 190

Amburgey Sisters, 85, 190, 339

Amburgy, Kash, 209

Amsterdam, Morey, 234

Anderson, Danny, 113

Anderson, Ray, 230

Anglin, Jim, 253

Anglin Brothers, 283

Anthony, Chubby, 141, 349

Arms, Danny, 98

Arnett, Charles, 368

Arnett, Daisy Mae, 368

Arnold, Eddy, 3, 51

Artis, Bob, 32–33

Atcher, Bob and Bonnie Blue Eyes, 198

Atkins, Ray and Lois, 94–95, **116,** 133, 160–61, 216–17, 350

Attaway, Buddy, 255

Austin, Harold, 96–97

Autry, Gene, 56, 325

Azinger, Norman, 33, 35

Bagwell, Wendy, 357, 368

Bailes Brothers, 43, 62, 133, 135, 202, 248, 249–58, **250,** 287, 331

Bailes, Walter, 32

Bailey Brothers, 169, 295

Bailey, Charlie, 32, 187

Bailey, Danny, 163–64

Bailey, DeFord, 63

Bailey, Green, 70

Bailey, Jay, 10

Baker, Billy, 98, 108–114, **109**

Baker, Howard Sr., 369

Baker, Kenny, 108, 163, 166

Baldwin, Bonnie, 245

Ball, Arthur, 257

Banks, Buck and Buddy, 306–7, 310

Banks, Roscoe, 303

Banner, Earl, 29–31

Bar Nothing Gang, 323

Barber, Roy and Carl, 135

Barbour, Burk, 15, 141, 227, 294

Barker, "Happy Go Lucky" Joe, 28

Bartenstein, Fred, 208, 359

"Bashful Brother Oswald" (Pete Kirby), 133

Basista, Frank, **28**, 31, 33

Bassett, Jay "Slim," 63–66

Baucom, Heath, 349

Baucom, Terry, 144

Baum, Clyde, 43, 255

Bava, John, 269

Beasley, Larry, 97

Beaucom, Luke, 139

Belcher, Finley "Red," 83, 287, 295

Belcher, Frankie, 96

Bell, Lloyd, 216–18, 220

Belton, Allie May, 17

Benson, Kristin Scott, 332

Berlin, Irving, 151

Berrier, Ralph, 17

Bess, "Big Jeff," 67, 287

Beverly, Bonny, 346

Biddix, Tyler, 363

"Big Slim, the Lone Cowboy" (McAuliffe, Harry C.), 201, 234

Birchfield, Wiley, 168

Blackweller, Beacham, 305

Blackwood Brothers, 356

Blair, Harry ("Horse Thief"), 323–24

Blake, Monte, 191

Blake, Norman, 8

Blake, Randy, 60

Blanchard, Lowell, 40, 308

Blanchard, Red, 326

Bloodworth, Owen, 314

Blue Grass Champs (a.k.a. Stoneman Family), 108, 317

Blue Ridge Quartet, 355, 357

Blue Sky Boys (Bill and Earl Bolick), 5, 29, 66, 68, 183, 187, 193, 248, 253, 292, 322, 330–31

Bluegrass Cardinals, 34

Bluegrass Kinsmen, 113

Boaz, Edgar, 70

Bohemian Orchestra, 323

Bond, Johnny, 16

Boone, Claude, 92–96, 115–121, **116**, 170

Bowles, Lori Lee, 86

Bowlin, David, 279

Boyd, Bill, 53

Bradley, Dale Ann, 209

Bradley, Owen, 51

Brady, Rafe, 15

Brammer, Troy, 312

Branham, Eddie "Kentucky Slim," 274–75

Branham, Ross, 9

Brewster Brothers (Frank and Bud), 95–96, 170

Briarhopper, Homer (Drye, Homer), 325

Briarhoppers, 318, 320–33, **321**, 349

Brock, George, 24, 208

Brotherton, Gary, 9

Brown, Bill, 15, 17

Brown, Frank "Hylo," 2, 4–10, **5**, 162, 170–71, 178, 274–75

Brown, Glenn, **344**, 348–49

Brown, Milton, 82

Brown's Ferry Four, 51

Brozi, Ed, 28

Brumley, Albert, 189, 362

Brumley, Albert Jr., 127

Bruner, Cliff, 307

Bryan, Eleanor, 325

Bryant, Billy, **28**, 30–35

Bryant, Ed, 314

Bub, Mike, 300

Buchanan Brothers, 330

Buchanan, Clato, 13

Buchanan, Frank, 343

Buchanan, Jim, 345

Bumgardner, Howard, 305

Bunn, Ollie, 305
Burge, Lloyd, 312
Burkhardt, Carl, 30
Burns, Jethro, 163
Burroughs, Gene, 314, 346
Busby, Buzz, 110–111, 297
Buskirk Family, 264, 293
Buskirk, Paul, 83, 160, 218, 264
Bussard, Joe, 61
Butler, Carl, 133, 137–38, 168, 228, 254
Butler Brothers, 131
Byrd, Robert, 125

Cactus Kids, 323
Cain, Benny and Vallie, 110
Calhoun, Bill, 41
Callahan, Alma, 261
Callahan, Betty, 339
Callahan Brothers (Homer and Walter), 11, 29, 88, 247, 259–66, **260**, 292
Calvas, Mary "Sunflower," 235–38, 20, 295
Campbell, Archie, 135–36, 143, 162, 168, 228, 367
Campbell, Cecil, 323–24
Cap, Andy, and Flip, 201, 204, 251, 293
Cap, Andy, and Milt, 223
Caplinger, Warren (of Cap, Andy, and Flip), 57, 62
Carlisle, Bill, 117, 324, 326–27, 366
Carlisle, Cliff, 115–117, 307, 326–27
Carlisle Brothers (Cliff and Bill), 32, 51, 248
Carney, Rev. Willard, 253
Carolina Tar Heels, 89, 261, 303
Carpenter, Boyd, 305
Carpenter, French, 124
Carr, Freddie, 125
Carrier, Randy, 347

Carroll, Bill, 110
Carroll, Eddie, 103
Carson, James, 350. *See also* Roberts, James
Carson, James and Martha (James and Irene Roberts), 143, 181, 183–94, **184**, 272, 365
Carson, Martha, 366
Carson, Mike, **28**, 30–35
Carter, Buster and Young, Preston, 40–41
Carter, Jack, 81, 251
Carter, Jason, 300
Carter, Joe and Janette, 331
Carter, Maybelle, 125
Carter Family, 7, 27, 38–40, 122, 127, 204, 287, 303–10, 317–18, 356
Carver, Will, 191
Carver, Willie, 311
Casey, Claude, 175, 323
Casey, Jack, 9
Cash, Johnny, 4, 10
Centers, Roy Lee, 208
Chambers, Bill, 163
Chance, Lightning, 218
Chaney, Charlie, 45
Chappelear, Leon, 65
Cheek, Earl and Jerry, 314
Cheshire, Harry "Pappy," 326
Chestnut, Ted, 70
Chief Powhatan's (Atkins, Floyd) Bluegrass Braves, 139, 143, 346
Childre, Lew, 65
Christy, Harold, 305
Chuck Wagon Gang, 353
Church, Porter, 108
Church Brothers, 33
Cianciola, Tony, 218
Clark, J. E. and the Lonesome Mountaineers, 91

Clark, Jim, 98

Clark, Joe, 280

Clark, Johnny, 202

Clark, Roy, 177

Clements, Vasser, 163

Clements, Zeke, 237

Clere, Slim, 57, 62

Clifton, Bill, 87, 139, 141, 145, 163–64

Cline, Charlie, 269

Cline, "Cousin" Ezra, 268. *See also* Goins Brothers

Cline, "Curly" Ray, 166. *See also* Goins Brothers

Cline, Ireland "Lazy Ned," 268–69

Cline, Kessler, 272

Coates, J. B., 187–88

Coffey, Inez, 339

Cole, Abner, 199–200

Cole, Dale, 41

Cole, James, 113

Cole, Maiford, 73

Colleran, William. *See* Martin, Mac

Collier, Chubby, 35

Collins, Charlie, 210

Collins, Curnie, 101

Collins, Eb, 97

Collins, Sonny, 7

Combs, Vince, 210

Cook, Bobby and His Texas Saddle Pals, 156

Cook, Joe, 116–117

Cook, John, 313

Cooke, Curtis, 108

Cooke, Hubert, 108

Cooke, Jack, 108, 110

Cooke Brothers, 108

Coon Creek Girls, 16, 159, 185, 263, 311, 318, 334–42, **335**

Cooper, Carol Lee, 197, 199, 203–4

Cooper, Wilma Lee, 172, 246

Cooper, Wilma Lee and Stoney, 16, 59, 67, 181, 195–205, **196**, 289, 345, 356

Copas, Lloyd "Cowboy," 57, 67, 88, 154–56, 205, 251

Cordell, Tommy, 349

Cortez, Froggie, 236

Cosby, John and the Bluegrass Drifters, 70

Cosse, Xavier, 190, 353

Cottrell, Jenes, 124

Country Gentlemen, 34

Country Pets, 349

Cousin Emmy [Carver], 201, 323

Cox, Billy, 27, 32, 62, 79–82, 124, 251, 293, 309

Coy, LaVelle "Bill," 43

Craft, Paul, 357

Craig, Wick, 86

Crank, Tommy, 208

Crase, Noah, 208

Crazy Buckle Busters, 325

Crosby, Bing and Dixie Lee, 327

Crowe, J. D., 44

Crowe Brothers, 248

Crutchfield, Charles, 323

Cummins, Jan, 341

Curless, Dick, 289

Dacus, Johnny, 144

Dalhart, Vernon, 304, 306, 321

Dalton, Jeff, 97

Dalton, Randy, 98

Dalton, Wanda, 357

Darby, Tom and Tarlton, Jimmy, 304, 306

Darling, Denver, 177

Daugherty, George (Earl of Elkview), 130

Davidson, Ken, 122–23
Davis, Big Bill, 323, 329
Davis, Gussie L., 304
Davis, Henry Gassaway, 195
Davis, Hubert, 52
Davis, Karl and Taylor, Harty, 39, 41, 65, 328
Davis, Lynn, 269
Davis, Shelby Jean, 65
Davis Twins (Honey and Sonny), 86
Dawson, Zeke, 204
Deaton, Bill, 314
Deese, David, 319, 344–50, **344**. *See also* Briarhoppers
Delmore Brothers, 14, 32, 51, 247, 259, 284, 331
Denny, Clyde and Marie, 96
Denny, Jim, 257
DePew, Jo, 339
Dickens, Hazel and Gerrard, Alice, 112, 211
Dickens, Little Jimmy, 58, 67, 135, 191, 251
Dillard, Doug, 127
Dillon, Bernard, 271, 273
Dillon, Jim, 313
Dirksen, Everett, 87
Dixie Bluegrass, **344**
Dixon, Howard, 308, 310
Dixon Brothers, 27, 40, 287, 304–6
Dockery, Henry, 174
Dodson, Tiny, 308, 310
Dominion Bluegrass Boys, 45
Domino, Fats, 350
Dorsey, Georgia Tom, 50
Drumwright, Joe, 6, 8
Dudgeon, Frank, 54
Dudley, Dave, 125
Duncan, Tommy, 53

Durham, Mel, 111
Dutton, Jim, 102

Eanes, Jim, 16, 141, 170, 275
Easter, Jeff and Sherri, 355–58
Easter Brothers, 24, 355–56, 358
Edwards, Billy, 8–9, 61, 171, 272–74, 314
Edwards, Tommy, 41
Elkins, Steven, 195
Elliott, James, 360
Ellis, Tim, 151–2
Ellis, Tony, 345
Ellison, Warren, 75
Ely, Brother Claude, 22, 212
Elza, Charles (Kentucky Slim/the Little Darling), 7, 93, 293
Epstein, Lou, 73, 75
Escott, Colin, 10
Estes, Mary Ann. *See* Starcher, Mary Ann
Estes, Milton, 67, 253
Ethridge, Floyd, 176
Evans, Dale, 326
Evans, Dave, 280
Evans, Gerald, 278

Faile, Tommy, 161, 350
Farmer, Dewey, 96
Feazell, Shelton, 210
Ferguson, Ernest, 253–57
Ferguson, Gene, 80
Fincher, Hubert, 306
Fincher, J. W., 39, 304, 306
Fincher, Rawhide and Shorty, 235–36
Fisher, Betty, 319
Fisher, Betty and Deese, David, 343–50, **344**
Fisher, Minnie Thomas, 257
Fishman, Lily. *See* Isaacs, Lily

Flannery Sisters, 65

Flatt, Lester, 42, **123**, 172, 174, 176, 309

Flatt, Lester and Scruggs, Earl, 1, 3,
7–9, 29, 36, 40, 122, 136, 139, 142,
168, 177, 253–54, 285, 287, 296–97,
299, 312, 350, 353, 363, 367

Fleming, Reece and Townsend,
Respers, 261

Florida Boys, 357

Flowers, Dennis, 347

Flowers, Doug, 361

Foley, Clyde, 339

Foley, Red, 51, 177, 263, 336, 338

Forehand, Blind Mamie, 356

Forrester, Howard "Howdy," 166, 179,
204, 296

Foster, Gus, 264

Foster, John and Rutherford,
Leonard, 40

Fowler, Wally, 17, 286, 354

Fox, Curly, 65

Foy, Jack and Jerry, 234

Frank, J. L., 43, 262

Franklin Brothers, 83

Franks, Tillman, 255

Freeman, Arville, 311

Freeman, David, 18, 32, 298

French, Bob, 297

Frizzell, Lefty, 41

Frizzell, Orville "Lefty," 265

Frog [Stack] and the Greenhorns, 126

Gabbard, Harley, 75, **147**, 275

Gabehart, Jim and Valerie, 182

Gainer, Patrick, 124

Gallion, Bob, 125

Gardner, Olen, 45

Garner, John Nance "Cactus Jack," 338

Gaskin, Dick, 360

Gately, Connie, 32

Gay, Connie B., 177

George, Uncle Tom, 59

Gibson, Don, 137, 370

Gibson Brothers, 248

Gillette, Lee, 286–87

Gillis, George, 348

Girls of the Golden West, 336

Glenville State College Bluegrass Band,
129

Gloria Belle [Flickinger], 45

Glosson, Lonnie, 226, 294

Godwin, William Henry (a.k.a. "Hiram
Hayseed"), 240, 245

Goff, Bob and the Bluegrass Buddies,
144

Goins, Conley, 125, **140**, 144, 277

Goins, Don, 268

Goins, Harold and Goins, James, 268

Goins, Melvin, 8, 125–26, 128, **140**. *See
also* Goins Brothers

Goins, Ray, 125, 128, **140**. *See also*
Goins Brothers

Goins, Willia, 125–26

Goins Brothers (Melvin and Ray), 125–
26, 139, 144–45, **147**, 248, 267–81, **268**

Golden State Boys, 111

Goodman, Happy Family, 354

Goodman, Herald, 264

Gordy, John "Papa," 369

Gosdin, Vern and Ray, 111

Graham, "Little" John and Cherokee
Sue, 82–84, 246

Grand Ole Opry, 2, 6, 27, 29, 50–53, 59,
61, 63, 89, 92, 104, 122, 128, 131, 136,
139, 146, 151–52, 156,172, 177, 181, 191,
198, 202, 204–5, 222, 237, 247–48,
252–54, 285, 287–88, 297, 308, 315,
345, 367

Grant, Bill, 358

Grant, Roy "Whitey," 350. *See also* Briarhoppers

Grant, Ted, 82

Grascals, 332

Graves, F. A., 356

Graves, Josh, 126, 130, 142, 201, 345

Graves, Tim, 204

Gray, Otto and His Oklahoma Cowboys, 79, 325

Grayfeathers, Doc and His Cowboys, 81, 251

Grayson, G. B. and Whitter, Henry, 303

Grayson, Shannon, 349. *See also* Briarhoppers

Green, Ben, 144

Green, Doug, 163

Green, Richard, 208

Greer, Tiny, 366

Griffin, Buddy, 122–32, **123**, **140**, 144, 151, 277–78, 361

Griffin, Rex, 65

Griffin, Richard and Erma, 122, 124, 131

Griffith, Andy, 16

Griffith, Harry, 86

Grindstaff, Randy, 97

Gustine, Frank, 33

Guthrie, Woody, 159, 311

Haddock, Kenny, 111

Haden Family, 323

Haerle, C. Martin, 97

Haggard, Merle, 178

Haley, Pete and His Log Cabin Girls, 323

Hall, Connie, 74

Hall, Jay Hugh, 11, 17, 47–48, 50, 308, 310

Hall, Marion, 312

Hall, Roy, 11–18, **12**, 47, 286, 308

Hall, Rufus, 11, 17–18

Hall, Tom T. and Dixie, 130, 203, 212

Hall Twins (Saford and Clayton), 14–17

Hamblen, Stuart, 191

Hamm, Bill, 278

Haney, Carlton, 346–47, 358

Haney, Lillie Mae. *See* Lillie Mae Whitaker

Hankins, Esco, 133, 193

Hankinson, Mel and Stan (the Kentucky Twins), 248, 283–89, **284**, 296

"Happy Gad," 15

Happy-Go-Lucky Boys, 47–49

Harmony Gospeleers, 67

Harper, Aunt Idy (Lillie, Margaret), 185, 337

Harrell, Bill, 31, 297

Harris, Homer, 219–20

Harris, Junior, 349

Harrison, Tex (a.k.a. Ray, Joe), 235

Hartman, Dick, 304, 324. *See also* Tennessee Ramblers

Hawkins, Hawkshaw, 191, 203, 288, 296

Hay, George D., 253

Hayes, Gabby, 15

Haynes Brothers, 166

Hays, Lee, 159

Hazel and Alice, 178. *See also* Dickens, Hazel and Gerrard, Alice

Hazel Holler, 212

Hazelwood, George, 97

Heathwood, Tom, 297

Heck, Del, 252–53

Heckels, The, 125

Hees, Irl, 362

Helms, Don, 369

Henderson, Dalton, 256

Henderson, Jack, 67

Henderson, Rex, 43

Henderson, Ted and Wanda, 67

Hendley, Fisher, 13, 303–4

Henry, Darrell, 220

Henry, Red and Murphy, 347. *See also*
    Hicks, Murphy

Hensley, Dennis, 23–24

Hensley, Lloyd, 208

Hensley, Walter, 23, 110

Herbert, Morris, 314

Herdman, Curly, 151

Hess, Clay, 361–62

Hewitt, Dolph, 83, 326

Hicks, Bobby, 52, 169

Hicks, Jack, 163

Hicks, Murphy, 347

Higgins, Bill, 29

Hill, Eddie, 215–16, 218

Hinshelwood, Jack, 114

Hired Hands, 331

Hiser, Rusty, 197

Hobbs, Shorty, 262

Hobbs, Smiley, 110

Hogan, Arval. *See also* Briarhoppers

Hogan, Clarence and Garland, 321

Hogan, Ed "Rattlesnake," 135, 293

Holden Brothers (Fairley and Jack),
    251, 263

Hollis, Richard, 348

Hollon, Noah, **100**, 101–2

Holmes, Billy, 24

Hooper, Gene, 288

Hooper, Russ, 110

Hoot Owl Holler Girls (Amburgey
    Sisters), 185

Hooven, Herb, 297

Hopkins, Doc, 5, 65

Hopper, Lonnie, 211

Hopson, Bob, 13, 15

"Horseshoe Mike" and "Cowboy Joe," 54

Horton, Vaughn, 330

Hoskins, Zeke, 208

Houp, Hall, 92

Houston, Cisco, 159, 311

Howard, Harlan, 61

Huey, Jim, 126

Hughes, Randy, 137

Hurdt, Walter, 116, 175

Husky, Ferlin, 191, 340

Hutchins, Sam "Porky," 110

Hylton, Randall, 357, 360

Ingram, Kenny, 45

Isaacs, Ben, 209, 361–62

Isaacs, Delmer, 209

Isaacs, Joe and Stacy, 182, 206–13, **207**

Isaacs, Lily, 24, 208–9, 212

Isaacs, Rebecca, 209

Isaacs, Sonya, 209, 211–12

Isley, Tex, 43

Ives, Burl, 159

Jackson, Harold "Shot," 8, 254–55

Jackson, Tommy (banjo picker for Betty
    Fisher), 347

Jackson, Tommy, 6, 33, 51, 327

Jam Up and Honey, 287

James, Sonny, 192

Jarvis, John Dill "J. D.," 2, 19–26, **20**,
    208

Jeffers, George "Sleepy," 86

Jenkins, DeWitt "Snuffy," 39, 308–9, 326

Jenkins, Gene, 191

Jenkins, Hoke, 92, 138, 169

Jenkins, Pee Wee, 365

Jenks, Orville, 58

Jennings, Gordon, 269
Jim and Jesse [McReynolds] and the
    Virginia Boys, 125, 128–29, 143, 148,
    151, 173, 176, 248, 330, 347
Johnnie and Jack, 43, 51, 140, 160, 370
Johnson, Carol, 99
Johnson, Geraldine "Jerry," 199
Johnson, Joe, 15
Johnson, Johnny, 199
Johnson, Lyndon, 87
Johnson Brothers (Clyde and Hack), 94
Johnson Mountain Boys, 34
Jones, Danny, 211, 277
Jones, George, 10
Jones, George and Montgomery, Melba,
    182, 211
Jones, Grandpa, 51, 57, 69, 162–63
Jones, Ramona, 162–3
Jones, Slim, 30–31
Jones Brothers (Lee and Bruce), 96,
    331, 347–49
Jones Sisters (Judie and Julie), 187
Jordan, Vic, 152
Jordanaires, 8
Jubilee Hillbillies, 176
Judds, The, 187

Keaton, Charles "Big Foot," 57
Keillor, Garrison, 127
Keith, John, 278–79
Keith, Leslie, 58, 166
Keller, Ralph, **344**, 348–49
Kennedy, John F., 86
Kentucky Travelers, 33
Kessinger, Clark, 124
Kincaid, Bradley, 5–6, 38, 133
King, Claude, 255
King, Curly, 17
King, Nelson, 60

King, Pee Wee, 237, 262, 328
King, Ralph, 24
King's Sacred Quartet, 51
Kirby, Fred, 324–25, 351–52
Kirk, Red, 136
Kirkpatrick, Floyd, 199
Klein, Ray, 326
Knight, Tom, 31
Koehler, Esther "Violet," 264. *See also*
    Coon Creek Girls
Krise, George "Speedy," 2, 31, 67, 133–
    40, **134**, 162, 179, 218, 227–28, 294
Kruger Brothers, 248

Laine, Frankie and Stafford, Jo, 137
Lair, John, 264, 335–40, 342
Lambert, Joe, 199
Lambert, Richard "Curley," 125, 139–45,
    140, 277, 370
Lambert, Robert, 43
Landers, Jake, 32
Lane, Christy, 127, 357
Lane, Lawrence, and his Kentucky
    Grass, 113
Lane Brothers, 296
Lange, Evelyn "Daisy," 264. *See also*
    Coon Creek Girls
Lanham, Marty, 204
Larkin Family, 360
Lattimore, Mike, 172, 204
Laur, Katie, 126–28, 278
Law, Don, 367
Lay Brothers (Lester and Howard), 303
Layne, Bert, 80, 156, 299
Leary Family, 196–97
Ledford, Charlotte "Rosie." *See* Coon
    Creek Girls
Ledford, Lily May, 222. *See also* Coon
    Creek Girls

Ledford, Minnie "Black-Eyed Susan."
    See Coon Creek Girls
Ledford, Steve, 158, 307–8, 343
Lee, Ernie, 69
Lehart, Slim, 125
Lehman, George and Glen, 138
LeRoy, Lance, 358
Lester, Bobby, 346
Lester, Chester "Butch," 86
Lewis, Little Roy, 130, 318; see also
    Lewis Family
Lewis, Wayne, 102, 211
Lewis Family, 19, 24, 67, 143, 318,
    351–63, **352**
Lilly, Charlie, 298–300
Lilly, Daniel, 298–300
Lilly, Everett, 177
Lilly, Everett Alan, 297–98
Lilly, Jiles, 297–98
Lilly, Mark, 298–300
Lilly, Mike, 151
Lilly Brothers (Everett and Bea), 29, 34,
    45, 135–38, 248, 288, 290–300, **291**
Lincoln, Abraham, 86
Lineberry, Audine, 45
Little, Keith, 35
Little, Tommy, 140
Little Roy and Lizzy Show, 362
Logan, Benjamin "Tex," 166, 200–201,
    295–96
Logsdon, Jimmy, 73
Logston, Corrina, 131
Lomax, Alan, 310–11
"Lone Pine" (Breau, Harold), 289
Lonesome Pine Fiddlers, 34, 248. *See
    also* Goins Brothers
Long, "Little Eller," 6
Long, Lizzy, 129, 361–63
Long, Rebekah, 129–30, 361
Louvin, Charles, 210

Louvin, Ira, 42–43
Louvin Brothers (Charles and Ira), 193,
    345
Love, "Daddy" John, 303–5
Loveless, Patty, 172
Lowe, Bill, 8, 274
Lucas, Bee, 44
Lulu Belle and Scotty [Wiseman], 51,
    181, 193, 326
Lumpkin, Ray, 346
Lunsford, Bascom LaMar, 261
Lunsford, Jimmy, 158, 161
Lunsford, Ray, 3, 72–74, 76
Lydick, Billie Jean and Red, 138
Lyle, Rudy, 177
Lyons, Ruth, 73

Macon, Uncle Dave, 89, 315
Magness, Tommy, 13, 15–17
Mainer, Carolyn and Mary, 313
Mainer, Glenn, 312–13
Mainer, J. E. (Joseph E.), 31, 49–50, 133,
    159, 247, 261, 301–14, **302**, 345
Mainer, J. E., Jr. "Curly," 312–13
Mainer, Julie, 171, 307, 314–16
Mainer, Wade, 3, 49–50, 111, 136, 158–
    59, 247, 253, 299, 301–16, **302**, 331
Mainer's Mountaineers, 324. *See also*
    Mainer, J. E. and Mainer, Wade
Malone, Bill C., 258
Manderson, Steve, 354, 356
Marsh, Eileen, 130
Martin, Asa, 70, 183, 185, 262
Martin, Benny, 67, 146, 166
Martin, Bob, 34
Martin, Grady, 6, 67, 287
Martin, James "Slim," 3, 42–43, 45–46,
    228
Martin, Jimmy, 6, 45, 51, 270, 281
Martin, Mac, 2, 27–36, **28**

Martin, Marion (Keyoski, Marion), **233**, 238, 240–44, 296
Martin, Roy, 247
Martin, Wilma, 43, 45
Masters, Gene, 270
Masters Family, 139, 143, 188, 192–93, 317–18, 350, 353, 364–72, **365**
Matheson, Buzz, 35
Mathis, Larry, 163
May, Rick, 278
Mayfield, Ed, 274
Maynard, Ken, 15
Mayo, Ralph, 141–42
Mayse Brothers (Budge and Fudge), 57, 82, 84, 288
McCall, Jim, 110
McCarroll, James, 221
McCarty, E. C. "Mac," 218, 228
McCormick, George, 204
McCoury, Del, **109**, 110–12
McCoy, Shorty, 6
McCurdy, Ed, 239
McEntire, Reba, 130
McGaha, Mac, 131
McGar, Mac, 68, 286
McGee, Sam, 368
McHan, Don, 148, 220
McIntire, Boat Whistle, 110
McIntire, Vernon, 23
McKellar, Mike, 97
McKenzie, Karen ("Punkin"), 243. *See also* Doc and Chickie Williams
McKinney, John, 129
McKnight, Gene, 156
McKnight, Luke, 128
McMahan, Ed, 91
McMichen, Clayton, 63, 153, 155–56
McNeely, John, 278–80
McPeak, Udell, 272–73
McPeake, Curtis, 8

McReynolds, Jesse, 129–30, 132, 357
McReynolds, Jim, 128–29
McReynolds, Keith, 152
Meadows, Ralph "Joe," 85, 124, 126, 146–52, **147**, 276–77
Medford, Joe, 43
Meechy, Montana and Myrtle, 54
Mesing, Ron, 34
Messenger, Ashley, 131
Mid-Day Merry-Go-Round, 93–94, 117, 136, 162, 168, 189, 214, 227, 293, 308, 327, 343
Milhon, Dan, 9, 61
Miller, Aaron, 130
Miller, Charles and Honey, 252
Miller, Curley, 245
Miller, Darnell, 125
Miller, Dave, 297
Miller, Emmet, 261
Miller, James, 103
Miller, Wendy, 151
Millsaps, Bill, 97
Milo Twins (Edward and Edwin), 237
Misenheimer, Junior, 305
Mix, Art, 326
Mix, Tom, 326
Monroe, Betty, 42, 44
Monroe, Bill, 1, 3, 27, 34–35, 37–40, 46, 50–51, 133, 139, 158, 174, 176–77, 199, 247, 271, 285, 289, 295, 312, 331, 345, 347, 350, 353
Monroe, Birch, 37–38, 43, 46
Monroe, Charlie, 2, 17, 32, 37–46, **38**, 160–61, 269
Monroe, Martha Gammon, 44
Monroe Brothers (Bill and Charlie), 27, 29, 34, 37, 39, 40, 45, 183, 193, 247, 259, 292
Montana, Patsy, 197, 222

Moody, Clyde, 3, 47–53, **48**, 176–77, 308–10, 331
Moody, David, 332
Moody, Dwight, 139–40. *See also* Briarhoppers
Moody, Ruby, 67, 201
Moody Brothers, 332
Moore, Bonnie Lou and Buster, 2, 67, 96, 136–37, 182, 214–21, **215**
Moore, Charlie, 49, 61, 139, 142–45, 178, 368
Moore, Frankie and the Log Cabin Boys, 262
Moore, Juanita, **56**–60, 200
Moore, Lee, 3, 54–62, **55–56**, 81, 171, 245
Moore, Roger Lee, 58
Moore, Thelma, 61
Moore Brothers, 166
Morgan, Ray, 269
Morganthau, Henry J., 328
Morris, Claude (Zeke), 11, 41, 49, 305–6
Morris, "Cowboy" Jack, 251
Morris, George, 11, 32, 158, 309
Morris, John, 44
Morris, Wiley, 11, 216–17, 306, 311–12
Morris Brothers (Wiley and Zeke), 158, 247
Moser, Mitchell, 97–98
Mountain Fury, 130–31
Mullins, Paul "Moon," 24, 44, 102, 275
Murphy, Megan, 130
Myers, Ray, 244

Napier, Bill, 61, 141–42
Narmour and Smith, 307
"Natchee the Indian" (Storer, Lester Vernon), 153–57, **154**, 251, 293
Nathan, Syd, 67, 142

National Barn Dance, 6, 65, 222, 335
Nelson, Ken, 4, 6, 188
Nesiti, Tim, 33
New Coon Creek Girls, 70, 341–42
Newman, Hank and Slim, 54, 251
Nichols, Eva, 16
Norman, Ben and Jessie Mae, 198
Norris, Kody, 114

Oberstein, Eli, 39
O'Day, Molly and Davis, Lynn, 32, 42, 59, 133, 135–38, 182, 199, 222–31, **223**, 251, 264, 293, 314, 328, 357, 366
Odell, Mac (McLeod, Odell), 2, 63–69, **64**, 136–37, 200
Odom, Glenn, 349
O'Neal, Uncle Jim, 313
O'Neill, Mattie (Amburgey, Opal), 185, 190–91, 229
O'Quin, Gene, 265
Osborne, Bobby, 131–32, 269–70
Osborne, Jimmie, 255
Osborne, Orne "Buddy," 43
Osborne, Sonny, 207
Osborne Brothers (Bobby and Sonny), 208, 248
Overcash, Floyd and Otis, 313
Owens, Buck, 40
Owens, Dusty, 169
Owens, Tom, 39

Pack, Billy, 299
Pack, "Cowboy" Loye, 82, 204, 294
Palmer, John, 8, 61, 170, 314, 346
Parker, Buck, 208
Parker, Byron and Mountaineers, 34, 39, 294, 307, 309
Parker, Mitchell, 310

Parker, Rex and Eleanor, 58, 62, 146, 269

Parmley, Don, 111

Parsons, Dorsey Ray, 86

Parsons, Penny, 360

Parsons, Phoeba, 124

Parton, Dolly, 163, 356

Patton, Danny, 300

Paul, Woody, 204

Paxton, Mike, 275–76, 281

Pearl, Minnie, 87

Pearson, Kirt, 340

"Peeper," "Poochie," and "Punkin," 236–37, 246. *See also* Williams, Doc and Chickie

Pennell, Zag, 58

Pennington, Glen, 339

Pennington, J. P., 340

Perry, Betty Sue, 371

Phelps, Jackie, 7

Phillips, Joe "Flapjack," 7–8

Phillips, Lewis, 355

Phillips, Marvin, 366

Phipps Family, 25

Pickelsimer, "Sister Ann," 57

Pierce, Don, 75, 119

Pierce, Webb, 257

Pike, Jim and Carolina Tar Heels, 251

Pike, Pete, 110

Pinetucket, 349

Pinson, Bob, 264

Pioneer Gang, 185

Pleacher, Smoky, 7, 243–44

Plyler, Larry, **344**, 348–50

Poole, Charlie, 11, 38, 303

Poor, Murrell, 82

Poplin, Sam, 329

Powell, Patti, 125, 130

Presley, Elvis, 4, 25, 148, 191

Pressley, Millard, 327

Prevette, Ronnie, 45

Price, Dewey, 325, 327, 329, 332

Price, James, 278

Price, Ray, 265

Prince, Paul, 43

Profitt, Louie, 8

Puckett, Riley, 63, 261, 303

Puntari, Albert, 270

Purdom, J. M. *See* Masters Family

Pursell, Bryan, 174

Queen, Carl, 9, 347

Queener, Monroe, 220

Raborn, Harvey, 327

Rackstraw, Ricky, 347, 361

Rainwater, Cedric (a.k.a. Watts, Howard), 29, 174

Rainwater, Jody, 296

Ramsey, LeRoy, 209

Randolph, Vance, 188, 237

Raney, Wayne, 68

Rangers Quartet, 328

Rarely Herd, 126

Rawlings, Bill, 276

Rebe and Rabe, 348

Rector, "Red," (William), 3, 7–8, 42, **116**–17, 136, 158–165, **159**, 170, 311

Rector, Roy, 329

Reid, Bill and Mary, 140–41, 149

Renfro Valley Barn Dance, 6, 41, 71, 99, 185, 226, 263, 318, 334, 337–39

Reno, Don, 2, 67, 122, 131, 178, 312, 357

Reno, Don and Smiley, Red, 122, 161, 307, 345–46, 350

Reynolds, "Barefoot Brownie," 73

Rhodes, Don, 347

Richardson, Deanie, 173

Richardson, Fred, 97
Richardson, Larry, 269–70
Richie, Jack and His Blue Ridge
    Mountaineers, 324–25
Ridge Runners, 168
Rigsby, Don, 130, 210, 279
Rigsby, John, 279
Rinzler, Ralph, 340–41
Ritchey Brothers (Galen and Melvin),
    288
Ritter, Tex, 15, 21, 286
Rivers, Jerry, 43
Robbins, Butch, 144
Robbins, Hargis "Pig," 357
Robbins, Marty, 34, 265
Roberts, Doc, 183–84
Roberts, James. *See* Carson, James and
    Martha
Roberts, Jeff, 126
Roberts, Louie, 220
Roberts, Marty, 73
Roberts, Pearl Arman, 191, 193
Rodgers, Jimmie, 38, 75, 261, 303
Ronstadt, Linda and Harris, Emmylou,
    187
Rose, Artie, 208
Rose, Billy, 280
Rose, Fred, 66, 137, 200
Roseberry, Dale, 58
Rosenberg, Neil, 111
Ross, Roy, 9
Rothman, Sandy, 208
Rouse, Ervin [and Brothers], 13,
    174–75, 179
Rusk, Leon, 330
Russell, Johnny, 125, 127
Russell, Roy, 45
Russell, Tony, 205
Russell Brothers, 70

Rutland, Robert "Georgia Slim," 81, 251
Ryan, Buck, 58
Ryan, Irene, 326

Saddler, Doug, 5
Salley, Jerry, 360
Salt and Peanuts (Kurtz, Frank and
    Margaret), 81
Samples, Mack, 130
Samples Brothers, 130
Samuelson, Dave, 91
Sanders, Price, 310
Sanderson, Jack, 23
Sassy Grass, 349
Satherley, Art, 48, 51, 200, 285–86
Sauceman Brothers (Carl and J. P.),
    168–69
Schneider, Doc and His Texas Yodeling
    Cowboys, 55
Scott, Leon, 115–17
Scott, Roy, 191, 244–45
Scott, Ramblin' Tommy, 41, 53
Scottdale String Band, 321
Scotty, the Drifter (Borg, Benny), 322
Scruggs, Earl, 3, 7, 86, 174, 176
Seagrave, Lea, 99
Seckler, Curly, 3, 41–43, 142, 172–73,
    309
Seeger, Mike, 341
Seiger, Mabelle, 169
Seldom Scene, 187
Shady Valley Boys, 110–11
Shamblin, Luke, 130–31
Shelton, Jack and His Green County
    Boys, 310
Shelton Brothers (Bob and Joe), 265
Shelton Brothers (Jack and Curly), 17,
    133, 308
Shenandoah Cutups, 166, **167**, 170

Shepherd, Riley, 330
Shepherd Twins, 7
Sherrill, Homer "Pappy," 39, 306, 331
Sholes, Steve, 187, 191
Shortridge, Bob, 57
Shuffler, George, 142
Shumate, Jim, 168
Shurtz, Mary Jean, 240
Sidle, Kenny, 151
Simmons, Vicky, 341–42
Sims, Benny, 136
Sims, Leonard, 234, 240
Singleton, Rachel, 130
Sizemore, Asher, 237
Sizemore, Herschel, 167, 171
Skaggs, Chief Dolpha and the
    Mountain Melody Boys, 57
Skeens, Dave, 277
Skeens, R. W., 277
Skillet Lickers, 38, 63, 303
Skinner, Esmer, 71
Skinner, Jimmie, 3, 8, 70–77, 71, 343
Smallwood, Bob, 144
Smathers, Ned, 311
Smik, Andrew, Jr. *See* Williams, Doc
Smik, Barbara "Peeper," 246
Smiley, Red, 9, 31, 67, 122, 124, 131,
    170, 347
Smith, Arthur "Guitar Boogie," 328,
    345, 350
Smith, Arthur Q. (a.k.a. Pritchett,
    James), 118
Smith, Blaine, 245
Smith, Carl, 34, 137, 168, 228, 370
Smith, Danny, 347
Smith, Edgar "Bud," 33–35
Smith, Fiddlin' Arthur, 237
Smith, Fred, 94, 136, 159–63, 311
Smith, George, 101–2

Smith, Harmie, 251
Smith, Jimmie, 55
Smith, Kenny and Amanda, 182, 210
Smith, Paul and the Tinker Mountain
    Boys, 15
Smith, Ray, 137
Smith Brothers (Tennessee and
    Smitty), 188
Smith's Sacred Singers, 183
Smoak, Jim, 7, 10, 170
Smythe, Kevin, 208
Snail, Curl, 126
Sneed, Roy, 190
Snow, Hank, 177–78
Sons of the Pioneers, 5, 15
Sovine, Red, 81, 251
Sparks, Larry, 24, 34–35, 125, 146, 151,
    208,
Speer Family, 355
Spencer, Fred, 23
Spencer Brothers (Maynard and
    Lance), 43
Spicher, Buddy, 130, 169, 361
Spinney Brothers (Allan and Rick), 248
Spottswood, Richard, 315
St. John, Al "Fuzzy," 139
Stack, Alan, 126
Staggs, Ervin, 81, 251
Stallard, Bill and Evalina (Indian Bill
    and Little Montana), 81, **154**, 155–56
Stamper, Art, 24, 124, 141, 276
Stamps Quartet, 183
Stanley, Carter, 281
Stanley, Ralph, 24, 144, 210, 275, 279,
    362, 372
Stanley Brothers (Carter and Ralph), 3,
    29, 31, 36, 67, 124, 139–45, 148, 179,
    199, 210, 267–69, 275, 363
Stanton, Jim, 199

Starcher, Buddy, 2–3, 32, 57, 62, 78–88, **79**, 146, 149–50, 246

Starcher, Mary Ann, 82, 85–86, 88, 150

Starrett, Charles, 326

Steele, Mel and "Blue-eyed Jeannie," 135

Stennett, Junior, **100**–102

Stevenson, Steve, 111

Stewart, Blaine, 200

Stewart, Nathan, 362

Stiltner, Haley, 363

Stoetzer, Joe, 234

Stokes, Leonard, 32, 309

Stokes, Lowe, 63

Stone, Harry, 237, 240

Stoneman, Patsy, 112

Stoneman, Scotty, 297

Story, Carl, 1, 19, 50, 89–98, **90**, 113, **116**, 117–21, 133, 136, 161–63, 169–70, 172, 176, 208, 328, 347, 356

Stover, Don, 290, 296–99

Strachwitz, Chris, 313

"Stringbean" (Akeman, David), 42, 92

Stripling, Pee Wee, 251

Stuart, Joe, 168, 347

Stuart, Marty, 300, 363

Stubbs, Eddie, 257

Sullivan, Hoyt, 354

Sullivan, John "Lonzo," 69

Sullivan Family, 363

Sunbrock, Larry, 155–56

Sunshine Boys, 357

Surratt, Cecil, 273

Sutherland, David, 275

Sutter, Smilie (Slater, Anthony; also "Crazy Elmer"), 81, 245, 294

Sutton, Tommy, 6

Swalley, Doc, 263

Sweet, Gene, 23

Swingbillies, 323

Tainaka, Robert and Jerry, 298

Tate, Clarence "Tater," 7, 9–10, 61, 96, 119, 126, 137–38, 164–65, 166–73, **167**, 204, 314, 346

Taylor, Earl, 110, 126

Taylor, Jake, 242–43

Taylor, Merle "Red," 6

Taylor, Paul, 293

Tennessee Barn Dance, 93–95, 168, 293

Tennessee Ramblers, 234, 323–25, 329, 331

Terflinger, Jeff, 126

Terry, Blind Sonny, 159, 311

Tew, Norwood, 306

Thacker, Ernie, 279

Thacker, "Southpaw," 136

Thomas, Billy, 24

Thomas, Evelyn "Little Evie," 252–53

Thomas, Gurney, 310

Thomas, Gus, 125

Thomas, Jennings "Flash," 250

Thompson, Bobby, 89

Thompson, Ernest, 324

Thompson, Jack, 177

Thompson, Uncle Jimmie, 89

Tibbits, Dennis, 348

Tilley, Dale, 347

Tobacco Tags, 39, 80, 139, 303

Todd, Clarence, 305

Tomlinson, Charlie, 110

Toomey, Welby, 70

Tripp, LaVerne, 357

Tubb, Ernest, 237, 286–87, 289, 328

Tuck, Marvin, 347

Tullock, Jake, 137, 169

Turner, Zeb, 68, 287

Turner Brothers (Red and Lige), 73

Tuttle, Curly, 24

Tuttle, Wesley, 265

Tweedy Brothers (Charles and Harry), 54
Two Gospel Keys, 22
Tyler, T. Texas, 251, 293
Tyler, Willie, 80

Ukelson, Lou, 75
Uncle Enoch and His Gang, 323
Uncle Henry's Original Kentucky
    Mountaineers, 5
Underwood, Marion, 70–71
Upson, Dean, 254–55

Val, Joe, 297
Van Winkle Brothers, 70
Vanderpool, Dale, 279
Vandiver, Pendleton "Uncle Pen," 37
Varney, Lowell, 9
Vaughn Quartet, 183
Vernon, Bill, 28, 30–32, 281
Vincent, Rhonda, 211, 362

Wade, Stephen, 315
Wagner, Bill, 29
Wagoner, Porter, 343
Wakefield, Frank, 178, 208
Wakely, Jimmy, 15, 64–65, 326
Waldron, Cliff, 171
Walker, Billie, 234, 237
Walker, Billy, 300
Walker, Cas, 59, 72, 168, 170, 193,
    214–16, 368–70
Walsh, Doc, 303
Ward, C. E., 96
Ward, George, 124–25
Ward, Preston, 343
Ward, Smokey, 6
Warrell, Lois, 17
Warren, Garnet "Hank." *See*
    Briarhoppers

Warren, Larry, 325
Warren, Paul, 160, 172
Watson, Doc, 97
Watson, Dud, 91, 118
Watson, Tex, 365
Watson, Wayne, 15, 17
Weaver, Lloyd "Cowboy," 265
Weaver Brothers and Elviry, 263
Webster Brothers (Audie and Earl), 192
Weisberger, Jon, 131
Weissburg, Eric, 95
Weldy, Quinton, 25
Welk, Lawrence, 59
Welling, Frank, 57, 62
Welling, Frank and McGhee, John, 304
Wellman, Curly, 57
Wells, Kitty, 6, 160
Wesbrooks, Cousin Wilbur, 50, 92, 176
Wheeler, Joe and Buddy, 177
Wheeler, Onie, 212
Wheeling Jamboree. See *World's
    Original Jamboree*
Whisnant, John, 90–91, 137, 168
Whitaker, Charlie, **100–104**
Whitaker, Lillie Mae and the Dixie
    Gospel-aires, 2, 99–104, **100**
Whitaker, Ron, 104
White, Asa, 65
White, Buck, Cheryl and Sharon, 163
White, Don (Whitsell, Walden). *See*
    Briarhoppers
White, Lee "Lasses," 264
White, Smokey, 137
Whitley, Ray, 15, 265
Widener, Art, 23
Wild, Lee Davis "Honey," 163
Williams, Blake, 24
Williams, Cy (Smik, Milo), 232- 40,
    233, 246

Williams, Doc and Chickie (Smik,
  Andrew and Wanda), 61–62, 182,
  201, 232–46, **233**, 289
Williams, Hank, 66, 177, 256
Williams, Jimmy, 141, 270
Williams, Landon, 125
Williams, Paul (Humphrey, Paul),
  270–71, 280–81
Williamson, Cecil "Skeets," 135, 222–25,
  227–28, 251, 263
Williamson, Dixie Lee. *See* O'Day,
  Molly
Wills, Bob, 178
Wilson, Red, 311
Wingfield, Craig, 143
Winn, George and the Bluegrass
  Partners, 346
Wise, Robert "Chubby," 8, 29, 50–51,
  166, 174–79, **175**, 296, 307
Wise, Rossi, 178
Wiseman, Lawrence, 175
Wiseman, Mac, 16, 31, 88, 126, 130,
  133, 135, 170, 177–78, 239, 269, 324,
  345–46, 350
Wiseman, Scotty, 329
Wolfe, Charles K., 111, 153
Wolfe, Kenneth "Pappy," 324
Woodettes, 126
Woodruff, Ducky, 191
Woods, Joe, 252
Woody, Lester, 140
Wooley, Sheb, 87
Woolum, Dave, 23
Wooten, Art, 137, 166, 176
Wooten, Mike, 204
World's Original Jamboree (*Wheeling
  Jamboree; Jamboree USA*), 7, 27,
  59–62, 125, 127, 130–31, 144, 169,
  171, 182, 191, 200–201, 237, 247–48,
  252–54, 285, 287–88, 297, 308, 315,
  345, 367

Yankovic, Frankie, 51
Yarbrough, Herman "Roscoe Swerps,"
  85–86
Yarbrough, Rual, 164
Yarbrough, Scott, 359
Yearwood, Trisha, 130
York, Rusty, 3, **20**, 23, 126
York Brothers (George and Leslie), 177
Young, Faron, 191
Young, Gib, 325
Young, Hayes and Stamper, Jimmy, 80

Zierath, Larry, 34
Zufall, Happy Johnnie and Handsome
  Bob, 54